CONSERVATION AND RESTORATION OF HORSE-DRAWN VEHICLES

Susan Green, Librarian
CARRIAGE MUSEUM OF AMERICA
Post Office Box 417
Bird-In-Hand, Pennsylvania 17505
phone 717-656-7019

©1997 Carriage Museum of America

ISBN 1-800499-05-3

Acknowledgments

Project director, Susan Green for the Carriage Museum of America-Library - General editor, Neil Fisher - Editor sponsored by Frank Morrow, trustee for the Carriage Museum of America - proof readers, Marjorie Everett, Mary Jane Green, Stewart Morris, Sr. and Bob Scott - technical advisor for the panel chapter Mr. and Mrs. Nick Wood - technical advisor for the wheel and axle chapter, Bruce Morrison - technical advisor for the trimming chapter Ralph Lane and Gregg Hunt - technical advisors for the brush painting chapter Tim Ragle and Joe Jennings - computer support Chris Harvey - authors for chapters Marc Williams, Norman Yoder, Darrell Shannon, James Martin, Dr. Gordon Cantle and Rick Bischoff - Financial support from Steve Osborn - Clearing the way Stewart Morris, Sr. Past projects that have given us inspiration Conservation programs at the Museums At Stony Brook, Tom Ryder's Restoration booklet, Rodale Press and Taunton Press books on wood finishing, George Isle's book on restoration.

Conservation and Restoration of Horse-drawn Vehicles.

Having examined many resources and interviewed many people, it quite evident there is a difference of opinion among leading professionals, so you must judge what works best in your particular situation. References are listed at the end of chapters for more exacting details. All instructions must be carefully studied and clearly understood before beginning any work. Products may vary as to quality, freshness, changing ingredients of manufactures, local conditions and personal skills. There are different options on conservation, spray and brush painting. Quality of air temperature, humidity, and conditions within materials are factors. Remember, only practice makes perfect. The Carriage Museum of America does not assume any responsibility for injuries or damages suffered from the information presented herein or from speeches or interrogatories of anyone associated with the Carriage Museum of America.

Board of Trustees

Stewart Morris, Sr., President/Chairman, Houston, TX
Richard McRae, Vice President, Jackson, MS
Owen Best, Secretary, Charlottesville, VA
Gloria Austin, Treasurer, Wiersdale, FL
Richard Nicoll, Williamsburg, VA

James A. Granito, Gardiner, NY
Kenneth Wheeling, North Ferrisburg, VT
Frank Morrow, Beaver Falls, PA
Dinwiddie Lampton, Jr., Louisville, KY
Stewart Morris, Jr., Houston, TX
Dr. William Cook, Jackson, MS

Front cover courtesy of the Carriage Association of America, reprinted from the Hub March, 1890

TABLE OF CONTENTS

INTRODUCTION	1
Background	1
Art And Skill Of Restoration	1
Where To Begin?	2
Your Ultimate Goal	2
CHAPTER 1 - RESEARCH AND RECORDING	5
Vehicles Without A Maker's Mark	5
Searching Patents	6
Vehicles With Maker's Name	6

SECTION I - CONSERVATION

CHAPTER 2 - GUIDELINES FOR SELECTING A CONSERVATOR	11
What Is A Conservator?	11
FAIC Conservation Services Referral System	11
What Questions To Ask Potential Conservators	12
What To Expect	12
Exercising Caution	12
Points To Remember When Selecting A Conservator	13
CHAPTER 3 - CONSERVATION TREATMENT OF HORSE-DRAWN VEHICLES	15
Pitfalls Of Restoration	15
Conservation To The Rescue	15
Self Treatment Versus Professional Conservation Treatment	16
What Is Conservation?	17
Conservation Ethics	18
Integrity Of The Object	18
Stable, Reversible Materials	19
Documentation	19
Single Standard	19
Uniqueness	20
Educational Responsibility	20
Carriage Technology	20
Causes/Prevention Of Deterioration	22
Composite Object	23
Before Treatment Documentation	23
Structure	24
Paint Stabilization	25
Varnish Cleaning	26
Varnish Removal	27
Inpainting Losses	28
Protective Coatings	29
Overpainting	29
Metal Components	29
Upholstery	30

TABLE OF CONTENTS

    Other Attachments — 30
    After Treatment Documentation — 31
    Routine Maintenance — 31
    Dusting — 31
    Dust Covers — 32
    Varnish/Paint Maintenance — 34
    Nicks And Scratches — 35
    Summary — 35
    Supply Resource List — 36

CHAPTER 4 - TECHNICAL EXAMINATION AND MICROSCOPIC ANALYSIS OF PAINTED HORSE-DRAWN VEHICLES — 37
    Surface Examination — 37
    Investigating Finish History — 38
    Determining Physical Properties — 38
    Studying Composition — 39

CHAPTER 5 - VARNISH FOR HORSE-DRAWN VEHICLES — 41
    Copal — 41
    Linseed Oil — 41
    Properties And Composition Of Linseed Oil — 41
    Turpentine — 43
    Properties And Composition Of Turpentine — 43
    Driers — 46
    Varnish Making — 46
    Different Recipes For Varnishes — 46
    General Considerations — 49
    Bibliography — 50

SECTION II - RESTORATION

CHAPTER 6 - AXLES — 55
    How To Make And Use An Axle Gauge — 55
    Axle Manufacture — 56
    Axle Types — 58
    Collinge Axle — 59
    Mail Axles — 61
    Bearing Axles — 62
    Plain Axles — 62
    Wooden Axles — 63
    Laying Out Wood Wagon Axles — 63
    Inspecting The Axles Before Buying and Restoration — 64
    Bibliography — 65

CHAPTER 7 - WHEELS — 67
    Patent Wheels — 68
    Getting Wheel Work Done — 69

TABLE OF CONTENTS

Dish In Wheels	70
Hubs	71
Restoration Hubs	72
Spokes	72
Felloes/Rims	72
Tires	74
Rubber Tires	76
Color of Rubber Tires	77
Bibliography	77

CHAPTER 8 - SPRINGS — 79

Taking Springs Apart	79
Having New Springs Made	79
Thickness Of Springs	80
Effects Of Stress On Carriage Springs With Comments On The Heat Treatment Of Spring Steel	80
Faults In Spring Fixing	80
Heat Treatment In General	81
Heat Treatment Of Spring Steel	82
Spring Manufacturing	83
Modern Spring Sizes	84
Subject Of Leaf Spring Fatigue	85
Bibliography	87

CHAPTER 9 - PANELS — 89

Beading And The Designing Of The Back Panels Of Bodies	88
Panels For Painted Vehicles	89
Natural Wood Panels	89
Different Methods Of Applying Panels	90
Replacing A Top Quarter Panel	90
Replacing Reed Moldings	91
Brass Bead Molding	91
Replacing Lower Quarter Panels That Have A Curve Edge That Fits Into A Rabbet	92
Replacing Rear Curved Panels Of Coaches That Have A Rabbet	92
Bending Panels	92
Replacing A Curved Back Panel In A Rabbet	94
Laminating Thin Layers	95
Cabinet Makers Paneling	96
Veneering Or Skinning	96
Repairing Panels By Inlaid	97
Bibliography	98

CHAPTER 10 - PREPARING FOR PAINTING — 101

Getting Started	101
Disassembling	101
Tip For Removing Rusty Screws	102

TABLE OF CONTENTS

Gluing	103
Paint Removal	103
Paint Remover	104
Decontaminating	105
Bleaching	106
Cleaning The Metal	106
Cleaning Small Metal Pieces	108
Sanding	108
Preparing The Wood	111
Finishing Springs	113
Finish	114
Bibliography	114

CHAPTER 11 - BRUSH PAINTING — 115

The Brush	115
Brush Care	116
Primer Coats	117
Color	118
Painting Wheels	119
Varnish	119
Applying Varnish	121
Glaze Coats	124
Getting Ready To Varnish	124
Some Problems of Varnish	126
Bibliography	126

CHAPTER 12 - SPRAY PAINTING — 129

Equipment Needed	129
Preparation	130

CHAPTER 13 - COLORS — 135

Corning Type Top Wagon	135
Cabriolet Or Panel Boot Victoria	136
Brougham	136
Landau	136
Surrey	136
Rumble Seat Basket Phaeton	137
Dog Cart	137
Wagonette Break	137
Private Coach Or Park Drag	137
Black Parts	138
Natural Wood Carriages	138
Bibliography	139
Paint Color List	140

TABLE OF CONTENTS

CHAPTER 14 - STRIPING, SCROLLING AND ORNAMENTING — 145
- Striping — 146
- Transfers — 149
- Modern Transfer Ornaments — 150
- Stenciling — 151
- Gilding — 151
- Bibliography — 152

CHAPTER 15 - CARRIAGE TRIMMING MATERIALS — 153
- Tools — 153
- Sewing Machine — 154
- Materials — 154
  - Bedford Cord — 154
  - Broadcloth — 154
  - Plush — 155
  - Tapestry Cloth — 155
  - Whipcord — 155
  - Camels Hair — 156
  - Luxury Fabrics — 156
  - Leather — 156
  - Patent Leather — 157
  - Gum Drill And Macintosh Cloth — 157
  - Artificial Leather — 158
  - Carriage Laces — 159
- Stuffing Materials — 160
  - Polyurethane Foam — 160
- Floor Coverings — 161
- Fringes — 165

CHAPTER 16 - UPHOLSTERY — 169
- Laying Out — 169
- Seat Falls — 171
- Door Trimming — 172
- Shafts — 174
- Poles — 176
- Bibliography — 177
- Splinter Bars — 177
- Valances For Seat Borders — 178
- Valances For Folding Tops — 179
- Some Suggestions For Clean-Up And Repair Of Old Folding Tops — 179

CHAPTER 17 - LAMPS — 180
- Lamp Covers — 180
- Obtain The "Correct" Lamps — 181
- Evaluating Lamps — 181
- Parts Of A Lamp — 182

TABLE OF CONTENTS

Restoration Plan	182
Accomplishing The Restoration	183
Hints	184
Use, Storage And Preservation	184
CHAPTER 18 - WICKER AND CANE WORK	**185**
Imitation Cane-Work For Painted Carriage Panels	185
Sham-Caning	185
Bibliography	187
Imitation Cane-Work Glued On	187
Bibliography	188
Modern Method Of Cane-Work	188
Routing The Cane-Work Pattern	189
Procedure	189
Woven Cane Work For Seats	190
Wicker Work	190
Willow	190
Reed	191
Bibliography	192
MUSEUMS	**193**
BIBLIOGRAPHY	**209**
Carriage Journal Articles	209
Book List	215
SERVICES, SUPPLIES AND RESOURCES	**217**
INDEX	**230**

CONSERVATION AND RESTORATION OF HORSE-DRAWN VEHICLES

INTRODUCTION

Background

Only those fortunate few who are owners of an original and authentic horse drawn carriage can truly appreciate the sense of beauty and the connection with history that such an experience affords. There is nothing that can compare with the satisfaction of stepping into this page of our American heritage and knowing that there is no compromise with authenticity, nor any flaw or imperfection for which to apologize.

And yet there are some uninitiated or novice carriage owners who unwittingly undertake improper carriage restoration and in so doing alter or permanently destroy the skillful design and workmanship of master nineteenth century craftsmen. With the revival of interest in owning and driving horse drawn carriages, in the past quarter century, and the sometimes haphazard approach to restoration, many fine examples of master craftsmanship are being lost forever. The purpose of this book is to encourage the goal of quality and authenticity in carriage restoration, and to offer helpful information on the proper steps and processes involved in conservation and preservation.

As James Garland, the celebrated authority on carriages, stated in his 1903 book, "It's the harmony and eternal fitness of things that create an object of beauty." Your pride of ownership will be enhanced tenfold when your carriage is restored with care for the harmony and fitness of each detail. The monetary value of a properly restored carriage is also greatly enhanced when compared with a less than careful restoration. At carriage sales throughout the country, the wisdom of a professional and authentic job of restoration is consistently rewarded by the top prices. And the joy of driving a fine, smoothly handling vehicle provides its own reward in the form of worry free operation. Nothing takes the place of knowing that your vehicle is in perfect working condition, ready to perform to your expectations.

The Art and Skill of Restoration

If you are now the owner of an original nineteenth century horse drawn carriage, you are indeed fortunate. You not only have a unique conveyance but an important historical artifact. You will be wise to reconsider your investment and the responsibility that goes with owning a item of history. As you recognize, most American carriages are more than one hundred years old, and antiques such as these are no longer being created. Only by careful and professional restoration can your carriage remain a genuine example of the early transportation history of America.

In all likelihood, when your carriage was originally crafted, its makers employed the best available materials and workmanship. The idea of economizing on either was virtually unthinkable in earlier times. It is only because of this that your carriage has already lasted a century or more. For this reason alone, you will be well advised to plan your restoration using only authentic materials and the best craftsmen.

In the past such materials and craftsmanship have been difficult to locate, due to the specialized nature of the market. However, it is the purpose of this book to assist in making your task easier. While there may be as many methods of restoration work as there are restorers, this publication will present the procedures of the most widely accepted and proven methods in the field. You will also find in the appendix a listing of craftsmen and the suppliers of the specialty materials needed for the work of quality restoration.

Before you do any work on your carriage, you will need to make some important decisions; decisions that will enhance the value of your investment or depreciate it; decisions that may well save your life or that of others; decisions that will bring admiration or disapproval from your fellow members in the carriage world. In the event that your carriage has not been altered and is in good condition, you may simply want to preserve it in its original state. Experience with resale values confirms that a carriage in original nineteenth century condition may be worth more than even a good restoration. So before you undertake any restoration work, make a careful appraisal of the condition of your carriage, then make your decision as to whether an extensive overhaul is necessary, or just a thorough cleanup.

Where to Begin ?

You wouldn't undertake to build a new house on a crumbling foundation, nor would you build a house without considering your needs and desires. By the same token, you will want to consider and decide what you plan to do with your carriage before you undertake any actual work. Will it be placed in a museum or in a display with your own private collection, to be viewed only and not to be driven? Or do you plan to drive it and if so to what extent? Will you be entering driving shows, or are you planning to enter driving competitions? The answers to these questions will largely determine the appropriate extent and quality of your restoration work.

A good place to start is with an inspection by a professional carriage authority or restorer to determine the vehicle's structural integrity. This will help determine the extent of the essential repairs. This phase is much more important than the cosmetic work, especially if the vehicle is to be driven. Wheels have been known to collapse, throwing the passengers out of the carriage; poles and shafts have broken under stress, causing serious accidents; carriages have even broken apart during a carriage show. Therefore, it is essential to have your carriage examined thoroughly for any areas of structural weakness. Now is the time to learn if any mechanical or structural repairs are needed.

Poles or shafts can be tested by placing the ends on a stand and sitting or bouncing on them. The same type of test can be applied to splinter bars, leader bars, yokes and other items. Also, examine the framework for soundness. More substantial carriages are built with hard wood bolted to steel rails; inspect this wood for dry rot or other deterioration. Examine the mortise joints for soundness, along with the axles, wheel boxes, hubs, spokes, felloes and rims. Inspect the king pin and other bolts, steps and all steel hardware for corrosion or deterioration.

While much of the time consuming work may well be done by the owner, certain jobs must be placed in the hands of experienced craftsmen with the proper equipment. For example, to replace the genuine patent leather on fenders and dashes requires a special sewing machine with a long reach - something that is very rare in this country. And certainly, you will want to employ professional wheelwrights, cabinet makers, painters, stripers, and other artisans with the special skills needed to complete your restoration.

Your Ultimate Goal

The goal of every serious carriage owner is to posses a vehicle that is uniquely superb. One that will provide the ultimate in pride of ownership in every sense of the term. It is a goal well worth striving for. But such excellence is achieved only by a sincere dedication to quality and authenticity. In the chapters to follow, you will find the help needed in guiding you to the kind of restoration that will produce this type of satisfaction.

The nineteenth century author, Francis Ware, put it best; "Correct appointments may be defined as genuine harmony of detail and outline, quietness of color and ornamentation and appropriateness of vehicle and equipment in every essential, resulting in the perfection of good taste, inconspicuous in every point yet competent for the purpose intended. Thus 'turned out', one is correct beyond dispute. True elegance is attained by presenting the graceful unity of flowing lines, dark colors and inconspicuous ornamentation.

The message is clear; authenticity is attained by paying close attention to every detail of construction and appointments. Don't be tempted to change the character of your vehicle or brighten the colors to suit a particular whim. Take care to choose the proper shade and texture of cloth materials, the proper paint color and application, the correct selection of hardware and appointments. These materials are seldom found from a single source, and so the appendix of this book includes a listing of the best known sources of such items.

By following these principles of care and correctness, you will have attained the goal of owning a vehicle that is uniquely yours, and indeed a source of unending pride and satisfaction.

Frank H. Morrow

Carriage Museum of America-Library
Post Office Box 417
Bird-In-Hand, Pennsylvania 17505
phone 717-656-7019

Decorative-Painters' Wagon
from the Hub March 1888

Physicians' Phaeton made by Golder & Post, of Newark, New Jersey
from the Hub February 1890
Painting.--Body and moldings, black; moldings striped with fine line of carmine. Gearing, black, striped with two fine lines of carmine.
Trimming.--Green goatskin. Mountings silver.

Stationary Top Phaeton
from the Hub September 1894
Painting.--Body: black, and beads striped a fine line of carmine. Carriage part: carmine, striped black.
Trimming.--Green cloth, style as illustrated, and carpet to match.
Finish.--Curved dash; seat rails painted; no lamps, an axle nuts silver plated.

Physicians' Phaeton
from the Hub October 1897
Painting.--Body: black; seat, deep green, including pillar and front bracket; spindles and moldings, black.
Trimming.--Green cloth; style, blocks throughout; raisers on fall and cushion front, and bound with same material.
Finish.--Plain silver-plated lamps; straight four-bar dash; five-bow closed top; square or round step pads, and carpet to match.

Stanhope Phaeton
from the Hub June 1896
Painting.--Body, quarter panels, pillars and back panel, olive green; remainder of body black. Moldings, black, striped wit light olive green. Gear, olive green, striped with 1/8 inch line of black and fine lined with carmine.
Trimming.--Light cloth. Back and cushions made in blocks, quarters diamond pattern. Finish, black.

Research and Recording
CHAPTER 1

RESEARCH AND RECORDING

Vehicles Without a Maker's Mark

Before beginning the restoration of a vehicle, it is wise to do some research and find out as much as possible about the company that made your vehicle, and when. This is a problem though for vehicles that do not have anything indicating who the maker was. With more than 7,000 establishments making vehicles in the 1900s. It is almost impossible to be certain which company made a vehicle if it does not have a maker's mark. For vehicles without a maker's name the closest information you might gain is to look through the old trade journals, The *Hub* and *Carriage Monthly*, for vehicles that match your vehicle as closely as possible. Starting around 1858, the monthly trade journals for the carriage industry published eight new designs for carriages, sleighs and commercial vehicles each month.

Cabriolet Phaeton with Canopy Top
Hub - May 1888
This plate represents a pattern of cabriolet-phaeton which may be looked upon as a standard, rather than a novel pattern. The canopy top is made to take off. The rockers are framed square, with bent corner-pillars and panel-quarters. The molding is worked on solid, 5/16 in. thick. Turn-under body, 2 ½ in.
Dimensions of woodwork.....
Dimensions of iron work......
Painting. Body, black, with fine line of carmine on moldings. Gearing, dark green, with double stripe of carmine.
Trimming. The back seat is trimmed with green cloth, and front seat with dull green leather. The curtains may be of 40 oz. rubber or enameled leather, lined with 13 oz. cloth.

Cabriolet Phaeton with Canopy Top
from the Hub May 1888
One of eight fashion plates for the month

The Carriage Builder's National Association was organized in 1872 and each year they tried to hold a convention and trade show besides the international trade shows that were held. Each year carriage manufacturers were opinionated about what were the best new colors and designs. Trying to do some research is important because over the years people have become rather opinionated about how they painted and upholstered carriages, etc. when in fact many different things happened to carriage styles each year. The Carriage Museum of America maintains a large file of these fashion plates sorted by vehicle type. The *Hub* and *Carriage Monthly* published many of these fashion plates with a description of paint colors, upholstery and dimensions. Other sources of information are manufacturers' catalogs to establish when a certain type of carriage was made. Some restoration projects require a great deal of perseverance in the search for information on pieces that might be missing, original colors and upholstery. When you have pieces that are missing, find a vehicle that is in more original condition then yours and take photographs and make drawings. Carriage Association members are helpful to each other and you might find someone who has a vehicle similar to yours, but in better condition : There are several large museums around the country that maintain carriages in original condition. The Museums at Stony Brook, Stony Brook, NY; Shelburne Museum, Shelburne, VT; Henry Ford Museum, Dearborn, MI. There are about 100 museums with smaller collections. Your county library should have a Museum Directory listing all the museums in the United States.

Research and Recording

Searching Patents

If you have a vehicle that is unique, you can sometimes trace information through patent records. This is an arduous task though if you do not have a maker's name or date. The horse-drawn vehicle industry took out close to 40,000 patents from 1790 to 1910. The Carriage Museum of America - Library maintains an index of these patents, but it does not include illustrations with them. For someone searching for a unique springing system the Carriage Museum of America-Library can provide a list of patents for springs and the carriage owner would have to search the illustrations. There are some fifty libraries throughout the United States called depository libraries that maintain U. S. Patent records.

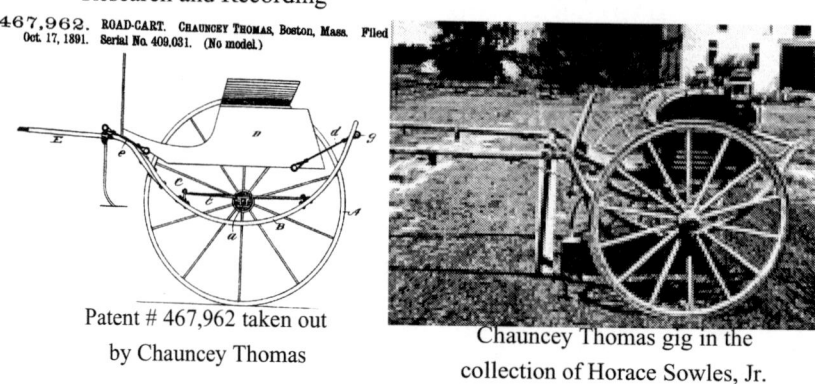

Patent # 467,962 taken out by Chauncey Thomas

Chauncey Thomas gig in the collection of Horace Sowles, Jr.

Manufacturer's photographic plate of Chauncey Thomas gig turnout

The Chicago Public Library also maintains a complete collection of British Patents. The United States Patent Office can send out the full specifications and drawings for $3.00 once you can give them the patent number. The patent index at the Carriage Museum of America is cross index, by inventors' names and patent dates, which allows you to obtain the patent number.

Vehicles With Maker's Name

It always seems to make a vehicle a little extra special when it comes with a maker's tag or name on it somewhere. Some better manufacturers sometimes stamped their name on the axle spindle, so that when you remove the wheel you might find a maker's name. The axle spindle could also be stamped with the name of the axle maker and should not be confused with the name of the maker of the vehicle. Many vehicle makers bought their axles from a company that specialized in making axles. Runabouts and buggies sometimes came with a paper label pasted under the seat cushion. Often carriages with oil caps have the maker's name engraved on them.

Carriage maker's tag with the name of the maker

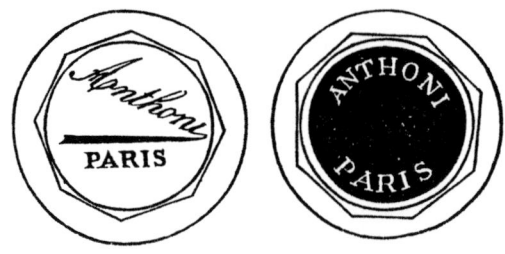

Oil caps wit the vehicle maker's name inscribed on them

If you have a maker's name for your vehicle, you can probably track down some history of the manufacturer, but not necessarily information about your particular vehicle. The first step is to send a self-addressed envelope to the libraries in the city where they made your vehicle and ask them when they listed that company name in the city directories. The American Library Directory found at your county library can be most helpful in this task. By having a list of all the libraries you can decide which libraries might be likely prospects. Most large cities have more than one library where the information might be, such as the public library, historical society and long established university libraries. Once a time period has been established for your vehicle, you can check out the old trade journals again for the fashion plates or history of the manufacturer. The Carriage Museum of America maintains files of information and catalogs for some vehicle manufacturers, but with more than 7,000 manufacturers a lot is unknown about the horse drawn vehicle industry. Archives are maintained for the following: the Brewster & Co. records at the New York Public Library and the Metropolitan Museum of Art, NY ; Studebaker Bros. Manufacturing Co., National Studebaker Museum, South Bend, Indiana ; Abbot-Downing Co., New Hampshire Historical Society Library, Concord, NH; Gruber Wagon Works, Wyomissing, PA. It can be very exciting to be able to trace the history of your vehicle.

Helpful Tip

As you are doing your research, it is a good idea to make up a file folder for your particular vehicle to keep all the information together and remind yourself what steps you have already covered. When you purchase the vehicle you should take pains to record any information the seller might have as to the vehicle's history. Take photographs of the vehicle right away, and if you take extra photographs of the vehicle these will be helpful in doing research. When asking for information about a particular vehicle good photographs make it easier for people to understand what you are talking about.

Four-seat Extension-top Phaeton--From the Hub August, 1872
This fashion plate was found to match a vehicle in the collection of Dinwiddie Lampton, Jr.

The lines of the body are simple, and the three seats on the door, when striped with a fine line, will make a really good effect. The proportions of the body are intended to be roomy and comfortable. The seats have round corners, and the back corner-pillars are also rounded, gradually lessening toward the top of box. This kind of square or straight phaeton we have found to be preferred by the majority of carriage-makers to the round-bottom style, the reason, no doubt, being that this body is less expensive and easier to make. DIMENSIONS: Width of body at door, out to out, 3 feet 2 inches width of toe-board 2 feet 11 inches--turn-under 1 ¼ inches on each side--width of hind seat, out to out, 4 feet--wheels 3 feet 5 inches x 3 feet 11 inches--Hubs 4¼ x 6½ inches--spokes 1⅛, inches, springs, 4 leaves 1½ inches wide--rocker plates 2¼ inches wide x ⅜, thick--axles 1¼ inches.

Furniture Car made by L. S. Burr & Co., Memphis, TN
From the new York Coach-Maker's Magazine May 1860

The extreme length of which is 18 feet 8 inches; width, 4 feet 6 inches; outside height, from bottom of sills to top rail, 2 feet 6 inches wide, with 9 leaves in side spring, and 11 leaves in cross springs. Will carry 5,000 pounds, axles 1½ inches.

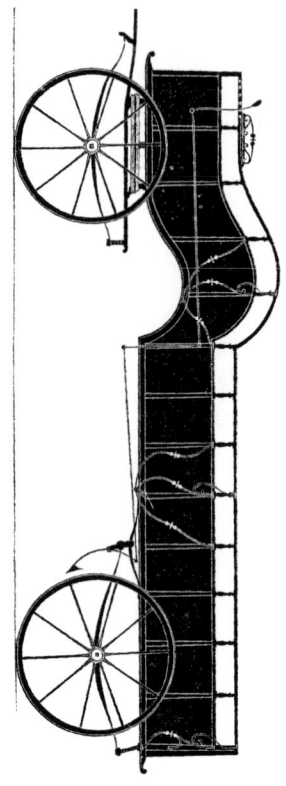

WAGONS ARE WHAT HELPED MAKE AMERICA A GREAT MANUFACTURING NATION. THEY CAME IN ALL SHAPES AND SIZES TO MOVE ALL KINDS OF FREIGHT AND GOODS.

Sebastian's One-Horse Truck built by J. Sebastian of New York, New York
From the Hub January 1877

Dimensions.--width of body outside, 4 feet 1 inch; length, 9 feet 10 inches... Painting.--Body, lake, striped with fine lines green and red, and one-eight line of gold. Gearing, wheels, varnished, striped gold, edged with red, and with distant lines of black; other parts light buff, striped wit broad line of gold, edged wit red, split with green. Trimming.-- Cushion of green morocco.

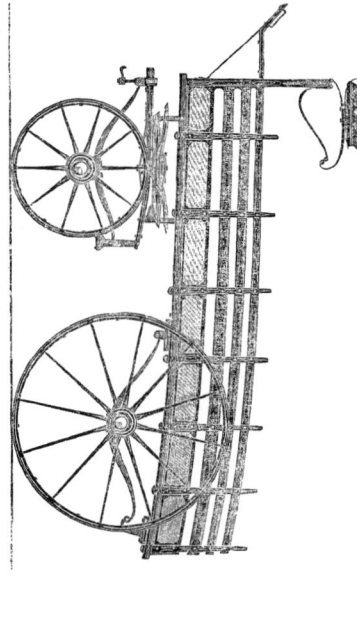

Light Two Horse Express Wagon made by Philip Ketterer, New York
From the Hub July 1878

Width of body, clear, 48½ inches, patent wheels, 3 feet 6 inches and 4 feet 10 inches...Painting.--Dark bluish-green body with vermilion gear; striping concord style. The lettering is done in gold and shade.

Studebaker Aluminum Wagon manufactured by Studebaker Bros., South Bend, IN.
From the Hub July 1893

Wheels, plain wood hubs, 3 feet 8 inches and 4 feet 6 inches. Diameter of hubs 8½ inches. Width of spokes at square end, face, 1⅜ inches. Length of gear from centers of hubs, 6 feet 8½ inches. Length of body at bottom, 10 feet 6 inches. Width of body, 3 feet 2 inches. Track, 4 feet 6 inches, center to center of tires on ground.

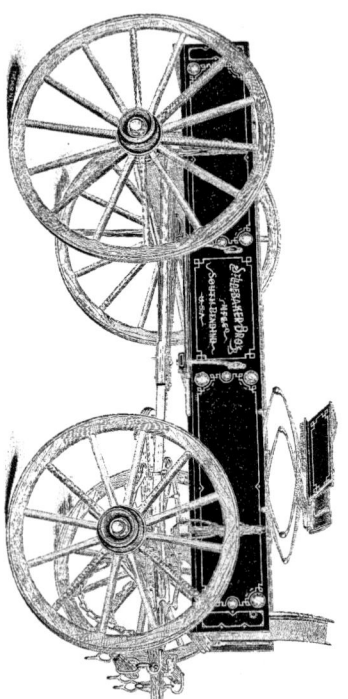

8

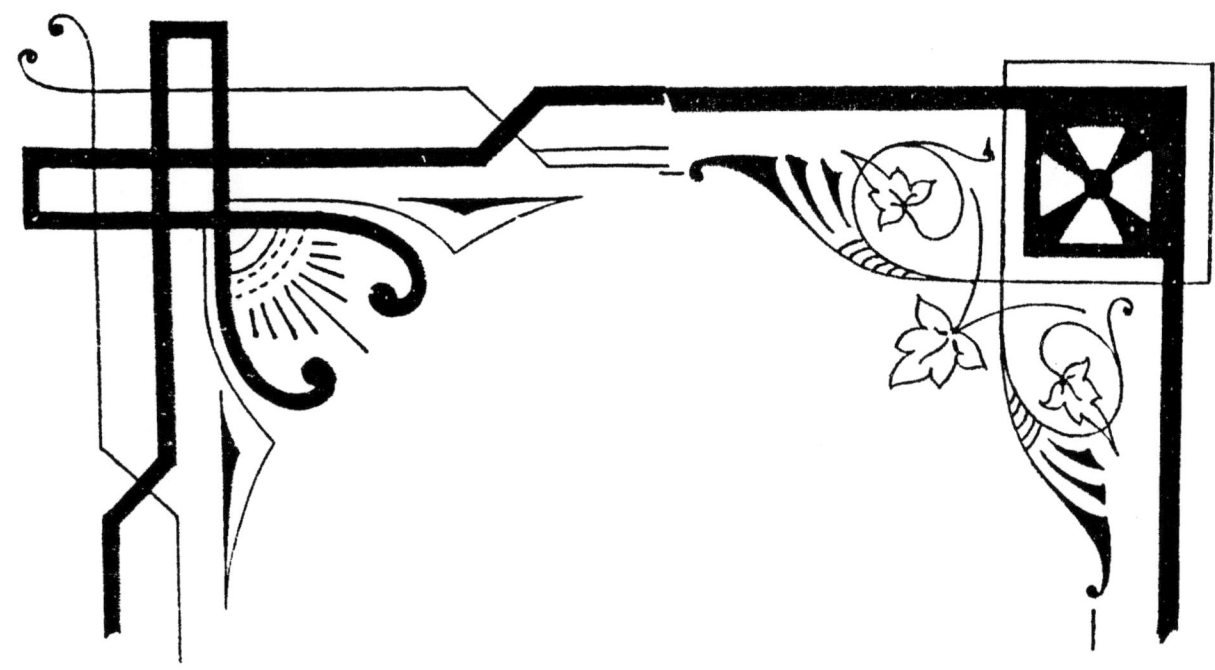

SECTION I
CONSERVATION

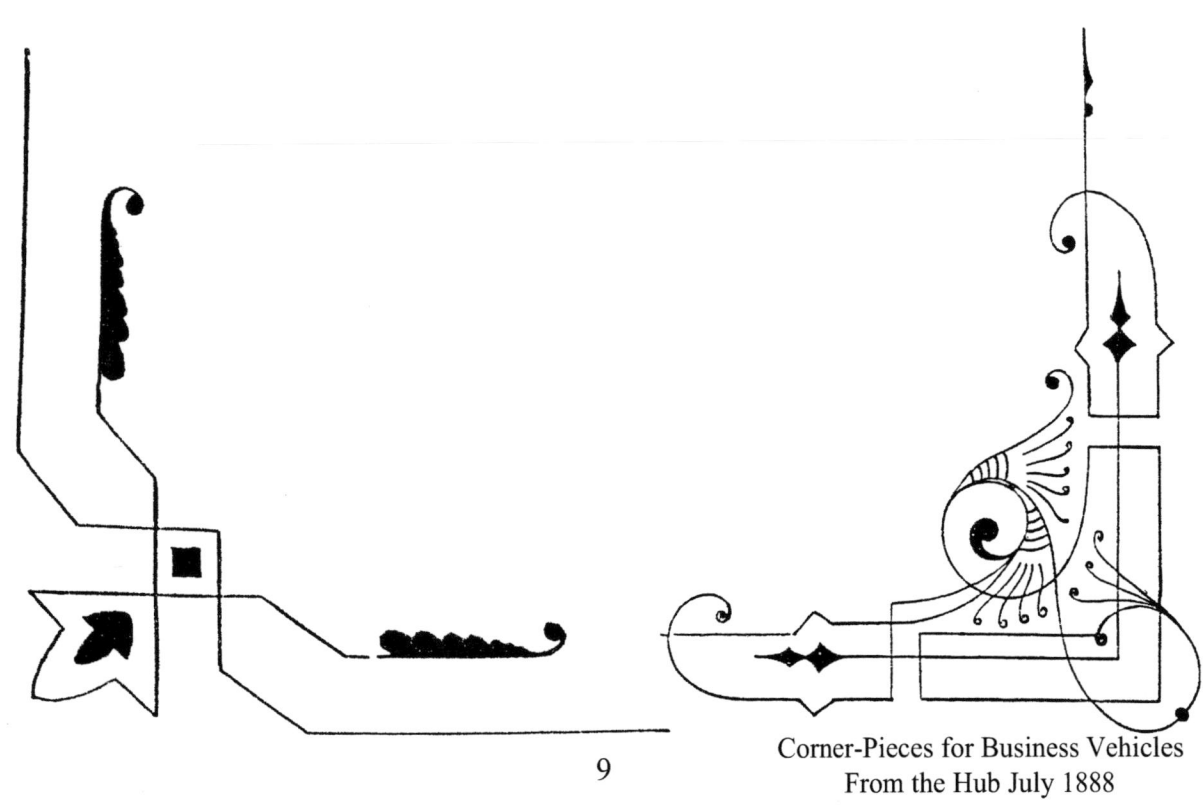

Corner-Pieces for Business Vehicles
From the Hub July 1888

BUGGY, RUNABOUT OR ROAD WAGON ARE ALL NAMES FOR THE MOST POPULAR AMERICAN HORSE-DRAWN PASSENGER VEHICLE.

Box Buggy
From the 1855 Coach Makers' Magazine

the sides are ¾ inch thick, of white wood. No rocker used, the bottom being fastened on the top side of the sill, inside. We consider these the most profitable buggy the manufacturer can make up, (owing to their simplicity of construction and at the same time the most room, convenient and durable vehicle of the kind that the customer can purchase.

Piano-Box Top Wagon On Four Elliptic Springs
From the Hub May 1872

Wagon hung on four elliptic springs, four very light iron pump-handles support the body; and in their place, two light iron spring-bars, running from side to side of body, the springs are 22 inches apart.

Square-Box Wagon On Side-Bars
From the Hub April 1881

Slanting molding and a corresponding finish for the riser; also a rocker of only the front slants up, and forms a kind of toe-board. Painting.--Body, chocolate brown; molding, black. The seat-skirt may be striped in imitation of Venetian blinds, using tints of the body color in connection with black. A fine line of vermilion glazed may be run along the molding. Gearing, black, striped with double fine line of vermilion glazed. Trimming.--Brown cloth. Mountings.--Silver.

Pneumatic Tire Road Wagon
From the Hub July 1895

Pneumatic tires on full height wood wheels, the suspension of the body being after the runabout style, with side springs instead of cross springs and side bars. Painting.--Body, black; gear, carmine, striped with two fine lines of black. Trimming.--Whipcord is used. The back is finished in two rolls. Cushion is made up in blocks.

These vehicles came in an endless variety of styles, different springing systems, (side spring, side bar, elliptic end spring, etc.), different tops (folding, standing, and no top), different seat styles (spindle, half back, & full back) and body styles.

CHAPTER 2

GUIDELINES FOR SELECTING A CONSERVATOR
from the American Institute for Conservation of Historic and Artistic Works

The conservation professional can diagnose present and potential problems, provide treatment when necessary, and advise on appropriate conditions for storage and exhibition. The choices you make will directly affect the objects you wish to preserve.

What is a Conservator?

Conservators are concerned with a number of factors in preserving an object, including determining structural stability, counteracting chemical and physical deterioration, and performing conservation treatment based on an evaluation of the aesthetic, historic, and scientific characteristics of the object. Conservation professionals have considerable practical experience, a broad range of theoretical and scientific knowledge, and a commitment to high standards and performance. A Conservator may be trained at a conservation graduate training program or by lengthy apprenticeship with experienced senior colleagues. Because of the increasingly technical nature of modern conservation, conservators usually specialize in a particular type of object, such as: paintings, works on paper, textiles, sculpture, furniture, rare books, photographs, or archaeological, decorative, or ethnographic materials. Conservators tend to work in private practice or for a museum, library, historical society, or similar institution.

Sometimes confusion arises about the terms "restoration" and "conservation." Restoration refers to the reconstruction of the aesthetic appearance of an object. Although restoration can be one aspect of conservation, the latter encompasses much more. Conservation involves examination, scientific analysis, and research to determine original structure, materials, and extent of loss. Conservation also encompasses structural and environmental treatment to retard future deterioration.

The careful selection of an appropriate conservator is particularly important, because the profession is not regulated by law. The American Institute for Conservation (AIC) is the national organization of conservation professionals. One of its goals is to define and maintain a high level of professionalism in conservation. This goal is reflected in the AIC Code of Ethics and Standards of Practice, copies of which are available from the AIC office.

FAIC Conservation Services Referral System

The Foundation of the American Institute for Conservation (FAIC) Conservation Services Referral System provides a systematic, consistent method of obtaining current information to identify and locate professional conservation services. The nationwide referral system enables you to address a wide range of conservation problems, whether your needs are long-range or short-term and whether your collection consists of thousands of valuable historic artifacts, one priceless work of art, or items of great personal value. In response to your inquiry, a computer-generated list of conservators is compiled and grouped by location, specialization, type or service provided, and AIC membership category (Fellow, Professional Associate, or Associate). AIC Professional Associates and Fellows have met specified levels of peer review and have agreed to adhere to the AIC Code of Ethics. Referral system information is provided free of charge.

What Questions to Ask Potential Conservators

Once you have obtained a list of potential conservators from the FAIC Referral System or have compiled one on your own by consulting conservation professionals, conservation organizations, or collectors, you must choose the most appropriate professional. When selecting a conservator to work on your object, seek sufficient information on the individuals under consideration. It may not be appropriate to restrict your search geographically, especially if the object presents unique problems. Many conservators are willing to travel.

Ask each potential conservator for the following information:
- training
- length of professional experience
- scope of practice (whether conservation is primary activity)
- experience in working with the kind of object for which you seek help
- involvement in conservation organizations
- availability
- references and previous clients

You are making a very important decision. Contact references and previous clients. The quality of conservation work is most accurately evaluated based on the technical and structural aspects of the treatment in addition to the cosmetic appearance; another conservation professional may be able to help you make this evaluation.

For time-consuming projects or collection surveys, you can advertise for a short-term contract conservator in a variety of publications, including the AIC News.

What To Expect

1. Procedures: A conservator will want to examine the object before suggesting a treatment. Prior to beginning a treatment, the conservator should provide for your review and approval a written preliminary examination report with a description of the proposed treatment, expected results, and estimated cost. The conservator should consult you during the treatment if any serious deviation from the agreed-upon proposal is needed.

2. Cost and Schedule: The conservator should be willing to discuss the basis for all charges. Determine if there are separate rates for preliminary examination and evaluation and if these preliminary charges are separate or deductible from a subsequent contract. Ask questions about insurance, payment terms, shipping, and additional charges. Conservators often have a backlog of work; inquire if a waiting period is necessary before new work can be accepted.

3. Documentation: The conservator should provide a treatment report when treatment is completed. Such reports may vary in length and form but should list materials and procedures used. The final report may, if appropriate, include photographic records documenting condition before and after treatment. Recommendations for continued care and maintenance may also be provided. Both written and photographic records should be unambiguous. All records should be retained for reference in case the object requires treatment in the future.

Exercising Caution

Conservation treatments are frequently time consuming and expensive. Be wary of those who propose to perform a quick and inexpensive restoration job, are reluctant to discuss in detail the materials and methods to be used, or will not permit you to see work in progress. If you have a large collection requiring treatment, you may wish to have one object treated initially before entering into a major contract. The added time or expense of finding the right professional will be small compared to the loss of future costs that could result from inadequate conservation treatment.

It is also important to note that conservators do not always agree. Ask about risks involved with certain treatment options. Speak to a number of conservators if you are unable to make a comfortable decision.

Points to Remember When Selecting a Conservator

Learn about the field of conservation.

Seek advice and recommendations through the FAIC Conservation Service Referral System and other professional organizations.

Contact a conservator's previous clients, and investigate references.

Request information regarding the conservator's background, training, experience, and professional affiliation.

Expect to receive the following from a professional conservator.

1. written preliminary examination report evaluating condition, proposing treatment, describing limitations of treatment, and providing an estimate of the treatment cost and duration.

2. notification during treatment of major changes in the proposal.

3. written and, if appropriate, photographic documentation of the treatment.

Prepared by Shelley G. Sturman with Martin Burke and Doris A. Hamburg, 1991

"Reprinted with the permission of the American Institute for Conservation of Historic and Artistic Works, 1717 K Street, NW, Suite 301, Washington, DC 20006; phone 202-452-9545, fax 202-452-9328

ANDERSON, HARRIS & CO., CINCINNATI, OHIO
From the Hub July 1884

SURREY, PARK PHAETON & EXTENSION TOP PHAETON ARE SOME OF THE NAMES FOR THE SECOND MOST POPULAR AMERICAN HORSE-DRAWN PASSENGER VEHICLES. SOME DAYS THEY JUST RAN OUT OF NAMES TO CALL VEHICLES SO THEY USED NAMES OF OTHER VEHICLES OR MADE UP NEW NAMES.

Odell & Waterman's Brett, New York, NY
From New York Coach-Maker's Magazine May 1860

The body is made without any side swell, with paneled or close seats, as seen in the draft, and a calash top to the back seat, and mounted on four springs. Heavy iron plates, well secured by screws to the inside of the rockers, are required in a job of this kind where no perch is employed.

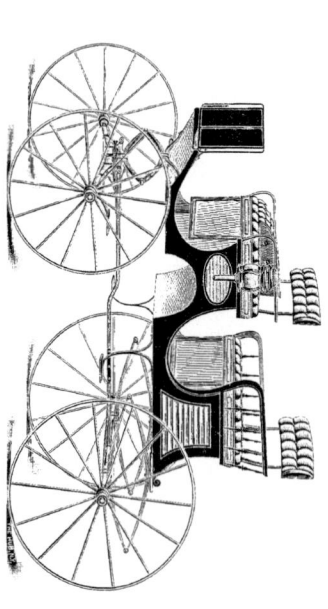

Tilbury Park Wagon--Designed by Quinsler & Co., Boston, MA
From the Hub July 1895

Painting.--Body, green; slats, light vermilion; molding, black. Gear, green, light red stripe. Trimming.--Green cloth, made in blocks, finished with black leather welts. Brass plated.

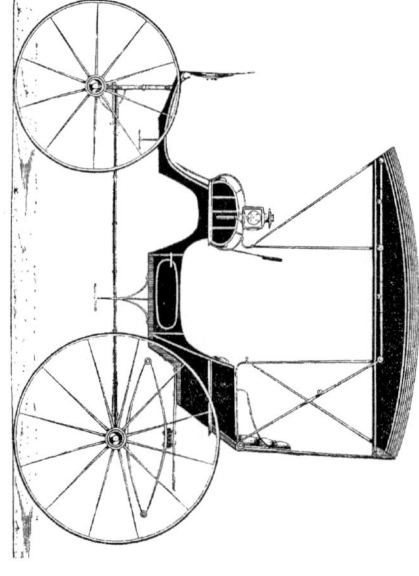

Three-Spring Extension Top Barouche--From the Hub April 1881
Painting.--Paint the front and back seats and door panel with burnt umber, and all other parts black. Stripe the moldings with a fine line of *le cuir* color. Paint the gearing with light *le cuir* color, and stripe with a "full stripe" of black. Touch up the spoke faces, bolt-heads, nuts, etc., with ornamental work (dots, etc.) In vermilion glazed. Trimming.--Brown cloth. Mountings.--Silver.

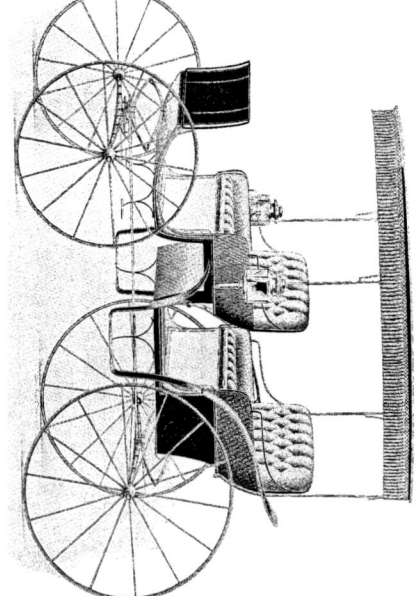

Cut-Under Surrey with Canopy Top
Built by Sturtevant-Larrabee Co., Binghamton, New York
From the Carriage Monthly 1910.

14

CHAPTER 3

CONSERVATION TREATMENT OF HORSE-DRAWN VEHICLES
Marc A. Williams, President
copyright, 1997

Treatment options for horse-drawn vehicles fall into three general categories: benign neglect; restoration; and conservation. Benign neglect of a vehicle that is *in a protected environment* often is the wisest choice when proper care cannot be given for financial or technical reasons. It is certainly a favorable option to a poorly-done treatment. However, benign neglect will not stabilize active degradation or improve the appearance of a vehicle.

Pitfalls of Restoration

Traditional restoration of horse-drawn vehicles has consisted mostly of repainting surfaces and remanufacturing components to produce a new-looking object. This approach is fraught with limitations.

* Original paints and finishes are destroyed, causing a decrease in historical and economic value.

* Repainting uses modern materials that can not replicate the depth of color or the complicated scheme of original paints and glazes.

* Original color schemes are misrepresented, due in part to a lack of understanding of the original application process and in part to insufficient analysis of the existing layering sequences.

* Original structural and decorative components are replaced, such as upholstery, wood and metal parts.

* The marks of use, wear and history are lost, with resulting surfaces often appearing much smoother and more polished than they were originally.

* Most restoration work of decorative surfaces is inferior in design and execution to the original.

The painted and decorative surfaces are a significant component of a vehicle and represent much of its visual impact. A vehicle that has lost these surfaces is little more than a reproduction, a shell empty of history. Fewer and fewer original surfaces exist due to over-restoration and we are in risk of losing this important part of our cultural heritage.

Conservation to the Rescue

Normally, original surfaces can be stabilized, preserved, and brought to a presentation appearance that is far more beautiful and accurate than a restored object. The scholarship, analytical capabilities, and technical ability exist to allow sensitive, ethical treatments of horse-drawn vehicles. This expertise has not developed within the carriage restoration field, but rather is part of the fine and decorative arts conservation professions.

This relatively new application of conservation technology to horse-drawn vehicles follows a progression that has occurred for other types of objects as well. Originally, conservation efforts grew out of a dissatisfaction with traditional restoration of paintings and fine art prints. In the

1920's, laboratories were established at several museums to pool the skills and knowledge of scientists, curators, scholars and restorers in the preservation of original fine art surfaces. The new breed of professionals who blended these skills were called conservators. By the 1960's, society's view of furniture, textiles, metalware and other decorative arts objects had changed to include them as important historic and cultural artifacts, not just utilitarian items. As such, they were considered worthy of the same quality of conservation treatment afforded to paintings. Today, these widespread attitudinal changes are reaching to horse-drawn vehicles, industrial machinery and automobiles. Conservation can help preserve the original components, surfaces, and integrity of these historic artifacts in many ways.

* Ultraviolet fluorescent microscopy can reveal the identity of intricate layering systems of paint, glazes and varnishes. Not only can colors be identified, but the nature of the paint types can be categorized. Additional appropriate analytical techniques, such as radiography, spectroscopy, and infra-red illumination, can provide information on the nature and condition of the surfaces.

* Custom treatments can be designed that remove later over-paint, revealing and preserving original layers, including the all-important glazing layers, that are lost during traditional stripping. Loose paint or varnish flakes can be reattached and stabilized. Missing areas can be inpainted to produce an unified appearance.

* The latest conservation materials can be used that are stable, identifiable from the original and removable in the future. Conservators realize that work done today will eventually deteriorate itself, and they make allowances for ease of future re-treatment.

* Preservation activities can reduce the risk of future deterioration. These can include application of protective coatings, as well as techniques for minimizing destructive stresses on composite materials.

* A team of conservators, curators and consultants can collaborate, each contributing specialized knowledge and skills.

* Condition Reports and Proposed Treatments outline specific detailed treatment needs of a vehicle, often listing several equally-viable treatment options. Meticulous written and photographic documentation of a treatment is provided to aid in future interpretation and re-treatment.

* Treatments adhere to the professional Code of Ethics of the American Institute for Conservation.

Neglect of horse-drawn vehicles, in consort with over-restoration, is threatening the survival of these wonderful ties with our past. It would be a tragedy for history to loose the contributions of these skilled artists and artisans. Conservation can help save the original surfaces of a vehicle, maintaining or increasing its value, while at the same time preserving an important part of our cultural patrimony.

Self Treatment Versus Professional Conservation Treatment

For owners and caretakers of historic vehicles, it is often difficult to know what treatment procedures need to be undertaken by a professional conservator, and what they can do themselves. Further complicating the problem are recommendations on care that are often conflicting. Even the definition of conservation itself, and the true abilities of self-reputed "conservators," are confusing.

As a general rule, if a person has the proper knowledge, skills, materials, and ethical outlook, they can safely undertake treatment of horse-drawn vehicles, whether they are a curator, conservator, or owner. However, obtaining the necessary abilities is very complex and requires extreme dedication. The greater the amount of experience someone has in conservation, the more self-obvious their skill limitations and knowledge shortcomings become. This paradox is responsible for a tremendous amount of unnecessary damage to collections objects. Too many people wrongly think they are sufficiently skilled and knowledgeable to perform conservation treatments. Understanding the history and ethical framework of conservation may help prevent some of this unfortunate damage.

What Is Conservation?

Stated simply, conservation is the *preservation* (minimization of future deterioration), *stabilization* (consolidation of existing deterioration), and *restoration* (repair of existing deterioration) of historic and artistic objects. The causes of deterioration are studied to better understand how they can be minimized. Environmental conditions are monitored and adjusted to approach the optimum level. Treatment materials and processes are tested for stability, safety with regard to the objects for which they are intended, and effectiveness. Hand skills and knowledge are developed constantly. Education and dissemination of information are promoted, as is fastidious documentation of treatments.

Early restorers used methods and techniques that were handed down from one generation to the next and were undoubtedly borrowed from the appropriate artistic and craft traditions. Due to the effect of the former guild system in Europe, many of these techniques and materials were kept secret and a mystique grew about restoration. In the second half of the 19th century, economic factors came into play. Values of historic pieces were rising and demand was high. Restoration ethics (or lack thereof) encouraged the execution of invisible repairs and visual "improvements" to pieces, culminating in an entire industry which produced fakes and pieces assembled from old parts.

By the early 20th century, artistic and historic objects were being examined in a more academic and scholarly manner. Their importance as cultural documents was being realized and, as such, the need to preserve them in an unaltered or "original" state became evident. A number of individuals in the museum world recognized the benefit of looking at deterioration and preservation from an interdisciplinary perspective. They noted that science, particularly chemistry, could be applied to better understand the compositional nature of a piece. This knowledge, combined with anthropological and art historical study of the object and its original production techniques led to a better understanding of deterioration processes. While the secrecy of traditional restoration had prohibited information exchange, early conservators became committed to open communication of ideas and techniques. For the first time, preservation and treatment processes could be examined objectively.

As the conservation profession developed, it borrowed techniques of examination and analysis from many different fields. These included the use of X-radiographs to view hidden areas of a piece, and the determination of an unidentified finish by infra-red spectrometry. Original conservation research added new information. All of this led to the realization that many traditional restoration techniques, while providing immediate visual or structural improvement, were actually causing long-term deterioration. Research and testing advanced at an ever-increasing pace.

Early training opportunities for conservators consisted primarily of hands-on experience similar to a traditional crafts apprenticeship. In order to fill a growing need for broad-based training, graduate conservation training programs were developed in the 1960's and 1970's. Requirements for admission to these Masters degree programs include a Bachelor's degree with significant course work in art history, chemistry, and studio art. Most programs also require experience as a technician or volunteer in a museum or conservation laboratory. The graduate programs generally include two years of courses in art techniques, materials science, methods of analysis, advanced chemistry, museum studies, conservation theory, and other related areas, in addition to hands-on work in the laboratory. Generally, the third year is an internship in a conservation laboratory under the supervision of a professionally-respected conservator in the chosen area of specialization. The great benefit of attendance at one of the programs is the condensation of information and opinions that might otherwise require a lifetime to obtain.

Most treatment of horse-drawn vehicles in the past has been greatly influenced by craft traditions that dictated smooth, "new" surfaces. Little attention was paid to original surfaces or materials, except to serve as a model for remanufacture or repainting, far too often executed in an inferior manner. A conservation approach to carriages is just beginning to have wide-spread impact. Eventually, a much greater number of original vehicles and surfaces can be preserved by utilizing a conservation approach to treatment.

Conservation Ethics

With the development of the conservation profession as we know it today, the need became apparent for a document outlining conservation attitudes. This was undertaken by the American Institute for Conservation (Washington, DC, 202-452-9545). The AIC Code of Ethics and Guidelines for Practice is embraced by all conservation specialties. This treatise represents and summarizes the essence of the conservation attitude which flavors every conservation activity and truly sets conservation aside as a unique profession. It is recommended that vehicle caretakers familiarize themselves with the Code and use it to guide their dealings both with conservators and with the objects themselves (copies are available from AIC).

The Code's Preamble nicely explains its entire concept:
> "The primary goal of conservation professionals, individuals with extensive training and special expertise, is the preservation of cultural property. Cultural property consists of individual objects, structures, or aggregate collections. It is material which has significance that may be artistic, historical, scientific, religious, or social, and it is an invaluable and irreplaceable legacy that must be preserved for future generations. In striving to achieve this goal, conservation professionals assume certain obligations to the cultural property, to its owners and custodians, to the conservation profession, and to society as a whole. This document sets forth the principles that guide conservation professionals and others who are involved in the care of cultural property."

Integrity of the Object

Perhaps the most important aspect of conservation ethics is an intense respect for the integrity of the object, which influences all activities of a conservator, from recommendations for exhibition to proposed treatments. ***The original or historic character and components of a piece must be preserved whenever possible.*** It is important to distinguish between original appearance and original components, which many times exhibit the effects of age and use. Returning a piece to original appearance may necessitate destruction of important information about the materials and techniques used by the maker, in addition to obliterating cultural information about how the piece was used and eliminating the subtle marks of age. Additionally, it should be noted that the original appearance is not necessarily the most important one. Alterations, both intentional or accidental, may have been made to the object that are important from an historic or cultural perspective. Examples include a sword slash on a table inflicted by Stonewall Jackson during the Civil War, wear on a chair rung, indicating generations of supported feet, or alterations to a carriage by the original maker a number of years after its manufacture.

Stable, Reversible Materials

Another important element of conservation ethics is the use of materials and techniques that are stable and well-tested. It is important to know that a material will not deteriorate quickly and, more importantly, that treatment processes will not damage the object. Many an object has been significantly harmed because an uninformed individual used a cleaner or varnish that slowly but steadily degraded the underlying surface. It is important to remember that such deterioration does not necessarily occur immediately, but over time its effects can be compounded severely.

Additionally, every attempt must be made to use processes and materials that are reversible or removable, both immediately following use and after aging. This is critical for several reasons. Materials used in conservation treatments are subject to the same deteriorative processes as is the object. They will not last forever and the object eventually will have to be re-treated. Reversibility also provides for implementation of new and better treatments in the future by allowing removal of the initial one without causing damage. Finally, there is always a chance something might go wrong during a treatment and reversibility insures being able to attempt it again.

Documentation

Documentation of a piece's initial condition and record of treatment is another important ethical issue. Conservators produce a detailed treatment proposal prior to working on a piece and a treatment report after completion of the project listing the specific techniques and materials used. These written records are usually supplemented with a series of photographs taken both before and after treatment. The tools of X-radiography, infrared and ultraviolet photography, microscopic cross-sectioning, and various analytical procedures are used as necessary to provide further documentary information. Documentation allows present and future owners to know exactly what has been done to an object and is especially helpful during future treatments or in the event of deterioration caused by previous treatments or improper care. It also prevents misrepresentation and confusion over what is original.

In a further attempt to clearly differentiate the work of the conservator from the historic components of the object, conservators will often choose to use materials and techniques that are easily detected as being modern. An extreme example of this would be the use of a plexiglass pedestal to support a coach wheel that is missing several spokes. In many instances, this treatment option would be considered too aesthetically and functionally severe. A more generally acceptable approach would be to make new spokes of the same or similar species of wood as the original, with coloration as necessary to produce a harmonious overall appearance of the wheel. Areas that are not normally visible would not be colored, allowing easy detection of the new wood.

Single Standard

In determining the proper treatment for a piece, the conservator must not consider the piece's value or aesthetic appeal. Each and every piece, regardless of age or rarity, deserves the same quality of treatment. In instances where time or funds are limited, the extent of the treatment can be adjusted, but never the quality. It therefore follows that a conservator can never answer the question of whether it is "worth" treating an object. Besides being unethical to consider the piece's value, it is obviously a conflict of interest for the conservator, since an affirmative answer will have a positive economic impact upon him/her. Only the owner or caretaker can consider value when determining whether or not to proceed with a treatment. If the owner is uncertain of the piece's value, he/she should consult with a competent appraiser and not with the conservator. Bear in mind that value is not only economic, but also includes historic value, cultural value, and emotional value as well.

Uniqueness

Each and every piece is unique. These differences may be subtle but they are extremely critical. Even if two identical horse-drawn vehicles were made at the same time by the same person, changes occurred that were dependent upon the total environment and history of each vehicle. Each one was probably made of slightly different materials which have somewhat different properties. If the vehicles had two different owners, the differing temperatures, relative humidities, light levels, and storage conditions will have caused differing degrees of deterioration. One owner may have used a cleaner, which affected the nature of the varnish, while the other did not. One carriage may have been subjected to daily abrasion, bangs, and water, while the other may have been used only for special occasions. Obviously, the vehicle receiving frequent use/abuse would have required more frequent repair and revarnishing, probably with materials that were completely different from the original, and possibly are not easily removable. Depending upon the abilities of the repairperson, it even could have suffered severe damage to its integrity and character.

For these reasons, the conservator must consider the specific needs and condition of each vehicle in order to determine an appropriate treatment procedure. Coupled with the fact that there are usually several equally acceptable treatment options, it becomes obvious that a conservator must personally examine an object before giving a suggested treatment. It is impossible to approach conservation from the perspective of a definite and consistent "cookbook" solution for each conservation problem. This is precisely why a conservator must have such a broad background of training and experience.

Educational Responsibility

It is the responsibility of the conservator to be aware of the latest information in their area of specialization in order to allow the best possible treatment of objects in their care. Additionally, conservators have an obligation to the profession to share their knowledge with other conservators, including the training of students in both formal academic settings and as apprentices and assistants. Education of the public and other non-conservators is accomplished through publications, lectures, workshops, and the answering of public inquiries.

These are several of the key elements of the AIC Code of Ethics. Numerous specific guidelines and concepts are generated from the use of these standards. The knowledge and application of these are the essence of the conservation profession. Anyone who is involved in the care and maintenance of vehicles is advised strongly to follow these standards as well.

Carriage Technology

In the United States, carriage building originated as a trade practiced predominantly by owner-builders. These individuals performed the arts of engineering, design, woodworking, blacksmithing, painting, varnishing and upholstery often alone in a small workshop. The degree of success in building the carriage depended entirely upon the ability of one individual. The variety of materials and techniques used for coach and carriage manufacture was vast and individualized. During the same time period in Europe, however, large manufactories existed. This allowed specialization of craftsmen in specific skill areas, resulting in a vehicle that reflected a very high degree of skill in all manufacturing operations.

In the United States, specialization in carriage manufacture grew progressively in the 19th century. By the second half of the century, large factories accounted for a high percentage of vehicles made. Along with specialization in skills came specialization in materials. Until this time, paints were individually ground and mixed by the painter. Each chose their own component materials based upon their personal successes and failures. By the second half of the 19th century, pre-mixed paints and varnishes were widely available. Experimentation by the larger companies led to an even greater variety of products used by the coach painter and varnisher, including both pre-mixed and individually-mixed materials.

In general, painting a vehicle consisted of the following steps.

    Primer coats. Often. this was white lead pigment in linseed oil, often with Japan or similar driers added. Sometimes varnish was added to the mix.

    Filler coats. These generally were inexpensive pigments in varnish. Drier and oil could have been added. Sometimes, left-over paint from other vehicles was used. Fillers were rubbed down between coats and after the final coat to a smooth surface.

    Color coats. The final color pigment was generally incorporated into oil or varnish, possibly with a drier added.

    Decorative painting, if any. This included striping, stenciling, and free-hand work.

    Varnish coats. Varnish generally consisted of natural resins such as copal and dammar, although oil-resin mixtures and even synthetics were possible. Pigment in small quantities could be added to create glaze layers. Varnish was rubbed down between coats, with the final coat applied as smoothly as possible and not rubbed out.

These procedures suggest two issues in the conservation of historic vehicles. First, the complexity of layers is great, even if only the original survives. Later repainting and revarnishing can make interpretation of the surfaces very difficult. And second, the nature of the paint layers may vary only in pigment content from the varnish layers, creating difficulty in, or even preventing, removal of one layer from another.

In addition to making vehicles, carriage makers also repaired them, including periodic revarnishing and repainting. The ravages of outdoor exposure eventually deteriorated the most expertly painted surfaces. The rapidity of this is illustrated by an advertisement from 1880 for a new and improved painting system for both carriages and railroad cars. "In one instance a Railroad...allowed *two years and ten months* to elapse after painting its first Car experimentally...(during all of which time the car did not return to the paint shop even for varnishing)."

Customarily, revarnishing was required every 1-3 years. Partial repainting and re-striping also were frequent. The light stability of pigments varied, and entire repainting could be needed in as few as 1 or 2 years, although most colors would last significantly longer than this. Repainting also occurred due to wear, damage or to keep up with the latest style. For commercial vehicles, repainting was done in the new owner's color scheme when used vehicles were sold.

When revarnishing, the old varnish could be removed either chemically or mechanically, or it could be left in place. Similar options existed for repainting. One of the most dramatic options was to burn the paint off to the wood surface. However, repainting also occurred with no surface preparation other than a light cleaning or sanding.

A primary issue in the conservation treatment of a horse-drawn vehicle is the determination of the presentation surface. Does the original painted surface survive? Do later paint schemes relate to the historic period of use? Is relatively recent repainting important or significant? Ideally, these sort of determinations are made by the curator, if the vehicle is owned by a museum, after reviewing the results of analysis and testing. However, if the object is privately owned, the conservator often must function in a quasi-curatorial role, attempting to guide the preferences of the owner into a responsible choice. Once a determination of the historic significance of each paint scheme is made, the condition of each of these layers can have an important contribution in designing a treatment. A later repainting that is in good condition may be the preferred after-treatment presentation surface. Remember, the vehicle was repainted for a reason. Often, this was due to degradation of the earlier layers. Additionally, the earlier layers may have been damaged in the surface preparation for the newer paint.

A final consideration is the technical feasibility of removing later layers from earlier ones. Often, the materials used are very similar in their composition. Removing a later sandarac-based paint layer from a similar earlier one can be extremely tedious and prohibitively expensive, or even impossible.

The majority of surviving horse-drawn vehicles dates from 1850 or later. Thus, the vast diversity of materials used in their decoration leads to equally diverse conservation challenges. The treatment approaches taken are specific to each individual vehicle and may or may not have relevance for other vehicles, even those of similar date and construction. ***Constant testing and re-evaluation is required for a successful conservation treatment!***

Causes/Prevention of Deterioration

Everything deteriorates, including historic vehicles, and nothing can be done to stop this eventuality. Must one, however, be resigned to a lifetime of restoration and repair? While it is true that deterioration cannot be stopped, it can be slowed significantly. It is the goal of the art conservation profession to do just that. By following proper maintenance and care procedures, owners, too, can contribute towards this end.

Wood, of which the majority of vehicles are composed, is an extremely complex material. Specialists have spent their entire careers studying one small aspect of wood and still do not understand it completely. While it is impossible, therefore, to predict exactly what will happen to a specific vehicle with the passage of time, a general understanding of the nature of wood allows determination of characteristic causes of deterioration. Wood is anisotropic - its properties are not uniform and are dependant upon the orientation of its cells. The most important of wood's many anisotropic properties to deterioration of objects is its dimensional response to variations in moisture content, determined primarily by the relative humidity of its environment. Movement in wood across the grain direction can exceed 10%, while longitudinal movement normally is well below 1%. As the relative humidity of the environment rises, wood absorbs moisture and expands. Conversely, when the RH falls, wood gives up moisture and contracts. This process occurs regardless of the age of the wood.

This dimensional variation with cycling relative humidity directly manifests itself as damage to vehicles. Boards allowed to move unrestrained will suffer, at worst, checking (small splits) at the ends of the boards. However, when the construction of a vehicle inhibits free movement, such as cross-grain attachment of wooden members to one another, degradation can result. If attempted shrinkage is prohibited, boards can split. Restricted expansion can result in compression setting of the wood - the physical squeezing together of the wood cells. Returning the board to its original moisture content results in a board that is permanently smaller and possibly split due to restrained shrinkage. The stresses generated by dimensional changes in wood are easily great enough to fracture glue joints with resulting joint looseness, and loss of parts. Prevention of damage to historic wooden vehicles from dimensional variation of wood can be accomplished only by stabilizing the relative humidity of the object's ambient environment.

Environmental factors other than temperature and relative humidity have deleterious effects on wood. Light will bleach the natural colorants found in wood, as well as the original paints and glazes applied by the maker. In addition, ultraviolet light can damage the cells on and near the surface of wood. Light will cause rapid degradation of varnishes, bleaching and crazing them and, in severe cases, will result in their cleavage and loss. Damage from light is not reversible, so vehicles should be kept in the lowest light level whenever possible. It is especially important to eliminate ultraviolet light, large proportions of which are contained in sunlight and most fluorescent light bulbs.

Dirt not only obscures the appearance and colors of the surfaces, but also contains chemicals that can attack varnishes, paints, and metal components. Insect infestation, commonly by the larvae of powder post beetles and of furniture beetles, can weaken wood so severely that it is unable to support its own weight. Early detection and fumigation are the solution to such infestations. It is important to bear in mind that adult beetles fly and females can lay eggs on wooden surfaces far from the infested one, so quick action once the problem is discovered is imperative.

Vehicles were built as utilitarian objects intended to be used, yet, unfortunately, even the most careful use hastens deterioration. Minimization of damage can be accomplished by understanding the limitations and weaknesses of each vehicle, and using it well within these limitations. In general, this consists of careful use, proper environmental conditions, correct maintenance procedures, and, when necessary, ethical and properly conducted conservation repair and treatment.

"Ideal" environmental conditions for the preservation of vehicles are constant relative humidity of 50% (this is appropriate for most of North America, with the exception of deserts and other dry regions), constant temperature of about 45 degrees F or lower, total darkness, no dirt or pollutants in the air, lack of insect infestation, and no handling or use. In most situations, these conditions are impractical. Therefore, it is important to vary from these levels as little as possible, with the knowledge that the amount of deterioration a vehicle will suffer will be directly proportional to the deviation from ideal environmental levels. If these ideals are approached, the need for additional care or maintenance virtually is eliminated. Rephrased, care and maintenance of vehicles consists, first and foremost, of providing the proper environment. Additional procedures only attempt to compensate for failings in the previous or current environments.

Composite Object

Horse-drawn vehicles are a consummate example of a composite object - one that is made of a whole host of materials. At a minimum, a vehicle consists of wood, metal, glue, and paint. In addition, it can also include varnish, glass, fabrics, under upholstery, plated metals, gold leaf, leather, oilcloth, wicker and other miscellaneous materials. Within each of these broad categories of materials, a wide variety of sub-types of materials were used. For example, it is not unusual to find three or four different types of wood utilized in a vehicle's construction.

Each material interacts with its environment in its own unique manner. Even one species of wood does not react the same as another species. Often, materials in association with each other react in conflict with one another. If the differences are sufficiently extreme, one will be damaged by the other. Perhaps the most common example is shrinkage or expansion of wood causing paint to detach from the wood and flake off. Another less obvious example is the acidic nature of some under upholstery materials causing the show fabrics in contact with them to become weakened and embrittled.

Thus, the overall nature of a horse-drawn vehicle is dictated by the interaction of the individual natures of the materials of which it is made. This is of extreme importance when designing a course of conservation treatment. A procedure that benefits and stabilizes one material may damage an adjacent one. Only an understanding of material properties coupled with careful treatment procedures can reduce the risk of damage to composite objects such as horse-drawn vehicles.

Before Treatment Documentation

The initial step in a conservation treatment is to fully document the existing condition of the vehicle. At a minimum, this consists of photographs of each of the sides with appropriate details (generally black and white negatives and color slides, as these are the most stable), and a written Condition Report. A Proposed Treatment Report will be provided also, which will clearly set out the intended procedures and materials for the entire vehicle. This will foster thinking about the treatment in a holistic manner and reduce the likelihood that treatment steps will be left out or that one step will negatively impact a succeeding step.

Depending upon the vehicle, further documentation and analysis may be needed. Low power microscopy will allow examination of surfaces to better assess their condition. On occasion, it may be necessary to conduct certain treatment steps while observing under magnification. High power microscopy can be used to evaluate the history of paint and varnish layers on a vehicle. Not only can sequencing of layers be observed from a paint and varnish cross-sectional sample, but also the gross characterization of the materials in each layer can be determined by using UV-fluorescence microscopy. For example, a natural plant resin can be separated from an oil, which can be separated from a synthetic resin. Very small samples are required for this type of examination. For most treatments involving surviving paint on horse-drawn vehicles, UV-fluorescence microscopy of several samples from different areas is critical to allow formulation of a treatment approach.

A number of other analytical techniques are available. Several of these are described briefly in the section of this book "Technical Examination and Microscopic Analysis of Painted Horse-Drawn Vehicles" by James Martin. Each technique can provide further information necessary for understanding the treatment needs of vehicles. Their usefulness depends upon the construction and condition of the specific vehicle undergoing treatment.

Structure

Conservation treatment of the wooden structure of horse-drawn vehicles is similar to conservation treatment of furniture and other wooden objects. Original parts should be stabilized as required and reinstalled. Splits and cracks can be glued in proper alignment with a hide-based glue, which is similar to the original adhesive used during the construction of horse-drawn vehicles. A good alternative is fish glue [see Appendix 1 for sources of supply for materials mentioned in this chapter], which is a liquid at room temperature and has a long working time, allowing gluing of more complex assemblies. Loose wooden parts can be glued also with hide glue. Spread glue on both parts or surfaces to be glued. Allow a few minutes for full saturation of the surface wood cells and apply pressure as required to properly align the pieces. If this is done correctly, a healthy amount of glue should be squeezed out of the repair, which can be cleaned up with a rag dampened with tap water. Resist the temptation to add nails, screws, or dowels to wood repairs. In nearly all cases, these split and fracture the wood and create a weaker repair. Gaps and losses in wood can be filled with a piece of wood of the same or similar species as the loss, using hide glue to attach the new piece. Any working or carving of the fill should not damage surrounding original wood. Smaller losses can be filled with an epoxy/micro-balloon mixture such as Araldite 1253. This material is carvable and can be finished and painted like wood. The advantage of the epoxy is that uneven losses can be filled without the need to "even up" the edges to produce a good join for a wood fill, thus preserving the maximum amount of original wood.

Wood degraded by fungal or insect attack can be consolidated with multiple brush coats of Butvar B-98 at about a 20% concentration in denatured alcohol. As with all solvents, be sure to use a respirator and provide adequate ventilation. Do not let the Butvar dry until the wood no longer absorbs any more Butvar, as penetration by additional applications is virtually impossible after drying. ***If the wood has paint or varnish on or near it, be sure to test them for solubility with denatured alcohol before applying the Butvar, or unintentional paint and varnish removal may result.*** If neighboring coatings are soluble, thorough masking off of these areas will be required.

When making repairs to wooden components, be sure that damage is not occurring unintentionally to the wood or to historically significant paints. For example, when clamping splits, be sure to use a pad beneath the clamp jaws that will prevent marring of the surfaces. Make sure that the pad does not stick to the surface due to glue squeeze-out by using a release agent under the pad. Waxed paper, aluminum foil, silicone release paper or plexiglass blocks can be used in most situations.

Paint Stabilization

Paint consists of three basic components, the pigments which impart color, the medium or binder which holds the pigment particles together, and the vehicle which allows the paint to be liquid and flow when it is applied. The vehicle evaporates after application, leaving behind the pigments in the medium. The earliest pigments were natural earths that were finely ground. Throughout time, many types of colored stones and other naturally-occurring compounds have been ground to produce pigments. Colors that did not occur naturally from these sources were produced by dying white pigments with the same types of dyes that were used for textiles. Called "lake" pigments, they generally were not as light stable as most of the natural pigments. By the end of the 19th century, synthetic pigments were being produced to complement those found naturally.

Mediums used for paint on horse-drawn vehicles were similar to those used for other types of paints. Drying oils such as linseed oil were one of the earliest mediums and generally were dissolved in turpentine. They produced a paint that became harder and less soluble as it aged. Accompanying this was a yellowing of the color. Oil paints were probably the most commonly used paint on vehicles in the 18th and early-19th centuries. As trade increased with the West Indies and other parts of the world through the 19th century, the use of natural plant resins for mediums increased. Most of the common natural plant resins were produced in tropical regions and included copal, dammar and sandarac. If they were dissolved in alcohol or turpentine, they were termed "spirit varnishes." Most plant resins remained soluble as they aged, unlike the drying oils. The primary animal resin used in the early- to mid-19th century in the United States was shellac, refined from the exudate of lac beetle larvae in Asia. While it was available as a medium for paints (dissolved in alcohol), its extent of use for horse-drawn vehicles is unclear since such as study has not yet been done.

By the mid-19th century, paint mediums were being made that incorporated a mixture of drying oil and natural plant resins. Generally, these were heated to produce a hybrid oil-resin medium that combines the properties of both. Most oil-resins were fairly hard, but yellowed and became less soluble as they aged. By the late-19th and early-20th centuries, intense experimentation in paint manufacture led to an extensive array of materials added to paints to change their appearance or performance. Development of synthetic materials also was occurring at this time, further increasing the variety of materials available to the carriage painter.

All of the materials composing the original paint on a vehicle, or making up repaint applied to it at a later time, have an effect on the conservation techniques that can be used safely and effectively. A procedure that works on an oil paint may completely remove a natural resin paint. ***For this reason, it is necessary to have as complete an understanding as possible of the existing paints and varnishes before beginning treatment.*** Cross-sections should be examined with UV-fluorescent microscopy. Armed with these results, small test areas should be done with swabs (Q-tips) in discrete areas with various solvents to determine their safety (see the Varnish Removal section of this chapter for possible solvents). Each different color or paint needs to be tested separately. Generally, the first step in treating paint is to set down any cleavage or lifted paint. A number of different adhesive agents can be used, depending upon the nature of the paint and the preferences of the conservator. For thin to medium paint, this author commonly uses Acryloid B-72, approximately 10%-15% concentration in toluene. As with all solvents, be sure to use a respirator and provide adequate ventilation. Test all affected paints and varnishes with toluene on a swab prior to application to verify that they are not affected by the solvent. Carefully apply the B-72 with a fine artists' brush beneath each lifted paint flake and set it down with gentle pressure. Use of silicone release paper can aid in this process. In some instances, a heated spatula may be required to assist in setting down the paint. Excess B-72 can be removed with toluene on cotton swabs. This author commonly uses gelatin or dilute hide glue to reattach thicker paint. Similar application and setting-down techniques are used. Excess gelatin or hide glue can be removed with water on a cotton swab.

Removal of later repainting from earlier historic paint is a process that requires extreme caution, knowledge and skill. In a few instances, it can be relatively easy, such as removing a natural plant resin paint from an oil paint. However, in the vast majority of situations on horse-drawn vehicles, safe paint removal can be extraordinarily complex and tedious. In some instances, it is simply not possible with the currently available technology. The future may hold solutions for today's enigmas. Removal of one paint layer from an earlier one should be referred to a conservator and should not be tried by owners of vehicles.

Varnish Cleaning

Varnish was applied originally to horse-drawn vehicles to optically saturate and enrich the paint colors, and to protect the paint from use, including from weathering. Varnish was applied as often as every 1-3 years, and it is common to find as many as 10-15 layers present on historic vehicles. Varnishes consist of a film-forming agent (essentially the same as the medium for paint) and a solvent that dissolves it and renders it the proper consistency for application. Natural resins (sandarac, copal, dammar, rosin and shellac) and oil-resin mixtures were the most common film-forming agents used to formulate varnishes for historic vehicles. However, similar to paints, by the late-19th century, numerous additives were being mixed in to change the varnish performance.

Normally, varnishes were applied in their natural color. However, on occasion, they were tinted to produce a specific shade or effect. Termed glazes, tinting was done by the addition of dyes dissolved in a solvent or thinly dispersed pigments. Most varnishes become more yellow as they age. If their thickness is sufficient, they can appear as an orange discoloration, or even as a brown layer that is opaque enough to hide completely the painted decoration. When varnish discoloration exists, it can be difficult to determine if this is the natural effect of aging, or if the varnish originally was tinted. Examination of cross-sections under the microscope will assist in answering this question.

Depending upon the thickness and nature of the varnishes applied to a vehicle, it may be possible to preserve them intact. This is preferred, since the varnishes usually date to the period of historic use, and thus are significant original components of the vehicle. Often, cleaning the surfaces of dirt will reveal an appearance that is fully acceptable.

Dirt on varnished surfaces *in good condition* may be removed with surfactants which are mixed in a dilute solution (1-2%) with distilled or deionized water. Common types are Orvus Liquid, Igepal, and Triton X-100. A small spot in an obscure area is tested with the solution on a cotton swab. All areas that appear to be a different surface coating or material must be tested separately. If the solution does not damage the test area, it can be used to clean the piece. A soft cloth or pad is dampened *slightly* and rubbed over the surface. Avoid excessive wetting of the surface, which may cause water damage. The cleaned surface should be wiped with a soft cloth/pad dampened slightly with plain distilled or deionized water to remove surfactant residues, followed by a dry soft cloth/pad. Varnished surfaces that show deterioration or bare wood *should not be cleaned* with water solutions of surfactants and should be referred to a conservator.

If a varnished surface is to be preserved, but has lifted or insecure varnish, these areas can be consolidated and set down in a manner similar to lifted paint. Test the varnish with toluene on swabs to verify that it is not soluble. Brush Acryloid B-72 under the insecure areas with a very fine artists' brush (use a respirator and adequate ventilation). Gentle pressure can be used to flatten the lifted varnish, utilizing a separator such as silicone release paper. Use extreme care, as lifted varnish can be very delicate. Excess B-72 can be removed with toluene on cotton swabs.

After a varnished surface has been cleaned and any insecure areas have been stabilized, a protective coating can be applied. If the vehicle will be kept indoors and use will be minimal, a coating is not required for protective reasons. However, it may be desired to optically saturate the painted surfaces and enhance the richness of the colors. If a vehicle is in less-than-ideal storage conditions or will be used, a protective coating should be applied. Additionally, application of a coating can consolidate powdery original varnishes and can eliminate hazing or blanching of the varnish. The success of this should be tested in a small area before applying a coating to large surfaces. See the section on Protective Coatings later in this chapter for further information.

Varnish Removal

If the original varnishes are too severely degraded or are too darkened, their removal may be desirable. Since varnish solubilities are often the same as paint solubilities, due to the similarity of materials used for their manufacture, removing a varnish from a paint can be very complex or even impossible. For this reason, it is necessary to examine cross-sections with UV-fluorescent microscopy to determine the gross nature of each varnish and paint layer. If, for example, the paint is oil bound and the varnish is natural plant resin, it should be possible to remove the varnish from the paint. However, if both the paint and varnish are made of plant resins, safe removal will be impossible with normal solvent application. Sophisticated techniques such as solvent gels may be effective, but these treatment processes should be utilized only by a conservator. Mechanical removal of a plant resin varnish from a plant resin paint may be possible, but is extremely tedious. Solvent removal possibilities are as follows for general types of paints and varnishes.

Paint - Varnish	Varnish Removal Possibilities
Oil paint - natural resin varnish	Yes, varnish usually can be removed
Oil paint - oil-resin varnish	Yes or no, depending upon the varnish Refer to a conservator if difficult
Natural resin paint - natural resin varnish	No - refer to a conservator
Natural resin paint - oil-resin varnish	No - refer to a conservator
Oil-resin paint - natural resin varnish	Yes or no, depending upon the varnish Refer to a conservator if difficult
Oil-resin paint - oil-resin varnish	No - refer to a conservator

If the paint/varnish natures allow solvent removal of the varnish, test small areas with different solvents on swabs (use a respirator and adequate ventilation). Do this in an area that will not show should one of the solvents produce unacceptable results. Each different color needs to be separately tested. Be particularly careful in areas of striping and decorative painting, as these are often natural resin paints, even if the body colors are oil paints.

The goal of varnish removal is to use the least aggressive solvent that will adequately dissolve the varnish without damaging the paint. A whole host of solvents and solvent mixtures is available to the conservator. However, a good understanding of chemistry is required to evaluate each individual situation and choose the best options. For this reason, the owner should limit his/her solvent options to a few solvents of known performance. These should be tested in order from least to most aggressive, as follows:

a) mineral spirits (will remove waxes and fresh oils)

b) toluene (will remove some modern coatings)

c) mixture of ½ distilled water and ½ denatured alcohol (alcohol is the solvent for most natural resins, and it may blanch [turn white] painted surfaces - generally, this will disappear when a protective coating is applied. Test to verify this, and stop if blanching does not disappear.)

d) denatured alcohol

e) mixture of 2/3 denatured alcohol and 1/3 acetone (acetone will dissolve most oil/resins and some oil films - use caution!)

f) mixture of 1/3 denatured alcohol and 2/3 acetone (this is more aggressive - use caution!)

g) acetone (use extreme caution as many paints can be dissolved by acetone)

If none of these solvents are both effective and safe to the painted surfaces, refer the vehicle to a conservator. Be sure to use a respirator and adequate ventilation whenever using solvents. Once a solvent has been selected, varnish can be removed by dampening a small cotton pad or cotton ball with the solvent and gently running it over the varnish surface. Work in a small area. Be constantly vigilant for signs of paint removal. Stop immediately if any problems occur. Be particularly careful around different paint colors, especially striping or decorative paint. In some areas, it may be necessary to work with solvent on cotton swabs in order not to damage the paint. If any questions or uncertainties arise, contact a conservator for advice. Most conservators are willing to provide expertise for a fee, but they will have to personally examine and test the vehicle.

Inpainting Losses

Once the paint has been stabilized and the varnish cleaned or removed, the next step in a treatment is to inpaint losses. Color matching is a very specialized skill. If the owner does not possess this ability, inpainting should be referred to a conservator. If the varnish has been removed, this author prefers to utilize two applications of an isolating coating. This saturates the paint colors, allowing a better color match and provides a protective layer between the original materials and the inpaint. Acryloid B-72, approximately 20% in toluene, is a good choice for an isolating coating (use a respirator and adequate ventilation). Apply two coats.

In most instances, inpainting can be done directly in the paint loss. Artists' acrylic paints in tubes are a suggested material. An excellent brand is made by Golden. ***Do not use oil paints***, since they become less soluble and discolor as they age. Colors can be intermixed until the exact shade is achieved. Depending upon the brand of paint, dilution may be required. Apply the paint only in the loss. Do not overlap on the surrounding original paint. When matching the color, be sure to allow for the slight color change when a protective coating is applied as a final treatment step.

If losses are deep, they may need to be filled prior to inpainting. This is a choice that depends primarily upon the aesthetic taste of the owner, and the willingness to spend what can be a considerable amount of extra time. Fills should be done after the isolating coating has been applied. For most applications, gesso can be used as the fill material. An alternative is a micro-balloon mixture sold in many hardware stores as low-density or light-weight spackling. Do not damage surrounding areas when applying and evening fills. Limit the fills to only the areas of loss and do not allow them to overlap onto original surfaces. After the fills have been leveled, inpainting can proceed as described above.

Protective Coatings

Once inpainting has been completed, a protective coating needs to be applied. This, in fact, replicates the original technique of varnishing the paint after its application, and produces an appearance that is more historically accurate than is possible with modern automotive lacquers. Several different coatings are possibilities, depending upon the nature of the paint and varnish on the vehicle, as well as what was done during the conservation treatment. Acryloid B-72, approximately 20% in toluene, can be used if the paints and varnishes are not affected by toluene (test first) and B-72 was not used to set down cleavage or as an isolating coating. Soluvar varnish (used undiluted from the bottle) and Acryloid B-67, approximately 20% in mineral spirits, can be used if the paints and varnishes are not affected by mineral spirits or if B-72 was used in a previous treatment procedure. ***Do not use other types of commercial varnishes***, since they will not be removable from the original surfaces in the future and will greatly complicate future preservation treatments. Protective coatings are usually brushed on with a minimum of two coats, since this produces an appearance similar to the original, although they can be spray-applied if all surrounding areas can be masked off to prevent coating deposition.

Overpainting

In certain instances, it is not possible to properly treat the original surfaces of the vehicle. This may be due to similarities in the nature of the paint and the varnish layers, not allowing the removal of a discolored varnish. Perhaps the original paint has been covered by a later inappropriate paint that can not be removed safely. These types of problems can not be solved with the current level of conservation knowledge. However, it is extremely likely that the future will hold solutions of which we can not yet conceive. For this reason, it is important to preserve the original surfaces, even though it may not be possible to reveal them. Reversible overpainting allows preservation while recreating an acceptable facsimile of the historic appearance. Do not decide cavalierly to overpaint, as removal of overpaint, even when it is designed to be reversible, adds time to future treatments, and somewhat increases their complexity.

Reversibly recreating decorative paint is a specialized skill. It is suggested that this phase of a treatment be referred to a conservator or to a decorative painter who is willing to follow conservation guidelines. ***Do not alter the surviving surfaces in any manner*** other than cleaning them of dirt. Apply two or more layers of a reversible isolating coating, such as Acryloid B-72, 20% in toluene (test first, and use a respirator and adequate ventilation). Repaint the body colors and decorative details over the isolating coating using artists' acrylic paints as described in the inpainting section. These paints are available in larger sizes for more effective mixing of body colors. After completing overpainting, apply a protective coating as described above. By using reversible materials for the overpainting, the vehicle can be re-treated in the future once the technology is available.

Metal Components

Metal components of horse-drawn vehicles are generally of two broad categories, those that were painted and those that were polished or plated. A common problem with painted metal is cleavage and detachment of the paint. Generally, the paint can be reattached by brushing on Acryloid B-72, approximately 20% in toluene, as a consolidant. Be sure to test the paint first to verify that it is not soluble in toluene, and use a respirator and adequate ventilation. Two or more coats can be applied as needed.

Iron components can rust beneath the paint. As iron is converted to iron oxide (rust), it becomes larger in volume, causing disruption of the paint. If disruption is mild or moderate, consolidation and reattachment of the paint is the recommended option. If the disruption is severe, it may be necessary to remove the paint and the rust beneath it. Since this is a loss of original material, choose this option only if absolutely necessary. Rust can be removed mechanically by brushing or with air peening using walnut shells or glass beads. Sandblasting is too severe to use on historic surfaces. These rust removal techniques can be applied to iron that no longer has its original paint surviving, or was never painted originally.

After the rust has been removed, application of several coats of B-72 will provide a protective layer on the iron that will slow future rusting. Iron that originally was unpainted can be left with just B-72. If the iron was painted, new paint can be applied with artists' acrylics directly over the B-72, followed by a final protective coating.

Rust can also stain the surface of historic paints and varnishes. While often this causes a permanent discoloration, sometimes the stain can be removed. However, mixing the stain removal agent is very complex, requiring laboratory equipment and supplies, so the assistance of a conservator is needed.

Other hardware was meant to be bright and shiny originally. Polishing of hardware, even with the mildest of agents, removes some of the surface metal. After repeated polishings, surface decorations and details can be lost and plated surfaces can be removed to the base metal. If the polish is not removed completely, residues can act as sites for corrosion of the metal. Some people prefer the appearance of oxidized hardware, while others prefer a shiny appearance. Polishing does not enhance preservation, so the choice to do it should be based upon personal aesthetics.

If you choose to polish, remove the hardware from the vehicle, being sure to note the exact location of each screw and nut. Polishing hardware on the vehicle abrades the surrounding varnish and paint, and allows polishing agents to run beneath the hardware where they can damage the metal and the adjacent materials. If removal is not possible, try to slip Mylar under the edges of the hardware and protect all adjacent materials from polish contact. After polishing with any good metal polish (Nevr-Dull, works well for most metals, commercially available jewelers cloths can be used on silver), thoroughly remove all residues by rinsing with acetone. Gloves must be worn when handling hardware to prevent fingerprinting. Latex surgical gloves work well.

Coat the hardware with Acryloid B-72 for pieces that are not used or handled, or with Acryloid B-48N for pieces that will receive use. These coatings will prolong greatly the time between polishings, perhaps for as long as 50 years, and they are reversible, allowing removal and repolishing in the future. If hardware is not polished but allowed to remain oxidized, application of a protective coating is suggested. Clean the surfaces first with a surfactant as described previously.

Upholstery

The treatment of upholstery is a very specialized area that should be undertaken by an upholstery conservator. Preservation of original under upholstery and show covers is of extreme importance. Preferably, these should be kept in place on the vehicle. Most reupholstery done commercially on horse-drawn vehicles is far inferior to the original in both materials and workmanship. Upholstery treatments can include cleaning, deacidification, stabilization of existing materials, and replacement of missing areas. If upholstery must be recreated, minimally-intrusive techniques can be applied that limit damage to the wood or other substrate materials. Please contact an upholstery conservator for details about these treatments and techniques.

Other Attachments

Several other materials are found commonly in association with horse-drawn vehicles. Common examples include leather, oilcloth, wicker, cane, and patent leather. Each of these has its own specific preservation and treatment needs. Generally, it is necessary to speak with a specialist conservator for each of these materials. Consult the American Institute for Conservation's (AIC) referral network at 202-452-9545.

While this author is not a leather specialist, several comments may help prevent unintentional damage to leather. Historic leather is quite different in nature and chemical composition from modern leather. Studies of commercially available leather treatments have shown that many actually promote damage over the long term, rather than preventing it. Additional research is needed, and contradictory advice is present within the conservation profession. The safest current recommendation is not to apply any treatments to historic leather.

After Treatment Documentation

The final treatment step is to record the materials and processes used in a Treatment Report. This document will allow future owners and conservators to understand how to properly care for the vehicle, and will provide vital information for re-treatment, since eventually this will be necessary. It will also allow real-time assessment of the success of the specific procedures and materials that were used. Photographs (color slides and black and white negatives) should be taken of the vehicle after treatment.

Routine Maintenance

Care and maintenance of vehicles consists, first and foremost, of providing the proper environment. Additional procedures only attempt to compensate for failings in the previous or current environments. Perhaps the most important factor to control is the relative humidity, since the vast majority of materials of which vehicles are fabricated are hygroscopic and give up or take on moisture from the environment. Each collection and storage building are unique and the specific solution chosen requires careful consideration of the properties of both. Generally, it is best to think of a target range of RH between 40%-60%, allowing the temperature to fluctuate as necessary to keep the RH more constant. When controlling an environment for stable RH, temperatures normally will fall within a 10 to 90 degree Fahrenheit range, which does not pose a problem for preservation of vehicles. Even greater stability of the RH, for example from 45%-55%, decreases the risk of damage to hygroscopic collection materials. Attempting to control both the relative humidity and the temperature significantly complicates control systems and makes them far more expensive to install, operate, and maintain.

Stability of conditions is important on a daily basis, as well as seasonally. Therefore, generally it is better to keep the RH and T stable day and night, rather than turning up the heat (if it exists) when people are present (forcing down the RH) and down when they leave (allowing the RH to rise). Generally, opening doors and windows for air circulation and ventilation is not a good idea for collections preservation. This promotes more rapid changes of T and RH, as well as access for dirt and insects. In fact, tightening the windows and doors by the judicious use of weatherstripping and storm windows and doors will help to hold more even RH and T in both the summer and winter. Added benefits are savings in fuel for winter heating, as well as reduced amounts of dust and insects infiltrating the building.

Clearly, eliminating moisture sources within a building is critical for preservation. Proper site grading that facilitates rain runoff, perimeter drains, and the use of gutters all promote moisture control. Eliminating roof leaks, making sure windows and doors fit tightly, and keeping flashing around chimneys in good repair also contribute. The first step in any program of environmental control is providing a tight, "dry" building envelope.

Designing simple environmental improvements is a service that many conservators can provide. Often the use of dehumidifiers in the warmer weather in combination with low-level winter heating (10-15 degrees F above ambient) can keep the RH within the desired 40%-60% range.

Dusting

Dusting may be done with soft cloths, either dry or moistened ***very slightly*** with distilled or de-ionized water to hold the dust. A misting sprayer directed at the cloth, not the object, works well. ***Do not use polishes or dusting aids***. An alternative cloth is the Dust Bunny™. It is woven of two different fibers that, when in association with each other, create a static charge and hold the dust to the cloth. The cloths are reusable and washable. Be sure to change them as they get dirty.

Do not dust surfaces with active cleaving and lifted paint or varnishes. Such areas may be able to be dusted with a clean natural bristle paint or artist's brush. Watch carefully for loss of surface and stop if it is observed, referring the problem to a conservator.

When moving or handling vehicles to allow dusting, wear clean cotton gloves to prevent corrosion and deterioration caused by hand salts, oils and acids. This is extremely important for metals and textiles.

If the storage building has an air handling system, consider installing high efficiency filters. Run the system fan continuously all year long. If an air handling system is not present, it is possible that stand-alone dust filtration units can aid in the collection of dust within the building. In order for any type of filtration to be effective, the building must be as tightly sealed as possible (including keeping the windows closed), or they will be trying to filter all the air in the surrounding region.

Dust Covers

The best type of dust protection is elimination of threats before they reach the vehicle. Dust can be filtered from the air with an air handling system, light levels can be reduced or eliminated, environmental conditions can be stabilized, leaks can be prevented, and birds, insects and other sources of liquid stains can be excluded from the exhibition or storage area. Dust covers should be used only if these factors are not controlled properly. In reality, very few owners will be able to achieve proper control, and some sort of protective dust covers must be used.

Dust protection of historic vehicles has as its primary goal the exclusion of dust and dirt from the surfaces of the vehicle. However, there may be several secondary goals, depending upon the specific dust cover used. These include partial light protection, moderation of environmental fluctuations, and shielding from leaks, bird droppings, and other liquids. Dust cover options include sheeting, of polyethylene, cotton muslin, Tyvek or Gore-Tex. Each has its advantages and disadvantages. These are summarized in the Table below.

Polyethylene is the least expensive. It provides protection from the finest dust, as well as from liquids. Polyethylene is a vapor barrier, thereby helping to stabilize the local environment of the vehicle. It has an additional advantage of allowing you to see the vehicle without removing the dust cover, thereby detecting deterioration, such as clothes moth infestation of upholstery. It does not provide light protection unless black polyethylene is selected, which obviously negates the visibility advantage.

Polyethylene is chemically inert and of neutral pH. Polyethylene can develop a mild static charge, causing it to cling lightly to surfaces and to attract dust. Additionally, since it is a vapor barrier, if moisture accumulates beneath it (such as in a flood or on a dirt floor that has poor drainage), the moisture will evaporate slowly, possibly leading to mildew growth. The risk of this can be reduced by keeping the polyethylene about 6 inches from the floor, thereby assisting with air circulation. Polyethylene is available in sheets or in large preformed bags. A light weight (1 mil thickness) is recommended, since it weighs less and conforms more readily to odd shapes. It is available at local hardware stores (sheets), or from material handling companies (large bags).

Unbleached cotton muslin sheeting allows the transmission of moisture and provides some degree of light protection, although this is not complete. However, fine dust penetrates easily to the vehicle surfaces, it does not allow any stabilization of environmental conditions since it passes moisture, and it will not protect from liquids such as bird droppings or leaks. If cotton is wetted, it can hold moisture against the vehicle surfaces, increasing the risk of mildew damage and surface delamination. Additionally, if the vehicle has sticky surfaces from heat, deterioration, or the past use of oil polishes, the cotton fibers can become embedded and create removal problems. Unbleached cotton muslin can be obtained at fabric suppliers and is moderately inexpensive.

Tyvek allows moisture vapor transmission, and provides some degree of protection from liquids, although this is not as great as polyethylene. It affords improved dust protection over cotton, but is not as effective as polyethylene. Tyvek assists in light protection, being similar to cotton muslin, and is less likely to stick to surfaces than cotton, although it is more likely to do so than polyethylene. Primary drawbacks are its stiffness - it does not drape easily over surfaces, and its moderate expense. Additionally, nearly all Tyvek is treated with an anti-static coating which purportedly is acidic and should not be used against sensitive surfaces such as upholstery. Tyvek is available in rolls 9 or 10 feet wide from building suppliers, where it is used as a house wrap to protect from wind infiltration. Purchase the brand that is white in color. It is also available in a special untreated version free from anti-static coating from Talas (212-219-0770), a preservation supplies vendor. Unfortunately, the maximum width is 45 inches, so seaming will be required for covering vehicles.

Gore-Tex sheeting transmits moisture vapor, yet prevents liquid penetration. It also excludes virtually all dust, and blocks some of the light. It is less likely to stick to tacky surfaces than cotton if the smooth side is placed against the object, but is not as resistant to this as polyethylene. Since it passes moisture, it is not effective in slowing environmental fluctuations. Its primary disadvantage is that it is extremely expensive. Gore-Tex is available from Talas as "thin Gore-Tex barrier." It, too, is only available in 45 inch widths and would require seaming for use on vehicles.

If funds are limited for dust protection, drape light weight polyethylene over the vehicles. Clear is preferred to black, thereby allowing easy inspection through the dust cover, with light control occurring at the windows (inexpensive pull-down room darkening shades work well). Be sure to allow at least 6 inches of air space between the end of the dust cover and the floor.

	Cost per 100 sq ft	Dust exclusion 1-10 best	Advantages	Disadvantages
Polyethylene	$2.	10	Smooth pH neutral Liquid protection Stabilizes T & RH Can see through it Large variety of widths/sizes	Slight static charge May trap moisture No light protection
Unbleached cotton muslin	$17.	4	Passes moisture vapor Some light protection	Passes fine dust No liquid protection Can't see through it No T & RH stability Can stick to surfaces
Tyvek	$14.	8	Passes moisture vapor Some light protection Liquid protection	Static charge (untreated) Narrow widths (untreated) Acidic (anti-static treated) Can't see through it Minimal T & RH stability Stiff
Gore-Tex	$514.	9	pH neutral Passes moisture vapor Some light protection Liquid protection	Can't see through it Minimal T & RH stability Narrow widths expensive

If funds are a little more substantial, construct frames to hold the polyethylene dust covers away from the surface of the vehicles. This increases the air circulation, and reduces the minor risks of sticking to the surfaces or condensation from trapped moisture. If the building floor is damp, unbleached muslin or Tyvek will have to be substituted for the polyethylene, to reduce the risk of moisture condensation. However, at best, this is a temporary solution, since long-term storage on damp floors will cause rapid deterioration of virtually all parts of a vehicle, even if they are covered with moisture permeable sheeting. The building moisture infiltration problem will have to be solved, or the vehicles must be moved to another building. Be sure to inspect the vehicle under the cover once a week to verify that insect infestation or other deterioration threats are not active.

If money is not an obstacle, use Gore-Tex dust covers supported by a frame. GoreTex can extend all the way to the floor, since it passes moisture vapor. Bear in mind that Gore-Tex will not assist in stabilizing the local environment around the vehicle, but if money is plentiful, an HVAC system should have been installed already to control the building environment. Also, be sure to inspect the vehicle under the cover once a week for deterioration threats.

Varnish/Paint Maintenance

Paint and varnish do not require any treatment to help preserve them other than provision of good environmental conditions. Polishes, such as furniture polish, lemon oil or proprietary mixtures, do not prevent deterioration. At best, they visually compensate for degradation that has already occurred and at worst, they rapidly accelerate varnish deterioration.

Oils in polishes are of two types, those that dry chemically (such as linseed oil) and are responsible for blackening of the surfaces of objects on which they are used, and those that do not dry (such as mineral and lemon oil), remaining oily and entrapping dust. Concurrently, as drying oils oxidize, they become very difficult to remove. Additionally, many polishes contain silicones and other additives than can cause future varnish or paint adhesion problems. Manufacturers are not required to disclose the contents of their products, so there is no way to judge their long-term effect on historic objects. Finally, contrary to advertising claims, these proprietary surface applications do very little to protect surfaces and prevent deterioration. They do not prevent dryness or "nourish" the wood, paint or varnish. The temporary improvement in appearance is not worth the risk of potential damage. For these reasons, polishes should not be used on horse-drawn vehicles.

The major exception to this is some degree of protection provided by wax from water damage for vehicles that are in use that have historic varnish surfaces. Even so, aesthetic enhancement is the major reason to apply waxes to historic items. Properly applied, paste waxes can raise sightly the gloss of the varnish, even varnish irregularities somewhat, and increase the saturation and depth of color. Unlike oils, they are removable in the future.

If waxing is chosen as an option, use only high quality *paste* wax such as Butcher's, Minwax, or Renaissance. Reapply wax no more often than every 1-10 years, in spite of more frequent application recommendations printed on their cans. Generally, between applications, buffing with a soft cloth will restore the luster. Avoid any product that contains silicones, as they are nearly impossible to remove from the surface once applied and will interfere with future treatment attempts by prohibiting the bonding of coatings and finishes. While not listed on the containers, generally, silicones are present in spray and liquid polishes, even those that are called "waxes".

Nicks and Scratches

Limit your treatment only to the specific damaged area. Do not let your work extend beyond the edges of the scratch or nick. Many nicks or scratches are obtrusive primarily because the varnish has been disrupted and the surface is no longer optically saturated. In-finishing the damage with Acryloid B-72 using a very fine artist's brush often will acceptably hide the disfigurement.

If this is not successful, application of color may be required. Utilize artists' acrylic paints on fine artists' brushes. Different colors can be mixed to produce the best color match with the damaged area. Since acrylics dry to a matte appearance, gloss can be increased by top coating with Acryloid B-72. Another coloring option is to mix dry artists' pigments directly in B-72 and apply them in the same manner as acrylic paints.

Do not expect to produce a completely invisible in-finishing or in-painting job. If your work is not obtrusive to the average person at the normal viewing distance, you have been successful. Remember, you will always see your repair, since you know exactly where to look.

Summary

This chapter has presented some of the basics on the conservation treatment of horse-drawn vehicles. Due to the complexities of material composition, aging histories, alterations through time and current physical conditions, no two treatments are the same. Thus, a significant degree of judgement is required in designing a treatment that is both successful and safe for the vehicle. Conservators spend a minimum of seven years in training, followed by additional years gathering practical experience. It is not rational to expect that an owner of a horse-drawn vehicle can make the same kinds of informed evaluations and decisions as a conservator. Therefore, the most important advice this chapter can provide is that it is always better to do nothing than do the wrong thing. Be constantly aware of the effects of each treatment procedure and stop immediately if problems or unusual results occur. Please contact a conservator for advice or assistance at any time that your lack of knowledge or experience may result in an inferior treatment.

Marc A. Williams is President of American Conservation Consortium Ltd. He is the former chief wooden objects conservator at the Smithsonian Institution and received his masters degree in conservation from the Winterthur Museum program. His firm specializes in conservation assessments, collections surveys, preservation consultation, and treatment of wooden objects, furniture, and horse-drawn vehicles. He can be reached at 603-679-8307.

Appendix 1
Supply Resource List

Acrylic paints - Golden

Acrylic resins (B-72, B-67, B-48N, etc.)
    Conservation Resources International
    8000-H Forbes Place
    Springfield, Virginia 22151
    Phone 800-634-6932
    Phone 703-321-7730
    Fax 703-321-0629
Email: criusa@conservationresources.com
www.conservationresources.com

Araldite 1253 epoxy/micro-balloon mixture
    Conservation Resources International

Butvar B-98
    Conservation Resources International

Cleaning surfactants (Orvus Liquid, Igepal, and Triton X-100)
    Conservation Resources International

Conservators' referral network
    American Institute for Conservation (AIC)
    Washington, DC
    202-452-9545.

Dust Bunny dust cloth
    New Pig Corporation
    800-468-4647

Dust covers - light weight polyethylene (1 mil)
    Elkay Products Co.
    35 Brown Avenue
    Springfield, NJ 07081
    201-376-7550 [800-631-7351]
    Item #116T for largest sofa size
    Local hardware store for sheets (1-4 mil)

Fish glue
    Lee Valley Tools
    Ottawa, Canada
    800-267-8767

Latex surgical gloves
    Local drug stores

Nevr-Dull metal polish
    Local hardware stores

Silicone release paper
    Conservation Resources International

Soluvar
    Local art supply stores

American Conservation Consortium, Ltd.
Marc A. Williams, President
85 North Road
Fremont, NH 03044
phone 603-679-8307

Corner Ornaments and Center-Piece
for a Large or Main Panel of a Business Wagon
From the Hub December 1889

CHAPTER 4

TECHNICAL EXAMINATION AND MICROSCOPIC ANALYSIS OF PAINTED HORSE-DRAWN VEHICLES
By
James S. Martin

Conservators and historians call on scientists for technical examination and scientific analysis to identify the materials used to construct, decorate, and protect painted horse-drawn vehicles. Another purpose of technical analysis is to assess the condition of vehicles, and to characterize the extent of visual and structural alteration. This information is used by conservators and historians when conserving, restoring, interpreting, authenticating, and dating vehicles. The tools used for technical investigation range from visual examination to sophisticated chemical analyses. This article will briefly describe the techniques commonly used for technical analysis of painted horse-drawn vehicles.

Figure 1. Photomicrograph of the surface of a Concord coach, as it would appear under visible light (left half) and ultraviolet light (right half). Multiple degraded coating layers are evident.

Surface Examination

The first step in technical analysis is visual examination of the surface of a vehicle. One makes an inventory of the different parts of the vehicle, the materials and techniques used to fashion these parts, and the general condition of structural members and of decorative or protective finishes. Strong visible light is used to examine color, reflectance, and texture, while a long-wave ultraviolet light is used to examine the visible fluorescence of finish layers and restoration. One then identifies a small number of areas that are representative of the whole vehicle for closer examination using a stereo microscope (fig. 1). When information is needed on finish layering or the composition of materials, small samples are removed for analysis, usually from the edge of existing damage.

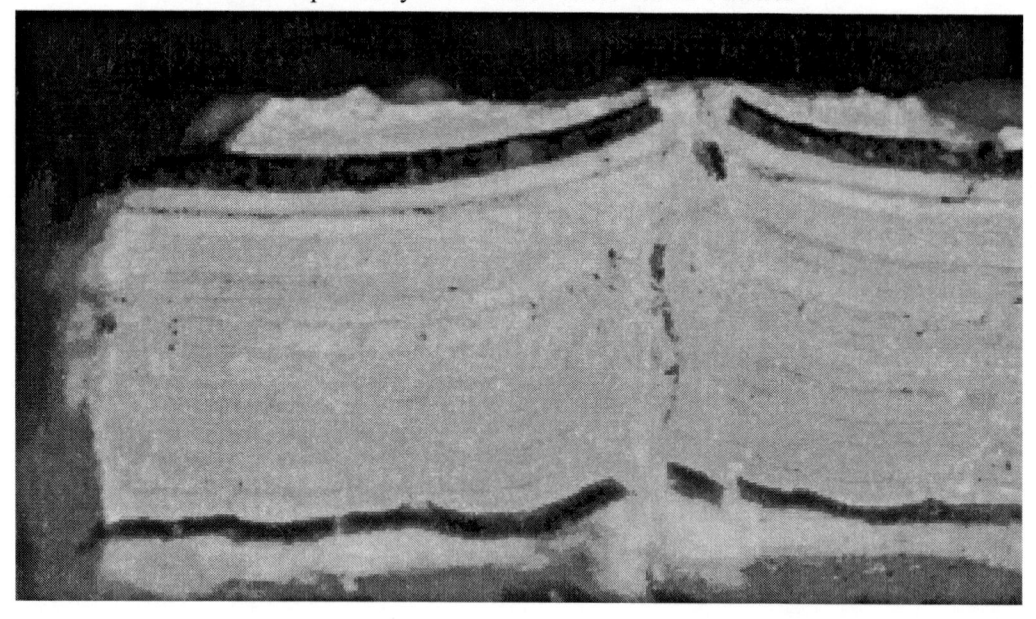

Figure 2. Photomicrograph of finish layers viewed in cross-section under ultraviolet illumination. The sample was removed from the area pictured in Figure 1. As many as thirteen coating layers are observed between the original red paint surface and the white/black repaint. Many of these layers are fissured, cracked, and covered with embedded grime.

Investigating Finish History

Painted horse-drawn vehicles are often decorated and protected with complex finishes consisting of paint, glazes, and varnish. Additional varnish is often applied when the surface becomes dulled by weathering and embedded grime. Color schemes might be changed to suit a new owner or fashion. Consequently, the layering of decorative and protective finishes on historic vehicles is often very complex and interesting.

In the same way that geological strata are studied using core samples, finish layering on vehicles is studied in cross-section using small layered samples removed from the surface (fig. 2). Layered samples are usually embedded in a rigid plastic, and polished or cut on edge to create a smooth cross-section of all layers. Individual paint and varnish layers are extremely thin (measured in thousandths of millimeters) and cannot be differentiated in cross-section without magnification. Light microscopes are used to examine layered samples. By varying the type of illumination, one may see the color, fluorescence, reflectance, and texture of layers. Layers of similar color, such as discolored varnish layers, may often be differentiated by their fluorescence color. Grime, which accumulates between varnish or paint layers, and weathering help to identify surface layers. Finish investigation usually focuses on the earliest extant finish layers, especially when there is a question about an original appearance, authenticity, or date of manufacture.

Determining Physical Properties

Solubility and melting point are two physical properties of paint and varnish that have a practical impact on conservation treatments involving cleaning, varnish removal, and consolidation. Before commencing treatment, conservators routinely test solubility and melting point directly on the surface of objects by applying a solvent-saturated swab or a heated tacking iron. These tests help conservators to select solvents for cleaning and consolidation, and temperature parameters for consolidation of lifting point. However, surface tests do not show which layer has dissolved or melted. Testing of individual layers can only be done using layered samples, or particles removed from specific layers, under a light microscope.

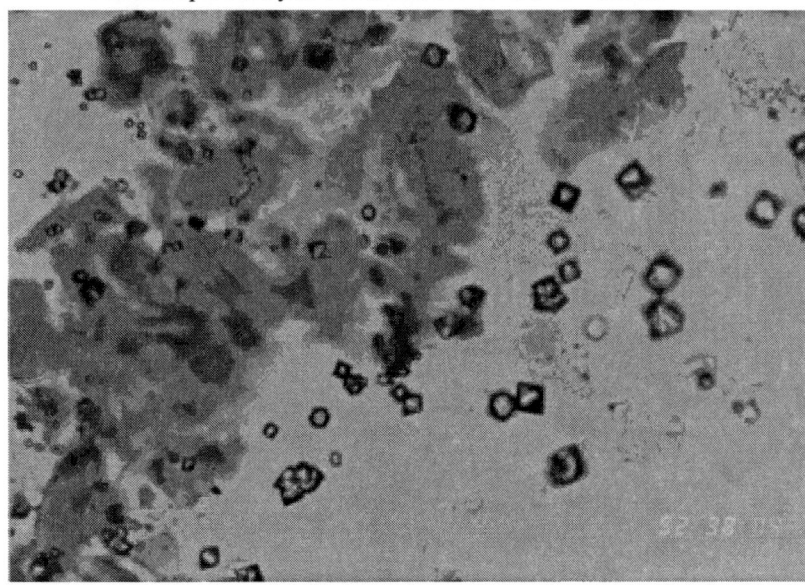

Figure 3. Photomicrograph of a microchemical reaction used to identify the blue glass pigment smalt. A minute particle of paint is dispersed in a solution of chloroplatinic acid. Formation of these orange isotropic octahedra confirms the presence of potassium, an elemental constituent of smalt.

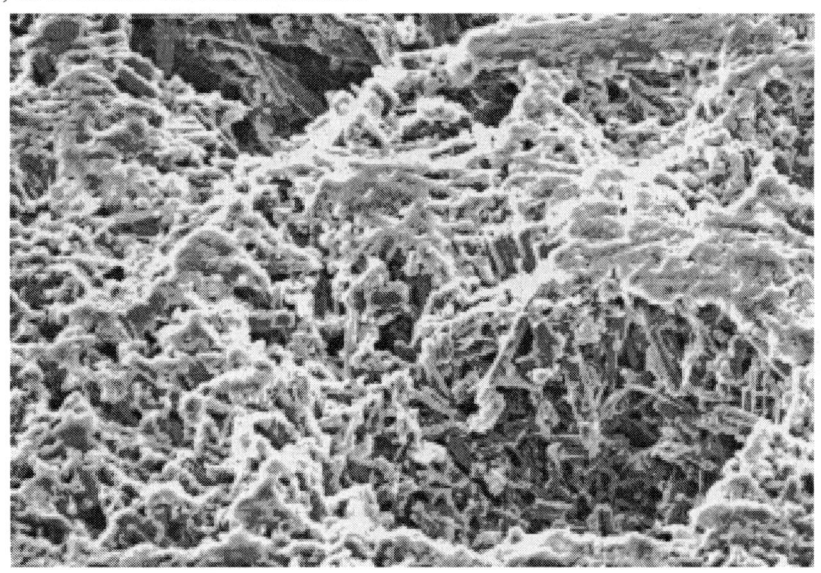

Figure 4. Scanning electron micrograph showing rod-shaped crystals of gypsum (calcium sulfate), a common ground pigment, lake substrate, and paint extender.

Studying Composition

Composition infor- mation enables conservators to tailor treatments to specific materials, thus saving time and needless experimentation on a vehicle. Composition information may reveal material anachronisms that provide conservators and historians with evidence of the origin, authenticity, or date of materials. Com-position information may also help to explain why a surface has faded, dis-colored, or otherwise altered.

The composition of materials cannot be deter-mined by sight. Identification requires analysis of small areas of a vehicle or microscopic samples using a variety of microscopic, spectroscopic, chromatographic, and other techniques. Fibers, wood, and many pigments exhibit unique visual features that may be observed using a light microscope fitted for polarizing light. Many fibers, wood samples, and pigments can be identified using polarizing light microscopy (fig. 3). Scanning electron microscopes provide far higher magnification and resolving power than light microscopes (fig. 4).

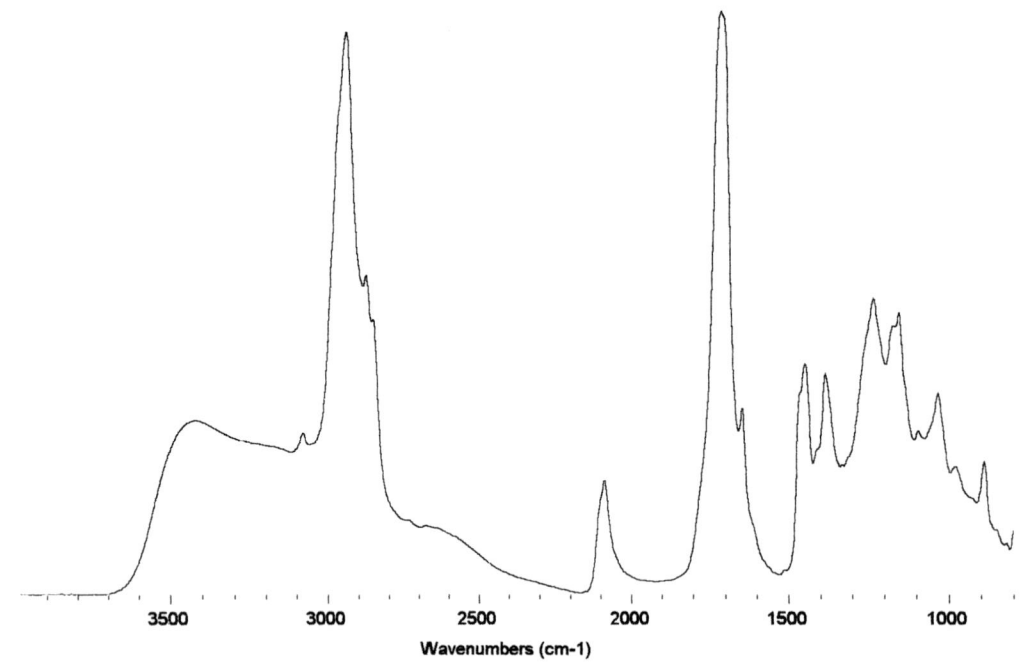

Figure 5. An FT-IR spectrum of a blue glaze layer containing copal resin and Prussian blue pigment.

Paint binders, varnishes, organic pigments, dyes, and metal lack unique visual features, and are identified by determining their elemental or chemical composition. Certain elements and chemical groups may be determined using microchemical tests, which are performed under a light microscope using minutes quantities of sample and chemicals. Microchemical tests are sensitive to very small concentrations, but are destructive and identify only a single element or chemical groups at a time.

Elements and chemical groups are also commonly identified using spectrometers. Spectrometers are instruments used to measure energy that is absorbed, emitted, or diffracted by a sample. Energy-dispersive x-ray spectrometry (EDS) is used to determine the elements present at the surface of samples viewed using a scanning electron microscope (SEM). SEM-EDS is used to identify metals and to confirm pigment identifications. Fourier transform infrared microspectroscopy (FT-IR microscopy) is used to determine the chemical, or molecular, composition of materials (fig. 5). Common applications of FT-IR microscopy include characterization of organic binders and varnishes, and identification of synthetic resins, pigments, dyes, and fibers.

JAMES S. MARTIN is Director of Analytical Services and Research, and Associate Conservator of Paintings, at the Williamstown Art Conservation Center in Williamstown, Massachusetts. Prior to joining the Williamstown Center, James earned an M.S. in Art Conservation from the Winterthur/University of Delaware Program in Art Conservation, and was a graduate fellow at the Hamilton Kerr Institute in Cambridge, England. James lectures on the scientific analysis of works of art at Williams College and the Conservation Analytical Laboratory's Furniture Conservation Program. His department provides analytical services to private conservators, museums, and collectors throughout North America and abroad. Postal address: Williamstown Art Conservation Center, 225 South Street, Williamstown, MA 0 1 267. E-mail address: imartin@williams.edu.Telephone: 413/458-5741. Facsimile: 413/458-2314.

CHAPTER 5

VARNISH FOR HORSE-DRAWN VEHICLES
condensed from
A Manual of Painters' Colours, Oils, and Varnishes by George H. Hurst, 1906 and 1913.

Most varnish used on horse-drawn vehicles was of the kind known as oil-varnish of which there are two kinds short and long oil. Varnishes of the long oil variety would have been made with a higher percentage of oil, and they were the preferred first quality varnishes as they maintained greater elasticity. The other two classes of varnish were know as Spirit varnish (the most common was known as Shellac) and Natural varnish (commonly recognized as lacquer). Spirit varnish and Natural varnish dried faster, but upon drying they were harder finishes making them undesirable for horse-drawn vehicles. For oil varnishes the main ingredients were resin (copal and the like), oil (linseed oil), and a solvent (turpentine). A fourth ingredient would have been driers.

Copal

Copal was the most commonly used resin in coach-varnish . It is a fossil resin exuded by tropical trees centuries ago. Lumps of copal were dugout of the ground during the rainy season in certain African countries. A grade used for coach varnish came from Sierra Leone and was imported as angular pieces, almost colorless or with a faint yellow tint. This was selected on arrival for use in cabinet and coach varnishes.

East African copal, known as "animi," mostly found in Zanzibar, was considered excellent for coach varnishes, being unsurpassed for brilliance and durability. Fossil animi was found at depths of from 1 ½ to 3 feet below the surface and an average of about one pound per man per day was usually found; consequently, this was the most expensive variety.

Linseed Oil

Linseed oil was the preferred oil for this type of varnish of which Baltic seed was said to have been the best quality for coach varnish.[1] This oil is obtained from the seeds of the flax plant, linum usitatissimum- which is cultivated both for its seed and for its fibre, which latter is spun and woven into linen. Baltic seed, comes from Riga and other ports on the Baltic coast of Russia. The English system of extracting the oil includes five operations:-1st, crushing; 2nd, grinding; 3rd, heating; 4th, pressing; 5th, refining. ...

Properties and Composition of Linseed Oil.

Linseed oil is sold in two forms, known as "raw" and "boiled" linseed oil; some text-books speak of a third form called "refined linseed oil," but the author considers this to be only a variety of the raw oil. Linseed oil as it comes from the press is rather turbid, of a dark colour, and contains some albuminous and mucilaginous matter. Before it is fit for use as a paint oil these must be removed, which is done by the methods detailed above; then it forms the "raw linseed oil" of commerce. The if "refined" linseed oil is mostly prepared for artists' use, and is obtained from the raw oil in various ways.

---

[1] Robertson, John. "Coach Varnishing" Papers Read before the Institute of British Carriage Manufacturers, 1883-1901. Bedfordshire, EN : Aspley Guise, 1902.

In some cases the oil is allowed to stand for some months to settle, and then the clear top oil is exposed in closed glass vessels to sunlight to bleach it. Sometimes a small quantity of litharge or acetate of lead is mixed with the oil, and then, after standing some time, the oil, which is clear, is run off and bleached as before; in other cases metallic lead is placed in the oil and left in contact with it for months; the lead seems to exert a kind of bleaching action, and at the same time causes the albuminous matter in the oil to settle out.

It may be laid down as a principle in treating oils that the simplest plan is always the best; in any case the use of too much chemical action should be avoided.

Raw linseed oil is a yellowish oil, having a brown hue, and possesses a characteristic odor and taste unlike those of any other oil. It is perfectly clear and limpid at all ordinary temperatures, but when subjected to moderate cold it thickens slightly, and solidifies at a temperature below -27'C. The viscosity of linseed oil measured in Hurst's standard viscosimeter at 70'F. is for the three principal varieties :-

Baltic oil,	.105
Black Sea oil,	.108
East India oil,	.112

The specific gravity of linseed oil at 60' F. (15'-5 C.) averages 0-935, but ranges from 0-932 to 0-937 ; Baltic oil is usually the heaviest. A sample of Baltic oil examined by the author had specific gravity of 0-9378, a sample of Black Sea oil a specific gravity of 0-9326, while a sample of East Indian oil had a specific gravity of 0-9339. At 212'F. (1OO'C.) linseed oil usually has a specific gravity of 0-8801.

Linseed oil is soluble in about 40 times its volume of alcohol at ordinary temperatures, and 5 times its volume at the boiling point. It readily dissolves in ether, petroleum spirit, shale naphtha, turpentine, chloroform, and similar solvents.

Sulphuric acid has a strong action on linseed oil, causing it to become thick and of a dark colour; large quantities of sulphur dioxide are evolved, while the temperature of the mixture is considerably increased, the amount varying somewhat in different kinds of linseed oil. Thus, with Baltic linseed oil the author obtained an increase of 120'C., with Black Sea oil an increase of 114' C., and with East India oil an increase of 106'C.

The action of nitric acid varies with the strength of the acid; a moderately strong acid converts linseed oil into a viscid yellowish mass, which is insoluble, or nearly so, in petroleum spirit or benzol; while strong, fuming nitric acid often causes linseed oil to take fire. Nitrous acid does not give a solid elaidin with linseed oil.

In glacial acetic acid it is readily soluble on warming, while the turbidity temperature ranges from 36' C. to 47' C.* according, to tile quality of the oil and the strength of the acetic acid.

Linseed oil combines very readily with bromine and iodine, absorbing a larger proportion of these bodies than any other oil; there are slight differences between the various kinds of linseed oil in the quantities of iodine and bromine that they will combine with, but it may be laid down as a rule that the better the quality of the oil, the more iodine or bromine will it absorb. Of iodine the average amount taken up is 156 per cent. of the weight of the oil, while of bromine the average is 98 per cent. That is 100 parts of linseed oil will combine with 156 parts of iodine or with 98 parts of bromine.

The property which gives linseed oil its special value as a paint oil is that when exposed to the air it gradually becomes hard, "dries up," in doing which it takes up from the atmosphere a large proportion of oxygen, forming a new compound of a resinous character, the properties of which have never been fully investigated. In this power of combining with oxygen, linseed is distinguished very markedly from other oils, which have little or no power of combining with oxygen. W. Foxt gives the following as the number of cubic centimeters of oxygen absorbed by 1 gramme of various oils:-

Baltic linseed oil, 191 - Black Sea linseed oil, 186 - East Indian Calcutta oil, 126 - East Indian Bombay oil, 130 - American linseed oil, 156 - Brown rape oil, 20 - Colza oil, 17-6 - Cotton seed oil, 24-6 - Olive oil, 8-2

Evidently, the quality of linseed oil depends very much upon its oxygen-absorbing powers; thus, Baltic oil, which dries better than any other variety of linseed oil, takes up more oxygen than Black Sea or East Indian, which latter takes up the least, and is the worst variety of linseed oil known. American linseed oil is not equal to Black Sea oil in its drying properties, but it is much better than East Indian, owing, as is clear, to its greater absorbing power for oxygen.

Turpentine

Turpentine for coach varnish is the resinous exudations from various species of pine and other coniferous trees of which American Turpentine was said to be of the best quality for coach varnish. It is derived from two or three species of pine, chiefly from the swamp or Georgia pine (Pinus australis), which grows in extensive forests in North and South Carolina, Georgia, and Alabama.

In winter, which extends from November to March, gangs of men proceed to the forests for the purpose of collecting the resin; for this purpose the trees are boxed, that is, a cavity is cut into the side of the tree, about 1 foot from the ground...

Properties and Composition of Turpentine

Turpentine is a hydrocarbon having the formula $C_{10}H_{16}$; there are, however, a number of isomeric compounds known which have the composition represented by the above formula. These bodies have been named the terpenes; they are derived, as well as the three varieties of turpentine already described, from natural resins or from various natural oils.

They closely resemble one another in their chemical as well as in many of their physical properties. The terpenes have been investigated by Berthelot, Tilden, Wallach and other chemists, and a number of them are known. Berthelot pointed out that French turpentine had some different properties from American turpentine, although their chemical composition was the same. He named the terpene of American turpentine, australene, and that from French turpentine, terebenthene; while he gave to the characteristic hydrocarbon of Russian turpentine the name of sylvestrene. Armstrong considers that American turpentine is a compound of two terpenes, one of which is the same as, found in the French turpentine and which rotates a ray of polarised light to the left; this he names laevoterebenthene. The other terpene has similar properties, only it rotates the ray of polarised light to the right; this he names dextroterebentbene; it is found in a very pure condition in the turpentine from *Pinus Khasyana*, a Burmese tree. Wallach describes nine terpenes which he names-1. *Pinene,* the main constituent of French and American turpentine. 2. *Camphene,* which differs from all other terpenes in being solid; it is not found naturally, but can be prepared by artificial means from pinene. 3. *Fenchene,* which is also obtained artificially. 4, *Cimonene,* found in the essential oils of various species of aurantiacece, oils of lemon, orange, bergamot, &c. 5. *Dipentene,* found in oil of camphor, Russian and Swedish turpentine, &c. *6. Sylvestrene,* the characteristic terpene of Russian and

Swedish turpentine. 7. *Phellandrene,* found in various essential oils. 8. *Terpinene,* found in several oils. 9. *Terpinonlene,* a rare terpene. The two most important of these are Pinene and Sylvestrene, which are found in the chief commercial turpentines.

Pinene is a colourless or water-white mobile liquid of a peculiar and characteristic odor, having a specific gravity of 0-8749 according to Tilden; Wallach gives it as 0-860. It boils at from 155' to 156' C. When dry hydrochloric acid gas is passed into it, combination ensues, and a crystalline body having the formula $C_{10}H_{16}HCl$ is formed; this closely resembles camphor in appearance and is known as artificial camphor; by heating, under pressure, with caustic potash this body is decomposed and the solid terpene, camphene, is formed. When pinene is exposed to sunlight in the presence of water **a** crystalline compound is formed which has the composition $C_{10}H_{18}O_2$, and is named by Armstrong, sobrerol. Pinene in contact with water gradually combines with it, formina, a crystalline hydrate, terpene hydrate, $C_{10}H_{16}3 H_2O$ which is soluble in alcohol, insoluble in turpentine, slightly soluble in cold water, a little more freely in hot water, and sparingly soluble in ether, chloroform and carbon bisulphide.

There are two varieties of pinene, which differ from one another simply in their action on a ray of polarised light. One variety, that in French turpentine, turns the ray to the left, and is distinguished as laevo-pinene, the other is found in American turpentine, and turns the ray to the right, and is named dextropinene. The air-oxidation and other products from the two terpenes differ from one another in the same manner. A mixture of the two pinenes, in equal proportions, would have no action on polarised light, and gives rise to inactive oxidation products. American turpentine contains both pinenes, the dextro variety predominating.

Sylvestrene is the characteristic terpene of Russian and Swedish turpentine, derived from the Scotch pine, *Pinus sylvestris.* It is a colourless, or water-white limpid liquid, having a specific gravity of 0-846 at 20' C.; it boils at 175' C. It has a dextrorotatory action on polarised light; the laevo-rotatory and inactive varieties are not known. Dry hydrochloric acid gas, when passed through sylvestrene, forms an hydrochloride, $C_{10}H_{16}HCl$, which is liquid. In this respect this terpene differs from pinene; it is also more easily -oxidised when exposed to air and light,

The other terpenes are of no practical importance to the painter. Commercial French and American turpentine is a water-white, limpid liquid, with a peculiar and characteristic odor that distinguishes it from all other bodies. The specific gravity ranges from O-864 to O-870, but usually is about O-867. French turpentine is a little more uniform than American turpentine in this respect. It begins to boil at from 156' to 160' C., and is completely distilled at 170' 0. If the sample be fresh, there is little or no residue left behind, but old samples generally leave a slight residue of resinous matter, which in any case does not amount to more than 1 per cent. of the turpentine.

Turpentine is readily combustible, burning with a smoky flame, a peculiar and characteristic odor being evolved. The flashing point of ordinary turpentine is 36' to 38' C. (97' to 100- F.)

Turpentine is readily miscible with ether, carbon bisulphide, alcohol, benzene, petroleum spirit, but it is insoluble in water. It is a good solvent for oils, fats, resins, &c.

On exposure to the air in bulk, turpentine absorbs oxygen slowly from the atmosphere, becoming thick and viscid or fatty in appearance. A prolonged exposure causes the turpentine to become resinous, part of the turpentine volatilising during the exposure. In thin layers, such as would be formed when turpentine is spread over a surface with a brush, a condition of affairs which occurs in painting, there is less oxidation, as a larger proportion of the turpentine volatilises away, and the oxidation of the residue is more complete, so that a hard resinous product is the result. This property distinguishes turpentine from all the other spirituous liquids used by the painter and varnish maker. These evaporate completely away, and consequently leave no residue behind which can act as a binding agent for the pigment or colouring matter of the paint; whereas, the resin left when turpentine is used, acts as a binding agent, and fixes or fastens the pigment of the paint on the surface over which it is spread. American has greater absorbing powers for oxygen than French turpentine.

Exposed to the air in contact with water, turpentine forms a solid crystalline product, having the composition $C_{10}H_{18}O_2$. This has been named sobrerol; the melting-point is 150' C. for the active variety, and 130-5' to 131' C. for the inactive variety. The crystals belong to the rhombic system, the inactive variety being of a different form to the active varieties. They are somewhat soft and flexible, and are soluble in alcohol.

When repeatedly distilled with strong sulphuric acid, turpentine becomes polymerised. Generally two bodies are formed. One of these has been named terebene, which has the same formula ($C_{10}H_{16}$) as turpentine, and, when pure, boils at 160' C. The other body has been named colophene, has the formula $C_{20}H_{23}$ and boils at 3OO'C. It constitutes the main product of the reaction. This property of polymerisation, which is essentially a conversion from a spirit boiling at a low temperature into a spirit boiling at a high temperature, distinguishes turpentine from any of its substitutes.

Nitric acid acts very energetically on turpentine, the result varying with the strength of the acid used. If strong enough, the turpentine may take fire; in any case, various oxidation products are obtained.

Chlorine, bromine, and iodine act with great energy on turpentine; great care must be taken in bringing these bodies into contact with one another or explosions may occur.

Turpentine has a strong action on polarised light, a property which distinguishes it from benzene, petroleum spirit, and rosin spirit. French turpentine rotates the ray to the left, its specific value being - 30, and is fairly constant, showing that French turpentine has a very uniform composition; this fact is also shown by its regular specific gravity and by its steady distillation temperature. The specific rotation of the pure terpene, terebenthene, is - 40. American turpentine rotates the ray to the right, but the variation of the value in different samples is very great; ordinary commercial samples give, specific values ranging from + 8 to + 16; the pure terpene has a specific rotation of + 21-5. It is quite possible that American turpentine contains a small quantity of a laevo-terpene, the quantity of which varies in amount and, consequently, the specific rotation must vary also. The air oxidation products (sobrerol) in their action on polarisecl light vary with the turpentine from which they are obtained; that from French turpentine rotates the ray to the left with a fairly uniform specific value, while that from American turpentine is rather variable and can be separated into two varieties, one with a + and the other with a specific rotation; while, by mixing the two in equal proportions, an inactive variety can be obtained. Burmese turpentine from *Pinus* Khasyana, which resembles French and American turpentine in its general properties, differs by having a strong and uniform + rotation.

Russian turpentine resembles American turpentine in many of its properties, such as solvent and soluble features, action of nitric acid, sulphuric acid, chlorine, &c. It is rather more variable in composition and specific gravity, which latter varies from 0-862 to as high as 0-873. It begins to boil at about 156' C., but is not completely distilled below 180' C., the great bulk passing over between 172' and 174' C.; this greater range of distilling temperature points to a more complex composition than that of other turpentines. It has an odor resembling that of American-turpentine, but differing slightly therefrom. It is rather more volatile. It rapidly absorbs oxygen from the atmosphere, becoming very viscid; partly on this account and partly on account of its stronger odor, Russian turpentine has not come so much into use in making paints. It is said to induce headache when being used; this phenomenon will depend a great deal on the physiological idiosyncrasies of particular individuals. The oxidation-product which is formed has, according to Kingzett, the composition $C_{10}H_{14}O_4$, and he has named it camphoric peroxide; on heating with water, this gives rise to the formation of camphoric acid, $C_{10}H_{16}O_4$, and hydrogen peroxide, H_2O_2. On this property of Russian turpentine is based its use in the preparation of the disinfectant, " Sanitas."

Russian turpentine exerts a strong rotary action on polarised light, the specific value varying as much as from + 15 to + 23, while the pure terpene, sylvestrene, has a specific rotation of + 19, which shows that the commercial turpentine must contain terpenes of higher rotary power, the amount of which varies in different samples. In all other properties Russian turpentine resembles American turpentine.

Driers

Driers are a class of bodies added to oil for the purpose of causing it to dry quicker than it would otherwise do. The bodies generally used for this purpose are salts of iron, lead, manganese, and zinc. The following list comprises all the compounds used as driers in paints and varnishes: - Red lead, litharge, lead acetate, lead borate, manganese oxide, manganesse sulphate, manganese borate, manganese oxalate, zinc oxide, zinc sulphate, and ferrous sulphate.

Of these, the lead salts are most in use ; the manganese compounds are largely used ; the others but rarely.

Varnish Making

Varnish making with the three main ingredients of the best quality this could amount to many different varnishes just by the variation of the amount of ingredient and the different processes in which they could be manufactured. For economical reasons the best ingredients were not always used and this would make for an even greater number of different kinds of varnishes used by coach painters. A typical varnish manufacturer's catalog might list from 12 to 20 different varnishes available for coach painters. The natural resins and some of the other ingredients varied so much that long years of experience was also a factor in making the best varnish along with the six steps of manufacture.

    1. "Gum running," or melting the resin,
    2. Boiling the oil and mixing with the melted resin,
    3. Boiling the varnish,
    4. Introduction of driers,
    5. Thinning,
    6. Clearing and aging ...

Different Recipes for Varnishes

The proportions are generally given as for a run of 8 lbs. of gum (copal).

Finishing Body Varnish for Coaches.-Run 8 lbs. of the best African animi, pour in 2 gallons of the best oil well boiled, set very slowly (by boiling for 4 to 5 hours until it strings well), allow to cool and add 3 ½ gallons of turps; strain and allow to age. This varnish is considered to be the best varnish made, but it requires considerable care in making it to obtain it of good quality; the best and palest gum and the best oil must be used.

Hard Drying or Flatting Varnish.-This is made by running 8 lbs. of gum animi, mixing with 2 gallons of oil, and, after boiling for 4 hours, thinning with 3 ½ gallons of turps. This varnish dries rather harder than the above and quicker i.e., in about 8 to 10 hours. It is chiefly used for the under coats of varnish on a coach body. This varnish is used for the surface coats of carriages, is pale in colour, and dries with a brilliant surface in about 12 hours. It is a very durable varnish, and will resist the destructive action of the atmosphere very well.

Varnish For Horse-drawn Vehicles

Elastic Carriage Varnish (1).-Run 8 lb& of good quality gum copal, mix with 2 ½ gallons of oil, add 1/4 lb. of dried copperas and 1/4 lb. of litharge, boil until it strings, then allow to cool and thin with 5 ½ gallons of turps. Run 8 lbs. of second sort gum animi, mix with 2 ½ gallons of oil, add 1/4 lb. of dried sugar of lead and 1/4 lb. of litharge, boil until it strings, allow to cool and thin with 5 ½ gallons of turps. The two lots are mixed together, strained, and allowed to mature. This varnish dries hard with a fine polish in about 5 hours in summer and in about 7 hours in winter. It is used for varnishing common carriages and also for cabinet work.

Elastic Carriage Varnish (2).-Run 8 lbs. of first quality gum copal, mix with 3 gallons of oil, boil for 4 hours until it strings, then, after cooling, add 5 ½ gallons of turps. Run 8 lbs. of best gum animi, mix with 2 gallons of oil, and, after boiling until it strings, thin with 3 ½ gallons of turps. Two pots of this running are mixed with one pot of the first running, and the whole is strained and allowed to mature. This varnish is much used as the finishing varnish for common coaches, and for the under parts of superior coaches. It dries brilliant and is durable. It is rather quicker in drying than No. 1, taking about 10 hours in summer and 12 hours in winter.

Elastic Carriage Varnish (3).-Run 8 lbs. of gum copal, mix with 2 gallons of oil, and boil until it strings, then thin with 3 ½ gallons of turps. Run 8 lbs. of gum animi, mix with 2 gallons of oil, boil as before, and thin with 3 ½ gallons of turps. Mix one pot of this running with one pot of the previous running, strain, and finish in the usual way. As good a quality of gums is not used in making this varnish as the last, so that it is usually rather darker, although it is quite as durable. It dries in about the same time.

Elastic Hard Carriage Varnish.-Run 8 lbs. of gum copal, mix with 2 gallons of oil, add 1/4 lb. of dried sugar of lead, and boil until stringy; thin with 3 ½ gallons of turps. Run 8 lbs. of gum animi, mix with 2 gallons of oil, add 1/4 lb. of dried copperas, and boil until it strings; thin with 3 ½ gallons of turps. Both runnings are mixed together and finished in the usual way. This varnish is used for the under coats in varnishing carriages; it dries hard in about 5 to 6 hours and gives a smooth surface.

Carriage Varnish.-Run 8 lbs. of second quality gum animi, mix with 2- 3/4 gallons of oil, add 1/4 lb. each of litharge, dried copperas, and dried sugar of lead, boil until it strings, then thin with 5 ½ gallons of turps, and finish in the usual way. This varnish is, used for varnishing dark-coloured carriages, the ironwork of coaches, and for ordinary cabinet work. It dries quickly in about 4 hours in summer and 5 hours in winter, with a hard and glossy surface. It is not so durable as the other varnishes described above.

Pale Copal Varnish.-Careful select 8 lbs. Of the palest gum copal; run well and mix with 2 gallons of pale boiled oil; boil the whole until it strings, then allow to cool down a little, and thin with 5 ½ gallons of turps. Strain and finish as usual. When well made this varnish is very pale, and dries with a lustrous, durable coat in from 8 to 10

Japanners' Gold Size.-Run 10 lbs. of gum animi and mix it with 2 gallons of hot oil; prepare two runs of this. In the set pot place 10 gallons of oil and boil it well for 2 hours; then add 7 lbs. of red lead, 7 lbs. of litharge, and 3 lbs. of copperas; the addition of these driers is best made in small quantities at a time, the whole mass being kept boiling all the time; when all the driers have been added the boiling should be continued for about 3 hours longer. Sometimes the addition of the driers causes the boiling oil to froth up very much; in such cases it is best to reduce the fire somewhat, and to take some of the oil out of the pot, adding it again as the frothing subsides. When the oil has been boiled for 3 hours the two runs of gum are added, and the boiling continued for 5 hours, when it will begin to string; the boiling is continued until the mass drops off the ladle or stirring rod in large drops, and strings well. Then allow to cool, which will take about 2 hours; pour in, in small quantities at a time, 30 gallons of turps.; as this is being poured in the whole mass must be thoroughly stirred up so as to get the turps and varnish well mixed; the mixing with the turps must not be done too quickly, or otherwise there is too great a liability to boil over; in fact, this applies to the mixing of turps in making all these oil varnishes. This gold size will dry in about 10 minutes, if well made; although sometimes it may take 25 minutes to dry.

Black Japan (1).-This is made in a very similar manner to the gold size just described. Into the set pot put 6 gallons of linseed oil, boil it on a slow fire for 2 hours, then run in a gum pot 10 lbs. of asphaltum, and mix with 2 gallons of oil: when mixed, pour into the set pot; then run three more lots, pouring each one as it is run into the set pot; then add 7 lbs. of red lead, 7 lbs. of litharge, and 3 lbs. of copperas, in small quantities at a time; keep the mixture boiling slowly for 4 hours longer; then allow to stand till the next day, when it is boiled until a small quantity taken out on a glass will, when rubbed or rolled in the fingers, set hard; it is now allowed to cool, and when sufficiently cold 30 gallons of turps are added. If after the Japan has become cold it is found to be too stiff, then it can be warmed up and more turps added until it attains the right consistency. This Japan is used for all kinds of ironwork about carriages which are to be black; it dries with a hard, durable lustrous coat in about 8 hours.

Black Japan(2).-A better quality of black Japan which will dry harder and more glossy is made as follows:-Melt 48 lbs. of asphaltum in the set pot, and when melted add 10 gallons of oil; run in the gum pot 8 lbs. of common gum animi, and mix with it 2 gallons of oil; pour the mixture into the set pot; then run 10 lbs. of common amber, and mix with 2 gallons of oil; this running is also added to the set pot, the contents of which is boiled for 3 hours longer, during which time 7 lbs. of red lead, 7 lbs. of litharge, and 3 lbs. of copperas, are added, and the boiling continued until the mass sets between the fingers into a bard mass. Allow it to cool; then thin with 30 gallons of turps, as before.

Black Varnish for Carriage Iron Work.-Run 48 lbs. of asphaltum in the set pot, and add 10 gallons of boiled oil, 7 lbs. of red lead, 7 lbs. of litharge, and 3 lbs. of copperas; run 8 lbs. of copal, mix with 2 gallons of oil, and add to the set pot; boil the whole for 4 hours; place on one side till the next day, and then boil until it sets hard between the fingers; then, after cooling, thin with 30 gallons of turps. This dries hard with a good surface in about 3 hours.

Brunswick Black (1).-This very useful black varnish is made in several ways. Run 45 lbs. of asphaltum for 6 hours in a set pot. Boil 6 gallons of oil with 6 lbs. of litharge until it strings well; pour into the set pot with the asphaltum, and boil the whole until it will set hard between the fingers; then allow to cool, and thin with 25 gallons of turps. This dries in about 4 hours with a good surface, having a brilliant gloss.

Brunswick Black (2).-A commoner Brunswick black is made as follows:-28 lbs. of coal-tar pitch and 28 lbs. of asphaltum are boiled together in the set pot for 6 hours; the mixture is allowed to stand all night, after which it is boiled up and 8 gallons of boiled oil are added; 10 lbs. of litharge and 10 lbs. of red lead are added in small quantities at a time, and the mass boiled until it will set hard between the fingers; it is then allowed to cool, and is mixed with 20 gallons of turps. This will dry in about 1 to 2 hours, and is a good black varnish for all kinds of ironwork.

Black Leather Varnish.-A very good black varnish is made by boiling 10 lbs. of linseed oil with 4 lbs. of litharge for about 5 hours, and then colouring with lamp-black. Other leather varnishes will be found described under spirit varnishes.

General Considerations.

The following general features concerning oil varnishes and their manufacture should be noted. An oil varnish should possess the following properties:-lst, good and free working; 2nd, drying hard and rubbing freely; 3rd, giving an elastic coating not liable to crack or bloom, and which is resistant to the destructive action of the atmosphere. It is difficult always to secure these features of a good varnish, especially to combine the second and third, as hardness and elasticity are somewhat opposed to one another.

In the preparation of these varnishes too much care cannot be exercised in carrying out the various operations. The materials should be carefully selected; good varnish cannot be made from a poor quality of gum, and, no matter how good this may be, the use of a bad sample of oil will spoil any varnish made from it; the quality of the turpentine used also has some influence. In the sections referring to these materials will be found information as to the qualities required in good materials. The better the gum or resin is run, the larger will be the quantity of varnish obtained, and this will be stronger and better for working. The boiling of the oil and resin together must be well done; if not sufficiently boiled, the resulting varnish does not work freely, and is sometimes liable to bloom. This latter defect also occurs in varnishes made from badly run-gums. The stringing or boiling should be done slowly, and at as low a heat as possible; if brought forward too quickly by the use of too much heat, then the resulting varnish is liable to be discoloured. It takes more turps to thin it down, and the varnish neither works so freely under the brush, nor gives such a smooth brilliant surface as a good oil varnish should do. The more oil there is used in the composition of a varnish, the more elastic and less liable to crack is the coat formed by the varnish. On the other hand, the drying is retarded by using too little oil. The more gum there is put into a varnish, the thicker, firmer, more quickly drying, and more brilliant when dry, is the coat formed; on the other hand, it is more liable to crack if there is too little gum. The varnishes made by the French method (which contain little oil) are rather liable to these defects of cracking, because of the want of elasticity in the coat they form.

Driers, especially copperas, when added to varnishes have a tendency to make the varnishes opaque, and to harden them. An oil varnish made with quick driers forms a coat which is hard, non-elastic, liable to crack, and of short duration.

The usual proportions of resins are for body varnishes about 1 1/4 to 1 ½ lbs. -per gallon; for carriage and cabinet varnishes, from 1 to 1 1/4 lbs. per gallon; for gold size and japans, from ½ to 3/4 lb. per gallon ; If, after making and cooling, the varnishes are found to be too thick, they can be reduced to the required consistency by warming (so as to render them more fluid) and adding turps.

Varnishes should be kept at least six months after making before they are used; this ageing causes a better amalgamation of the constituents of the varnish, increases the ease with which it works under the brush, and causes it to form a smoother and more lustrous coat.

Varnish For Horse-drawn Vehicles

FOR MORE INFORMATION ON HOW PAINTS, VARNISHES, ETC. WERE MADE.

Hurst, George H. Painters' Colours, Oils, and Varnishes : A Practical Manual. London, England : Charles Griffin & Company, 1906 & 1913.

For information on how horse-drawn vehicles were painted.

Arlot, M. A Complete Guide for coach painters : to which is added an appendix, containing information respecting the materials and the practice of coach and car painting and varnishing in the United States and Great Britain / translated from the French of M. Arlot coach painter, for eleven years foreman of painting to M. Eherler coach maker Paris, by A. A. Fesquet, chemist and engineer. American edition. Philadelphia : Henry Carey Baird & Co., 1905. xvi, 173 p., 32 ; 21 cm. Includes index 169-173.

Baird, Henry Carey. The Painter, gilder, and varnisher's companion : Containing rules and regulations in everything relating to the arts of painting, gilding, varnishing, glass-staining, graining, marbling, sign-writing, gilding on glass, and coach painting and varnishing; tests for the detection of adulterations in oils, color, etc. and a statement of the diseases to which painters are peculiarly liable, with the simplest and best remedies ... colors and coloring- theoretical and practical, comprising descriptions of a great variety of additional pigment, their qualities and uses, to which are added, dryers, and modes and operations of painting, etc. together with Chevreul's principles of harmony and contrast of colors / by Henry Carey Baird. Sixteenth edition, (1872). Philadelphia : Industrial Publisher, c1869. 356 p., 24 : ill. ; 20 cm. Includes appendix 241-339. Includes index 341-356.

Baker, Jennifer D. "Understanding Antique Carriage Finishes." Driving Digest Magazine no. 90 (1995/4) pp. 8-16, 56.

Boag, Alfred. Boag's practical guide to coach painting / by Alfred Boag. Newcastel-on-Tyne, England : P. J. Jackson, 1890. 224 p. : ill. ; 22cm.

The Coach painter's handbook and guide / by a coach painter of thirty years' experience. London : Henry J. Drane, [1895]. 131 p., [6], [2] leaves of plates : ill. (I col. & 1 b&w plate) ; 19 cm. Six pages of advertisements in back of book. Priming, priming second coat, filling up, rubbing, first coat of paint, stopping lead, facing, ground colour, varnishing second coat, varnishing third coat, carriage, wheels, shafts, etc., japan and how to use it, leather covered carriages, how to treat them, colours, lining, choice of colours, mixing colours, touching up and revarnishing, matching colours, leather heads or tops, how to touch up and revarnish, painting iron work, varnished work, basket carriages or wicker work, tradesmen's carts and vans, brushes - their selection and care, why varnish goes bad, and how to prevent it, blistering and cracking, railway carriage painting, locomotive engine painting, writing scrolling, scrolling, ornament, table to assist the writer in the choice of colours for blocking, work-time tables, table for best painted work, table for varnished work, table for japan work, table for tradesmen's carts and vans.

Cognard, Paul. Traite theorique et pratique de peinture en voitures / par Paul Cognard. Paris, France : Artistiques & Industrielles, [190+]. 90 p., 24 leaves of plates, : col. ; 32cm. In French.

Gannon, William Louis. Carriage, coach, and wagon : the design and decoration of American horse-drawn vehicles. Iowa : State University of Iowa, Ph.D., 1960. 404 p. : ill. ; 21cm. Eighteenth century, formative years 1800 to 1830, imports and innovations 1830-1865, designs for the west 1830-1900, town and country carriages 1865-1900, ornamented and special wagons 1865-1920, end of the industry.

Gardner, F. B. The Carriage painters illustrated manual : containing a treatise on the art, science, and mystery of coach, carriage, and car painting, including the latest improvements in fine painting, copying, lettering, scrolling, and ornamenting, with an appendix, containing useful suggestions, receipts, etc. : a list of the principal varnish makers and dealers : a correct list of carriage and wagon-makers in New York City / by F. B. Gardner, A practical New York coach and ornamental painter. New York : S. R. Wells, c 1 871. 126 p., [14] p. : ill. ; 16 cm.

Green, Susan. "Carmine." Carriage Journal. vol. 33 no. 4 (Spring 1996), 144-146.

Green, Susan. "Varnish Making." Carriage Journal vol.34 no. 2 (Fall 1996) pp.71-73.

Hillick, M. C. Practical carriage and wagon painting : a treatise on the painting of carriages, wagons and sleighs embracing full and explicit directions for executing all classes of work, including painting factory work, lettering, scrolling, ornamenting, varnishing, etc. with many tested recipes and formulas. Chicago, IL : Press of the Western Painter, 1898. viii, 161 p., ix-xxii : ill. ; 26cm.

[Monograms and heraldic designs] / [by the Wilkinson, Heywood & Clark Limited.]. London: Wilkinson, Heywood & Clark Limited, [188?]. [10] p., 165 plates : ill. (most in col.) ; 31 cm. Large amount of color plates with monograms, lettering, color samples, and heraldic designs.

Schriber, Fritz. The Complete carriage and wagon painter : a concise compendium of the art of painting carriages and wagons and sleighs, embracing full directions in all the various branches including lettering, scrolling, ornamenting, striping, varnishing and coloring, with numerous recipes for mixing colors / by Fritz Schriber. New York : M. T. Richardson Co., 1907. 177 p. : ill. ; 21cm. Includes index 171-177. The shop and how it should be constructed, combining pigments to form colors, lead color method, wood filling method, care of materials, failures in varnishing, wagon striping, colors employed on wagons, wagon lettering, laying out work, shading, wagon scrolling, stenciling, good foundation, dusting and cleaning work, painting lumber wagons, touching up repair work, how to paint a cheap job, how to revarnish a carriage, forms and colors in the painting of vehicles. transfer ornaments-how made, monograms.

Simpson, William. Treatise on coach painting : re-edited and brought up-to-date by the technical staff of the coach builders,' wheelwrights' and motor car manufacturers' art journal / by William Simpson, edited by G. A. Thrupp. Thrupp. London: J. & C. Cooper, 1905. 179 p. ill. ; 1905. Includes appendix with illustrations 157-175.

H. R. PARROTT, President.   F. W. PARROTT, Treasurer.

THE PARROTT VARNISH CO.,

MANUFACTURERS OF

Fine Coach and Car Varnishes,

BRIDGEPORT, CONN.

From the Carriage Monthly September 1894

Varnish For Horse-drawn Vehicles

VALENTINE & COMPANY'S STORE,
323 Pearl Street,
SHOWING THEIR FACILITIES FOR PROMPT SHIPMENT OF GOODS.

From the Hub August 1876

SECTION II
RESTORATION

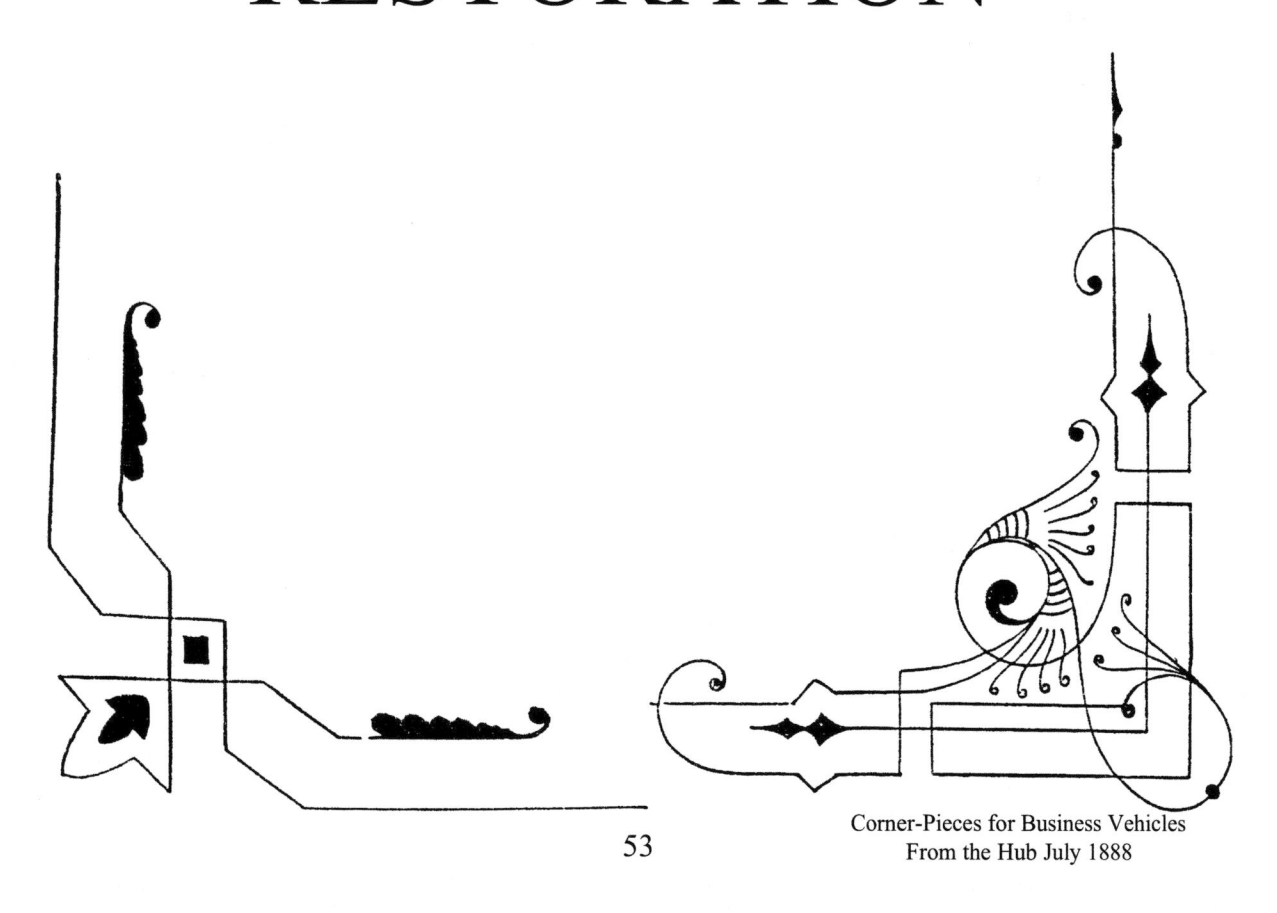

Corner-Pieces for Business Vehicles
From the Hub July 1888

Huber's Patent Adjustable Axle-box Reamer.

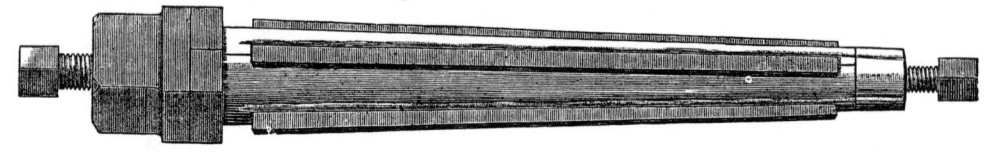

This is beyond question one of the most useful tools ever offered to the carriage-maker. By means of tapered set screws the cutters can be set in or out at either end. With this reamer any carriage-smith can fit new boxes to old spindles, or replace a broken box as perfectly as it can be done at the axle factory. Two sets of cutters accompany each reamer. Half Patent and Imp. boxes can be reamed as well as plain taper. Cutters can be be taken out or replaced with the greatest ease.

No. 1 will ream ¾ to 1⅛, boxes inclusive; two sets of cutters, . . . $7.00
No. 2 will ream 1¼ to 1⅝, boxes inclusive; one set of cutters, . . . 12.00

R. M. BRINTON, 406 Commerce-st., Philadelphia, Pa.

From the Hub June 1882

Buffalo Patent Axle and Wheel Company,
MANUFACTURERS OF
A PERFECT SELF-LUBRICATING AXLE.
OFFICE, 202 Main Street.   FACTORY, Auburn Avenue,
BUFFALO, N. Y., U. S. A.

Perfect Lubrication,
More Durable,
Noiseless,
Absolutely Clean.

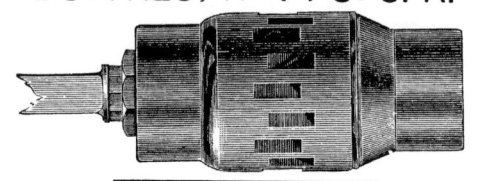

Much Stronger,
Better Material,
Very Simple.
No grit can enter or oil escape.

No More Setting of Wheels;
No More Greasy Hubs;
No More Breaking of Axles;
No More Trouble of any kind;

If the axles of the BUFFALO PATENT AXLE AND WHEEL COMPANY are used exclusively, and properly oiled four times per year.

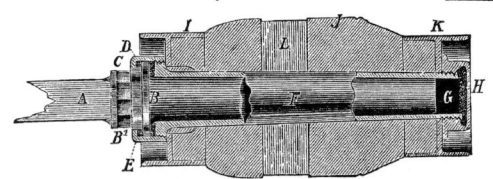

A—Axle.   B—Axle Bearing.   B1—Fixed Collar.   C—Flanged Collar.   D—Movable Flange.   E—Swivel Nut.   F—Axle Box
G—Oil Chamber.   H—Nut.   I—Inside Hub Band.   J—Hub.   K—Outside Hub Band.   L—Mortise.

We Invite Correspondence   Send for Sample Set.   Price List and Terms Furnished on Application.

From the Carriage Monthly April 1889

CHAPTER 6

AXLES

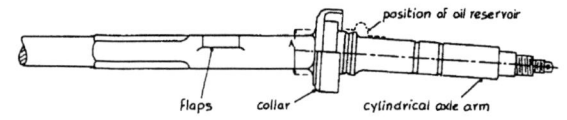

Axle arm or spindle with taper giving the axle the proper gather for the wheel to run true.

The subject of axles would make up an entire book by itself, as to the number of different kinds of axles and wheel combinations, and the making of different types of axles over the last 100 years of the carriage era. This chapter will mention some of the main types of axles of which there were many variations. In combination with wheels that had what was called dish, axles had what was called gather. The ends of the axle-arms are bent forward, away from the center line of the axle. Having the right gather for an axle allowed the wheel to run true without the wheel boxing pushing on the collar of the axle excessively or the opposite would be the wheel boxing pushing on the axle nut and wearing the axle nut. In setting or bending to the proper gather, solid collar axles, neither the collars themselves nor the spindles should be heated, and the set should be given directly back of the collar.[1] If the axles are set by the spindle there is a great risk of damaging or springing this surface where the wheel boxing

---

How to Make and Use an Axle Gauge from the *American Blacksmith*, June 1915
Ed. J. Hoffer

The engraving shows an easily made axle gauge that is inexpensive and yet serves the purpose. To make it, take a piece of hardwood about one inch thick by 1 ½ inches wide and about as long as the longest axle that comes into your shop. In one end of this piece cut a long slot or hole as at A in the engraving and at the other end bore a hole as at B.

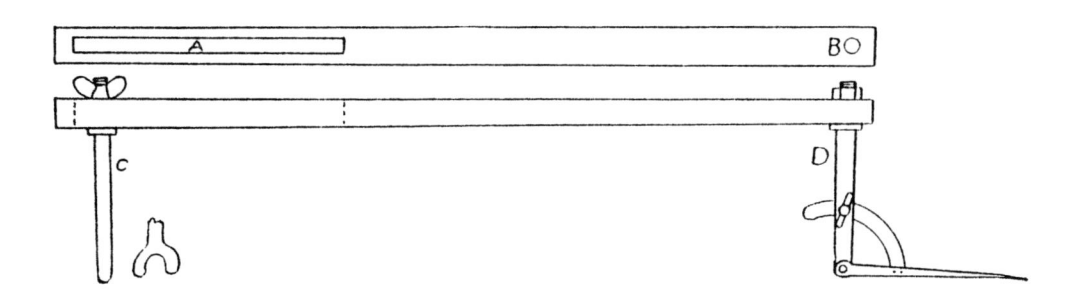

Now forge a forked rod as shown at one end forming the fork and the other end being threaded to take a thumb nut. A washer is welded on to the threaded end of this rod so that with the aid of the thumb screw it will grip the wood tightly when in use. This rod is shifted along on the wood bar to accommodate different lengths of axles.

The rod D is made from an old buggy top joint. This rod is fitted with washer and thread the same as the forked rod. If not long enough it may be lengthened by welding a piece on at the upper end. The joint is then fitted with a quadrant similar to a pair of dividers, the stationary part of the rod being fitted with a thumb screw at the point where the quadrant passes through it. This arm is arranged in this way so as to allow for different adjustment to different angles.

In use, place the rod C on the spindle of the axle and against the collar. The other end D is placed on the other spindle with the joint of the rod up against the collar. When the axle is set just right, mark the quadrant at the thumb screw. Then get the gather and mark that on the other side of the quadrant. You now have a guide for any other axle with the same dish of the wheel and for the other end of the axle, and by this means you can save yourself much time.

Axles

comes in contact with it. This can result in wheels being heated fast or broken axles because of improper turning of the wheel. For different axle gauges and information on setting axles, one reference is "Practical Blacksmithing" by M. T. Richardson.

Axle Manufacture

There were a number of ways in which axles were manufactured. Some were formed from one solid piece, while others were welded together in different steps, with the axle flaps or spindles welded on separately. For the better part of the carriage era, iron was thought to be the better material for axles even though steel had come into use for other carriage parts. The largest French axle manufacture, Lemoine, had this to say about the material in 1890. "The axles, properly stated, should be of iron. Considering that the axles should have sufficient resistance to the side motion of the wheels, the weight of the vehicle, the tendency to change of form and the reaction of the wheels against many obstructions, the material should possess a great deal of elasticity. It should be sufficient, in fact, to resist all the combined influences of shocks, accidental or otherwise, without deforming the axle. Under these requirements we must conclude that iron, which is soft and fibrous, is the best material for the purpose. Iron of the best quality is granular, and the process of forging improves it and renders it fibrous.

Steel offers, in the construction of axles, great advantages from an economical point of view, notably in the importance of reducing the weight and size, and the facility with which the spindles may be hardened. But when the influences to which axles must submit in service are considered, objection must be urged not only against the employment of steel, but also of iron having the nature of steel."[2]

The leading French and American axle makers were also of the opinion that first quality axles were made from one solid mass. The following description of axle making is taken from the booklet of the Dalzell Axle Company of South Egremont, Massachusetts, one of America's leading axle manufactures since 1845. The location of Dalzell Axle Co. allowed their axles to be made from a local supply of iron from the Salisbury mines. Dalzell introduced a method of forging axles and collars from the solid bar instead of using welded collars. Other makers had tried forging the collars by the process known as "upsetting", that is by making a swell in the metal at the desired place by means of heat and end pressure; the Dalzell method was to start with metal of

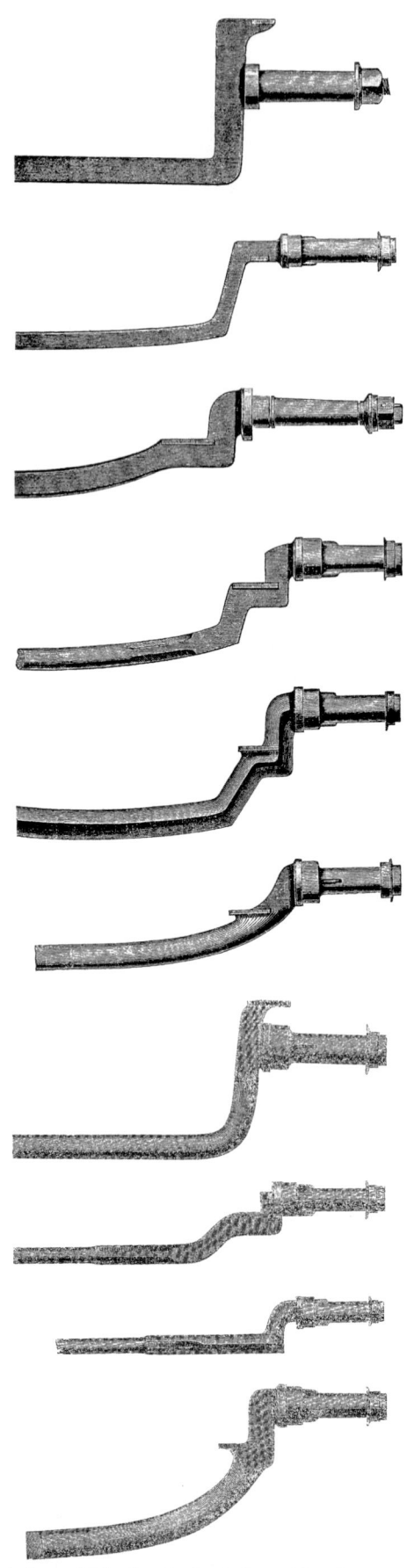

Axles exhibited at the Paris Exposition from the Carriage Monthly May-June 1890

the required diameter for the collar and then to draw out the axle-arms or spindles by forging. He also adopted the case-hardening process which rendered the arms less susceptible to wear, and he overcame the tendency to fracture that other users of this technique had experienced. Another specialty was the case hardened wrought iron axle-box.

The axles were made from bars of iron or steel in the forging shop where, after being cut to length, the bars were heated in a petroleum-fired furnace and drawn down to form the axle-arms or spindles. The largest of the several power hammers used had been made by Dalzell, and so finely was it adjusted that it could deliver a mighty blow of 1,500 pounds or a gentle tap of a few ounces. The accurate work done in the hammer department meant that in the turning room the lathes had but little metal to remove. Axles with cylindrical arms, such as the Collinge's, were tuned on engine lathes, but those with tapered arms or spindles were turned on special axle turning machines, called "rams", constructed like turret lathes with special cutting knives. Also in the turning room were machines for cutting oil grooves, and for milling the edges of the collars, nuts, etc.

Axles

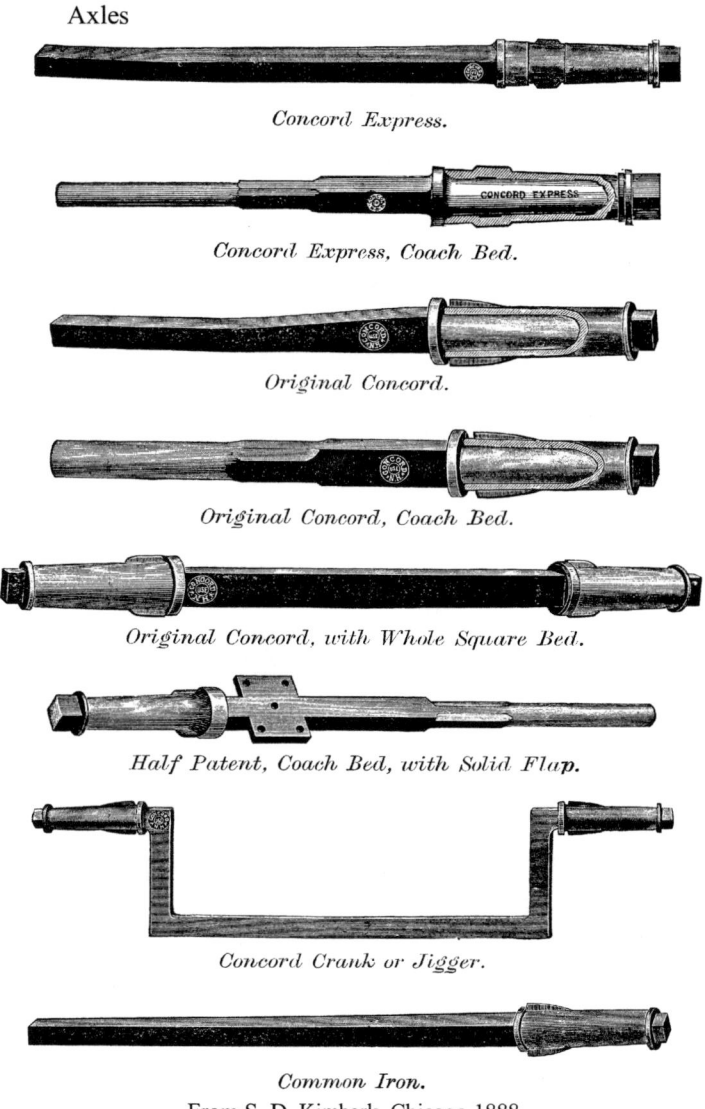

Concord Express.

Concord Express, Coach Bed.

Original Concord.

Original Concord, Coach Bed.

Original Concord, with Whole Square Bed.

Half Patent, Coach Bed, with Solid Flap.

Concord Crank or Jigger.

Common Iron.
From S. D. Kimbark, Chicago 1888

The next process, known as "ground fitting", was done by a special Dalzell method in which the axle-arms were polished with oil and emery to a standard size and a mirror-like finish. In most other factories each box was ground to its own axle-arm by means of oil and emery, but the Dalzell process produced much greater uniformity with a perfect a fit.

The final process was that of tempering and hardening, and for this as many as a dozen or so axles were packed in a retort with a ground bone and carbon mixture, and heated in a charcoal furnace to cherry heat for three to four hours according to size. The axles were then taken out and dipped in water. It was claimed that this process produced hardening to a greater depth than the old case-hardening process. Ten thousand bushels of charcoal a year were needed for this part of the operation.

The wrought iron boxes were made out of wrought iron gas piping, cut to suitable lengths in an automatic machine. The pieces were then heated and "upset"[3] to form the collars. Following this the boxes were drilled out with fluted reamers, the outsides turned on engine lathes and then put through the tempering process. Lastly they were carefully ground with oil and emery to make a prefect fit, the insides being made as smooth and true as a gun barrel.[1]

---
[1] For the term "upsetting" see Weyger, A. G. The Modern Blacksmith, 1974, p. 29.

Axle Types

In dealing with horse-drawn vehicles there are about five main types of axles: wooden axles found on Conestoga wagons, heavy dray wagons, and farm wagons. Collinges axles found on quality pleasure carriages such as breaks, traps, broughams, park drags, landaus, etc. Mail axles are found largely on public road coaches and occasionally on other vehicles such as mail phaetons, and Stanhope gigs. Plain axles, or the common axles, were found largely on buggies and heavy commercial vehicles. Bearing axles come in a wide variety from ball bearing to tapered roller bearing, and they were found on surreys and similar vehicles. They are now used largely on newly made vehicles in place of traditional Collinges axles and plain axles.

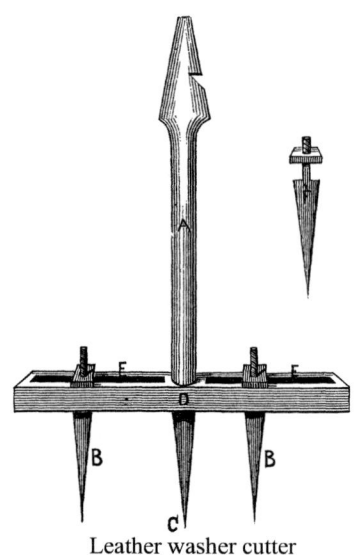

Leather washer cutter from the Coach Makers's International Journal April 1872. Modern washer cutters have much the same appearance

AXLE WASHERS.

Sole Leather.

Leather washers sold by S. D. Kimbark, Chicago washers were also made out of felt and cork. Most agreed leather was best.

This type of leather coil was commonly sold & used for Plain axles.

With all these axles it is advisable to fit a leather washer to the front and back of the hub box. Leather washers help prevent the wearing down of metal surfaces and they help keep the lubricant oil or grease in the hub box. It is the responsibility of the owner of the vehicle to make sure the axles are tended to and in good order, unless there is a professional coachman to look after the carriages. Even if a carriage is sent out for restoration the owner, on getting the carriage back, needs to make sure the axles have been attended to properly. Hand cut washers using the leather washer cutter are usually required for the larger size axles such as Collinge, mail and large plain axles. Someone who owns this type of vehicle should own a leather axle washer cutter in order that the best fit of the leather washers is obtained. If you depend on someone else to cut the washer from measurements that you give them or you send them the old washers it does not necessarily mean you will get tight fitting washers back. For small plain buggy axles leather washers are available in a coil, and just need to be cut to length for this type of axle. Leather washers should be cut from russet colored leather that is vegetable tanned or oak tanned, therefore the leather will not have any dyes or chemicals in it that would be corrosive to metal.

Other essential equipment for carriage owners is a carriage jack for jacking up the vehicle. Or, if you use a modern hydraulic jack you will need an assortment of wooden blocks of different thicknesses to place on the jack platform to make up the space that can't be reached by the jack and also to prevent scratching the axle. An assortment of wooden blocks or wedges will be needed for chalking the wheels. **Never jack up a vehicle without blocking or chalking off the wheels.** For very heavy and large wheels it is safer to have two people taking the wheels off. Carriage jacks are made new and can be found at carriage suppliers or plans for making your own carriage jack can be found in the Driving Digest (1990/4, no. 60).

COLLINGE AXLE

One of the finest axles for carriages is the Collinges axle named after it inventors' John and Charles Collinges of England, who patented their new axle design from 1792 to 1833 it used oil for a lubricant and it only needed to be attended to every six or nine months. The Collinge Axle is precision machined and the various parts are not interchangeable, and each part will be found to have an identifying mark stamped on it. A common complaint about these axles is that they stick fast if not properly attended to. This most often occurs in transporting the carriage. Even though it does not

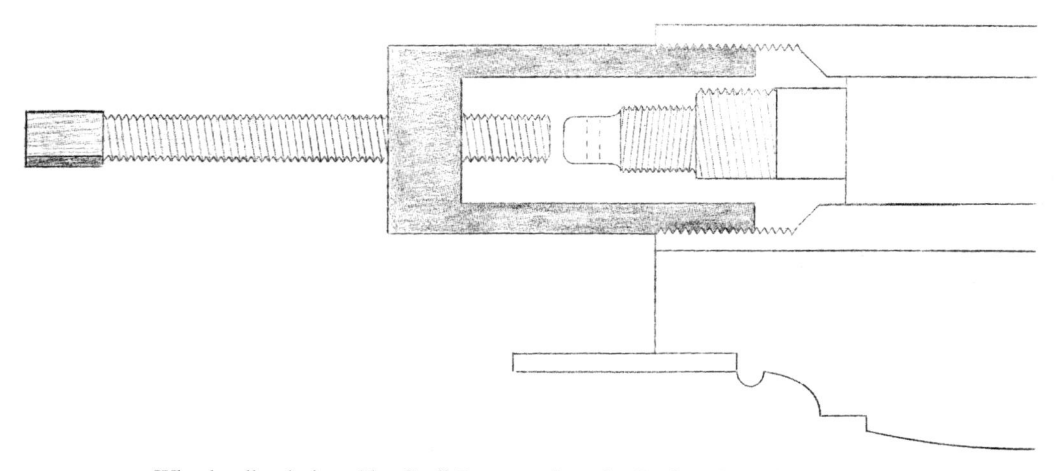

Wheel puller designed by Cecil Ferguson from the Carriage Journal Vol. 7 No. 1

have a horse pulling it, it is still in motion oscillating or vibrating on the truck and trailer without the benefit of the wheel rotating to move the oil about and over the axle arm. Carriage manufacturers found this a problem when shipping carriages by rail and they recommended that before shipping, the oil cap be filled all the way with oil, rather than the normal half full when it was to be used.

Another precaution might be to have a wheel puller made up for your carriage if you do a lot of transporting and being able to have your carriage in running order when you get to an event is important to you. In order to remove a wheel that has been stuck fast you need to remove the oil cap and take it to the machine shop along with a drawing of the kind of wheel puller you want. Have the machine shop thread a piece of pipe matching the threads on the oil cap. Then have a long bolt that can be threaded through a nut fastened to the opposite end. Once you have the wheel puller, put it in position on the wheel. Slowly work it loose pulling the wheel straight off. Do not rotate the wheel, try working it loose with the use of with the use of some WD 40®.

ADVICE ON CLEANING AND OILING COLLINGE AXLES

1. Locate a wrench to fit the axle cap and inner nuts. If you can't find an original, this may require two trips to the auto supply store to first get a socket to fit the oil cap. When you have the oil cap off, a deep well socket is needed to fit the inner nut or nuts. It was proper carriage etiquette that every vehicle should have its own axle wrench that stayed with it. There was usually some kind of space provide that a wrench could be carried along.

2. Place cardboard or paper on the floor, underneath the wheel if you want to keep your floor preserved from oil stains.

3. **Block wheels before jacking**, then remove the oil cap, cotter pin and inner nuts. As you pull the wheel off, reach inside and locate the collet, so that it doesn't drop out accidentally and get lost somewhere.

4. Clean all parts thoroughly, especially the oil reservoir which is the deep groove inside of the box. George Isles recommended paint remover for cleaning the axle arm and parts and then washing with alcohol.

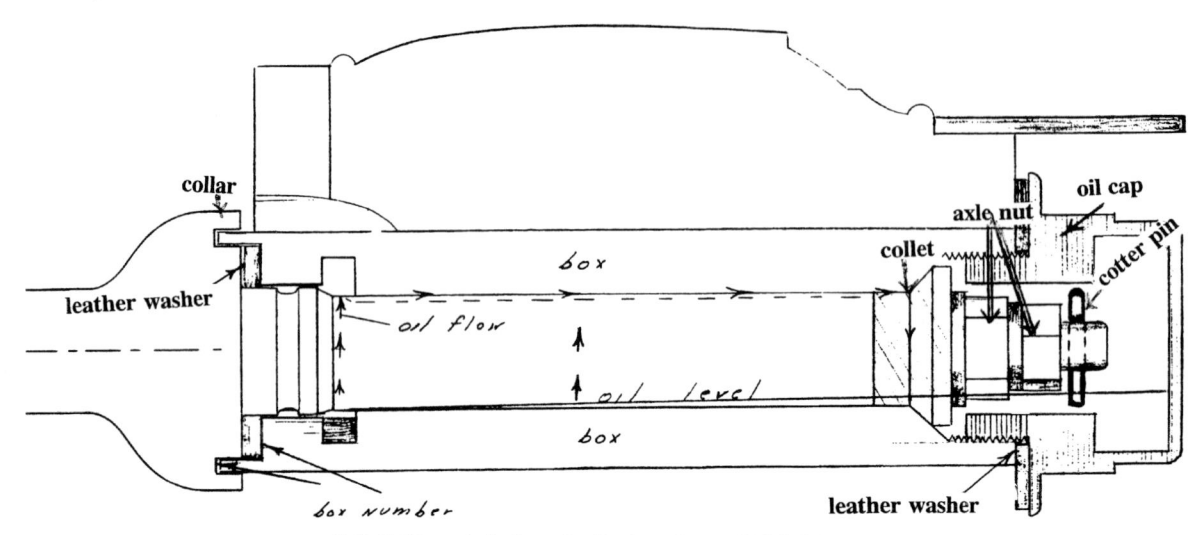

Full Collinge Axle from the Carriage Journal Vol. 7 No. 1

5. Inspect parts for condition. If the wheel was heated fast, make sure the surfaces are again smooth. Check the axle, box, oil cap, collet and nuts for corresponding numbers or letters.

6. Cut new leather washers, unless you are only inspecting a job that has recently been done.

7. Set the leather washer in position at the collar. This washer is usually cut out of 8 to 10 oz. leather making it a thick washer. Apply oil freely on the axle spindle with an old paint brush. Oil the inside of the hub box, filling the reservoir to capacity. There were historically many different kinds of oil recommended, but present day motor oil SAE #20 or #30 non detergent will serve the purpose.

8. Set the wheel on the axle arm, having the collet and nut ready at hand so the wheel does not slide off. When your collar washer is fitted in the wheel box, if it is tight fitting it may require a quick thrust to push the wheel back.

9. Apply oil to the collet bearing surface in the box, insert collet; next turn on the first axle nut by hand and then tighten with the wrench while rotating the wheel, until the wheel just starts to bind. When the wheel starts to bind back off the nut from 1/8 to a half turn.

10. Set the lock nut in position, tightening with moderate pressure. Check that the wheel turns freely. This nut will tighten in the opposite direction on the first nut. Some oil axles may only have one nut.

11. Insert the cotter pin. The cotter pin should be only the length of the opening of the oil cap. If you need to replace the cotter pin you might need to buy a pin that is the right size for the cotter pin hole and then cut it off to the length of the opening of the oil cap or a little less. It is not necessary to bend the cotter pin over. When the oil cap is put in place it will keep the pin in place.

12. Put the newly cut leather washer around the oil cap. This leather is usually 3 to 5 oz. leather and not very thick. Practice screwing the oil cap on, by making sure which way it turns. Tilt the oil cap to an angle of about 45 degrees; fill it about half way with oil; hand tighten and then

tighten with the wrench, but not to such an extreme that you break the brass threads off the axle cap. Some believe that the axle cap should only be filled half way, this way it helps prevent oil from leaking between the boxing and wooden hub.

13. Wipe oil off front and back of the hub with a rag soaked with benzine, and put new paper on the floor under the wheel until you are sure there isn't any leakage. (Taken in part from the Carriage Journal article Collinge Axle by George Isles).

MAIL AXLES

Mail axles are considered the safest axle that was made for horse-drawn vehicles. This axle came into common use on the mail coaches of England. Although it was the safest axle, it never became very popular, because it was difficult to maintain. Fairman Rogers had this to say about Mail Axles, "It is not tapered, but the arm is cylindrical. It is not long enough to extend through the hub or the wheel, and it has at the back end a wide collar against which the back of the hub bears. The box in the hub is turned to fit the cylindrical axle-arm, and the two are ground together, or ground by gauges, so as to fit with accuracy. This box is closed at its outer end, and there is neither nut nor

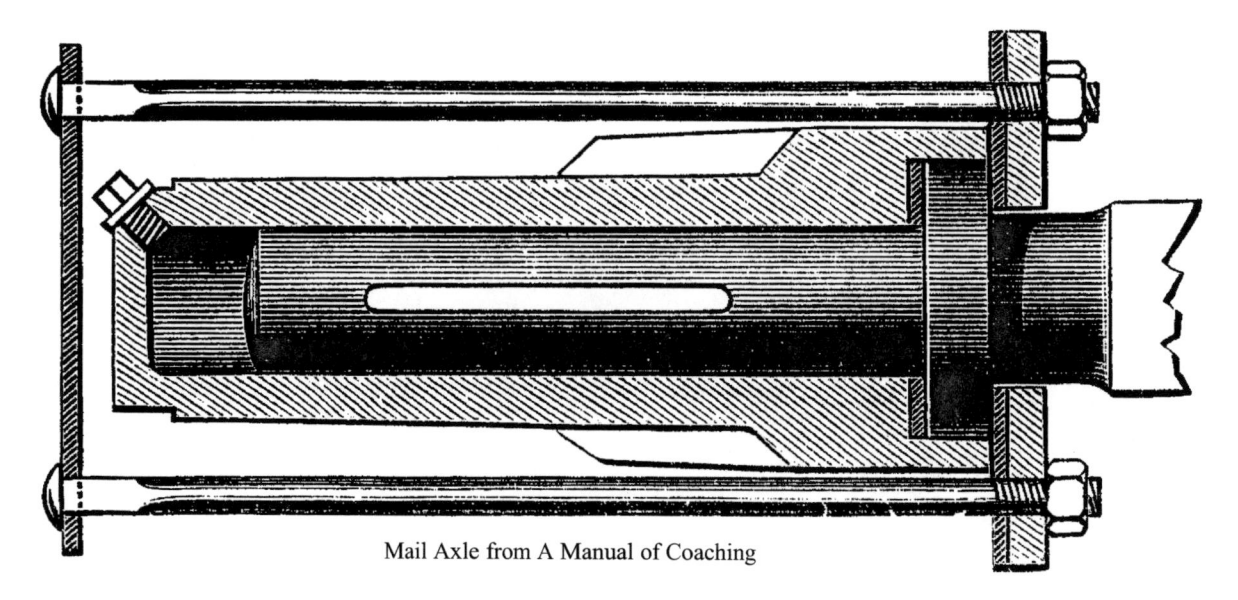

Mail Axle from A Manual of Coaching

linchpin. Behind the collar of the axle there is a loose circular plate, called the moon plate, which has been put on before the axle is welded together in the middle. Around the edge of this plate there are three holes; three bolts run entirely through the hub from the front and pass through the holes in the moon plate, terminating in threaded ends, on which there are nuts. As will be seen in the figure of the "Mail Axle" these bolts held the wheel, by drawing the moon plate toward the back of the hub, the collar of the axle being between them, so that the wheel cannot come off unless all three bolts break, and even if the axle breaks, the wheel will not release unless the fracture takes place behind the collar. . . . The mail axle requires oiling every one or two weeks, which is not only troublesome, but necessitates the constant unscrewing and screwing up of the bolts, which wears the threads and ruins them if it is not done with much care." These axles must also have carefully fitted leather washers.

BEARING AXLES

Ball bearing axles are an early invention, but really didn't become a popular idea for carriage axles until about the mid 1890's. Tapered bearings seemed to be even more popular for carriage axles around the 1900's, and ball bearing axles became less desirable. The literature in the trade journals is not clear as to what you should use for lubricant. Some axle manufacturers called for oil while others said they ran fine on such lubricants as Vaseline. If you should have

a bearing axle that needs replacing the modern carriage trade uses this type of axle in their carriages. Some manufacturers claimed that the axles could go for two years before they needed looking after.

THE BAKER BALL BEARING AXLES THE MOST NEARLY PERFECT ANTI-FRICTION AXLES IN THE WORLD

The Simplest
Most Durable
Most Practical
And Best

Are constructed on scientific principles. The bearings are guaranteed to carry any load that axle to which they are attached will bear. Our bearings reduce friction to a minimum, and have been thoroughly and successfully tested.

We would like to tell you more about these bearings, and a request will bring you our catalogue.

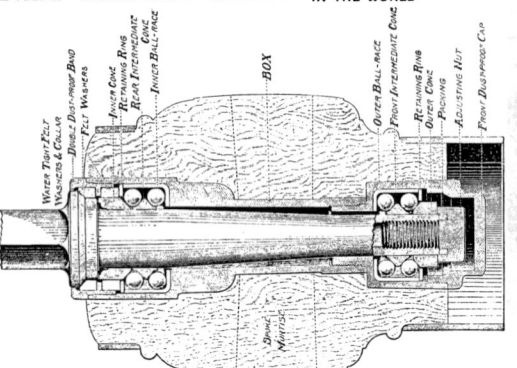

THE UNITED STATES BALL BEARING CO., Washington, D. C.
This Ball Bearing Axle required a felt collar washer.
From the Carriage Journal Spring 1986.

Tapered Roller Axle that became popular towards the end of the carriage era. from the Hub June 1907

PLAIN AXLES

These axles, also known as the common axle or "old style," were the simplest form of an axle found largely on buggies and wagons. The axles require frequent inspection and periodically they should have new washers and be thoroughly cleaned in order that they be free of dirt and grit. In answer to the problem of having to frequently grease the axles a modification was made with a groove on top of the spindle in which a strip of felt could be placed that was soaked in oil. Inventors patented quite a number of different variations of this idea, and several of them became popular with carriage builders. These axles would then use oil and we recommend a heavy weight oil. Leather washers for these axles are available in a coil and you cut off the length you need. The axle nuts turn on so that as the carriage moves forward the axle nuts would be tightening. When using grease, a lithium based grease is a good modern grease to use.

Brewer Longitudinal
AXLE LUBRICATOR.

This type of Plain Axle had a felt pad that was to be soaked in oil and the manufacture claimed it would run for 3 to 6 months without oiling.

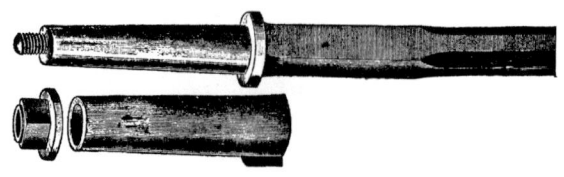

Plain Axle or Common Axle requires leather washers and frequent maintenance, using grease.

WOODEN AXLES

The wooden axle is the first type of axle used on horse-drawn vehicles with the main structure being made of wood. The spindle could have either metal strips or bands around it to help prevent the surface from abrading. For the boxing, metal bands were inserted into the front and back of the hub opening to keep the axle spindle from wearing away at the wooden part of the hub. The wheel was fasten on with a linch pin running through the end of the axle spindle. These axles coexisted with other types of axles until about 1850 - 1860 at which time they were largely replaced by the thimble skein over a wooden axle with an axle nut. This more sophisticated axle style stayed extremely popular to the end of the horse-drawn vehicle era being used on farm wagons and heavy dray wagons. Lubricant for these axles was anything that was available; horse fat or soft tallow, and a mixture of tar. This type of axle requires cleaning and greasing and how often it is done can depend on how often the vehicle is used and under what conditions.

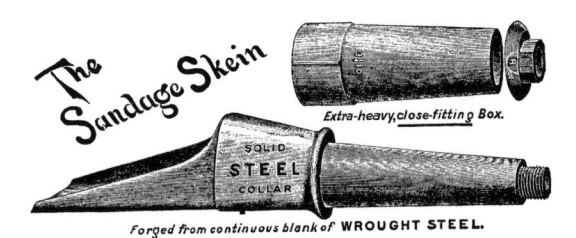

Wooden Axle showing the metal plates to help prevent wear.

THIMBLE SKEINS.

S. D. Kimbark catalog 1888.

Laying Out Wood Wagon Axles.

The best and most convincing method of obtaining the most correct results is to make a drawing as we illustrate in connection with this article, or at least one-half divided with a center line. We illustrate on the left side the finished wheels, and on the right side we take particular pains to show the size top and bottom of spokes, with the plumb line going through the center of the spoke.

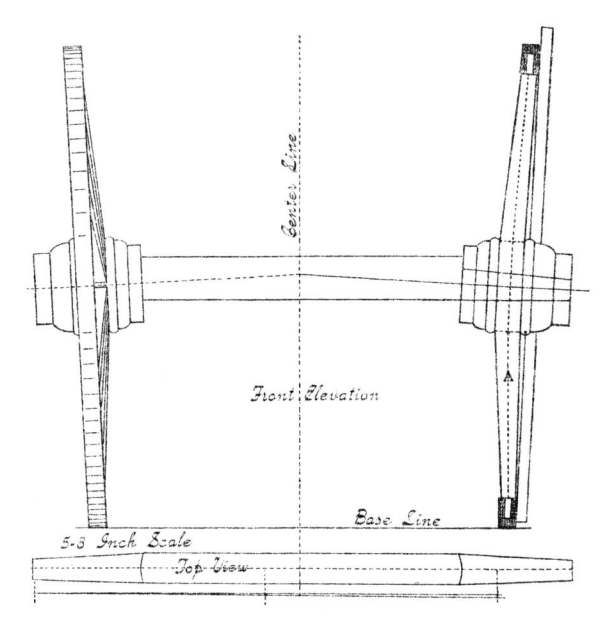

To set steel or iron axle arms, we must have the tired wheels, and the width of the track, which is reproduced in the position as shown in illustration. Plumb spoke in vehicle building is that the plumb line must pass directly through the center of the wedge shaped spoke or staggered spokes. This plumb line is indicated by dotted line A on the right side. The illustration is drawn to B\, inch scale, and the dimensions are as follows: Diameter of wheels without tires, 52 inches; with tires, 54½ inches; diameter of hub bands outside, 10 inches front and 10 ¾ inches back; length of front end to center of spokes, 8½ inches, and length of rear end to center of spokes, 7 inches, showing that the hubs are shorter on rear end than on front end, which is right. The size of spokes at hub shoulders is 1B\, x 3 ½ inches; and at felloe shoulders 1M\, x 2C\, inches. The size of felloes is 2 ½ x 2 M\, inches, and size of tires, 1 ¼ x 2B\, inches; amount of dish, ¾ inch full

From these dimensions draw the wheel full size, as shown on the right side, and be very particular with the position of the lower spoke so that the plumb line goes through the center of the spokes. The plumb position of the spoke is most important, as it makes the wagon run easier and wears equally on under surface of axle arm. To obtain the dish of the wheels which affects the spread on top, lay on straight edge on front side of felloes and take distance from straight edge to dot on dotted line and same on felloe, and reproduce exactly the wheels on the drawing; also the length of the hub from dotted line to rear end. This will give the axle shoulder, which is beveled, and also the horizontal or under surface of axle; also the taper of the skein. If the wheels should have more dish than on this illustration it would increase also the taper in proportion to the dish, but the taper on skeins is not alike, when the different makes are concerned. They may have more or less taper which will affect the horizontal line, and again they may just fit for the dish of the wheels.

There are two ways to equalize the taper of the skeins in the hubs. One is to change the direction of the horizontal line, or under surface of axle arm. The taper may affect the under surface, either front or rear end of hub, depending on the taper of the skeins.

The other way is if the horizontal under surface is desired, to give more or less spread to the wheels on top. By doing this it will throw the spokes more or less out of the plumb line, which does not make much difference on heavy tapered spokes as shown on this illustration.

To obtain the length of the axle stock, mark the width of the track from out to out or center to center of tire, and if the wheels are in the right position, the length and bevel of the axle stock is most correct. If for heavy or light carriage wheels, use the same method. Make the drawing full size, draw the wheels or wheel correctly, let the plumb line pass directly through the dodged spokes on heavy coach wheels where the axles are rigid; but when the wheels are light underset must be given. For 1¼ inch spoke inch underset for each wheel is correct, which makes 1-16 inch underset directly under the hub down to base. If the carriage is loaded, the wheels will spread from the load, and the spoke will run in a plumb direction. For 1 inch spokes, 3-16 inch for each wheel is given, making 3-32 inch on under surface of hubs.

The rule is, all dished wheels should have gather when in motion and when loaded. The higher the wheels and the broader the tires, the more gather.

The spreading of wheels in front is caused by the load on the contact of tires on the road. Wagon wheels, as shown in this illustration, do not spread, but the axles are not as well fitted in the skeins as the coach axles, and the tendency in its forward motion will always be toward spreading, consequently provision must be made to give some gather. In our opinion, if the axle arms are fairly well fitted, each wheel should have about inch gather for entire diameter of wheel. Below the wheels we show the top view of axle stock, and below the axle stock the gather line inch on the length of 54 inches makes less than 1-64 inch on the length of axle arm. From the *Carriage Monthly* March 1909.[2]

INSPECTING THE AXLES BEFORE BUYING AND RESTORATION

When deciding to buy a vehicle or getting a vehicle ready for restoration the axle should be inspected to make sure it is not bent and the spindles are not worn to such an extent that it interferes with safe operation of the vehicle. Excessive play of the wheels causes stress on the axle arm making it more prone to excessive wear. Vehicles with wooden axles, need to be inspected for dry rot or other damage to the wood, by poking around with a penknife. Having to replace a wooden axle is not uncommon if the vehicle has been outside for many years. There are only a few people that can still make this type of wooden axle, so you might want to check the expense before starting this type of project. Abnormally bent axles are often a result of a wreck and it is a comparatively easy job to straighten axles. An axle gauge should be used to make sure the gather of axle remains true. Worn

---

[2]For additional information on wooden axle making refer to - Richardson, M. T. Practical Blacksmithing. Weathervane Books, NY p. 128-146.

spindles can be checked while the wheels are on the vehicle, move each wheel back and forth to see if there is excessive play. If there is, it means either that there has been excessive wear on the spindle or it could mean simply that it needs leather washers. Next block the wheels and jack up the individual wheels and spin the wheels and check for wobble. Then take off the wheels. Check for wear on both sides of the spindle. A flat spot on the underside of the spindle is a good indication that the spindle or axle will have to be replaced. If there are no signs of wear put on new washers, one in the nut and one in the rear at the collar, lubricate the axle spindle and replace the wheel, tightening the nut. Then rock the wheel back and forth to see if it still has play in it. Some wheels may have slight movement even if the spindles are ok because there is wear on the inner part of the hub boxing or hub face. This can be corrected by adding another washer in the rear or by having a wheelwright cast hot lead alloy in the worn area to make it flush again. Spindles which show excessive wear, will also have wear on the boxings. Someone planning to buy or restore such a vehicle should figure the repair costs into the their project.

There are two choices for worn spindles and boxings; one can replace the axle and boxing or replace the axle spindle and boxing. Usually the latter choice is cheaper. In replacing the spindle and boxing there are also choices; does the person want to keep the axle/wheel style as authentic as possible or do they simply want a usable safe vehicle. Missing parts for Collinges axles can be machined such as axle nuts, collets and oil caps. If the hub boxing and the axle spindle combination is a wooden or a patent type (Sarven type) there is not much of a problem, as there are a few people who supply these materials. Many people, when faced with this choice assume, or are told by a wheelwright that doesn't know any better, that their only choice is to replace the damaged spindle with a roller bearing type of arrangement. Roller bearing wheels, while cheap to put on and functional, can take away from the value of a fine vehicle. There are several types of roller bearing axle spindles and hub boxings available. Each has a different appearance and uses different spokes. Probably both are equally functional. It is very important that this job be done by a qualified person who will maintain the proper gather. Some owners make the mistake of assuming that a roller bearing hub is naturally superior to the hubs which came with their vehicle. They have them changed even when the original axle spindle/hub boxing were in fine condition. Unless a person is going to put on tens of thousands of miles a year, the original axle spindle/hub boxing, if in good condition, will give excellent service. In fact some drivers prefer the slight resistance offered by the traditional type axle spindle/hub boxing combinations. Notes from Bruce Morrison

Bibliography and additional references for axles

"[Ball Bearing Axle]." Carriage Journal. Vol. 23 No. 4 (Spring 1986), p. 188.

Cantle, Gordon. "Mechanics Of Wheel Setting." Carriage Journal. Vol. 27 No. 4 (Spring 1980), pp. 174-176.

Cantle, Gordon. "On Axle Flaps." Carriage Journal. Vol. 28 No. 1 (Summer 1990), pp. 3-5.

"[Different Oil Axles]." Carriage Journal. Vol. 25 No. 3 (Winter 1987), p. 146-147.

"Historical References To Axle Lubrication." Carriage Journal. Vol. 27 No. 4 (Spring 1980), p. 176.

Isles, George. "The Collinge Axle." Carriage Journal. Vol. 7 No. 1, pp. 22-25.

Isles, George. The Restoration of Carriages. London, England : J. A. Allen & Co., 1981.

Lemoine. "Notes on Manufacturing Springs and Axles." Carriage Monthly. Vol. 26 No. 3, Vol. 26 No. 4, Vol. 26 No. 5, Vol. 26 No. 6, Vol. 26 No. 7(June 1890, July 1890, Aug. 1890, Sept. 1890, Oct. 1890) pp. 78, 118-119, 150-151, 182-183, 214.

"A Man Of Ideas : The Story of Henry Timken, Carriage Builder and Founder of a World Wide Enterprise." Carriage Journal. Vol. 17 No. 4 (Spring 1980), pp. 185-191.

Axles

"What Is The Best Lubricant For Carriage Axles." Carriage Journal. Vol. 20 No. 4 (Spring 1983), p. 193.

Ryder, Tom. "Mail Axle." Carriage Journal. Vol. 27 No. 3 (Winter 1989), pp. 133-135.

Ryder, Tom. "Carriage Axles." Carriage Journal. Vol. 15 No. 3 (Winter 1977), 327-330.

Endnotes

1. Ware Bros. The Handy Shop Book. Philadelphia, PA : Ware Bros., 1902 p. 42.
2. Lemoine. "Notes on Manufacturing Springs and Axles." Carriage Monthly. Vol. 26 No. 3 (June 1890), p. 78.
3. "The Dalzell Axle Company of South Egremont, Massachusetts." Carriage Journal. Vol. 15 No. 3 (Winter, 1977), pp. 331-333.
4. "How Carriage Axles Are Made." Carriage Dealers' Journal. Vol. X No. 9 (Jan. 1900), pp. 19-24.

Dalzell's Improved Collinge-Axle.

Patented Sept. 6th, 1870.

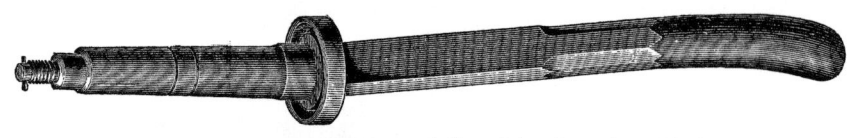

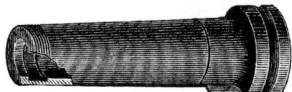

A new Coach Axle in which the essential points of that valuable Axle, the "English Collinge," are preserved, while the construction is made more simple and cost reduced. This Axle is more easily cared for, not so liable to rattle, and a more thorough and well distributed lubrication is secured. Its leading features, as illustrated, are in the bridge and oil chamber in front end of box. The Axle proper is practically the "Collinge," but by using this box we have a broad washer bearing on front end of box, with a leather washer which dispenses with the brass washer or D plate, the single nut and pin taking the place of the two nuts, as this single nut can be set up to the shoulder, requiring no lock or jam nut, making it much easier to remove the wheel and lubricate; while the oil cup when on the job gives it the appearance of, and it is practically, a Collinge Axle.

These Axles are perfectly finished, and owing to the fewer pieces used in manufacture, the cost is reduced below that of *first quality Collinge Axles*. They are in use by some of the best carriage builders in the country, and have in all cases given perfect satisfaction.

For further particulars apply to **Dalzell & Co., South Egremont, Mass.**

MANUFACTURERS OF FINE AXLES.

From the Hub April 1883

CHAPTER 7

WHEELS

The making of wheels was a whole industry or trade in itself. From English Pleasure Carriages by William Bridges Adams in 1837 he had this to say about early wheel making. "The result of this mode of making a wheel is, that it is very imperfect when finished. Scarcely any two wheels are alike." Early craftsmen that were able to make good wheels by hand were well-respected tradesmen. Wheel making before the industrial era was a very labor intensive job. To make the spokes for a set of four wheels by hand took up to a day and a half, this made a vehicle an expensive item for the average workmen before the 1850-1860's. William Adams gives the following description of making wheels by hand. "When the nave (hub) of elm wood has been turned to its size in the lathe, it is marked for the spoke mortises, and firmly fixed at a convenient height at such an angle with the horizon as corresponds to the intended dish of the wheel. Two holes are then bored in each mortise in succession, after which they are squared out with proper chisels.

Truth of eye and skill of hand are the workmen's only guide in this operation; though it is evident that it is the most important operation of the whole, as upon it depend the accuracy and solidity of the wheel when finished. The tenons of the spokes--which are portions of dry rent oaken saplings-- are then cut to fit the mortises, parallel in their thickness and slightly wedging in their width. The other parts of the spokes are only partially prepared. Every alternate spoke is then driven by blows of a maul, the workman guiding it as well as he can in a proper direction till it abuts upon the shoulder. But it is evident that the position which each spoke will take is by no means certain. The spokes are driven very tight, and wood, not being of a homogeneous texture, will yield more in one part than another: and the mortise, cut as it is by sleight of hand, must be uncertain. Every alternate spoke being driven, the remainder are then driven in between them in the same manner. After this, the spokes are finished to their proper form; and the lengths being measured from the nave, the outer tenons are cut to a cylindrical form, leaving the back shoulder square, to abut on the felloe with more firmness. The back of the spoke is rounded to a semicircular form in nearly its whole length behind; in front it is worked to a knife-edge, for the sake of a light appearance. The felloes are then fitted on the spokes, and jointed together. Holes are then bored in the ends of the felloes, and a small piece of wood, called a dowel, is inserted, which serves as a tenon to connect them together. The felloes being then driven home, wedges are inserted in the ends, of the spokes to keep all firm. After this, the tire, welded into a solid hoop, is heated and put on. As it shrinks in cooling, the wheel cracks and compresses beneath the force. Iron pins are then driven through tire and felloe, one on each side of every joint, the points being riveted inside the felloe upon a small round plate of iron called a burr."

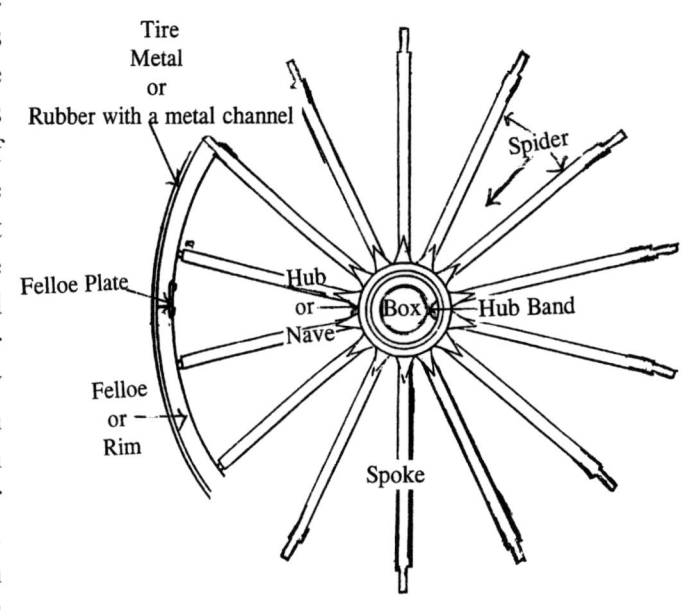

Parts of a Wheel

Wheels

Around the 1860's wheels started to be made with more labor saving machinery. Large wheel making factories appeared all across the country, and after awhile very few vehicle makers made their own wheels, they purchased either wheel parts or fully assembled wheels. The largest wheel factory on the east coast the Hoopes Bros. and Darlington listed some 80 steps to make a wheel from selecting the timber to having it painted. Each step of making a wheel had it's own specialized machine; coarse, medium and fine sanders that finished spokes, finish machines that only finished felloes, power hammers that drove in the spokes, powerful hub mortising machines, etc. These mass produced wheels meant higher quality and more uniform wheels.

Patent Wheels

There were a great variety of wheels with many ideas of what made the best and most economical wheel. Between 1790 and 1910 there were an estimated 8000 patents taken out for the design and construction of wheels, this does not include axles. There were two main types of wheels ; wheels with wooden hubs and patent wheels. Wooden hub wheels were the traditional wheels with either staggered spokes or in line spokes all made out of wood. Patent wheels usually involved an extra metal support system for the hub. A landmark patent for wheels was issued on June 9, 1857 to J. D. Sarven of Columbia, TN. In order to give the wheels sufficient strength, a large hub was necessary, which was thought clumsy upon light carriages. To overcome this defect, Sarven conceived the idea of making a strong but light wheel, by using a very light wooden-mortised hub. Instead of staggering the spokes to give them strength, as had always been done on light wheels, he mitered the shoulders, so as to form a solid arch on the outside of the hub, and, in order to give lateral support to the spokes forming this arch, he brought a metallic flange to bear on each side, and connected them together by rivets or bolts; thus making a strong wheel. In the Sarven patent the flanges were forced on after the spider[1] had been made. Mr. Sarven was unable to put his patent into use and he sold his rights to the Woodburn & Scott, of St. Louis and the New Haven Wheel Company and later other wheelmakers. It wasn't until the 1870's that this wheel started to become popular and this type of wheel has remained popular today with people building new vehicles. Although not as popular as the roller bearing wheels today.

SARVEN PATENT WHEELS.
DIAGRAM SHOWING THE CONSTRCTION OF THE "SARVEN PATENT" WHEEL.

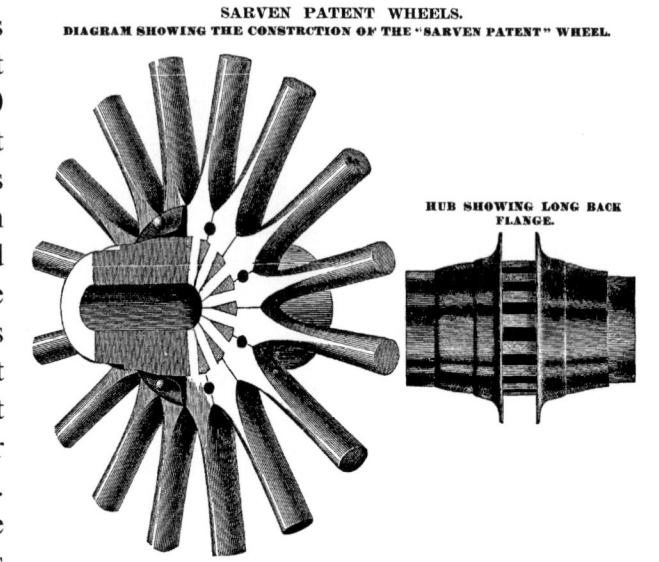

HUB SHOWING LONG BACK FLANGE.

From the catalog of Bradlee, Hastings & Co., Boston.

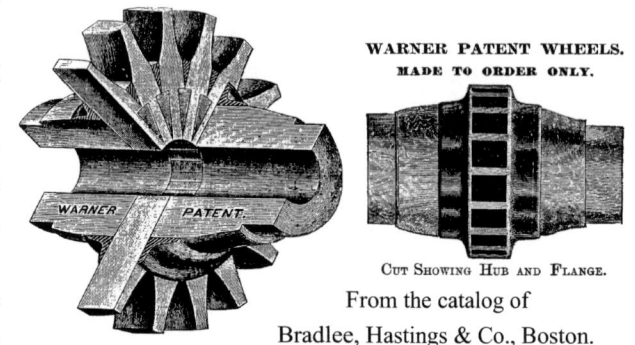

WARNER PATENT WHEELS.
MADE TO ORDER ONLY.

CUT SHOWING HUB AND FLANGE.
From the catalog of
Bradlee, Hastings & Co., Boston.

---

[1] A "spider" refers to the assembled hub and spokes with out the felloe or tire.

Another type of patent wheel that became popular and remains in use to this day is the Warner patent, issued Feb. 5, 1867 to Almon Warner of Belvidere, New Jersey. The Warner patent has the spokes mortised through cast metal mortises for support, with the metal flanges being forced onto the wood core before it is mortised. The rights for the Warner patent were sold to the Elihu Hall & Co. of Wallingford, Connecticut and it became a popular wheel on the market. The Sarven patent was renewed for seven years in 1872 and a lawsuit occurred against the Warner patent in which the judge ruled *a wooden hub, into which spokes entered by a mortise and tenon, having any metallic support for the spokes outside of the hub* was an infringement of the Sarven patent. Between 1872 and 1877 the Sarven patent maintained a virtual monopoly, with only modifications and improvements by various licensees. The Warner patent came back on the market after 1877 along with other patent wheel designs. The Warner and Sarven patents became the two most popular patented wheels. Today much of the large factory machinery for making wheels has gone to the scrap yard, with only a few places left that keep some of the machinery in operation. Some of the suppliers of wooden parts for wheels have adapted modern wood working machinery for turning spokes and hubs and mortising and tenoning.

Getting Wheel Work Done

There is a big difference in the way wheels with wooden hubs and staggered spokes and wheels with metal hubs (patent wheels) are constructed. Not all present day wheelwrights make all kinds of wheels. Wheels with staggered spokes and wooden hubs have a certain artistic design and craft to them which would be destroyed by sending them to a wheel wright that can only makes patent wheels. Even among patent wheels different jigs and shaped spokes are required for all the different varieties of patent wheels. If you have a wheel that is unusual you should not assume that it was never meant to be that way and change it to a more acceptable and common type wheel. Try to do some research and keep it as close to the original as possible. Listed at the end of the chapter are some references for wheels, *Wheelmaking* edited by Don Peloubet is so far the most comprehensive book on wheels in print.

If you are going to need wheel work done, you will need to give careful consideration to where to best get this done. Just as with mechanics, there is a difference both in scope and level of competency of wheelwrights. There are some who are simply not very good. Among those who are competent, many can do Sarvens, some can do Sarvens and roller bearings and a few can handle wooden hubs with staggered spokes. Similarly many wheelwrights are not competent or willing to do large wagon wheels either of the common old style or the large Sarvens or Archibalds. If a person is going to have a wheel done it would be wise to not only to look at the persons work but also to ask for the names of other customers to see if they were satisfied with the person's work. Good wheelwrights always stand behind their work. The price charged for the same work varies to a large degree, both within a particular region and across the country. notes from Bruce Morrison.

When you get your wheels back there are several things you can do to make sure the job has been done properly. First lay a straight edge across the felloes and measure to the spoke shoulder on each wheel to check the dish. It should pretty much be the same on each wheel unless their is a great difference in size. Secondly, check that the two front wheels and the two back wheels are of the same diameter, that is, the front wheels are the same and the back wheels are the same. Thirdly, make sure that the shoulders of the spokes are seated evenly at the hub and where they join at the felloes. There should be no gaps between the felloes and the spoke shoulders. Fourth, check to make sure the spokes are straight, that is that none of them bulge indicating that the spoke is too long. Fifth, look for excessive burning between the tire and the wooden felloe. This is often caused by forcing a tire on the felloe. Large amounts of wood filler between the felloe and the tire are often used to hide this problem. Sixth, check to make sure the hub boxing is centered and tightly secured in the hub. Seventh, check the wheels on the vehicle to make sure they have the correct amount of dish to line up center again with the break blocks.

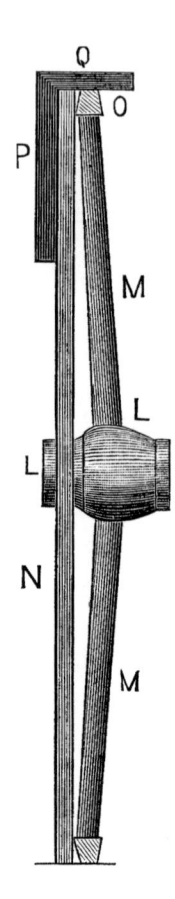

DISH IN WHEELS

Among all the aspects of wheel making, none provoked more discussion and disagreement than the subject of dishing, (curvature of the wheel), whose prime purpose was thought to be that it added greater strength to the wheel. In fact, the amount of dish required for certain types of vehicles, and the reasons for dishing, are still debated to this day. The debate seems to focus around the issue of whether the emphasis should be placed when the tire is put on or when the spokes are put in. Those who favored the tire tightening approach while using spokes with some angle on the tenon, rely on the felloe-tire relationship to produce the dish through contraction of the tire. These wheels sometimes have a problem of reverse dish either through a sharp blow when driving, or the spokes reseating themselves (driving further into the mortises through use) after the wood shrinks. The people focusing on setting the dish when you put in the spokes, cut the angle, often 2 %, of the tenon before inserting them into the hub. On many hubs the mortice is also angled when it is made. This is particularly important in wooden hub wheels with staggered spokes. But it can be done with other wheels as well. The felloes are set without much of a gap and the tire is just an of an inch under the felloe size. The tire then, holds it all together and protects the wheel but doesn't dramatically force the dish as the other procedure does. Good wheelwrights, who understand the process of creating dish, use a little of both methods depending on the wheel. While the best way to set the dish is setting the spokes properly, if it isn't quite right, they will cut a little more from the felloe joint and measure the tire accordingly. Correcting the dish in a wheel is something any qualified wheelwright can do. Notes from Bruce Morrison

The most important reason for dishing is that it aligns the bottom spoke that contacts the ground (referred to as a "plumb" spoke), so that no matter how much weight is applied (within the limits of the vehicle), the spoke has the tendency to remain vertical and be less vulnerable to side thrust and subsequent breakage. The spoke on the bottom of the wheel is acting as a lever on the hub as it comes in contact with the ground and it has greater strength if it is vertical as this lever action is applied. Other reasons for dishing are: that a dished wheel is less likely to become rim-bound as the wood shrinks, the tire remains tight with wear, mud is thrown away from the vehicle, allows for greater width of the body, a properly dished wheel along with the set of the axle (called the gather) runs true rather than causing excessive wear on the axle collar or axle nut. Some vehicle makers would set their wheels so that they wore on the collar of the axle rather than taking a chance of the wheel boxing wearing on the axle nut and causing the wheel to come off.

The dish of the wheel can be obtained by: 1. a slight angle on the shoulder of the spoke tenon, which is driven into the hub mortise, kicking the spoke toward the front of the hub. 2. how tightly the iron tire is set 3. the angle on the tenon of the spoke and the hub mortise.

Normally the concave surface (dish) faces the outside of the vehicle. Recent research has shown that Brewster & Co. made two wheeled vehicles with a dish inch back on some of their carts that were ordered by customers.[2] It is unknown why these wheels had a backward dish. If you are restoring a Brewster vehicle, you should always check the original specifications when available.

Wheels
HUBS

The preferred wood for hubs was elm, because it had just the right elasticity, an exception to this was the use of locust for the hubs of ice wagons because they didn't rot when the ice melted. Early wheel makers seasoned or dried elm hubs by putting them under hay for a whole year, or more depending on the diameter. They dried very slowly and were said to produce good results. In the more modern factories after the 1870's, the hub blocks were sawed to the various necessary lengths, and these lengths dipped in a soluble resin to keep the air from penetrating too suddenly into the ends of the hub thus keeping them from splitting. After this they are placed above the floors on racks, lying on top of each other in two rows, and left there until dry, and turned into shape. Other methods of drying hub stock included boring a hole in the center and then dipping the ends in paraffin or resin. Some were said to dry their hubs at 90 degrees Fahrenheit.

Some wheel makers believed that once the hub was mortised you should never let it sit about, because moisture would get into the hub through the mortise and the spokes should be put in place as soon as possible. Some wheel makers thought that temporary hub bands should be applied to the hub to prevent the hub from splitting, other wheel makers applied the hub bands when they set the tire, while other applied permanent bands as soon as they started making the wheel.

Today some of the technology of how hub blocks were dried without splitting seems to have been lost. Elm is no longer readily available due to the large use from wheel makers, the present decline of forest land, and Dutch Elm disease. With new technology some hub manufacturers use laminated hardwood to make hubs.

There are two major types of wooden hubs-common or old style and the patent hub. Common hubs are usually made with an in-line or staggered spoke pattern. Patent hubs started to become popular around the 1870's and there were many different types of patented hubs that coexisted with the common hubs. Patent hubs are reinforced with a patented malleable iron sleeve, or band. Some professional wheel makers thought that staggered spokes gave the wheel greater elasticty and they refused to acknowledge that the patent wheel had any merit. Both were equally popular though with wheel makers and consumers. Better quality vehicles and upper class carriages are generally seen with common hubs with the in-line spoke pattern or the staggered spoke pattern. In the in-line spoke pattern an excessive amount of wood is removed thinning the mortise wall in a defined area. While

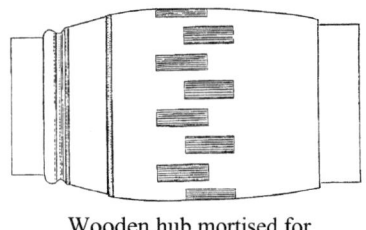

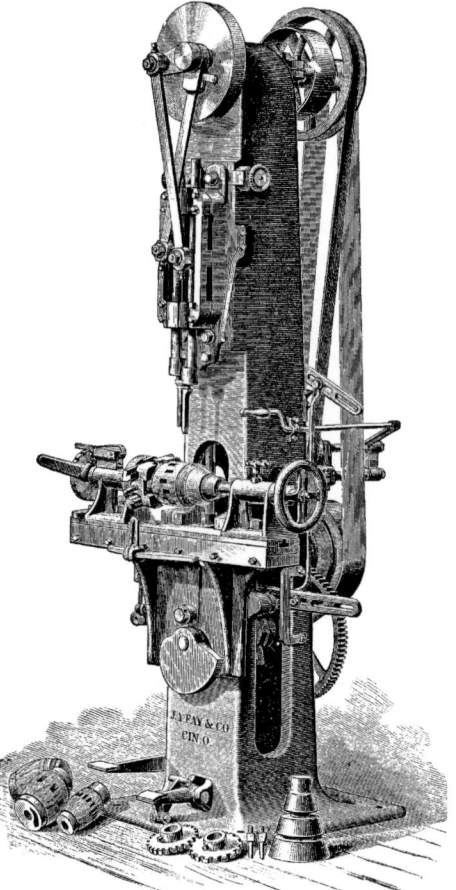

Wooden hub mortised for staggered spokes

Wheel with staggered spokes

Double-Chisel Hub-Mortiser and Borer, from the Hub Sept. 1886.

this was a problem for carriage hubs, wagon wheels using an in-line pattern solved the problem by putting a metal band on either side of the mortice as well as at the ends of the hubs.

Restoration Hubs

Wooden hubs should be checked in various ways depending on the type of hub. Those with bands should have the bands checked for looseness. Check for a loose boxing in the hub, check for deep cracks and other cracks with extend into the spoke mortice. If unsure of the significance of a crack check with a wheelwright. Sarven hubs tend to be alright if all the spokes are in place and tight even if they are broken off from the felloe. The spokes keep out the moisture and thus the dry rot. Normally if a wheelwright is replacing the majority of the spokes in a Sarven hub they take the flanges off to check the hub just to make sure it is alright. Non professionals are advised not to remove the flanges from a Sarven hub because if it is not put on correctly the integrity of the wheel will be affected. Notes from Bruce Morrison

SPOKES

The preferred wood for spokes was hickory for light wheels, but this was not until about the 1840's, when a more successful spoke turning machine was put into use at the Amos Carter factory in Newark, New Jersey.[3] The use of hickory, the strongest and hardest American hardwood, is said to have given American wheel makers the edge on the international wheel market, because they could make a stronger and lighter wheel.

White oak is mentioned as being used for heavier wheels in wagons because it didn't deteriorate as quickly as hickory under adverse conditions of moisture, and proportionally hickory didn't add any greater strength when used for large wheels. The large use of hickory also caused a national crisis, and it was found to becoming extinct in some parts of the country. Spoke tenons for the felloe can be cut either oval, square or round. Round tenon ends seemed to be the most widely accepted.

FELLOES/RIMS

The hand-method of wheel making practiced in the early wheelwright shops involved cutting the felloe sections from rough planks with a felloe saw, a type of frame saw with a narrow center blade that cuts on a curve. A felloe pattern was used to mark the planks for each size and type

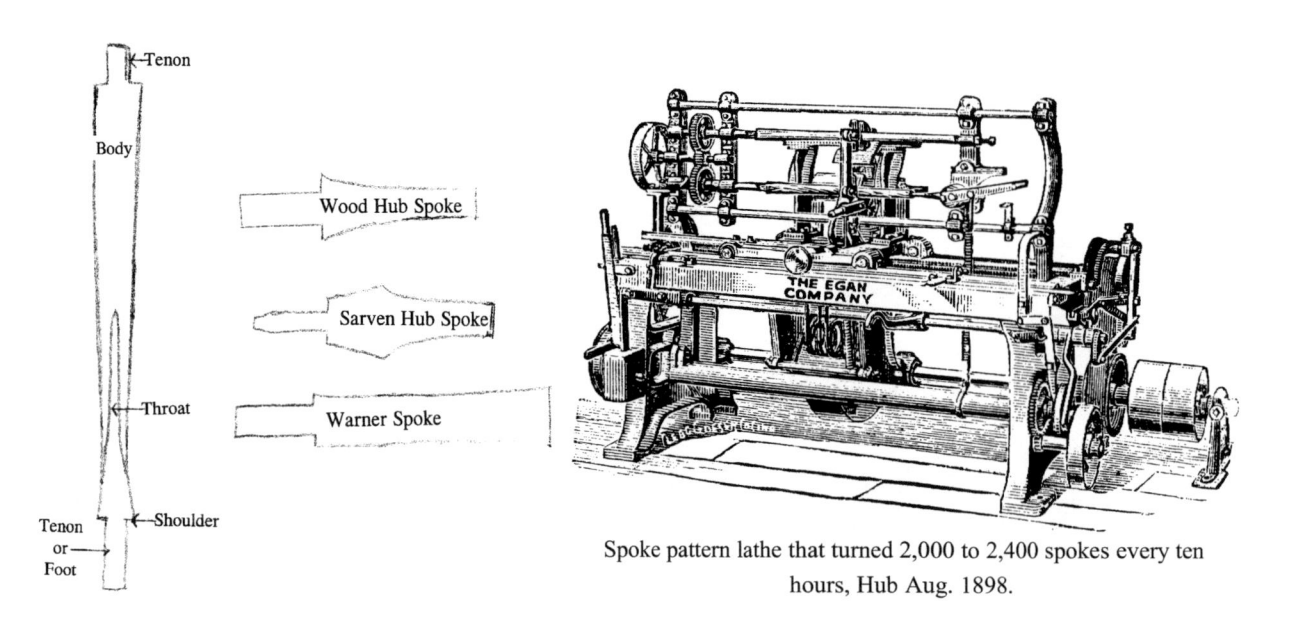

Spoke pattern lathe that turned 2,000 to 2,400 spokes every ten hours, Hub Aug. 1898.

of wheel with each section covering two spokes. Blacksmith shops doing wheel work usually keep patterns for the most called for sawed felloes hanging on their walls. After cutting, the felloes were smoothed with a compass plane and rounded or chamfered with a spokeshave.

The first bent rim in one piece was believed to have been made in America by James Hansen of Saugerties, New York in 1835. In the same year Edward K. Reynolds of St. George, Delaware attempted to make two section bent rims available to the trade but his method of wood bending was not very practical. It wasn't until 1856, with the introduction of Thomas Blanchard's wood bending machine, that the two section bent rims became practical with less breakage of oak, ash and hickory.

Felloes come not only in different diameters but also in different widths and thicknesses. The dimensions varied depending on the type of vehicle and the uses to which it was put. The late Pete Leach who studied Brewster carriages, identified 5 different felloe patterns they used. One of the Brewster's trade marks was a felloe with a slightly rounded side wall. To replace this type of felloe would take special care. Felloes in different sizes are readily available from carriage supply shops and if your project has special requirements, wider than normal felloes would have to be ordered. The carriage restorer might have to take the responsibility to take the felloes to a wood working shop to have the taper put on the side walls before the wheelwright puts the wheels together, or have the wheelwright modify them.

A common problem of wheels was the joint between the felloe and spoke becoming loose. Some old remedies for loose wheels were to soak them in the water trough or the stream. This would swell the wood and tighten the wheel up again. It was not uncommon for people that were near a blacksmith's shop to have the tires reset. Another way was to soak the felloe in a specially made wheel trough filled with linseed oil, and this was the practice of some manufacturers before painting the wheels. Many professionals of the carriage era were of a different opinion about adding linseed oil to the wheels first. Some thought it made the situation worse while others made a great practice of it.

We would not recommend any of these procedures for a restoration job that you want to last for many years. The best solution is for a wheelwright to reset the tire by cutting and rewelding the tire to the proper size. Swelling the wood in the wheel is only a temporary solution, it would cause moisture to be trapped under your paint job lifting the paint later on, and once the wood dried out the wheel would come loose again.

The best wheel makers gave important consideration to the moisture content of the wood used in making wheels, so that the wheels didn't dry

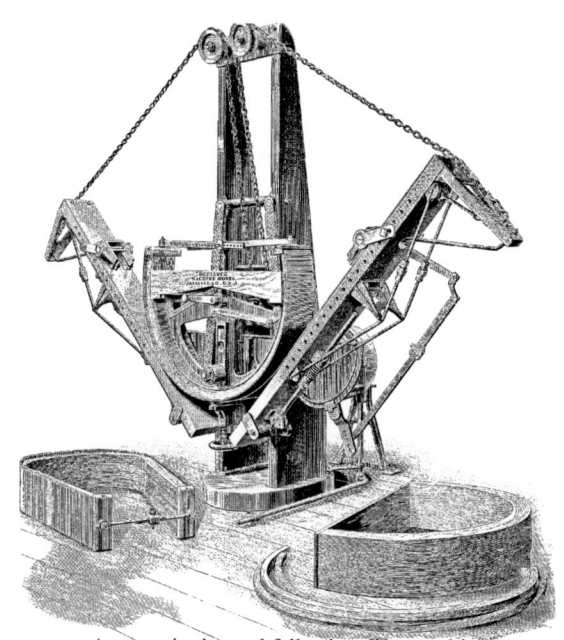

Automatic rim and felloe bending machine, Hub June 1892.

and shrink later on causing it to come loose. This is still a problem today when having new wheels made. People in the dry western areas ordering wheels from a wheel maker on the east coast may find the wheels come loose once they start to be used in the west if the wheelmaker has not specifically dried the wood for that part of the country. Wood is a material that is able to take on moisture and its well being is affected by Relative Humidity and temperature. Having wheels made on the middle east coast where the Relative Humidity is around 50 degrees and shipped to south west were the RH maybe less then 20 degrees is a huge difference to wood. You may want to try to have wheels made in your region or check to see if the wheelwright not in your region can dry the wood out for your Relative Humidity

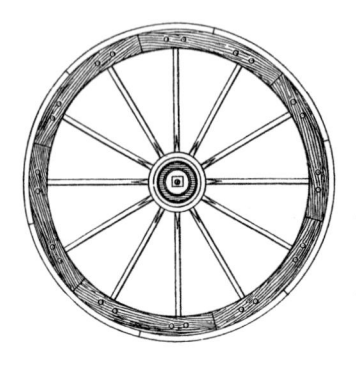

TIRES

Check to see if the tire is set tight. One way to check to see if the tire is tight is to drop the wheel about 12 inches onto to a cement surface, by listening to the sound the wheel's makes you can determine if the wheel is tight. A wheel with a tight tire will make a solid thumping sound and a loose tire will make a ringing sound. Lift and drop the wheel several times in several different places.

On very old wheels, and especially those on cannons, the tires were made in as many parts as there were felloes, and were so divided that each sectional piece of tire was jointed always in the middle of each felloe. This was done to strengthen the felloe joints, and facilitate the removal of felloes and tires when it was necessary to repair by replacing with new ones. Very few people now do this kind of tiring and Ron Vineyard the master wheelwright at Colonial Williamsburg has documented this procedure in a *Carriage Journal* article. The sectional tire was called straking and it was replaced by the continuous iron tire that still maintained the square edges. J. W. Britton is believed to have introduced steel tires on Brewster carriages in 1863 importing the steel from England. Steel tires are stiffer, lighter and wear twice as long. By 1874 only steel tires were used. Carriages having tires with rounded edges, and tires with square edges stayed in general use with wagons.[4]

Strake tire from the Hub Sept. 1891.

The tiring of wooden wheels involves five main steps. First, the wooden wheel is measured by rolling the traveler (a small wheel affixed to a handle) around the circumference. As the traveler goes around the wheel the number of rotations are counted along with any faction of a rotation, and then transferred to the iron strap. Secondly, the iron strap is bent to fit the wheel. In the early rural shops, an old wheel or millstone was used to bend the iron tire into a circle. It was later replaced by the roller type bender, which was turned by hand.

From the catalog of Bradlee, Hastings & Co., Boston.

In the third step, welding the tire, the ends are scarfed or upset, to avoid a weak butt joint, then drilled and pinned, in preparation for forge welding.[5]

The thickness and width of the strap varied with the type of vehicle for which it was intended, some of the big wagon or dray tires were inch or more thick. With metal tires the wheelwright usually allows for an inch overhang on the tire to protect the wheel from the road (that is inch on each side of the felloe. While channel tires were often flush with the felloe (but not always). Notes from Bruce Morrison

The fourth step of the process is tire setting or hooping. In the early shops, the tire was heated just enough to expand it, in the blacksmith's forge or a fire pit. Once the heated tire was placed on the wheel, it usually had water thrown on it to keep it from burning the wood and to contract the tire, so it would be set tight on the wheel. The contracting of the tire would help to establish the amount of dish in the wheel, and the amount of dish that could be gained by a contracting tire, was largely estimated by years of experience in setting tires.

While early tire furnaces were fueled by coal or wood, the introduction of the more efficient gas furnace in 1874 allowed expansion of the tire with a more even heat, and they were faster and cleaner. Tires heated in the gas furnace did not become so hot that they charred the wood when the hot tire was put on the rim and some wheel makers eliminated throwing water on the heated tire. Some wheel makers believed that the use of water caused an adverse effect by swelling the wood in the wheel which later dries out and makes the wheel loose. The practice of heating tires to excess was thought to be used by wheelwrights who set the dish solely by the tire. In order to set the dish solely by the tire required the tire to expand a greater distance to fit over the wheel then contract, and large amounts of water were used to cool the tire. A tire heated in a furnace cooled and contracted on its own pulling the wheel tightly together.

The invention of cold-tire setting process was thought by some to be a great improvement over setting tires hot. The possibility of charring the wood and swelling the wood with water was eliminated and a gauge could be used to determine the amount of dish more accurately.

According to the patent records the idea of cold tire setting probably started around the

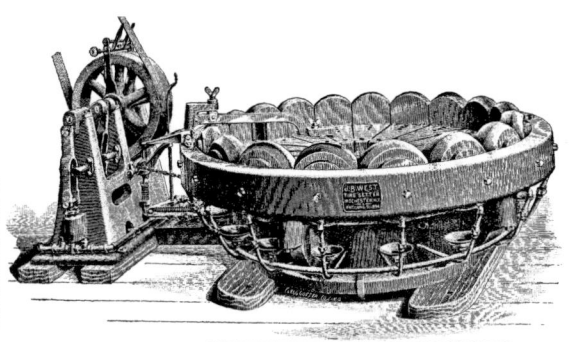

1870 West's Tire Setter from the Carriage Monthly Aug. 1898.

West's Tire Setter in 1898, operated by hydraulic pressure, sets 500 to 700 tires per day from the Carriage Monthly Aug. 1898.

1860's, and had evolved by the 1870's to J. B. West's American Tire Setter. By 1891 there was a cold hydraulic tire setting machine that more evenly set the tire and was more accurate in controlling the amount of dish.

In the final step of tiring, regardless of the method used, the tire is fastened to the wooden rim with tire bolts. The number of tire bolts used on a wheel varied from company to company, the usual number was one every other spoke. The heads are countersunk in the tire, so as to be flush with the outer surface. In addition, wheels for vehicles expected to negotiate rough terrain often had rivets put into the felloe on either side of the spokes to keep the felloe from splitting.

The nuts for the tire bolts should be square with a small metal washer put on underneath. A good restoration job should have all the nuts turned in a straight line with the felloe. Although a few shops have hydraulic tire presses and propane furnaces today, by and large, most tires are still heated over a wood fire outside of the shop.

RUBBER TIRES

Restoration Rubber Tires

If you plan to have new solid rubber tires put on your wheels, and the wheel is already fitted with a channel it might be helpful to sand blast and prime the channel with some rust preventive primer before sending them to the wheelwright, especially if you are going to get the white rubber tires. Rust under the tire channel can leave rust stains later on if the wheel gets wet or damp. In order to sand blast the channel and edge of the channel you would need to mask off the wooden rim with some duct tape. If you have any old paint that needs to be removed, it would be easier to take it off before sending the wheels for new rubber tires. Once the paint has been removed make sure the wood is free of all chemicals that might have been used as the result of paint remover. Sand and clean the wheels applying a coat of paste wood filler and then a coat of sanding sealer. We would not recommend having your wheels prepared any more than this before sending them for new rubber, as for some reasons they get dented and damaged by transporting and handling. Once your wheels come back with the new rubber the wheels should be wiped down with a degreaser. In applying the rubber, tire grease or other lubricants are often spread in the channel before tightening the tire. It invariably gets on the outside of the channel and sometimes on the felloes. When applying additional coats of paint the rubber tire can be masked off with masking tape. Do not leave masking tape on too long or it will be hard to get off. You will have to remask the rubber if it is going to take several weeks to paint your wheels.

The rubber tire was a vast improvement for city use over the conventional iron or steel tire, resulting in a more comfortable carriage ride. The three main forms of rubber tires developed were, the solid rubber tire, the cushion rubber tire and the pneumatic rubber tire.

Pneumatic Tires

The first pneumatic tire was invented in England in 1845, however after several market tests the public was just not ready for the idea of an air filled tire. The pneumatic tire was reinvented in 1888 by an Irishman, John Dunlop, for his son's bicycle. The pneumatic tire in America began to be successful with carriages around 1892-1893. If you have a carriage with pneumatic tires, you will have a very difficult task, as we do not know of any source to have pneumatic tires custom made at this time.

Restoration Tip for Pneumatic Tires

The following tip comes from Robert Babcock as to how he cleaned up and preserved the pneumatic tire wheels on his vehicle. "We took the tires on the wheels to a local truck tire recap plant and they did an injection process of hard rubber into the tires inside the original pneumatic tire. This process is primarily used on equipment like fork lifts used in scrap yards or high tire danger zones. So basically I have 4 hard rubber tires inside the original pneumatic tire. The price was reasonable. I recommend the process for static display and general rolling rather than an operational horse operating vehicle. We sandblasted our wheels first

Pneumatic tires made by Hartford Rubber Co., on wooden spoke wheels, from the Carriage Monthly June 1894.

then used metal primer, then had the injection process. There was minimal clean up, then we painted the wheels.

Another course of action that I saw done at Harrahs Auto Collection on a car with similar tire problems was, they wrapped the tire with an appropriate fabric type tape then filled it with probably foam or hard rubber. Again, it was display only."

Solid Rubber Tire

In America the solid rubber tire had a limited number of market tests as early as 1856, but it wasn't until the 1880's that if became a popular and practical idea. The first solid rubber tire in Philadelphia was reported to have been in 1875 when Fairman Rogers ordered a set from W. D. Rogers of Philadelphia, for a dog cart.[6] The introduction of solid rubber tires on vehicles was a great benefit in absorbing shock, resulting in less breakage of wheels and a longer life for the whole vehicle.

Color of Rubber Tires

It is a popular belief that rubber tires were black for horse-drawn vehicles, but in fact carriage tires were white for the greater part of the carriage era. The first rubber tires made used zinc oxide as a reinforcer for the rubber which colored the tires white or grey. The rubber tire industry states that it wasn't until 1904 that the first patent was taken out by S. C. Mote of England to reinforce rubber with carbon black. It was not practical until 1912 for rubber tires to be made with carbon black, and the first commercially produced black tires were made by the Diamond Rubber Company which was purchased by B. F. Goodrich in the same year. It still took several years of a mass advertising campaign by the rubber tire industry to convince consumers that black colored tires were just as good as white or better.[7]

Many vehicles came with a choice of either rubber or metal tires and for people buying a vehicle today for use it is a relatively simple process to change metal tires to rubber or vice versa. The carriage parts suppliers list about 20 different rubber tires available. Many people traveling on hard surfaces prefer rubber tires because it is quieter and smoother.

Bibliography for more information on wheels.

For those who want to rebuild their own wheels, sometimes proprietors of carriage shops will teach wheel making for a fee. Organizations such as the Western Canadian Development Museum (Saskatoon, SASK) offer wheelwright courses to the general public.

Cantle, Gordon. " Development Of Solid Rubber Tires For Carriages." Carriage Journal. Vol. 29 No. 2 (Fall 1991), p. 75-76.

Cantle, Gordon. "Fundamentals Of Fitting Tires." Carriage Journal. Vol. 27 No. 1 (Summer 1989), pp. 10-12.

Cantle, Gordon. "Assembling A Wheel For Tiring." Carriage Journal. Vol. 26 No. 3 (Winter 1988), p. 114-115.

Cantle, Gordon. "Tire Bending Segment Extant In North Yorkshire." Carriage Journal. Vol. 26 No. 2 (Autumn 1988), p. 77.

Cantle, Gordon. "On Dishing And Staggering." Carriage Journal. Vol. 25 No. 1 (Summer 1987), p. 39-40.

Foggett, John S. 1881. "The Manufacture of Carriage Wheels." Carriage Journal. Vol. 15 No.1 (Summer 1977), pp. 236-242.

"Proportions Of Wheels In Relation To Their Tire." Carriage Journal. Vol. 13 No. 2 (Autumn 1975), pp. 102-105.

"[Staggered Spokes]." Carriage Journal. Vol. 24 no. 3 (Winter 1986), p. 150.

Ryder, Tom. "The Manufacture of Carriage Wheels Part II-Factory Made Wheels." Carriage Journal. Vol. 15 No. 2 (Autumn 1977), pp. 268-274.

Wheeling, Ken. "Rubber Tires And The Carriage Industry Part I-Solid Rubber Tires." Carriage

Journal. Vol. 28 No. 1 (Summer 1990), pp. 6-8.
Wheeling, Ken. "Rubber Tires And The Carriage Industry -Part II-Pneumatic Tire." Carriage Journal. Vol. 28 No. 3 (Winter 1990), pp. 102-105.
Wheeling, Ken. "Rubber Tires And The Carriage Industry - Part III-Contemporary Scene." Carriage Journal. Vol. 28 No. 4 (Spring 1991), pp. 138-140.
Vineyard, Ron. "Straking." Carriage Journal. Vol. 28 No. 1 (Summer 1990), pp. 17-20.
"[Wheel Chart For Proportions]." Carriage Journal. Vol. 26 No. 1 (Summer 1988), pp. 39-40.

Books

Bailey, Jocelyn. The Village Wheelwright and Carpenter. Aylesbury, Bucks, U.K.: Shire Publications, 1977.
Byorlykke. The Craft of The Wheelwright. England : Profile Books Limited, 1983.
Cantle, Gordon, A Collection of Essays on Horse-Drawn Carriages and Carriage Parts. Bird-In-Hand, PA: Carriage Museum of America, 1993.
DeWitt, Melvin L. The Art of The Wheelwright. Moscow, ID: Melvin L. DeWitt, 1975.
DeWitt, Melvin L. Wheels, Wheels, Wagons and More. Moscow, ID: Melvin L. DeWitt, 1984.
Green, Susan. Horse-Drawn Vehicle Wheels : United States Patents 1790-1910. Bird-In-Hand, PA : Susan Green, 1996.
Peloubet, Donald. Wheel making. Mendham, NJ: Astragal Press, 1996.
Richardson, M. T. Practical Carriage Building. New York: M. T. Richardson Company, 1892. reprinted edition available.
Smith, Peter Haddon. The Industrial Archeology of The Wood Wheel Industry in America. Washington, DC. : George Washington University, 1971.
Sturt, George. The Wheelwright Shop. Cambridge, U. K.: University Press, 1923,1934, 1942, 1943, 1948.
Thompson, John. The Wheelwright's Trade. Fleet, Hampshire, U. K.: John Thompson, 1983.

Endnotes

[1].Brewster & Co., New York, New York, records 24032 Small Stanhope Gig, 25783 French Two Wheeled Cart.
[2].FitzGerald, William N. "The Rise and Progress of the Carriage Industry of the United States." The Hub. (Nov. 1882), 495.
[3]."Tires on Wagons and Carriages." Carriage Monthly. (Nov. 1892).
[4].Peloubet, Donald. Wheelmaking. Mendham, NJ : Astragal Press, 1996.
[5]."Evolution of Today's Pneumatic Tire." Rubber & Plastics News. 18 no. 2 (August 22, 1988), 26-28.

CHAPTER 8

SPRINGS

Taking Springs Apart

If your vehicle is in fairly sound condition have your friends over to sit in your new vehicle, this way you can check to see if the springing system is still good. Some heavy vehicles after many years of sitting around may have sagging springs and the springs will have to be retempered or replaced. When taking springs apart it is a good idea to use a c-clamp to hold them together while you loosen the bolt that holds the leaves together. Some springs used in the modern buckboard of the 1880's are under tension and they will fly apart. It is a good idea to use some kind of a dot system for marking the placement of springs leaves within each set. Not all springs would have to have a hole directly in the center so there may be a front and back placement of springs. Use a punch or a small drill bit to make a number of dots for each set of springs on the underside where it will not show, on the same side of the hole for each spring leaf in the set. Loop a piece a wire through each set of springs to hold the leaves together while they go to the sand blaster or spring maker. Try to explain your system to your spring maker so that he keeps each set of springs together. Double check when your springs come back that each set of springs is together the way you marked it.

Having New Springs Made

If the original springs are missing and they must be replaced with more modern springs, it will take close supervision to fabricate springs to match the original. Modern spring stock is no longer the size of carriage springs. You will have to have the spring maker cut to length the required lengths for new springs. You will then have to take the lengths of spring leaves to a machine shop and have it milled to the desired thickness and width. Take back the milled spring leaves to the spring maker to make up the springs. If your carriage needs major spring work, it will be good to refit the springs to the carriage to make sure everything is going to fit properly before starting the restoration.

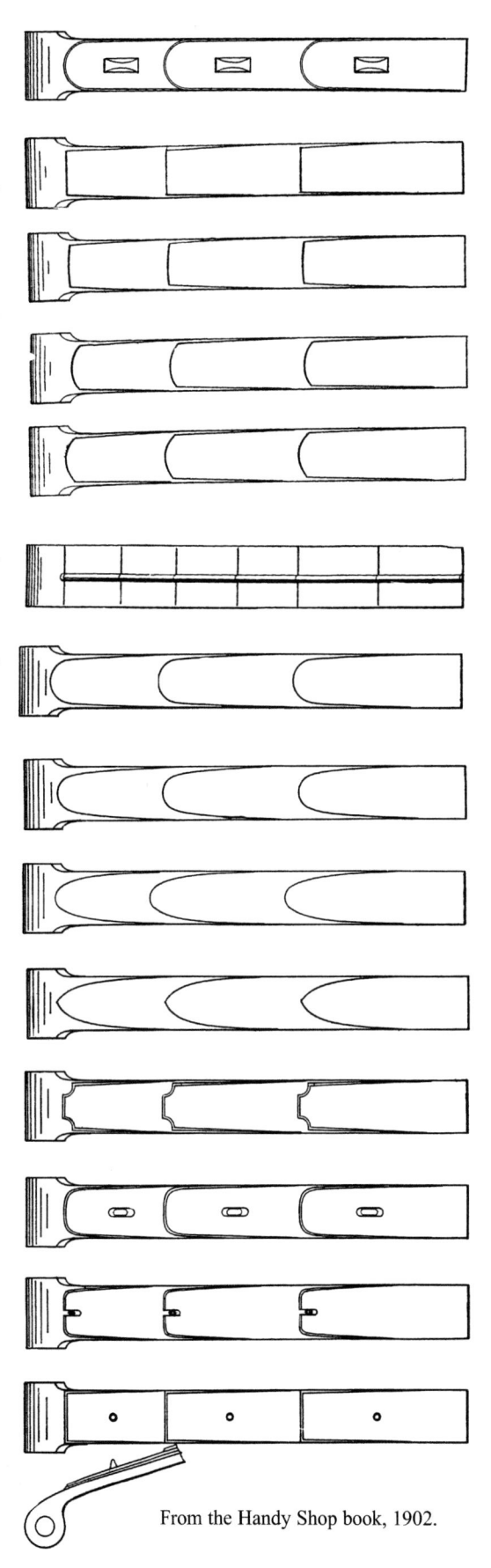

From the Handy Shop book, 1902.

Thickness of Springs

The thickness of springs was referred to by a numbering system and usually the long plate was made thicker and some of the shorter plates were made thinner.

SIZES OF STEEL IN AMERICAN SPRINGS	SIZES OF STEEL AS USED IN FRANCE
No. 1 steel, 10/32 inch	8 millimeters = about 5/16 inch
No. 2 steel, 9/32 inch	7 millimeters = about 9/32 inch
No. 3 steel, 8/32 inch	6 millimeters = about 8/32 inch
No. 4 steel, 15/64 inch	5 ½ millimeters = about 15/64 inch
No. 5 steel, 13/64 inch	5 millimeters = about 13/64 inch
No. 6 steel, 6/32 inch	4 ½ millimeters = about 6/32 inch
No. 7 steel, 5/32 inch	4 millimeters = about 5/32 inch

THE EFFECTS OF STRESS ON CARRIAGE SPRINGS WITH COMMENTS ON THE HEAT TREATMENT OF SPRING STEEL

by Dr. Gordon S. Cantle

from the Carriage Journal Vol. 26 No. 1

Carriage springs may cease to function effectively over a period of time or else collapse suddenly due to a broken leaf or plate. In the former case there is probably little amiss with the spring apart from requiring resetting and heat treating, having yielded permanently in shape due to exceeding the limits of elasticity of the steel. A broken plate however, can arise from either inappropriate heat treatment, faulty fixing, or a combination of both.

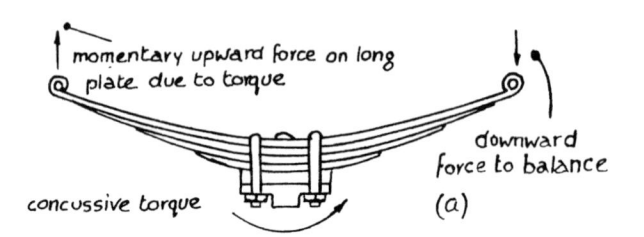

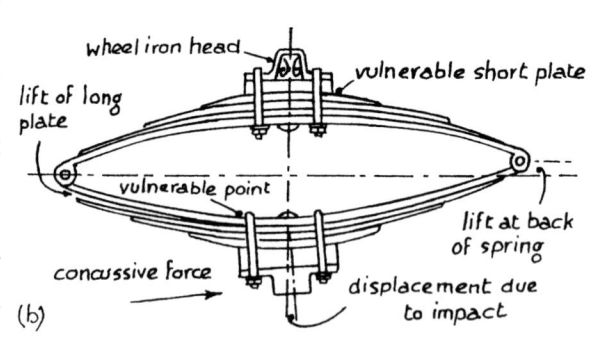

Faults In Spring Fixing

A laminated spring such as that shown in (a) is designed to provide resilience against a downward load at the eyes, each plate being supported elastically by the plate beneath, apart from the short plate which has a rigid support. If the load becomes reversed as by the application of the torque shown, the long plate is unsupported for almost half its length which results in a potentially high stress in the plate at the rigid clips which secure the spring. Such a reversal of a load can occur in an elliptic spring since an approximately horizontal concussive force at the road surface, or impact between a wheel or outer nave (hub) band with a rigid object, applies a concussive torque to the spring about its upper fixing as shown in (b). This is resisted primarily by the fore half of the bottom long plate and the hind half of the top short plate which are, in consequence, the plates most vulnerable to breakage if precautionary measures are not taken. Accordingly, the short and long plates will frequently be found to be of slightly heavier gauge, say 2, compared with 3 for the remaining plates which is about 1/64 inch increase in thickness. Having provided this extra thickness in the short and long plates, however, carriage builders often secured such springs with bolts rather than clips, so reducing the cross section of the plate at the bolt holes and increasing once again the probability of breakage at that section. Further, if at one end of the axle, the wheel iron head and axle flaps are parallel but at the other end they are inclined to one another, then tightening the clips gives the springs an initial torque which at one end of the axle supplements the stress arising from concussive impact.

A quite different source of stress increase affecting the long plate occurs when the spring is subjected to a twisting action. This arises when (I) the body sways or rolls, (ii) when the span between the wheel iron heads is different from that between the axle flaps and (iii) when a cross spring is fitted and the right-angled shackles have limited or zero rotation as in (c). In each case the stress caused by the twisting of the plate combines with that due to concussive forces to give a still greater total stress within the plate, which, while not necessarily causing breakage could exceed the elastic limit and result in ductile deformation.

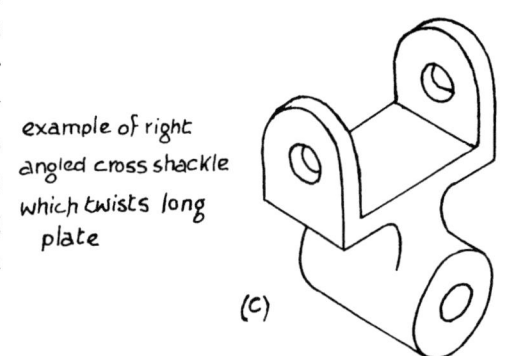

example of right angled cross shackle which twists long plate

(c)

Heat Treatment In General

Heat treatment of steel for use in springs is not only essential for strength and elasticity but must be correct otherwise the steel may become too brittle, giving rise to premature cracks, or too ductile, allowing the plates to change shape from their original curvature thereby diminishing the resilience of the whole spring.

Steel is an alloy of iron and carbon. In its manufacture, steel cools slowly during the rolling processes and the finished steel is described as 'annealed'. The effect of only a small proportion of carbon in the steel, up to 1.8%, is quite significant, the hardness and ability to deform elastically both increasing with carbon content while the ductility, or plastic stretching without rupture, diminishes. Also, above about 0.25% carbon, the steel, when heated to redness, that is 800 degrees C or so, and quenched in water, will harden and become brittle, whilst below 0.25% this effect is inappreciable. Without involving metallurgical terminology this difference in behavior is due to the state in which the carbon exists in the iron, some being combined chemically with the iron to form iron carbide whilst the remainder is left dispersed through the steel as what XIXth century metallurgists called 'hardening carbon', a concept which conveys a convenient mental picture. The degree of hardness depends upon the relative amounts of carbon present as carbide and as hardening carbon, the hardness increasing with diminishing carbide. Heating to 800 degrees C in the hardening process dissolves the carbide already existing in the steel and the subsequent rapid quenching prevents the carbide re-forming, the resulting high proportion of hardening carbon making the steel hard and brittle. If this is followed by heating to a lower temperature than that required for hardening, the carbide gradually re-forms, reducing the hardness while increasing the strength and elastic limit to values exceeding those of the original steel. This state is then stabilized by quenching or by simply allowing to cool. Such reheating and cooling is the 'letting down' of tempering process and the rate at which the carbide re-forms depends upon the tempering temperature which provides, therefore, a control over the final properties of the tempered steel.

Heat Treatment of Spring Steel

Consider now, spring steel in particular. Steel with a low carbon content that is 'mild steel', does not harden appreciably and therefore cannot be tempered to increase its strength. On the other hand, a 'high' carbon steel, although harder and more elastic in its manufactured state, is too brittle for use in tensile shock conditions and more so when hardened. Spring steels, therefore, have a compromise range of carbon from about 0.25% to 0.6% and are classed as 'medium' carbon steels.

To harden such steel is heated to the temperature mentioned above, that is 800 degrees C or slightly more, which is a distinct red when viewed in the shade, It is then quenched in water, or, for a carbon content at the upper end of the medium carbon steel range, in oil, which cools the steel more slowly and avoids possible water cracks in the hardened state. Tempering gives rise to a choice of hardness and elasticity, but the final physical properties depend upon a number of variables in addition to temperature, namely, initial carbon content of the steel, speed of the hardening quench, method of heating to tempering temperature, and variation of cross section of plate from middle to points.

Of these variables, the total carbon content, in the early days of steel manufacture, was somewhat unpredictable but became more controlled in the subsequent Cementation, Bessemer and Open Hearth processes. Even so, the spring maker, if in doubt, should verify that the steel is within the range of medium carbon steel either by a saw cut, a spark test on a grinding wheel or a preliminary hardening test. Having established that the carbon content is satisfactory, the plates are forged with central hole, slot, nibs and points or eyes, then heated to hardening temperature, set to shape, quenched and tempered. If the carbon content is known with more accuracy than that given by the tests above, the tempering temperature should be chosen accordingly, otherwise tempering 0.6% carbon steel at too low a temperature may result in a brittle plate while too high a temperature with 0.25% carbon may be too ductile.

Originally this temperature was attained by passing the plate lengthwise through an incandescent hollow fire sufficiently slowly for the surface of the plate to achieve a temperature at which it would ignite wood, usually the handle of one of the rod tools. However as the plate has a varying cross section, the core of the thickest part of the plate would not necessarily be tempered at as high a temperature as the surface, so giving a hard core enveloped in a strong elastic skin. On the other hand, the tapered ends of the plate which heat more rapidly could be ductile, leading to the opening up of the points in use. Notwithstanding these variables, the experience of the spring smith ensured a statistical probability that a satisfactory plate would result.

Much of this difficulty can be removed if the carbon content is known more exactly and a gas heated muffle, oil bath or fused salt bath is used to heat the plate to a uniform tempering temperature of between 220 degrees C and 300 degrees C according to carbon content. Subsequent cooling then gives a more consistent strength and elasticity throughout the length and thickness of the plate.

There are, of course, numerous alloy steels used for springs which contain other elements such as silicon, manganese, molybdenum, vanadium and tungsten, chromium and nickel in various proportions. While the principles of heat treatment of such steels is as described above, the temperatures used are generally higher than for medium carbon steels. The tempering temperature, particularly, is in the region of 550 degrees C and heat treatment is carried out in uniformly heated pyrometrically controlled muffle or reverbatory furnaces or a more modern electric induction furnace. Thus, it must be pointed out that a medium carbon steel inadvertently tempered as an alloy steel will have properties approaching those of the annealed state, that is, ductile, with a modest elastic limit, and would therefore have a short effective life in a laminated spring. end of article by Dr. Gordon Cantle

SPRING MANUFACTURING
by Wana Coach & Company.

Today's process of manufacturing leaf springs for horse-drawn vehicles has incorporated quite a bit of the old and new techniques. Because of the uniqueness of each spring leaf in length, thickness, taper of the ends, and curvature, it demands a lot of the old hand to eye techniques. Incorporating the old controlled-gas fired furnaces, quality oil & polymer quenchants will definitely produce springs of consistent high quality. Of course this all depends on the accumulated knowledge of the manufacture in these techniques and the ability to apply them. Incorporating the art of a blacksmith and that of a modern heat treater makes spring manufacturing wonderfully successful, and getting these two together is more wondrous yet.

5155H spring steel; is used extensively by today's spring manufacturers with results that exceed the old high carbon spring steel. When a spring maker is working daily with modern alloys and then suddenly switches to working on an old high carbon spring he will most likely run into frustrating problems. These problems occur because of unknown carbon content and the inconsistency of it.

Instead of trying to retemper old collapsed springs it is recommended to have new ones made if at all possible. Especially if the carriage is to be used on a regular basis. There are a couple of alternatives for an individual who is very concerned in keeping the original geometric design of a restoration project. Usually the main leaves are the ones that set the trend of uniqueness for any individual spring. These are also the ones most complicated to reproduce because of odd sizes of width and thickness, or the forged eye & socket on the ends. The width and thickness can be reproduced by machining, and the sockets by welding, grinding and hand forging. Providing you can find someone capable to do this, you will find all of this very time consuming and expensive. The leaves on top of the main ones vary quite a bit from spring to spring in length and thickness of taper, shape of the ends, and alignment features. This is all fairly easily reproduced by today's spring makers with a little added hand work and grinding.

It has been quite successful to use the two main leaves without trying to retemper them but maybe re-arch them somewhat in a cold process. Then have the remaining leaves made new according to the original ones. Better yet is to cut the old forged ends off and weld them to new steel. If the welding is done right and the whole leaf annealed before heat treatment, you will end up with excellent results.

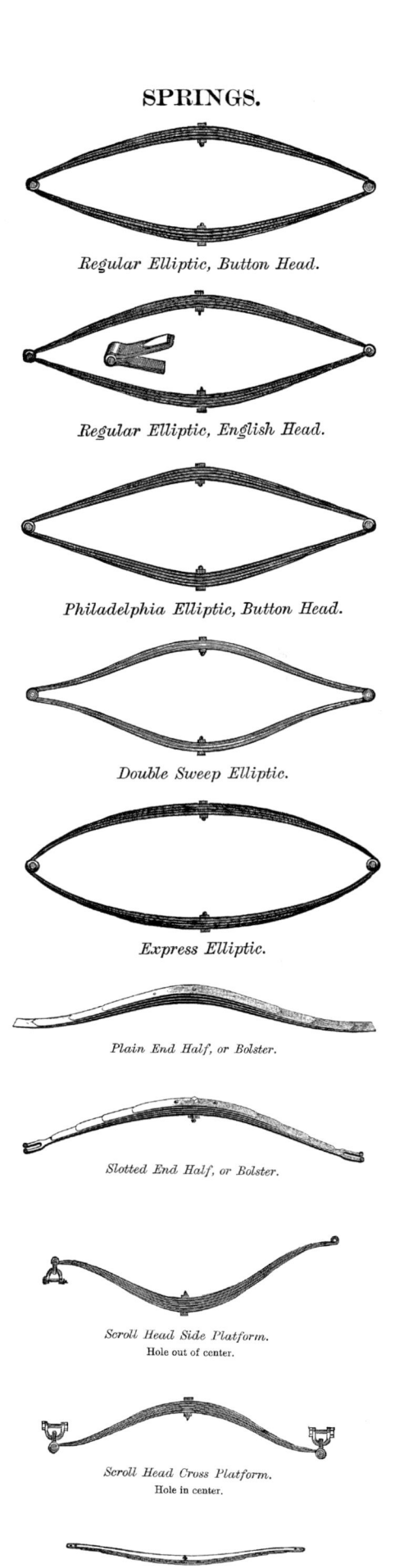

SPRINGS.

Regular Elliptic, Button Head.

Regular Elliptic, English Head.

Philadelphia Elliptic, Button Head.

Double Sweep Elliptic.

Express Elliptic.

Plain End Half, or Bolster.

Slotted End Half, or Bolster.

Scroll Head Side Platform.
Hole out of center.

Scroll Head Cross Platform.
Hole in center.

Side Bar.

From S. D. Kimbark, 1888.

Springs

Modern Spring Sizes

Some of the spring steel sizes that are readily available today are:

Round Edge 5155H
1¼" wide x .250" thick
1½" wide x .204" to .375" thick
1¾" wide x .204" to .499" thick

High Carbon
1¼" wide x ⅛"-³⁄₁₆"-¼" thick
1½" wide x ⅛"-³⁄₁₆" thick

2" and wider is also available in the 5155H steels. Some of the old springs were made from 1⅜" and 1⅝" wide steel. These sizes are no longer available so consequently the next size larger steel has to be machined as previously mentioned.

Today's process of manufacturing carriage springs is fairly basic and similar to bygone years. First the spring steel stock has to be cut to length, holes punched, and alignment features added to the customers preference such as, nib & slots, center ridge, or side tangs. There was a span of many years when these features were not available without doing them specifically by hand. After getting the ends of one of the main leafs up to working temperature the eyes are then rolled with a hand operated eye machine or with a powered machine. For the socket, the other main leaf is then slightly bent on the ends to the curvature of the eye and a heavy washer type plate welded on the sides. A lot of the new springs being built today have cast sockets welded on instead of the welded plate. The tapering of the spring leaves are most generally done with tapering roller mills or sometimes with a power hammer. The leaf ends are squeezed together edgewise or trimmed off before tapering to allow the material to spread in the tapering process without exceeding the original material width. The arching and hardening process can usually be done with one heat. When the spring leaf comes up to the correct temperature it needs enough soak time according to the steel thickness so that the inner core is the same temperature as on the outside. It is then taken over a pre-arched form, clamped to the form, slightly quenched with lukewarm water to set shape, then dropped in quench oil to finish the cooling process. This is an interrupted type of quench using two different kinds of quenchants, water and oil. In this process there is a critical time, temperature, transformation period that has to be met to reach full potential hardness of the steel that is being used. Magnetic particle inspection for quench cracks, stress tests, lab analysis after heat treatment as well as modern computer

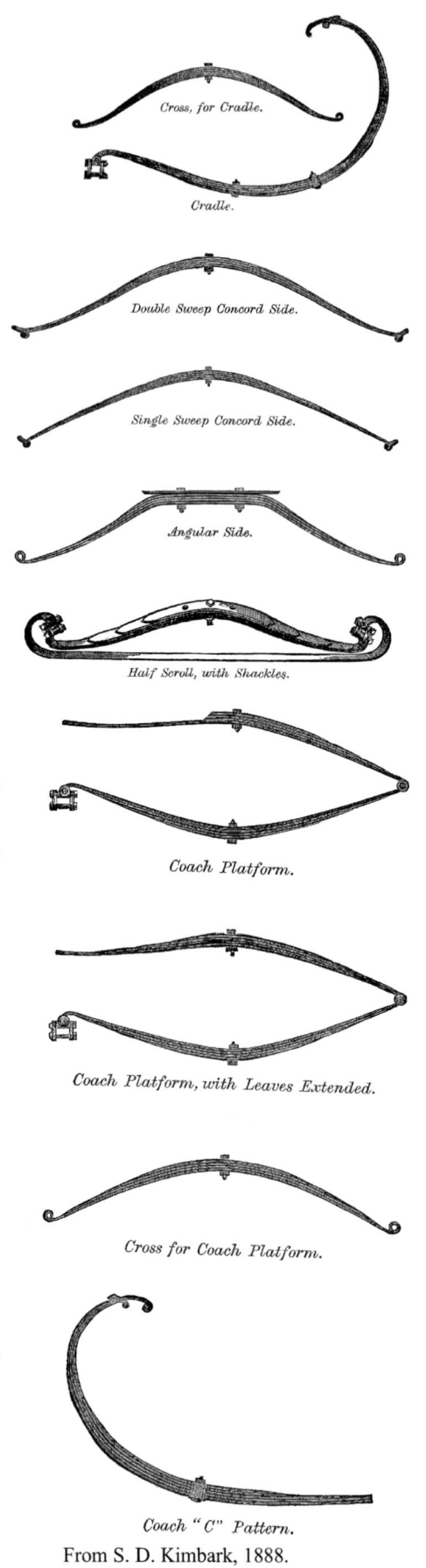

Cross, for Cradle.

Cradle.

Double Sweep Concord Side.

Single Sweep Concord Side.

Angular Side.

Half Scroll, with Shackles.

Coach Platform.

Coach Platform, with Leaves Extended.

Cross for Coach Platform.

Coach " C " Pattern.

From S. D. Kimbark, 1888.

programs has proven this process to work. When the steel has cooled well past the TTT point it is then put back into a batch type furnace at a lower temperature to heat treat or draw the spring back out of it's brittle stage to a flexible condition. The heat treating process and the correct hardness varies for each type of steel being used. Usually your steel supplier or heat treater can supply that type of information. After cooling the leaves are descaled with a hand grinder, shot blast, or tumbled with an abrasive media. The springs are either fitted with hammering when still warm or with hydraulic presses and hammering when cold. Usually each leaf gets a coat of a good metal primer before assembly.

To fix a broken spring leaf it is of course recommended to replace it with a new piece. If in an emergency or for whatever other reason it needs to be welded, do not however expect outstanding and lasting results. If a strict welding procedure is followed you can end up with a fairly decent result, but we must mention again, it is very seldom lasting. When welding the broken leaf do not apply the bead on top of the splice but take the broken ends and grind them on an angle and then fill it in with a high alloy welding rod. Afterwards it should be annealed, hardened, and tempered for the best results on a welded spring.

If heat treating is not available then be sure to take extra caution in the welding process. It is recommended to use a non-cracking high alloy welding rod similar to the EUTECTRODE 680 which has a tensile strength of 120,000 psi. When using DC, set the welder on reverse polarity. The recommended amperages are 75 to 125 when using 1/8" welding rod. Deposit the weld at the highest possible speed, one bead at a time. Between each pass let it cool and peen the area quite vigorously to relieve internal stresses. Let the welded piece cool slowly and do not quench it with water or anything else that would speed the cooling rate. The welded spring leaf is more likely to hold if it is supported top and bottom with other leaves.

Of course this is written with the consideration that there is equipment available other than the anvil and coal forge.

The Subject of Leaf Spring Fatigue

There is always the question on what causes fatigue in leaf springs and in what way can a collapsed spring be fixed. The general opinion is that the spring steel has lost its temper. This is not correct unless the steel has reached temper. This is not correct unless the steel has reached temperatures exceeding approximately 600 degrees. There are a couple of basic factors causing fatigue which I'll try to explain.

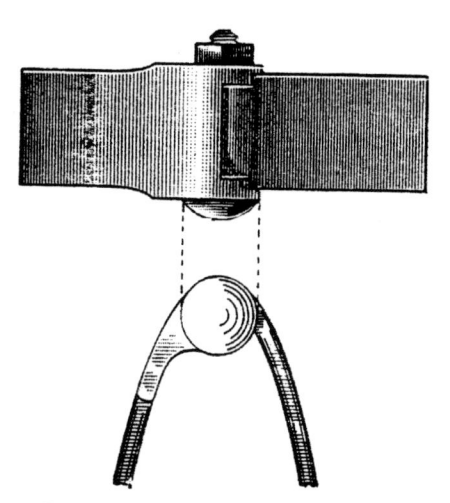

Pear Head with Semi-Shoulder for Elliptic and Platform Springs

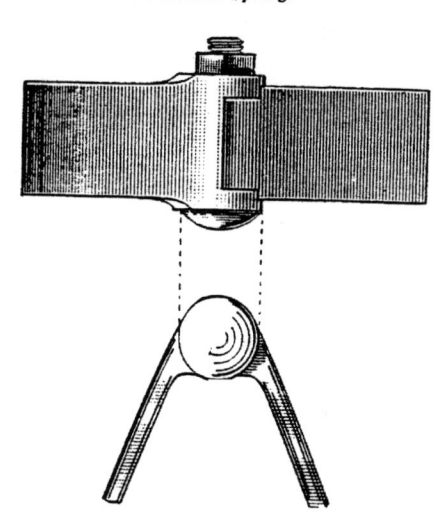

English Elliptic Head with Half-Shoulder

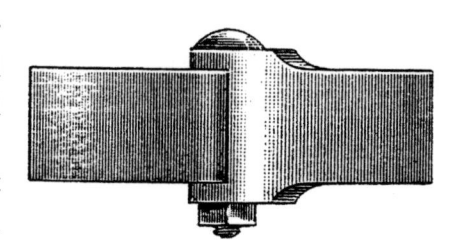

Full English Head for Side, Elliptic and Platform Springs

From the Handy Shop Book, 1902.

Springs

Improper hardening and tempering of the spring steel during manufacturing will cause fatigue and failure in different ways. Each failure occurs according to what it's own unique fault was. To insure the maximum performance of the steel, the heat treater has to deal with a very narrow margin of error in the final hardening process. Even the slightest variance in any one of the many factors involving this process will alter the internal structure of the steel. Basically when the steel is too soft it will not take the stress of flexing and will set (bend). Neither will it take the stress if the steel is too hard, this causes small stress cracks in the material and will eventually break through completely. There are so many factors contributing to faulty heat treatment that there are books written on that subject alone.

A correctly tempered spring can flex tremendously and still return to its former shape. If it flexes past the maximum point of flexibility it will move the grain structure of the steel and cause fatigue. This is probably the number one cause of fatigue. Usually the spring can be re-arched but will not solve the problem if the same load is put back on.

We see a lot of old springs with rust pits all over them, even after sandblasting. This will take away from the spring in such a way that it can never be its former self again.

There is an ideal height of arch for a spring which will cause the spring to bottom out before it reaches the over stressed point. Over arched springs can easily be overloaded causing them to exceed the maximum flex point. Under arched springs will bottom out before you get the full benefit from the spring.

You cannot correctly make the spring steely harder or softer to get a stiffer or more flexible spring. You can do it somewhat, but not without losing your full value of the steel. The amount of steel being used is the main principle that decides the load factor of your spring. The close running 2nd principle is in the design of your spring, a person definitely has to corporate the amount of steel to be used with the design of the spring to end up with something that will do the job.

The history of leaf spring manufacturing goes back a long ways. Have you ever wondered why the old carriage and automobile springs were tapered leaf springs instead of one solid bar or even a solid bar tapered out? It would be a lot easier to hammer out one solid bar than to hammer out and fit 8 different ones to the shape of one. There are a lot of reasons, factors and mathematics in designing leaf springs which I will not undertake to try and explain at this time. The main function of a leaf type spring versus a solid bar spring with the same amount of steel is that it can flex further without over-stressing the steel.

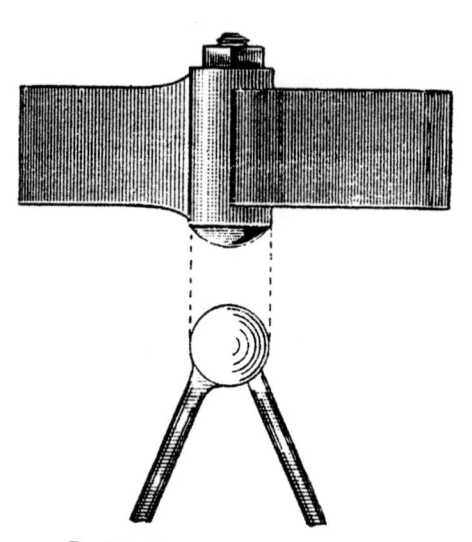

English Shoulder Head for Elliptic and Platform Springs

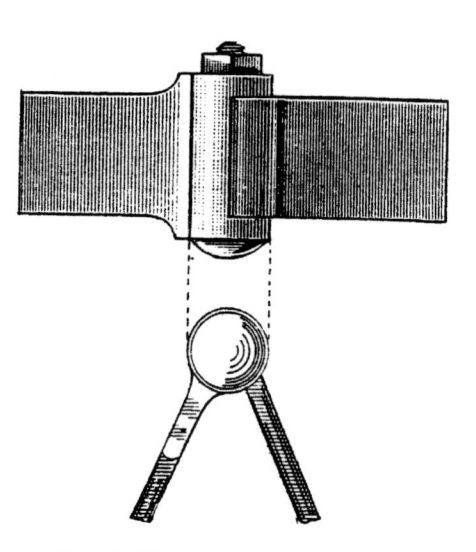

English Elliptic and Platform Head

Open Head Semi-Shoulder for Elliptic and Platform Springs

From the Handy Shop Book, 1902.

Springs

There is another interesting function in the performance of a leaf spring. The rubbing action of each leaf rubbing against its neighbors both top and bottom caused the dampening of movement, (or shock absorbing action). A car which is much faster than a buggy causes a lot more action in the springs and in the cases of early cars a wedge type clamp made to pry the leaves apart was used to keep them regularly greased. Today the auto industry has moved up in technology to higher quality shock absorbers.

Bibliography for Springs

"A Man of Ideas : The Story of Henry Timken, Carriage Builder and Founder of a World Wide Enterprise." Carriage Journal. Vol. 17 No. 4 (Spring 1980), pp. 185-191.

"[Brewster Side Bar]." Carriage Journal. Vol. 21. No. 3 (Autumn 1983), p. 70.

Cantle, Gordon. "Sleigh Springing." Carriage Journal. Vol. 32 No. 3 (Winter 1994), pp. 111-113.

Cantle, Gordon. "End Fastenings for Side Springs." Carriage Journal. Vol. 28 No. 4 (Spring 1991), pp. 144-146.

Cantle, Gordon. "Observations on "Straight Spring" Carriage . . . " Carriage Journal. Vol. 31 No. 1 (Summer 1993), pp. 6-8.

Cantle, Gordon. "On Spring Curvature." Carriage Journal. Vol. 30 No. 2 (Fall 1992), pp. 61-63.

Cantle, Gordon. "On Body Loops and Pump Handles." Carriage Journal. Vol. 27 No. 2 (Autumn 1989), pp. 78-81.

Cantle, Gordon. "Effects of Stress on Carriage Springs With Comments on The Heat Treatment of Spring Steel." Carriage Journal. Vol. 26 No. 1 (Summer 1988), p. 26-27.

Carriage Monthly. "Spring Rusting." Carriage Journal. Vol. 9 No. 3 (Winter 1971), p. 119.

"Elliotts Specification." Carriage Journal. Vol. 1 No. 4 (March 1964), p. 118.

"Improvements in Side-Bar And Side-Spring Carriages at The Centennial." Carriage Journal. Vol. 14 No. 1 (Summer 1976), pp. 43-45.

"Names of Carriage Springs and Their Combinations." Carriage Journal. Vol. 24 No. 3 (Winter 1986), p. 141-143.

"Notes on Manufacturing Springs and Axles." Carriage Monthly. (Oct. 1890, Nov. 1890, Dec. 1890), p. 214-215, 246-247, 290-291.

Ryder, Tom. "Steel Carriage Springs." Carriage Journal. Vol. 27 No.4. (Spring 1978), pp. 367-369.

Ryder, Tom. "Steel Carriage Springs." Carriage Journal. Vol.16 No. 1 (Summer 1978), pp. 21-23.

Ryder, Tom. "Steel Carriage Springs." Carriage Journal. Vol. 16 No. 2, p. 99-101.

Ryder, Tom. "Steel Carriage Springs Part IV-American Designs." Carriage Journal. Vol. 16 No. 3 (Winter 1978), pp. 141-146.

Ryder, Tom. "Suspension of American Carriages." Carriage Journal. Vol. 22 No. 3 (Winter 1984), pp. 145-149.

"[Shuler Spring]." Carriage Journal. Vol. 24 No. 1 (Summer 1986), p. 29.

Panels
BEADING AND THE DESIGNING OF THE BACK PANELS OF BODIES
Condensed from the Hub July 1895

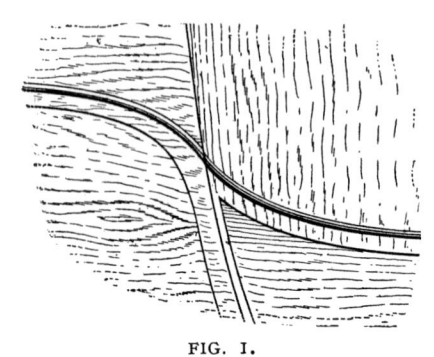

FIG. I.

In Fig. 1 shows the design of elbow and back curve.

The beading of carriages in large shops is done by a man kept especially for the purpose. In large cities a coach plater is called in to do it, and this accounts for this class of work being done so excellently when turned out of a first-class establishment; however, all cities are not large, and coach platers as workmen are never seen in such centers; hence it falls to the duty of body makers to bead the bodies, either when covered with leather or on painted surfaces. In some shops trimmers put the bead on, but where much exactitude and expertness is required in making the joints, the work is at variance with trimming, and properly speaking, more in keeping with the body maker's duty, because it's work that requires the greatest care in bending to the required curves and in fixing as well. It will be as well to commence the fixing of the bead with the knowledge of its composition, which is lead, brass and silver. Lead melts at 612 degrees Fahr..; brass melts at 1,869 degrees Fahr.., and silver melts at 2,233 degrees Fahr.. We thus see how it is that we can hold a piece of plated bead over a gas and melt the lead so that we may shift the pins or put in fresh ones where it is necessary to do so, without injury to the brass or silver.

The bead being lined with *lead* enables us to bend it easily without causing kinks in the curve required, as it toughens the action of the brass in bending, by acting as a buffer to the pressure, and of course the lead is necessary to the bead to hold the pins by which it is fixed to the body. On bending bead round a quick curve sideways it is advisable to take the pins out and refix them after the bead is bent to the required curve.

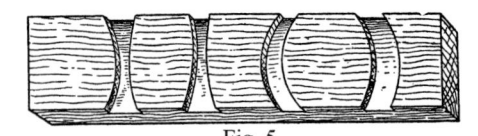

Fig. 5

In Fig. 5 is shown a sketch of a *bead block,* in which is made recesses of different curvature in which to bend the bead to the required shapes sideways. This block is made

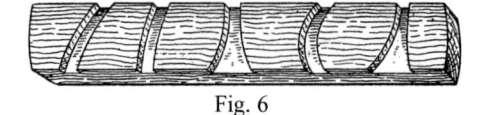

Fig. 6

to clamp on to the bench, out of a piece of C\v birch and the curved recess pieces are fixed on to the top with screws. Fig. 6 shows a narrow block made in the same way, or may be made of a thick piece of ash and the recesses cut out; this block is made narrow, for bending bead into quick curves.

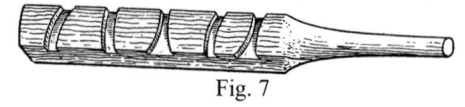

Fig. 7

Fig. 7 is a hand block, made to use with the hand when bending the bead in the blocks, either on the bench or in the vice.

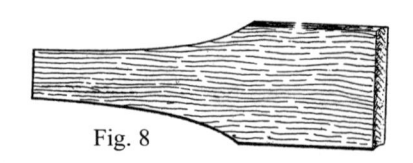

Fig. 8

Fig. 8 shows a bead driver. This is made of a piece of lancewood about B\, of an inch thick and three inches wide. The bead should be driven on with a light mallet.

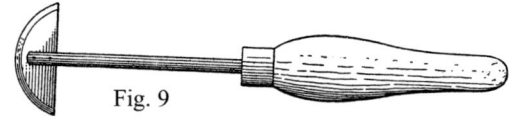

Fig. 9

Fig. 9 shows a handy little tool made after the shape of a coal-rake. This tool is made of thin steel and beveled on each side of the flat edge. This tool is for easing the bead-off the body when a point wants easing to allow the surface to go home. A piece of patent leather should be placed to the painted surface before using this easing tool, to lift the bead back with to prevent damaging the painting, and the bead eased off with the tool from below, but great care must be used in doing so. The additional tools necessary to those given are a pin awl, an eight inch flat file and a thin lock file. To rise a joint with plated bead it should be put on to a body before the trimming is nailed in, so that a hammer can be held to the framing during the time the head is being driven on, more so on a brougham body, to prevent the bead rebounding from the panel, which it often does in this class of body if the framing is not held rigidly. The holes for the pins should be driven well up with the awl, which ought, of course, to be a little smaller than the pin in the head. If the pins drive hard into the wood they are apt to be forced through the lead and show themselves on the plated surface, which, of course entirely spoils it. In beading back rests or parts where the bead has to be drawn over in its flat direction, it ought to be pulled tight and the pins pitched at an angle with the pliers, to give a draw to the bead on knocking it down to its place with the mallet.

THIS CAN BE APPLIED TO THE BEADING ON LEATHER VALANCES FOR TOPS AND SEATS

CHAPTER 9

PANELS

Panels For Painted Vehicles

Whitewood (Poplar) was used by American vehicle builders as the preferred wood for painted carriage and coach panels. Whitewood is a fine, close-grained timber, sufficiently flexible to resist damage from the twisting and jarring of the body; and yet it can be bent easily and retains its shape when curved panels are needed. The best quality has a greenish appearance with a narrow white "sap" and extremely fine grains.[1] The best grade should be used for panels free of "wind checks," "water streaks" and "twig curls." English and European body builders preferred using Honduras mahogany and walnut for coach and carriage panels. A wood of even greater quality for panels was basswood, the preferred wood for the complex curves of Albany and swell body sleigh panels. In our modern era it seems to be unknown how some of these sleigh bodies were originally made from solid wood being bent into complex curves.

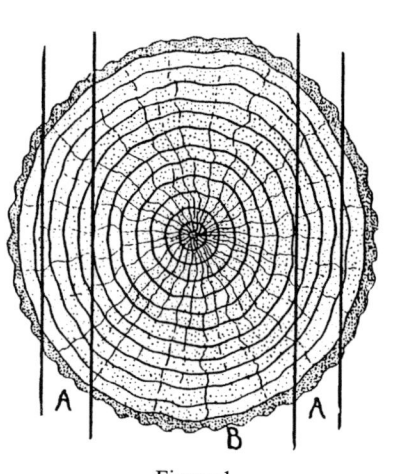

Figure 1

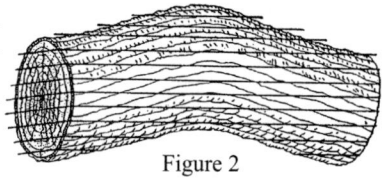

Figure 2

Natural Wood Panels

From the *Hub* of Jan. 1894 the following information was given on the selection of wood for natural wood panels that had become popular in the 1890's. The lumber for the panels of these vehicles was carefully selected for the well-mottled grain pattern and color. "Ordinarily it is difficult to obtain well-mottled and grained panels, except from planks cut from the log in a manner that will permit the side of the larger grains to show.

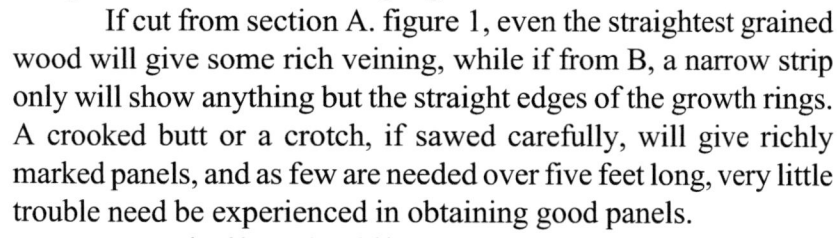

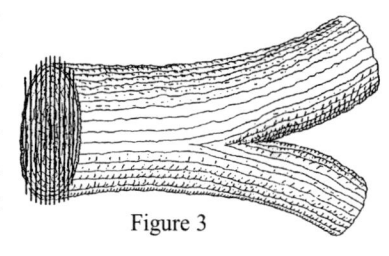

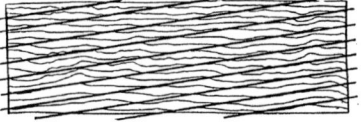

Figure 3

If cut from section A. figure 1, even the straightest grained wood will give some rich veining, while if from B, a narrow strip only will show anything but the straight edges of the growth rings. A crooked butt or a crotch, if sawed carefully, will give richly marked panels, and as few are needed over five feet long, very little trouble need be experienced in obtaining good panels.

Figure 4

A crooked butt should be sawed as shown by figure 2, while a crotch will give the best results if cut as shown by figure 3. When it is not possible to obtain logs such as described, fairly good results may be obtained by sawing up thick planks, as shown by figure 4. Some nicely marked panels are procured by sawing around a log as shown by figure 5, the cutting being steamed and straightened afterward.

Edge jointing often enables the worker to get a finely-grained panel, but for carriage work this is a bad plan except when the thin panel is backed up by another with the grain running directly at right angles with the first. If possible, always make the

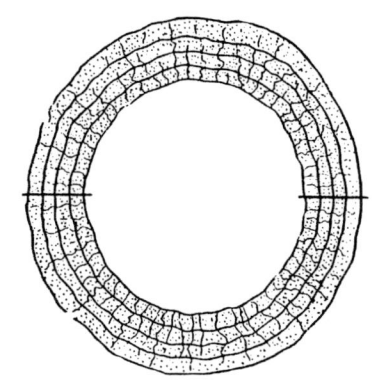

Figure 5

outer side of the tree the outside of the panel.

When ordering direct from the sawyer, instruct him to cut panel stock from crooked butts and to saw them in a way that will cut across the greatest number of growth rings and irregularities. Knurls, branches, knots, etc., are all to be sought after, if solid, as they insure the greatest amount of irregular graining.

Ash is the most popular wood, but hard elm, oak, maple, button wood, black walnut and butternut all give rich markings, and, if care is taken, rich natural colors as well."[2] (end of quote from the Hub Jan. 1894).

Different Methods of Applying Panels

Coach panels were glued over framing with nailing around the edges where moldings were applied over the edges, or the panels could be fitted into a grove with a molded edge. Panels for buggies or runabouts were manufactured with screw holes and it was a common vexation of carriage builders, how not to have screw holes show. The gluing of wooden plugs over screw holes would oftentimes show shrink marks. Screw holes showing was believed to be caused by the glue touching and rusting the screw head, causing the wooden plug to expand.

When panels of a coach or carriage were to be covered by upholstery on the inside, the inside surface of the panel and framing was covered with a piece of canvas that was glued to the interior surface. The cloth had a mesh like texture like burlap and was oftentimes linen. The inside was further coated with paint. Usually the paint was anything that was cheap and left over. Once the upholstery was installed, this would help prevent moisture from being absorbed on the back-side of the panel. Another method used by body builders in order to prevent cracking, warping, swelling and splitting of panels was to glue 1 ½ to 7/8 inch square blocks, 3/8 to 1/4 inch thick at right angles to the grain of the panels, to the interior of the panel, between the framing where it would be covered by upholstery. Inside panels that were not going to be upholstered were usually just given a good coating of paint, minus the linen cloth and glued blocks.

Great care was taken by body makers in the selection of wood that was of the best quality, cut on the right grain and dried in the right way for panels. Still the cracking of carriage panels was a vexation to body builders.

There is no known way of repairing cracked panels so that the cracks do not show up in some way or the other later on in the restoration job. For the traditionalist the first choice in dealing with a cracked panel is to replace it with a similar wood.

Panels that are just glued on the framing and secured around the edges by a molding on the top of the panel are the easiest to remove and replace. Most top quarter panels of coaches are applied this way.

Replacing a Top Quarter Panel

Step 1. If the upholstery has been removed, cut the inside edges of the linen cloth away from the paneling with a utility knife.

Step 2. Carefully remove the moldings so that you do not damage the surface surrounding the old panel. If you break up the molding, it is a simple job to make new moldings, but it makes extra work if you dent the surrounding surface.

Step 3. Split the old panel off with a floor chisel from the face side.

Step 4. Next clean away any old glue with a sharp scraper or sharp wood chisel. Hot vinegar should help to loosen the glue. Clean the back of the framing so you can again apply a protective coating.

Step 5. Using a piece of brown paper or drafting paper, draw a template of the panel with a pencil or by creasing it with your fingernail.

Step 6. Cut out the template, and refit it to make sure you have the correct size, making allowances for a 45 degree angle if you have a corner to miter. Draw around the template on your piece of lumber to be cut out.

Step 7. Cut the straight edges out about 1/16 inch bigger than needed. Cut the curved edge next. Then make the 45 degree miter for the corner edge on the planer or the table saw.

Step 8. Then work the straight edges down with a sander or planer until you get an exact fit.

Step 9. Hold the panel in place and from the back mark where the framing is going to come. Take the panel off and using a glue brush, brush the glue in between the lines on the panel and brush glue on the framing.

Step 10. Glue the panel in place using furniture clamps for the back corner and C-clamps for the door frame corner. When using clamps, you will need to use blocks of wood underneath or pieces of leather to keep the clamp from marring and denting the surface of your new panel. In addition to the blocks, use wax paper if you think the glue might ooze out. This will prevent your blocks and leather pieces from sticking fast. Scrape up any excess glue that can be seen to have oozed out.

Step 11. Once the glue is dry remove the clamps and coat the back of the panel. Elmer's white glue or Elmer's carpenter glue thinned with a little water will make the glue pliable enough to soak a piece of cloth in the glue solution. Soaking the cloth in the glue first allows the cloth to pre-shrink. Some builders thought the canvassing, as they called it, pulled the panel in unevenly when the cloth and glue dried. There would be any number of things you could use presently to seal the back of the panel from moisture. Modern resins and fiberglass used in automobile repair and boat making will work just as well.

Replacing Reed Moldings

It is only a simple task to replace the moldings when reed is used.

Step 1. Buy some reed, as used in wicker work, the diameter of the old molding and run it through the planer until it is shaved to a half round molding.(Be sure to use a push block and not your fingers to push the molding across the planer).

Step 2. Cut your molding pieces to the desired length and drill very tiny holes about every two inches. This thin material has a tendency to split, especially towards the ends when you are putting little brads in to tack it fast. If you are going around a curve you might want to soak the molding for a few minutes to make it pliable.

Step 3. Run a little bead of glue on the backside of the molding and fasten it to the panel using small brads and a nail punch.

Step 4. After everything is dry, touch up the nail holes with spot putty or paste wood filler since they are such tiny holes.

Brass Bead Molding

European, English, and better class American carriages have been found to have used brass bead molding rather than reed. This presents a more difficult job to try and replace this kind of molding. Originally these molding were made in the same way as the beaded molding on seat valances and top valances. Strips of brass sheeting were bent into a half hollow tube then lead was poured in and nails were set in the lead. This way there would not be any nail heads showing on the top surface. An alternative to this is to get half round solid brass rods and drill out the back about every two inches with about a 3/16 inch hole and then solder brads in the holes. If the molding goes around in a curve you will need to make a form and heat the brass to bend it in a curve. The brass should be anneal for bending and not a red heat, as brass tends to collapse very easily and it is impossible to handle if it gets to hot. The pins should be put in after the curve is established.

Replacing Lower Quarter Panels That Have a Curve Edge That Fits Into a Rabbet

These panels can be replaced with ease as long as the rabbet does not go all the way around the panel so that it can not be removed without taking the body apart.

Step 1. Start by cutting the linen cloth loose from the back framing with an utility knife.

Step 2. Draw a template of the hole using brown paper on drafting paper. Then lay your pattern flat on the work table and add the additional width needed for the panel where it fits into the rabbet.

Step 3. Carefully remove the panel, using a floor chisel. You may have to break up the panel into smaller pieces in order to ease it out of the rabbet without breaking the molding of the rabbet edge.

Step 4. Trace your template on to the piece of lumber for the new panel. Cut out your panel leaving a little extra on the straight edges. Then gradually work the straight edges down by planing or sanding till you get an exact fit. You have to use judgement in whether you need to taper the edge of the panel to fit into the rabbet.

Step 5. Fit your panel in place and mark the backside with a pencil where the framing is. Make up some thin wedges that can be driven behind the panel if need be in order to make sure the panel fits tight against the rabbet on the front side.

Step 6. Take the panel off and brush glue on both surfaces to be glued. Put the panel in place, clamping and wedging as needed.

Step 7. Once the glue is dry, coat the back of the panel by canvasing or fiber glassing, and replace any moldings.

Replacing Rear Curved Panels of Coaches that have a Rabbet

Panels that have a rabbet or groove all the way around the edges would have been put in place by the body maker as he was framing and building the body. This could be a problem requiring the dismantling of the body in order to replace this kind of panel. There are other problems if these panels are curved. Some are even compound curves. The rabbet may have been cut on a straight angle, but when all the pieces come together, the panel fits in on an angle. The panel might need to have tapered edges and also wedges placed behind it to bring it flush with the outside edge of the rabbet.

Bending Panels

Early carriages show a great inclination by body builders to make vehicles with curved panels. Before the piano box buggy, even the ordinary buggy or runabout such as the Goddard style body and the Coal box buggy had curved panels, all seemingly trying to outdo the previous styles as to the number of curves. Most of us are now in awe as to how and why the body builder and carriage designers would take such great pains to make such an abundant number of complex curves in a vehicle. Many of these curved body styles went out of fashion in later years for carriages, while curved bodies were still fashionable for sleighs. Toward the end of the 19th century there was somewhat of a revival for carriage designs with curved panels again, but never to

Scroll Coupé of 1857
from the Coach-Makers' Magazine

the extent seen in the early and mid 19th century.

The following table was devised by a London builder to list the bending capabilities of panels using the best woods for bending: pine, whitewood, open grained cedar, Honduras mahogany, walnut, wych-elm, and many American woods of the maple species. Under the dual action of heat and water, or steam, the curvatures in circles of various thicknesses of panels are shown in the following table.

TABLE OF CURVATURES

Thickness Panels	Diam. Circles
1/8 inch will bend to	4 inch circle
3/16 inch will bend to	5 inch circle
1/4 inch will bend to	6 inch circle
5/16 inch will bend to	8 inch circle
3/8 inch will bend to	12 inch circle
1/2 inch will bend to	16 inch circle
5/8 inch will bend to	20 inch circle
3/4 inch will bend to	26 inch circle
1 inch will bend to	32 inch circle[3]

When bending panels, you will first need to determine which is the easiest way for the panel to bend. The heart side should be the concave curve and the sap side would be the convex curve. To determine the heart and sap side, plane the end of the panel off so that the growth rings show. The larger rings will be on the sap side. This way you will be bending the panel with the law of nature so that panel will warp naturally. The heart side would need to be contracted and the sap side would need to be expanded. This was accomplished by swelling the sap side with water (hot water is best in some cases) and applying dry heat to the heart side.

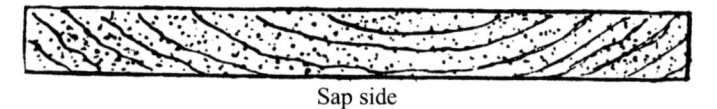

Sap side

Early body panels were laid on the shop floor overnight with wet sawdust on the top of the panel that would be the outside curve, and heat would then be applied to the dry surface to bend the panel around. This practice is thought to have caused too much moisture to be absorbed swelling the wood to an extreme so that when it dried, it was prone to splitting and cracking later on. The saturation of the outer surface of the wood should not be more than two-thirds the thickness of the panel, according to a London builder. Any more moisture would neutralize the bending efforts and cause the panel to crack and split latter on.

Where the bend is slight, it is best to shrink the inside by heating, without wetting the outside. When the bends are more pronounced, the panels need to be bent over a form, using edge pressure, so as to upset the grains on the inside.

Other primitive methods of bending were to work the panel on top of the stove with the sap side down, applying water and a wet rag to steam the wood and swell it. In order to try to eliminate the sinking of panels in the middle after being applied to the carriage,

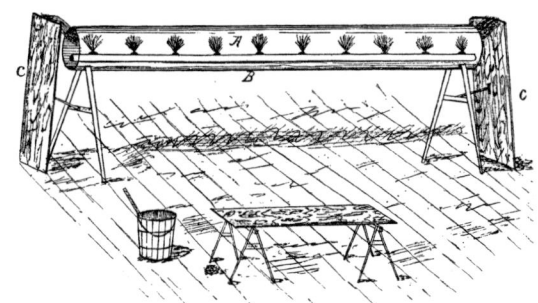

Gas Heated stove pipe

some body builders heat only the ends of the panel at the stove, in order to warp the ends ever so slightly. More advanced methods of bending the panel were to heat the panel over a heated stove pipe, sometimes red hot. Moisture was applied to the top side of the panel while the heart side laid on the stove pipe. This sometimes caused the panel to be charred. By 1888 many of the more modern shops had a stove pipe that was heated by a series of gas jets.

Panels

By 1893 the practice of bending panels over a stove pipe is reported to have been abandoned in all good shops, steam bending being the preferred method. Steam bending of wood was largely practiced by carriage builders for bending shafts, wheel rims and other heavy timber parts of vehicles that required bending. The wood was placed inside a closed container called an autoclave or steam box, where steam was then piped into the container. The steam is not required to be under pressure and people have built steam boxes out of almost anything : PVC pipe, pine boards, metal barrels, and old refrigerators.

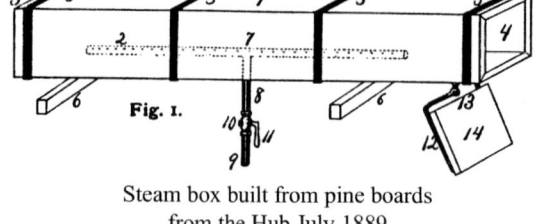

Steam box built from pine boards from the Hub July 1889

The wood then becomes plastic and is taken from the steam box and quickly placed in a form or mold to the desired shape. Part of the skill of wood bending is having the proper form or molds and techniques for bending. The outside curve needs to be supported as well as the inside curve or you will have breakage and splitting. The time that the wood is plastic when taken out of the steam box is very limited so it must be worked quickly, and once clamped to a form, it must be left to dry until the wood can retain its bent shape on its own. Once the bent wood is taken from the form, temporary strips are attached until the bent wood is put to use.

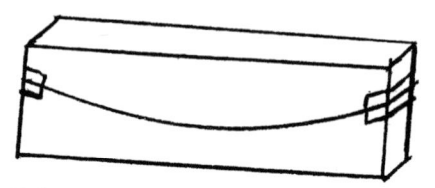

Using 2 x 6s cut the curve of the panel out

Cut notches on the ends of the curves for narrow straight pieces

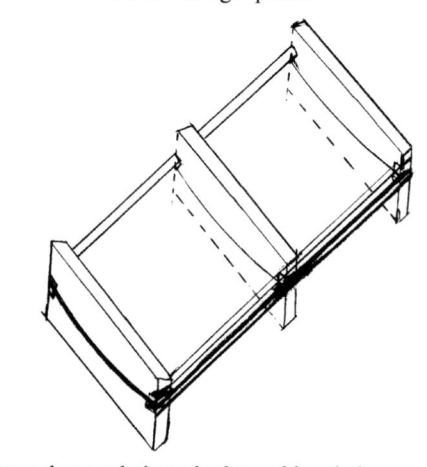

Replacing a Curved Back Panel in a Rabbet

Step 1. When replacing a curved panel, make a template, by using brown paper or drafting paper before disassembling the panel. Crease the paper into the edges to mark.

Step 2. Lay your pattern flat on the work table and draw around the crease lines and cut out your pattern. Refit your pattern to the panel to make sure you have the correct fit and make any adjustments if it does not fit exactly.

Step 3. Once you have disassembled the vehicle and measured the depth of the rabbet, draw another template adding the depth of the rabbet to the second template.

Press the panel pieces in the mold and clamp together securely

Step 4. Cut out the new template and draw it onto the panel stock and cut out the panel

Step 5. Bend the panel by using forms that you have made by making a template or pattern of the body curve. Using your pattern, cut out forms of some two inch thick lumber. Depending on your curve, you can use some two by fours. Two by sixes of pine or hardwood might be called for in some cases. You will need at least three sets of forms. Each set should have a top and bottom. You will need a form for the ends and one for the center. Bend and clamp your panel in the form.

Step 6. Let the panel dry at least 24 hrs. clamped in the forms. Leaving it in the form up to a week or more can't hurt it any. If you have very humid weather, you will want to make sure it is dry and cured before taking it out of the form.

Laminating Thin Layers

An alternative to bending a solid wood panel would be to laminate thin layers together. From a speciality lumberyard or plywood manufacture you can get 4 foot by 8 foot (grain crosswise) sheets or 8 foot by 4 foot (grain lengthwise) sheets of bending plywood 1/8 inch thick called Italian poplar. There is an extra thin aircraft plywood for bending with Finnish birch on both sides that comes in 3 ply, 1/16" x 24" x 24" and 24" x 48" sheets and a 5 ply, 1/8" x 24" x 24" and 24" x 48" sheets. Available in a 3/8" bending plywood is a wood called Luan, in 4 x 8 and 8 x 4 sheet. This wood has a more open grain and it would require the extra finishing of open grain woods.

You can use the same kind of forms as used for bending a solid wood panel.
For a panel with a curve in two directions or an extreme curve, it might be necessary to wet the bending plywood. Lay several layers of cloth on the floor and put the panel on top. Saturate the plywood with water, starting from the center and working to the sides, wetting about every 15 minutes, and after about an hour or two it should be pliable enough to bend. Put the layers needed for the thickness of your panel in the forms and clamp without gluing. Let the paneling dry sufficiently so that you have a dry surface on which to apply glue. Unclamp the forms and apply glue between the layers according to the glue manufacturers directions. Put your layers with the glue back in the form until the glue is set. When gluing layers together on a curve, you might experience some difficulty in getting the edges even. A good idea might be to give yourself some extra width when cutting the layers out and once they are glued, trim off any excess.

Take your panel out of the form and fit it in the rabbet. Some body builders thought that a curved panel fitted into a rabbet should not be glued in and they set the panel in white lead that was mixed with lamp black. This way the groove would be sealed from moisture but the panel could contract and expand.

In some cases the rabbet to receive the panel was cut wider than the thickness of the panel. Once the panel was set in place, wedges were then driven into the space between the back of the panel, forcing the panel against the outside edge of the rabbet. In other cases the rabbet might have been cut smaller than the panel and the outside panel edge was beveled to fit the panel in the rabbet.

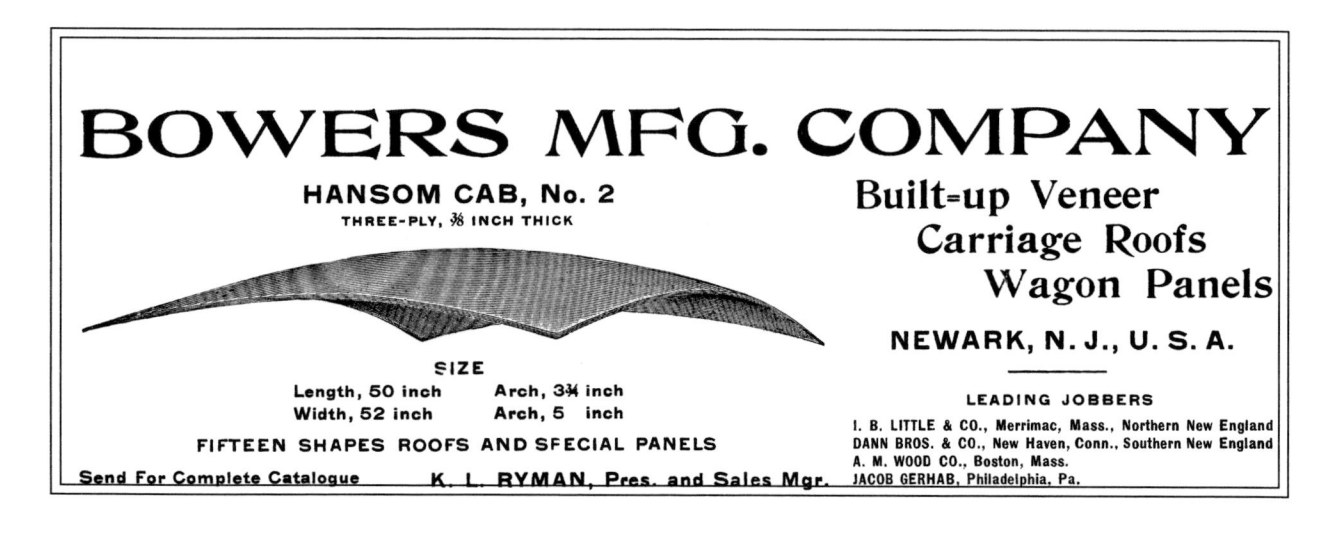

BOWERS MFG. COMPANY

HANSOM CAB, No. 2
THREE-PLY, ⅜ INCH THICK

Built=up Veneer Carriage Roofs Wagon Panels

NEWARK, N. J., U. S. A.

SIZE
Length, 50 inch   Arch, 3¾ inch
Width, 52 inch   Arch, 5 inch

FIFTEEN SHAPES ROOFS AND SPECIAL PANELS

Send For Complete Catalogue   K. L. RYMAN, Pres. and Sales Mgr.

LEADING JOBBERS
I. B. LITTLE & CO., Merrimac, Mass., Northern New England
DANN BROS. & CO., New Haven, Conn., Southern New England
A. M. WOOD CO., Boston, Mass.
JACOB GERHAB, Philadelphia, Pa.

From the Carriage Monthly Sept. 1900

Cabinet Makers Paneling

A second choice to replacing panels with solid wood would be to use cabinet makers paneling, sometimes known as Baltic Birch or Finland Birch. It comes with a smooth finished surface and several solid laminated layers, which makes the edge easy to finish when the edges show. Standard thicknesses and constructions are 1/8" - 3-ply, 5/32" - 3-ply, 3/16" - 4-ply, 1/4" - 5-ply, 3/8" - 7-ply, ½"9 - ply, 15mm - 11-ply, 5/8" - 12-ply, 18mm - 13-ply, 3/4" - 14-ply, 1" - 18-ply. Standard sizes are 4' x 4', 5' x 5', 61" x 61" and it is also available in 4 or 5 ft. lengths and in widths from 6 ft. up to 12 ft. The best quality is known as "A" selected, one-piece face, very even and light in color. Other qualities are "BU", "S", "BB" and the lowest quality is "WG" with firm knots and patches allowed. For panels that are going to be painted, a lesser quality than "A" can be quite satisfactory. The use of cabinet makers paneling has become a popular choice with many restorers for replacing panels because it is easier to use and more durable than solid wood panels. Lumber for wide solid wood panels is harder and harder to come by and there is always the risk of splitting and cracking again. Cabinet makers paneling may not come in the exact thickness of your old panel so you might have to cut a piece out and take it to a wood working shop and have it milled to the right thickness on one side. Have it milled through a thickness planer that uses sandpaper rather than cutting knives. This will do the nicest job. Laminated plywood was used in the carriage era and it was historically called built-up wood. It was three layers each 1/8 inch thick. The two outside layers had the grain running lengthwise and the inner layer had the grain running crosswise.[4] In 1884 E. F. French of New York advertised built-up wood for all types of vehicle roof. It was said that it "never cracks or shrinks, and rarely stirs from its plane."[5]

It is not uncommon to find a Portland sleigh that used this built-up wood. Often times it has come unglued. Sometimes furniture restorers can reattach loose veneer by using a hot iron. This remelts the glue between the layers. It wouldn't hurt to try some different techniques before you decide to replace it with a new panel. You could try using a syringe with glue to get behind loose layers and then clamping them together.

Veneering or Skinning

A third choice in dealing with cracked panels is to use a veneer and glue it over the entire panel that is cracked. This is probably an option for some jobs when you do not want to take the whole carriage apart in order to get to a panel to replace it. The veneer can be a number of things, thin aluminum sheeting, Formica, fiberglass and resin, and canvas, but canvas would be harder to paint. The draw back to this procedure is that you are adding additional thickness to the panel and you may loose the sharp definition of the moldings surrounding the panels. The 1/8 inch or 1/16 inch thick plywood could be used in cases where the thickness of the panel is not critical. Probably the thinnest and strongest would be a piece of paper thin aluminum sheeting. Applying canvas is known to have been a traditional way of finishing some panels on vehicles. Canvas has been found applied to the under side of sleigh dashes of small sleighs. Some European carriages had their upper quarter panels covered with canvas and then painted to match the rest of the vehicle so that you wouldn't have known canvas was even used.

Step 1. In using some type of skinning or veneering it would be wise to try and get to the back of the panel in order to secure it from any further contracting and expanding. If you are able, remove the upholstery and get to the back of the panel. Grind about a one and a half inch wide surface on either side of the crack with a small grinder using coarse sandpaper.

Step 2. Once you have made a new wood surface, glue a three inch strip over the crack. You might have to hold it fast by countersinking some wood screws into the three inch strip and the panel.

Step 3. Once you have secured the back of the panel and the glue has dried, use a sharp wood chisel or utility knife to clean the crack to a new surface, and then fill up the crack with auto body filler or similar epoxy.

Step 4. Next make a template of the panel using brown paper or drafting paper.
Clean off the surface of the old panel to new wood and you might even want to rough it up with coarse sandpaper if you are using contact glue or a similar adhesive. Apply the contact cement according to the manufacturer's directions. The easiest way to spread out thick contact glue is to use a squeegee. You will probably need to have a small roller or block handy to press the two surfaces together. Apply fiber glass according to the manufacturer's directions or any automotive paint store will have some handbooks on auto repair showing the use of fiberglass and how to prepare it for painting.

In the case of sleigh dashes where both sides of the panel show, you will need to skin or veneer both sides. In most cases skinning only one side will still show a crack on the other side, if you try to fill the crack with putty.

Repairing Panels by Inlaid

A fourth choice of repairing panels is to follow the directions for veneering or skinning by first securing the back of the panel, except in the case of sleigh dashes when both surfaces will show. For panels whose thickness you do not want to change and which cannot be removed, you can try routing a half inch groove on both sides of the crack about 1/3 the thickness of your panel. Next make up a strip of wood to fit in the routed out section of the panel and glue in place using clamps. On a sleigh dash you will have to rout out a groove on the opposite side of the panel. Try making it only 3/8 of an inch wide on each side of the crack. In some cases you might not be able to get a

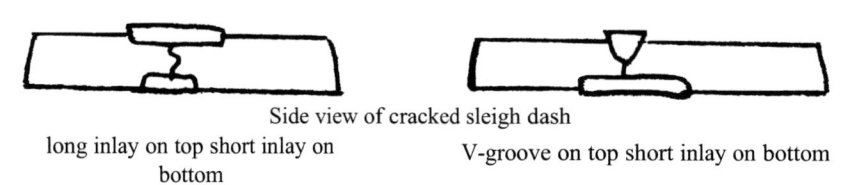

Side view of cracked sleigh dash
long inlay on top short inlay on bottom

V-groove on top short inlay on bottom

router to fit into the space, so you would need to score a straight line on each side of the crack with a knife and use a good sharp wood chisel and to make a groove by hand. Fit and glue a piece of wood into the groove.

Another alternative is to make a simple v- groove and glue and clamp in a v shaped strip. Once it is dry it can be finished off flush with the surface of the panel. You should let this type of repair cure a long time in order to prevent shrink marks showing later on in the restoration job. If you have nice hot dry summer days it will not take as long to cure and thoroughly dry as trying to work on a project during the winter.

One known cause of panels' cracking is storing vehicles in a building that gets too hot or cold and the relative humidity is below 50 degrees for extended periods of time. This causes the panels and carriage to dry out to an excess. Other conditions that are not good for carriage panels is moving them all of a sudden from a warm environment to a cold environment or vice versa with a sudden change of over 20 degrees. Proper care sometimes helps prevent panels from cracking. Therefore if you need to bring a vehicle in from a cold barn to a warm shop, you might want to be careful not to change the relative humidity and temperature all of a sudden.

Panels
Bibliography

"Bending Solid Wood To Form." Washington, DC., 1957. (Bulletin of the United States Department of Agriculture, Forest Service, Agriculture Handbook No. 125.) "Bent Wood Members." Madison, WI, August 1951. : (Bulletin of the United States Department of Agriculture, Forest Service, No. R1903-3.)

"Gas Heating Apparatus For Bending Panels." Hub. (May 1888), p. 104.

"How to Repair a Checked Panel, How to Warp a Door Panel, How to Face Off "Stuff.", How to Smooth the Surface of a Panel." Hub. (Dec. 1881), p. 469.

"How to Determine the Way In Which a Board May Be Warped." Hub. (Nov. 1881), p. 391.

Isles, George. "The Restoration of Carriages." London : J. A. Allen, 1981. pp. 54-76. (Some step-by-step instructions were taken in part from this book).

"English Methods of Panel Bending For Bodies." Hub. (July 1896), p. 251-252.

"Natural Wood Finish." Hub. (Jan. 1894), p. 817.

"Selecting Panels." Hub. (Dec. 1893), p. 733.

Stevens, W. C. "Machinery and Equipment Used For Bending Wood". London, England : His Majesty's Stationery Office, 1938.

"The Woodworker: Why are Panels Canvased?, Bending Panels, Bending Lower Back Panels ..., Why Panels are Blocked, Why Gluing Panels In to the Grooves is not Practical, Should Panels be Braded On Carriage-Bodies?" Carriage Monthly (May 1885), p. 160.

For further information on glueing & clamping.

Fine Wood Working on Bending Wood. Newtown, CT : Taunton Press, 1985.

Spielman, Patrick. Gluing & Clamping : A Woodworker's Handbook. New York, NY : Sterling Publishing Co., 1986.

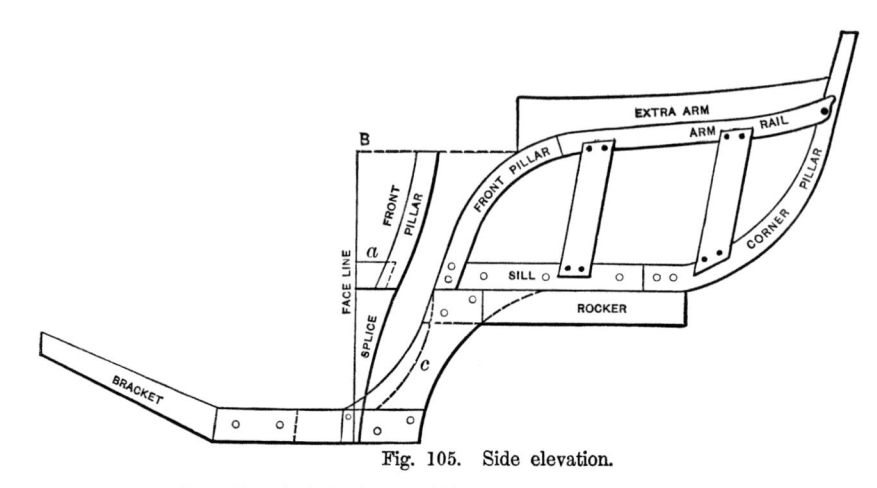

Fig. 105. Side elevation.

From Practical Carriage Building by M. T. Richardson, 1892.

Endnotes

[1]."Selecting Panels." Hub. (Dec. 1893), p. 733.

[2]."Natural Wood Finish." Hub (Jan. 1894), p. 817.

[3]."English Methods of Panel Bending For Bodies." Hub. (July 1896), p. 251-252.

[4]."Built-Up Wood In Carriage-Making." Hub, (April 1884) pp. 23-24.

[5]. E. F. French. "Whole Roofs of Built-Up Wood for Carriages, heavy and light, and for Trade-Wagons." Hub, (April 1884).

Panels

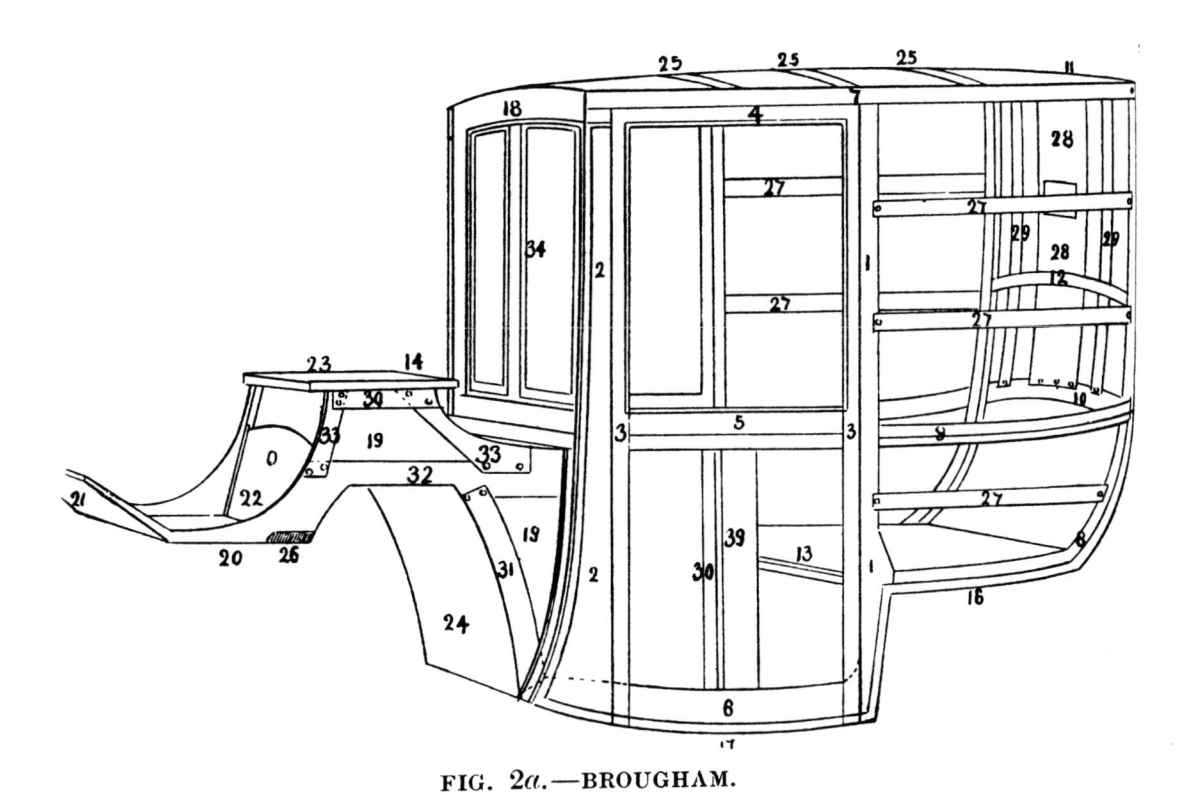

FIG. 2a.—BROUGHAM.

From the Art and Craft of Coachbuilding by John Philipson, 1897.

1. Standing or hinge pillar
2. Front or lock pillar
3. Door pillars
4. Door top rail
5. Door fence rail
6. Door bottom rail
7. Cant rail
8. Corner pillar
9. Elbow rail
10. Back rail
11. Back top rail
12. Back cross rail
13. Seat rail
14. Boot cross rail
16. Seat bottom-side
17. Rocker
18. Front rail
19. Boot side
20. Bracket
21. Boot footboard
22. Heelboard
23. Seatboard
24. Arch panel
25. Roof sticks
26. Boot bar
27. Quarter battens
28. Back-light board
29. Back battens
30. Door battens
31. Boot contracting piece
32. Boot neck
33. Boot side framing
34. Upright front rail

Preparing for Painting

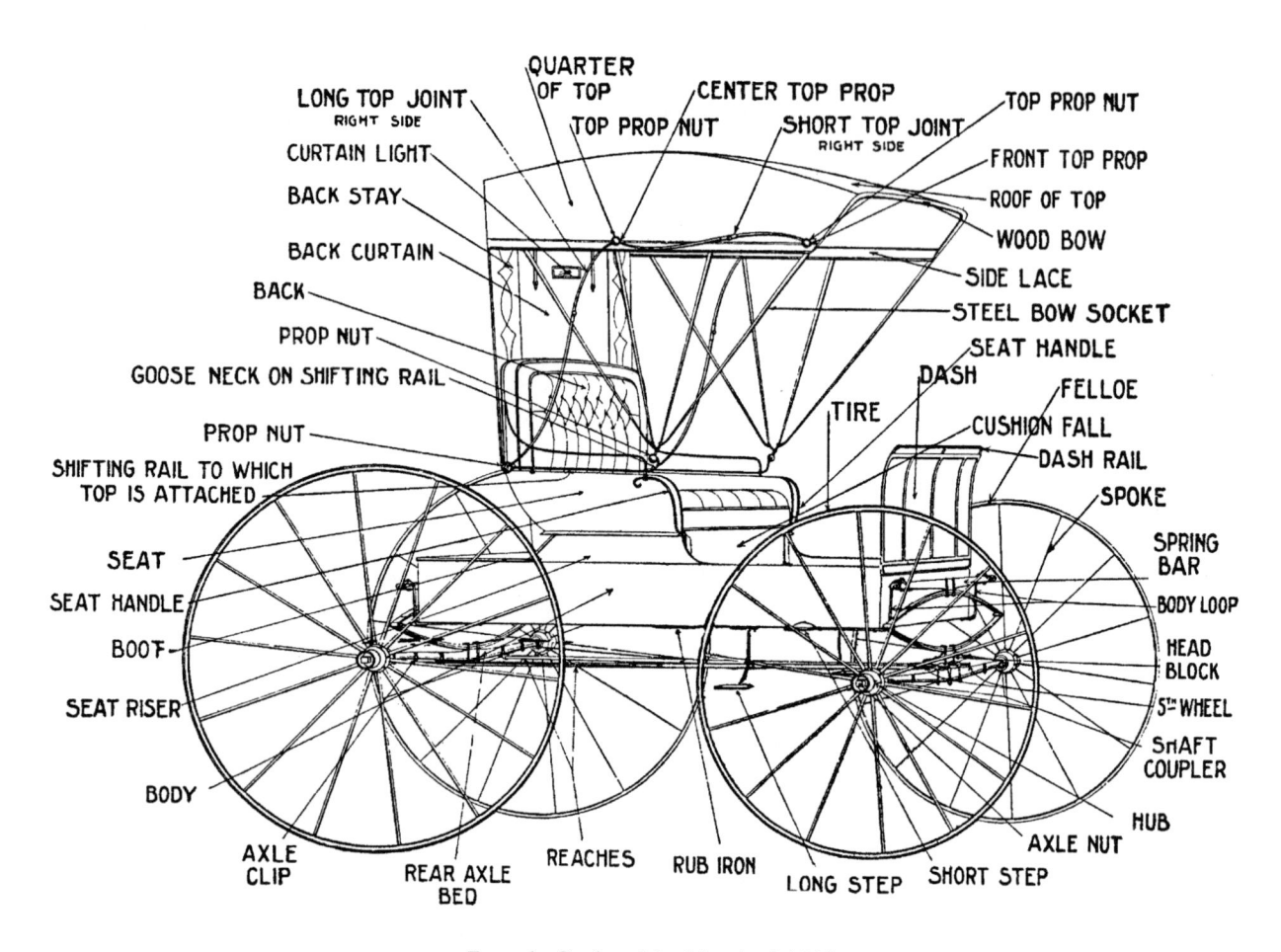

From the Carriage Monthly--April 1914

Preparing for Painting
CHAPTER 10

PREPARING FOR PAINTING

Getting Started

The first step towards physically starting on your project is taking lots of photographs of the vehicle before you begin your work. As time goes by, it is easy to forget the exact details of striping, crests, upholstery and other construction details. Even if you are not starting a restoration project it is important to take photographs and keep them in a file as soon as you acquire a vehicle. It is always good business to keep good records and as a carriage is an investment in an historical artifact, you should have photographs on hand to show your friends, other reasons being in case of fire, theft, trailer accident or other disaster.

If your vehicle has a lot of striping and ornamental designs you might acquire a roll of Drafting Vellum or some clear tracing film and trace off the exact location and size of different striping and designs. Cut a piece of drafting vellum to fit the panel or part of the carriage, hold it in place on the carriage with some masking tape if desired and trace around the designs with a pencil. This way you will have a good record between color photographs and your tracings to show the person who is going to be painting the art work back on. Take many close-up pictures of the carriage details as well as over-all shots. You may even get better photographs once you separate your project into sections, so you may want to take more close-ups mid way between disassembling.

In starting a restoration project it can be important to plan at least a year in advance for some vehicles. Many quality shops have a year's waiting list for customers orders. If your project requires such things as custom made wheels, springs, or special fabric, it is advisable to pick out these details that are going to cause waiting and special attention, so that your

project goes along smoothly.

Disassembling

After all the preliminary work is out of the way, you may begin to dismantle the vehicle. Remove all the upholstery, leaving as much as possible intact, to serve as a reference for the trimmer. Any metal work that is practical to remove should be detached from the body. It would be important to label the position of the axles, springs, lamp brackets. When removing bolts once the threads are cleaned it makes the job go back together faster if you hand turn any

Take lots of photographs of construction details before and during disassembly.

Take lots of photographs of painting details.

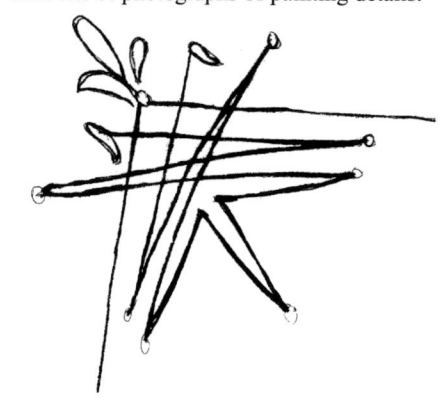

Using tracing film trace off any designs as to their exact location and size.

101

Preparing for Painting

nuts back on the bolts right away. A small triangular file is a handy tool in touching up any damaged threads. Replace any stripped or badly worn or corroded bolts. Now days you might need to special order square nuts, or get them from a carriage parts supplier. The most common grades of bolts carried by the hardware stores are grade 2 soft to grade 5 harder. It is important to replace carriage bolts with the proper strength bolts. Shafts coupling bolts need to be extra strong for obvious safety reasons. If the hardware store does not have what you need, some bolts can be still ordered from specialty bolt manufacturers. When extracting old bolts that are a bit stubborn use patience , Liquid Wrench®, and heat. Do not hit on the thread end of bolts with a hammer as this will damage the threads. Always use a punch smaller than the diameter of bolt for removing bolts. A small specialty torch may also come in handy in freeing stubborn screws and bolts.

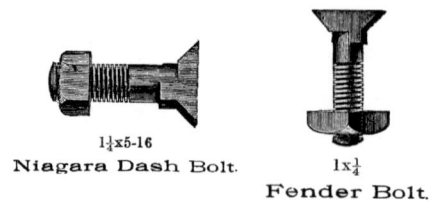

1¼x5-16
Niagara Dash Bolt.

1x¼
Fender Bolt.

2½x5-16
Buffalo Dash Bolt.
From the Carriage Monthly Nov. 1890

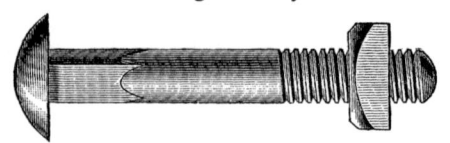

Common Carriage Bolt, Oval Head
From S. D. Kimbark 1888

Tip For Removing Rusty Screws

In trying to remove badly rusted wood screws from a vehicle, I've evolved a system that seems to work well. From previous experience in working with antique furniture, I use a hot soldering iron placed on a tight screw to loosen it. But horse-drawn vehicles were used in rain and storms so capillary action caused moisture to penetrate deeply in the screw holes. I take an iron washer with the hole just the same size or slightly smaller than the screw head. With an oxyacetylene torch turned down to a needle point, one is able to quickly heat up the screw with little charring of the wood. Of course this procedure is best done before stripping off the old paint as this protects the wood.

I learned of an epoxy that is used to restore architectural decoration in historical preservation projects. It is called Abatron, Liquid Wood® and Wood-Epox®. The Liquid Wood reconstitutes rotten wood by slow penetration and is the primer for Wood Epox which is used to build up the missing parts. These products work so well that the Illinois State Railroad Museum used them to restore the window sashes on their coaches and parlor cars.

After removal of the rusty screw, I use an old horse wormer syringe and pump the Liquid Wood into the hole. After a few days to allow this to penetrate, I thin Wood Epox with Liquid Wood and use this in another syringe to fill the hole. After one week one can re-drill new screw holes.. from Chester Stegman, Carriage Journal Summer 1987.

Have a bucket of water or a water-soaked rag handy to keep from charring the wood when heating stubborn screws and bolts. If the slot in a screw becomes damaged you can cut a new slot using the dremel tool and cutting disc attachment.

Depending on the vehicle and the weight of the body decide whether it is easier to lift the body off with the wheels on or off the vehicle. To remove the wheels, from the undercarriage always remember to **block the wheels before jacking up.** Always keep safety in mind and use good size blocks that will not tip over to support the undercarriage and body while taking the connecting bolts out. Once the connecting bolts are removed that attach the body to the undercarriages a hoist or pulley system would be ideal for lifting the body. The next alternative is to have some help to lift the body from the undercarriage. Putting the body on sawhorses or two rolling dollies that are about

30 inches high makes it easy for the body to be worked on.

Gluing

If the body and undercarriage need repairs with glue, do this first in order to give any glue jobs ample time to dry. Glue drying under a new paint job will cause shrink marks. In order to glue old wood back together you should always make a new surface for gluing. If something is splintered off you can glue it back together by drilling holes through the two surfaces and pinning and gluing them with wooden dowels. Old glue joints that have come loose can be cleaned with hot vinegar. For carvings and moldings that are chipped away, glue on little pieces by making a new surface. These little pieces can later be shaped with the dremel tool if need be. Plastic wood is not recommended as it has a tendency to chip out and shrink as time goes on.

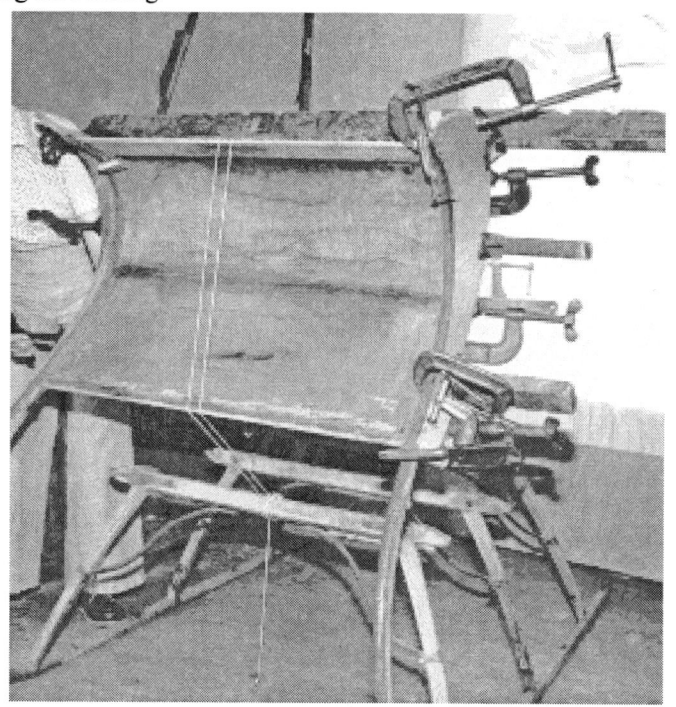

It is important to do the glue work as soon as possible in your restoration plan.

If you have a carriage that has been upholstered several times it probably has a multitude of tack holes. A good idea is to go around with a bottle of Elmers® glue or a two part liquid wood filler and fill up the holes using toothpicks for larger holes. This works better than plastic wood, which tends to chip out when you start putting tacks in again. The other alternative is to use bigger tacks to hold the upholstery, which will soon cause very little solid wood to be left.

Paint Removal

Once you have your vehicle disassembled into sections and as much of the hardware as possible removed from the wooden parts you can start to remove the old paint from the wood. The two most acceptable procedures are scraping and paint remover with methylene chloride. **WARNING**: As you remove the old paint you should keep in mind carriages were largely painted with lead putty and lead paint, and scraping causes dust that can be inhaled. The methylene chloride paint remover attaches itself to metals and it can be absorbed through the skin if you aren't wearing protective clothing. If the condition of the old paint lends itself well to scraping there are various kinds of paint scrapers available at the hardware store or in specialty catalogs for wood workers. You should wear a dust mask and protective eye wear. The draw back of scraping is that you need to be careful not to scratch or gouge the wood. Always scrape with the grain. For finishing natural wood carriages you need to be careful not to mar the natural aged patina of the wood. For the various parts of the carriage, it will be helpful to have several different types of scrapers that are well sharpened.

Wheels can easily be scraped by laying them on sawhorses or a strong metal trash can that has been padded.

Preparing for Painting

Paint Remover

The preferred method of removing paint by finishers of fine furniture is with paint remover containing large enough quantities of methylene chloride to do the job. Paint removers with sufficient quantities of methylene chloride are faster acting than water base paint removers and caustic solutions, therefore they are less harmful to the wood by not raising the grain as much and loosening glue joints. **WARNING** : Paint removers with methylene chloride do give off a rather obnoxious and harmful odor, and when it is inhaled, the body metabolizes it, creating carbon monoxide. It is not recommended for use by people with a heart condition. Ideally it should be used outside in the summer in the shade at about 75 degree F weather with a light breeze. If you work with it inside you should have lots of fresh air and an exhaust fan. If dizziness occurs, get some fresh air. We live with carbon monoxide from our motorized vehicles everyday, so the same common sense should apply when working with paint removers with methylene chloride. Other safety precautions when working with paint removers containing methylene chloride are to wear neoprene gloves when handling it, with cuffs rolled up so that it can't drip down your arm. A long shirt and eye protection is additional protection.

Paint removers with methylene chloride act as a "bottom up" stripper penetrating through the layers of old finish to the wood line, allowing the finish to peel off in sheets.

For your paint removing project you should start by laying out some old newspapers or cardboard, (plastic tarpaulins could be melted by some removers), on the area underneath in order protect the floor or ground surface, and secondly to collect the sludge and properly dispose of it, since some areas now have regulations on disposing of old paint. It is then a good idea to mask off such things as the rubber tire or any plated hardware that was not removed from the wood, in order to prevent it from getting slopped up with paint remover. The paint remover usually comes in paste, or liquid form. It is easiest to start with paste and for a final wash liquid can be used with steel wool or nylon scrub pad to remove any remaining paint in the grain.

Shake the paint remover can well and then put a rag over the top of the can when opening and slowly twist off the cap. Once open, pour some of the paint remover in an old can or glass jar and then apply the paint remover with an old natural bristle paint brush. Brush the paste on very heavily, avoiding brushing over more than once, (more of a daubing operation). If dry spots should appear, go back and daub a little more on to the dry spots. The paste paint remover is chemically engineered so that a thin

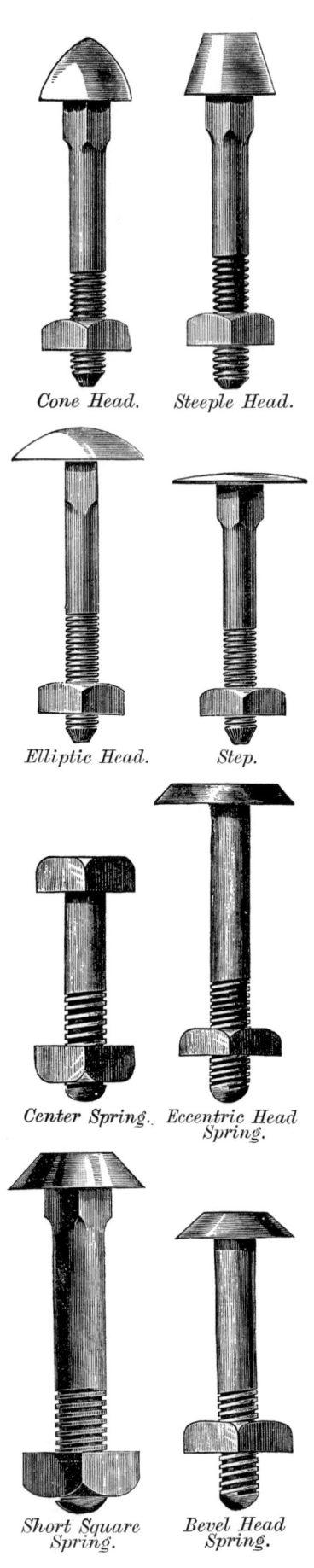

Cone Head.   *Steeple Head.*

Elliptic Head.   *Step.*

Center Spring.   *Eccentric Head Spring.*

Short Square Spring.   *Bevel Head Spring.*

S. D. Kimbark, 1888.

crust raises to the air exposed surface of the remover. This thin crust prevents the rapid evaporation of the paint remover. Therefore the paint remover absorbs into the old paint. Excessive brushing disturbs the crust causing the remover to evaporate rather than absorbing into the old paint. After application most paint removers require 10 to 15 minutes to do its job. With a putty knife scrap away the old paint while it is still wet. For turnings you might have to use a series of nylon brushes, and for heavy ornamental work it is helpful to scrub the area while it is still soft and gooey with wood shavings, and with a stiffer brush to scrub out the loaded shavings. Other useful tools for getting paint out of corners and carvings are dowel sticks sharpened to a point. Soft brass bristle brushes are available for really stubborn paint that doesn't want to come out of the grain. Especially time consuming is wicker work that has been painted with some really stubborn paint. You just need to keep applying successive coats of paint remover keeping it very wet while soft brushing it between applications. (Sometimes it is just not possible to get out old paint that is stained into the wood or wicker.) Once it looks like you have removed all the old paint wipe the work down with a wash of liquid paint remover using steel wool or nylon abrasive scrubbing pad and finally wipe with rags or paper towels.

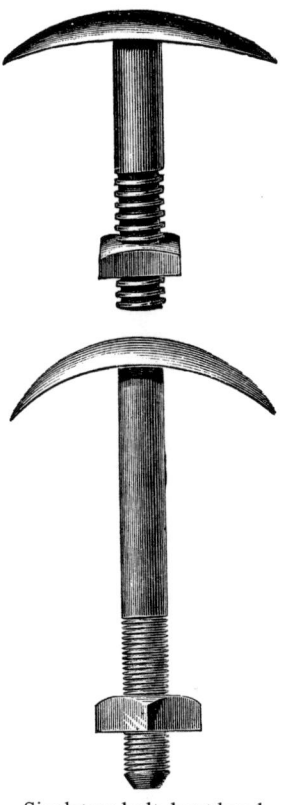

Singletree bolt, bent head, round neck.

Decontaminating

Unseen to the eye there may be chemicals left on the surface of your carriage parts that are contaminants, such as residue paint remover, grease, wax, oil and silicone which is a very stubborn contaminant that plays havoc with new finishes. We have often seen people rubbing their carriages down with Liquid Gold® furniture polish or similar polishes to make their carriages more presentable and brighter. Silicone can be found in furniture polishes and in the long run is damaging to painted carriage surfaces, plus plays havoc when trying to apply new finishes. Once you have removed the old paint from your vehicle parts you might want to clean them with a series of washes to make sure that they are free of possible contaminants. Using an abrasive scrubbing pad or steel wool, wash them first with a liberal amount of lacquer thinner. For the second wash use alcohol, and for the third wash use mineral spirits or naphtha. If your project is suspected of being contaminated with silicone, first scrub and wipe the wood with mineral spirits, then with an ammonia solution (1 cup of ammonia in 1 gal. of warm water). One end of the ammonia molecule will attached itself to the silicone, pulling it away from the wood, and the other end of the ammonia molecule to the water, allowing the silicone to be mopped up. Work as quickly as possibly with the water and then dry the wood thoroughly in order to keep the grain from raising.

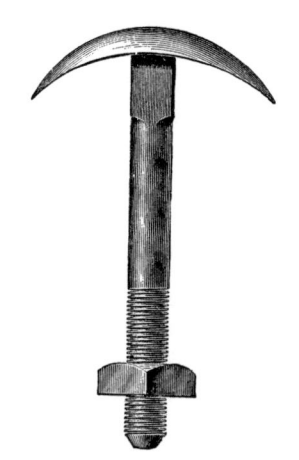

Singletree bolt, bent head, square neck.

Singletree bolt spur head.
From S. D. Kimbark, 1888.

Bleaching

You should now be ready to start the finishing process unless you're trying to finish the vehicle in natural wood. You might have to do some further preparation of the wood with bleach to remove various stains. Sometimes though, once a vehicle has been painted, it is almost impossible to get out the residue left saturated in the wood. Some aniline stains can be removed with a saturated solution of chlorine sold for pools (usually 65% to 85%) in the form of either calcium hypochlorite or sodium hypochlorite. Add the white crystals to warm water in a glass container until the water will not dissolve any more crystals. Wear rubber gloves and apply the bleach solution liberally with a synthetic sponge to the wood surface and let it dry overnight. Wash the surface the next day with plenty of clean water, then dry it well. If some of the stain does appear to be bleached out you can repeat the application two or three times.

Oxalic acid is bleach that works on a wide variety of stains: water rings, ink stains, silvered wood, and stains made by iron. It can be bought at most hardware stores in 1 lb. boxes. Wear a dust mask, gloves and eye protection when mixing and using this product.

Mix 2 oz. of oxalic acid with 1 quart of very warm water and stir. Once the acid is dissolved, apply the mixture liberally over the entire surface and let dry overnight. Wash the next day with liberal amounts of water and dry the surface thoroughly. If any improvement is shown you can repeat the procedure.

Both these bleaching treatments require the liberal use of water. Dry the wood as quickly as possible, but not so quickly as to cause the wood to crack or warp. Do not place it in the sun or use excessive heat. Having a fan blowing moderately temperate air over the surface of the wood is advantageous in drying your project well. Once the surface is dry you will probably need to sand it with 220 grit paper or finer.

Cleaning the Metal

The best way to clean the metal parts seems to be sand blasting. You get rid of any rust and create a new clean surface for the paint to adhere to. There are a number of commercial sandblasters listed in the yellow pages. You will need to organize your time so that you can drop off the metal parts with the sandblaster the night before, have the sandblasting done the following morning, and then pick up the work in time so that you can prime the work right away. It is not a good idea to leave your valuable metal carriages parts with the

Tire bolt

Countersunk Head.

Bastard Head.

Shaft coupling bolt, plain pattern for round holes.

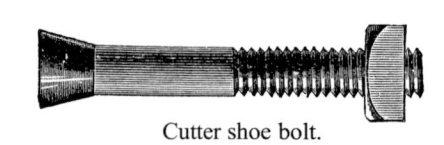

Cutter shoe bolt.

Shaft Coupling bolt, square neck pattern.

Preparing for Painting

sandblaster for days at a time until he gets to sandblasting them because with such an assortment of parts, things could get lost. When readying the pieces to go to the sand blaster you must pick through and see that pieces sent can not be damaged by the commercial sandblaster.

The axle spindles should not be sand blasted. Clean the axle spindles and wrap them up securely with some bright colored duct tape to protect them. Kerosene or similar cleaning solvents can be used to clean grease, oil and dirt from axle spindles. Once the axle parts are cleaned wipe them with some WD 40 ® to keep them from rusting until you put the vehicle back together. By wrapping the axle arm, and nut, or nuts, with paper or a bread wrapper and using duct tape over the wrapper, the axle spindles will be safe from sandblasting and future painting operations. Try not to let any tape surfaces touch the axle spindles, because as time goes on tape tends to stick itself fast to the surface and you will need solvents to clean it off. Other parts that should not be sandblasted with the iron carriage parts are soft metals such as brass oil caps and door handles. To protect the threads of bolts from being worn by sand-blasting the nuts should be threaded back on the bolts. Spring leaves need to be separated so they can be sand blasted in between the leaves. You could tie the spring leaves together with a large coil of wire, so the leaves can be moved around for sand blasting between the leaves.

You might want to sand blast some of the more delicate pieces where there is still wood

Duct tape any wood surfaces next to metal before sandblasting.

attached to the metal with a small sand blasting unit. If you don't have one you can rent one. The wheels should not be sent to a commercial sandblaster. To sand blast the metal on the wheels, such as the rubber tire channel or steel tire and metal hub bands, you will need to mask off the wooden surface around the metal with duct tape. When sandblasting you should always wear a sandblast hood, heavy leather gloves and long sleeve shirt and pants. If you do sandblasting for extended periods of time it is recommended that a sand respirator be worn to prevent breathing large amounts of the abrasive. To increase your chances of having a trouble free day sandblasting you should never try to sand blast in humid weather and the sand must always be perfectly dry. A very fine grade of silica sand the same size as table salt, blasted at 80-90 p.s.i., is the most trouble free. Greater pressure than 90 p.s.i. will sometimes pit old metal which will then require more filler to get a smooth finish. If the metal has been severely rusted it may require filling up the pit marks. Pettit's Filler #7125 ® or Duro's Epoxy Cement Filler ® are recommended.

Preparing for Painting

Cleaning Small Metal Pieces

Small bolts and screws can be cleaned in muriatic (hydrochloric) acid, available at most hardware stores. Rubber gloves, eye protection, and a good supply of fresh air are essential when working with this acid. Place all metal parts to be treated in a glass jar and carefully pour in the acid until it covers all the parts. The acid works slowly, but about one-half hour usually does the trick. Then pour the acid and the bolts into a large pail of water to dilute the acid. You can dispose of it without hurting your plumbing. Muriatic acid has water in it and this will rust the metal again quite quickly so you must place the parts in a jar of lacquer thinner to remove the moisture. After about ten minutes, remove the parts, wipe them carefully with a towel, and let them sit for several hours in a warm place to dry. When dry, you will notice a yellow residue on the parts. This can be removed by using a wire wheel in a variable speed drill or a wire brush wheel on a bench grinder. A pair of vise grips will be needed to hold small parts. Then prime the same as the other metal using metal primer. (from Tim Ragle)

Once metal pieces have been sandblasted or cleaned, the metal must be primed immediately, as bare metal will start to oxidize when exposed to air. A good way to get everything primed is have an assortment of screw eyes with nuts. Put these through the bolt holes in spring leaves and other parts with bolt holes and, using some wire, hang them up. Other pieces you can just wrap a piece a wire around a couple of times to hang them up to prime.

Before priming, the metal should be wiped over with a good grease solvent such as Dupont Reducer 3011S®. The first coat of primer may be brushed on, and for this, zinc chromate, or proprietary products such as Pre-parakote®, Rust-Oleum® Red Primer, etc., may be used. Taking the time to brush the parts at this point leads to better adhesion, and any successive coats can either be sprayed or brush painted.

Sanding

This is probably where the true and dedicated carriage enthusiasts are separated from the people who have had a carriage in pieces for several years. Sanding is everything to a good restoration. One of the most time consuming parts of carriages restoration is good sanding, between the many layers of coatings.

Axle clip yoke or tie.

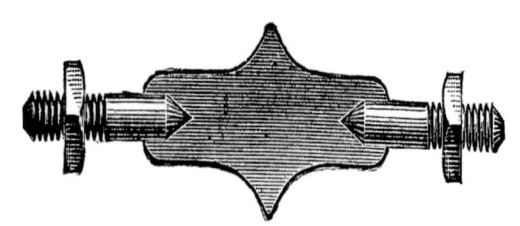

Sleigh clip bolt, point center.

Axle clip--Seward's Heavy Wagon & Rockaway.

Saddle clips--Half round pattern.

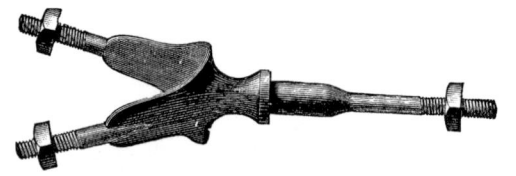

Clip King Bolt--flanged with finished ends.
From S. D. Kimbark, 1888.

108

Preparing for Painting

It is money and time saving to buy good sandpaper. Of the several kinds of sanding paper, the most popular used for sanding on wood is garnet (which is orange-to-red in color), and aluminum-oxide paper, (which is tan-to-brown). Aluminum oxide is a man-made material made in an electric furnace. This hard, man-made material gives it a longer life and good cutting properties that make it last longer than garnet. Some of the trademark names for aluminum oxide paper are Production ®, Three-M-ite®, Imperial®, Cutrite®, Aloxite®, Metalite® and Adalox®.

Sandpaper is graded by a numbering system that designates the number of grids per inch that the granules were screened through. The coarsest is 40 and it goes up to 220 for very fine for garnet and aluminum oxide sandpapers. In sanding there should always be a progression from the coarsest to the finest, with never more than a 80-100 point difference. If you start out with an 80 grit sandpaper it would be a waste to go to 220 grit paper to finish it off, because the scratch marks left by the 80 grit paper are too deep to be taken out by the 220 grit paper. So in the first step of sanding and smoothing down the wood you usually need to go through a series of three progression. These are coarse (60-80), medium (100-120) and fine to very fine (150-180-220) if you are starting with new wood, such as new wheels. If you are starting with wood such as the soft wood of the panels that you have just cleaned off with paint remover and you have not raised the grain of the wood you probably could start with a medium grit and then go to fine. In sanding large flat surfaces by hand it is helpful to fold the paper around a block of wood. There are also several kinds of flexible pads and cork rubbing blocks sold commercially. This way you get more surface area of sandpaper working than if you were just using your fingers. A sand paper block helps to prevent valleys or ridges from your fingers. You can make your own cork rubbing blocks in various sizes to suit your different needs by gluing a 1/4 inch thick piece of cork to a wooden block.

If you use a power sander for flat surfaces it really isn't any faster, just easier. An excellent light-weight sander for carriages is the electric block finishing sander with a sanding surface area of about 4 1/2 x 4 1/2 inches. This has a perfect square which fits nicely into corners, and it also has a foam sanding pad which is very good for use on curved surfaces such as curved dashes of sleighs, wheels or shafts. Garnet paper breaks down faster, so it's best to use Aluminum-oxide paper for power sanding.

STAY CHAIN HOOKS

BOLT PATTERN

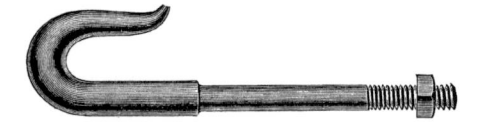

Cleveland Hardware Co.

WAGON CHAINS.

Pole.

Stay.

Lock.

S. D. Kimbark, 1888.

Preparing for Painting

Read the manufacturers directions for your power sander as to what rate you should move the sander in order to prevent oscillating marks from the sander. Using the power sander makes each grit more powerful than when sanding by hand. So if you were using a 180 grit with the power sander it would be like using a 200 grit by hand. For getting into tight places and carvings there are a number of flexible pads and sanding sponges. If you have a carriage that has turned spindles around the seat there are a number of abrasive cords for sanding around the sharp crevices of turnings. To get into the corners and between spokes try using the sandpaper folded over a small plastic ruler. Always sand well in the corners as a build up of paint will have a tendency to crack later. One sign of a good restoration job is that the molding and corners have good definition, so sand those corners and joints of the wheels. As you are sanding, periodically knock the dust out of the sandpaper to keep it cutting longer and brush or blow the dust off your project to keep it from building up unto the sandpaper. You will save time by knowing when it is time to change your sandpaper, rather than letting it wear away after it has lost its cutting edge. Sandpaper deteriorates rather rapidly so changing it often is more efficient. Use aluminum oxide paper for the first couple of steps in the finishing process of your carriage, sanding down the sanding sealer and paste wood filler. When sanding on finishes you are likely to get clumps of finish sticking to the sandpaper in little circles. Keep checking the sandpaper for these and scrap them off with a knife or your fingernail. These clumps of finish prevent the sandpaper from touching the surfaces, cutting the efficiency of the sandpaper. Aluminum oxide paper is also made in closed-coat and open-coat sandpaper. Closed-coat sanding paper has 100% of surface of the paper covered with grit, making it the fastest cutting on bare hardwood. Open-coat sandpaper has only 40% to 70% paper covered with grit, making it much slower to clog, so that even though there are fewer granules of grit it will cut faster and last longer when you are sanding finished surfaces or softwoods.

An alternative to open-coat paper offered by some companies is a sandpaper with special coating that reduces clogging. This paper is usually white or grey in color. Sanding coats of primer and finishes can sometimes be trying, as it keeps clogging up the sandpaper. Once you have gotten several coats of paint on and you are safe from sanding into bare wood you have the option of using a more powerful cutting paper know as silicon carbide. This paper can be used for wet sanding and along with a bar of Fels Naptha® soap in the water bucket this paper does not clog up as fast. This paper is primarily used in only the finest grades, from about 220 fine to ultra fine 600 grit, even through coarser and finer grits are available. Silicon carbide paper is a very uniform blue-black color. It uses a waterproof adhesive to adhere this grit to a water proof paper to be used dry or wet for sanding. In addition to dry/wet sandpaper silicon

WHIFFLETREE COUPLINGS

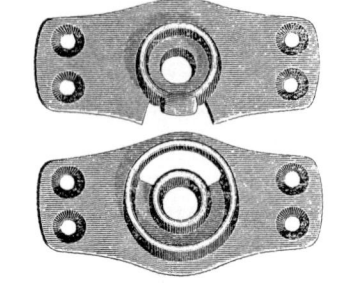

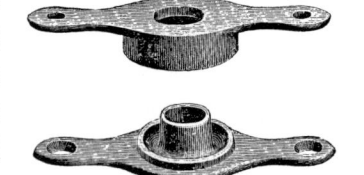

S. D. Kimbark, 1888.

Preparing for Painting

carbide paper can come as a dry paper with a special preloaded dry lubricant to eliminate clogging and heating. This paper is white to grey in color.

Wet sanding helps to prevent the sand paper from clogging up and eliminates the dust associated with dry sanding.

After each sanding it is important to clean all the dust or sludge off. If wet sanding, rinse water over the job with a sponge and with tooth brushes clean around the joints and moldings. Wring your sponge out dry and wipe the job so that it dries off quickly. Added help might be to use the air compressor to blow air around the joints and moldings. When dry sanding you can wipe your job clean with a dry clean rag or a rag with some solvent that you are going to use in your next application of finish. Brush the dust from the project, vacuum, or blow off with compressed air. Compressed air is probably the best way to get all the dust out of the grain and cracks. The disadvantage is you blow dust all over your shop and unless you have a finishing room you need to get all the dust out of the shop before applying finishes.

Preparing the Wood

After all the wood has been thoroughly sanded, decontaminated, and free from dust, it makes the job of brushing or spraying of successive coats go along a lot faster if you use a sanding sealer and paste wood filler. Open grained wood such as oak, ash and hickory should be rubbed with a paste wood filler. There are prepared wood fillers available in colors or if your project is to be finished in natural wood you can buy a neutral color and tint it to the color of your project. Using a paste wood filler saves time by not having to try and fill up the grain of the wood with layer after layer of primer. Filling the grain prevents the top coats from shrinking into the grain later on and showing the grain. It is important to pick a paste wood filler that will be compatible with the rest of your coats of finish. An oil base-filler is most likely for carriage restoration when you are brush painting carriages and for spray painting see if there is a recommended wood filler from your automotive paint supplier.

In applying paste wood filler, first stir it up thoroughly in the can and then portion some of it out into a clean container. Some paste wood fillers come the consistency of custard and some people are able to work with it that way. Others prefer to thin it by adding turpentine, naphtha, or mineral spirits, bringing it to the consistency of heavy cream. Brush the filler on with a large stiff brush, and allow it to become partially dry about 20 to 30 minutes. Then work it into the grain by rubbing across the grain with a piece of burlap, nylon abrasive pad or open mesh sandpaper. A circular rubbing motion can also be used. Work one area at a time, so that you are able to wipe off the excess before it dries completely. Remove the excessive filler

WEAR IRONS

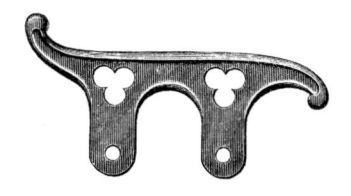

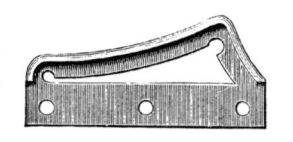

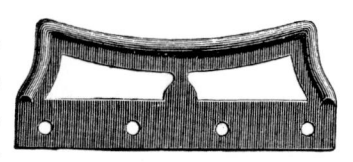

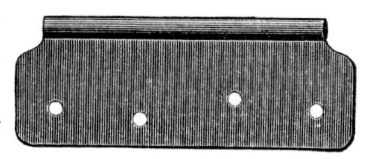

S. D. Kimbark, 1888.

Preparing for Painting

with the burlap and then give it a gentle wipe with the grain, using a lint free rag. Let it dry at least 24 hours or up to three days.

There does not seem to be any hard and fast rule about which to apply first, the sanding sealer or the paste wood filler. In only rare instances is it important to apply the sanding sealer first then the paste wood filler. There are a number of prepared sanding sealers on the market or you can make your own by thinning shellac with denatured alcohol or ethanol. True Value Hardware® sells Enrich® Interior sanding sealer. Brush on for the best adhesion, or some people use a rag to wipe on shellac when it is thinned for a sealer. Prepared shellac has a shelf life of only six months, and if you should buy a can that is too old it will be difficult to get it to dry. Shellac flakes are available at specialty houses for wood finishers or through mail order catalogs and you can mix your own sealer. A sanding sealer should be very thin so that it is able to penetrate the wood for good adhesion and be fast and hard drying so that it is easily sanded. Sanding sealer also helps stop the migration of the moisture from the wood to painted surfaces. Applying the paste wood filler first makes it easier to get the grain filled up, but if your are trying to get a certain look with a project that you want to finish in natural wood you might want to apply the sealer first.

Carriage restoration is a rather unique type of restoration and it differs from other restorations mainly because you are dealing in a large part with wood and metal being combined into one artistic artifact. Metal and wood contract and expand at different rates under varying conditions of humidity and heat. A carriage is different from a furniture restoration. Not only is the metal and wood contracting and expanding at different rates by natural forces, but all these small parts are put into motion when the vehicle is moved by a horse over a road surface. Carriages are different from car restorations after the 1910's, because with cars you don't have to worry so much with the undercarriage showing and being a piece of artistic work. This point we cannot stress enough. If you want to do a good restoration job that lasts a long time you need to do good preparatory work. Originally all the small individual parts of carriages, even the nuts and bolts and undersurface that you never saw, were coated with a protective coating to help prevent rust on metal and moisture entering wood. This was known to be a lead base coating in most cases. This was done with all the better class carriages and then after much preparation all the little parts nuts, bolts, screws and spring leaves, etc. were assembled. This lead base primer seemed to be the perfect solution for carriage painting, it was long lasting and elastic. In order to prevent the paint from cracking between the joints of metal and wood and spring leaves, you need to have as much work done as possible on the little pieces before assembling.

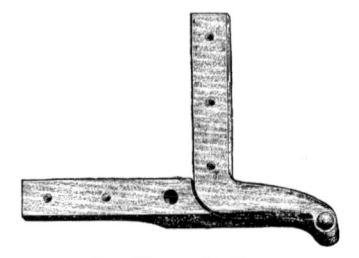

BOTTOM DOOR HINGES.

New Haven Pattern.

COACH HINGES.

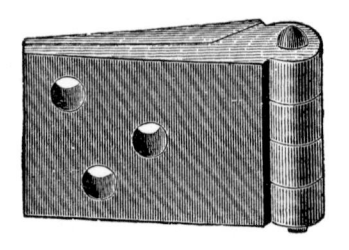

Malleable Iron. Double Joint.

COACH LOCKS.

Phœnix Pattern.

French Pattern.

S. D. Kimbark, 1888.

Preparing for Painting

Finishing Springs

Each spring leaf should have been primed and sanded smooth and have a coat of color on it before assembly. Be prepared in carriage restoration, if you want a good job, to do lots and lots of sanding. If you rely on layers and layers of paint to build up a smooth surface you will run the risk of the paint cracking as the vehicle contracts and expands. Have several tooth brushes handy to clean out the corners of moldings and joints of wheel spokes as you are sanding between coats, since any sludge left in the cracks and corners will cause poor adhesion for the successive coats. Sand in the corners well to avoid build up of paint. Once you have all your parts prepared you can assemble them. Sand any nicks and scratches that occurred in assembly Then put on a final light coat of color and, if brush painting, the successive coats of varnish. Springs should be put together with a small amount of grease applied between the leaves. After assembling the leaves make sure any excess grease is wipe away with degreaser to avoid contamination for future applications of paint and varnish.

BODY STEPS.

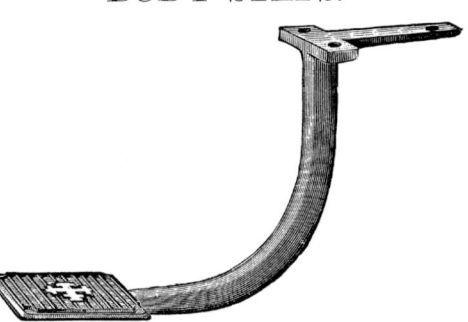

Brewster Pattern. Finished Yoke.

FRONT BODY STEPS.

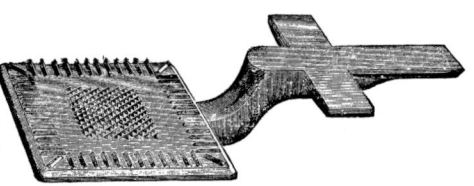

Diamond Pattern, Forged.

The Finish

There are several ways of obtaining a high gloss finish on a carriage. The old coach painters based their method of finishing with several coats of varnish, and no modern system can produce a finish to match the sheen and elegance of first class varnish work. But nothing looks worse than a poorly done job. All of the work was done by brush, of course, and the procedure is described in several old handbooks. One advantage claimed for the old way is that the finish is more resilient and less likely to chip or flake off due to movement where wood and metal meet. However, anyone trying to follow the old methods today will encounter many difficulties; the old materials are hard to obtain; a paint mill and other special tools are needed; a dust-free and temperature-controlled environment is needed for the final finish with slow drying varnish; and the skill acquired through a long apprenticeship under a master painter is necessary. Brush painting, using readily obtainable materials, can be done and it has some advantages over spraying, so both systems will be described.

SHAFT STEPS.

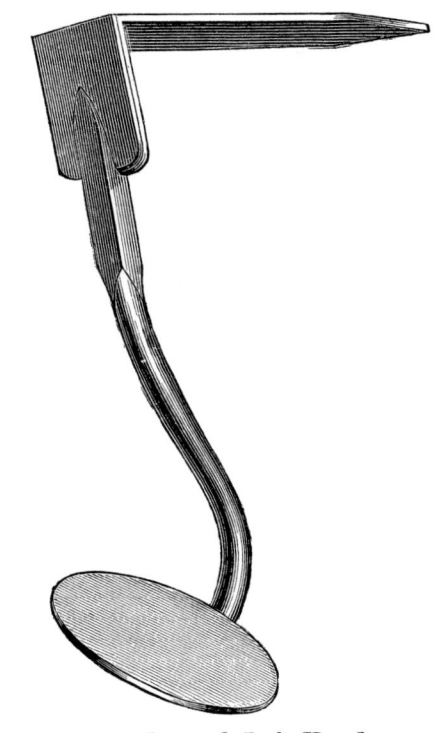

Oval Pads. Right and Left Hand.

S. D. Kimbark, 1888.

Preparing for Painting

The principles of surface preparation are the same for both methods; the aim being to get a perfectly smooth surface before beginning the color coats. After using the sanding sealer and paste wood filler, coats of primer are needed to additionally prepare an absolutely smooth surface. Use oil base or alkyd enamel primer for brushing and an automotive spray primer enamel if spraying. It is a good plan to have the first coat of a different color to subsequent coats, called the guide coat, so that, when rubbing down, if the first coat is exposed one knows it is time to stop rubbing. Any color left by the guide coat might mean that the surface needs to have the small pin holes and dents filled with spot putty. The spot putty sold at the automotive paint store is good for both the brush painting method and spray painting method. It is made to go between layers of paint and relatively fast drying. Spot putty is not for large size holes and it will shrink away, so if you are trying to fill a larger hole you should use an epoxy or reapply the spot putty and give it more time to dry. Apply the putty as level as possible with a flexible putty knife and when it is dry sand all the spots level.

Bibliography and further references:

Dresdner, Michael. Wood Finishing Book. Newton, CT : Tauntom Press, 1992.

Flexner, Bob. Understanding Wood Finishing. Emmaus, PA : Rodale Press, 1994.

Ragle, Tim. "Authentic Carriage Restoration." Carriage Journal. Vol. 26 no. 4 (Spring 1989), pp. 161-167.

Spielman, Patrick. Gluing and Clamping : A Woodworker's Handbook. New York, NY : Sterling Publishing Co., 1984.

The Carriage Museum of America wishes to acknowledge and thank the following for information used from their publications.

Some information reprinted from Understanding Wood Finishing, copyright 1994 by Bob Flexner. Permission granted by Rodale Press, Inc., Emmaus, PA 18098-0099

Some information excerpted with permission from The Woodfinishing Book by Michael Dresdner copyright 1992 by The Taunton Press, Inc. All rights reserved.

CHAPTER 11

BRUSH PAINTING

Brush painting is thought by some to be the better way of painting a carriage because the materials used for brush painting (oil-base varnishes) are reactive finishes and inherently elastic. Reactive finishes are paints and varnishes, that when exposed to the air a chemical reaction is set in motion within the finish as the solvent evaporates. This causes the finish to dry slower and more flexible. Evaporative finishes (shellac and lacquer) when exposed to air the solvent evaporates from the finish causing no chemical reaction within the finish. These finishes dry very hard, and non-elastic.

Brush painting is probably the more cost effective for people who are only restoring a few carriages. To spray paint, you need an air compressor and spray gun (which can be rented if need be). But these days there are so many strict regulations that must be followed, that for an individual to set up his own spray operation for a few vehicles is prohibitively expensive. Brush painting has it problems too. There are now regulations in many areas on the use and disposal of many solvents used for brush painting. Besides the use of solvents the negative side of brush painting is that it takes longer for the finish coats to dry, and requires more careful housekeeping practices. Dust landing on the finish is always a problem. Carriage factories a hundred years ago had a room specially reserved for varnishing. Fresh air was allowed to enter through specially fitted dust proof screens over vents and windows.

The Brush

The most important tool of brush painting is the brush. Natural bristle brushes are used with carriage painting and modern synthetic brushes are designed for and work better with water base paints. Some people have expressed a liking for the new modern disposable foam brushes, but they probably won't replace the brush entirely because there are still people who prefer a good brush. Good brushes are expensive, but they can more than pay for themselves in the quality of work they perform and they can become your long time friend if you treat them right. Natural bristle brushes are made of bristles glued together at the top with a setting compound of glue or epoxy and held to a wooden handle by a wrapping called a ferrule. The setting compound used to bind the bristles can vary and can be dissolved by some strong solvents such as lacquer thinner, thereby destroying the brush. There are three different physical forms of bristles: 1. Non-tapered bristles are square on the tip end. This is most often caused by the brush manufacturer not taking the time to sort the bristles and they are just cut off to make an even edge. 2. Tapered bristles start out a thicker diameter at the handle end and taper to a point at the tip of the brush 3. Flagged bristles are tapered bristles with fuzzy hairs on the tip end, much like the condition of split ends in humans. Only in this case it is a desirable quality because it allows the paint brush to load up more paint at the tip of the brush.

The most common commercially sold natural bristle brush is known as China Bristle. This brush has hair that comes from a hog, usually raised in France, Russia, India or China. The best bristles, come from the hog's back and they are washed, boiled, sterilized and, for softer bristles, bleach is used. The bristles are then sorted into different grades of soft, thin, silky, stocky, black and white bristles etc., so among China Bristle brushes there is going to be quite a selection from cheap brushes to more expensive brushes. These brushes have flagged bristle tips which are better for working with thin paints and low solid varnishes.

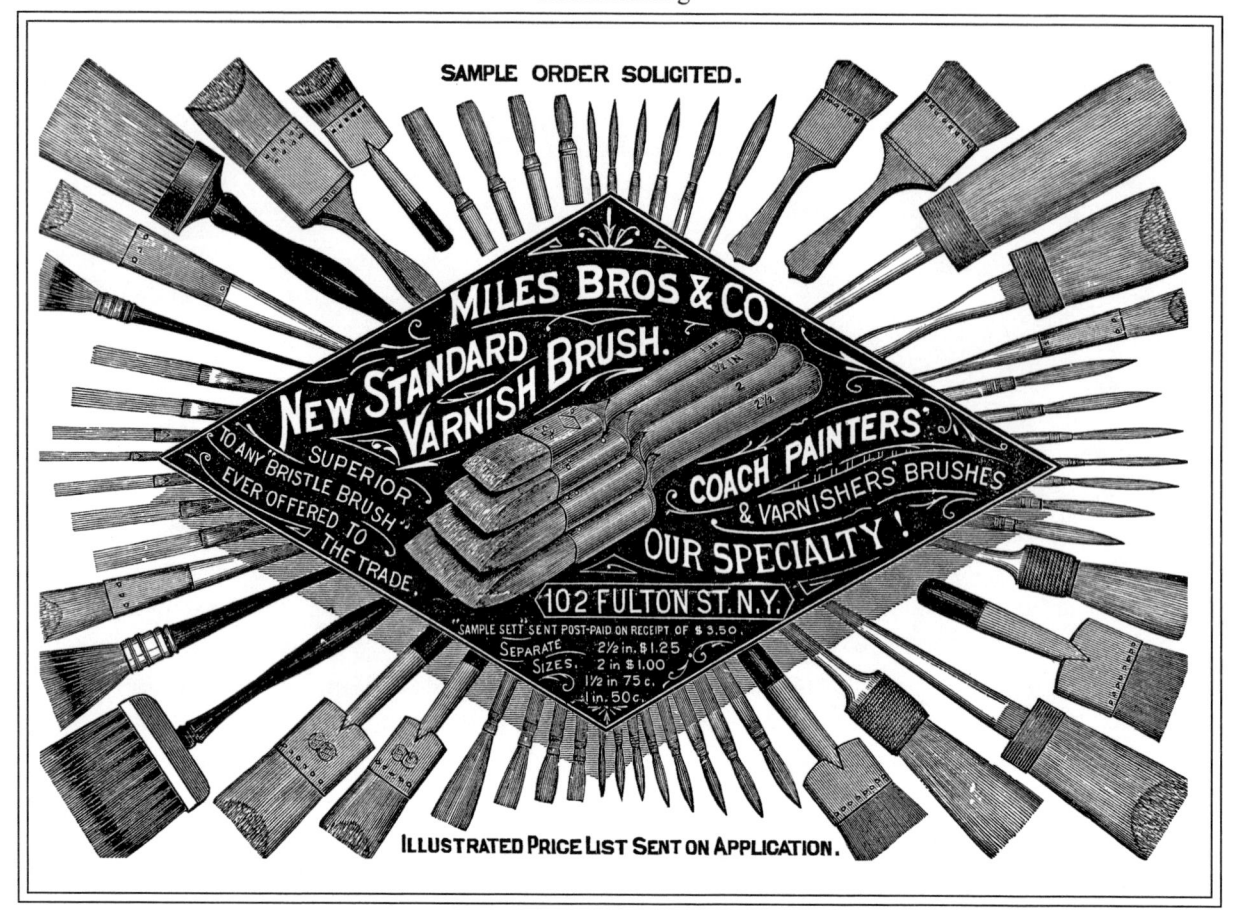

From the Carriage Monthly November 1885

The old carriage painters' manuals often speak of badger hair brushes for varnishing. A varnish brush made of real badger hair would cost over a hundred dollars. The best brush that replaces the badger brush is the Corona 16055®, recommended by Quill Hair and Ferrule. While not made out of 100% badger hair, it looks and feels like the badger hair brush. It has tapered bristles to allow heavy solid varnishes to flow out. Other desirable qualities are that the bristles are arranged to what is know as a chisel edge, rather than all the bristles being arranged square at the tip.

Brush Care

In order to have your brush as a long time friend, proper cleaning and storage is essential. After use, wipe the excess paint out by brushing it on a scrap piece of wood or a piece of cardboard or gently squeeze the excess out between some paper towels or rags. Then rinse the brush out gently by swirling and swishing it in a container of turpentine or mineral spirits. Repeat this operation as often as needed until there is no longer any evidence of varnish or paint coming from the brush. When cleaning, never push the brush to the bottom or hard against the sides of the container. This can damage, break or bend the bristles

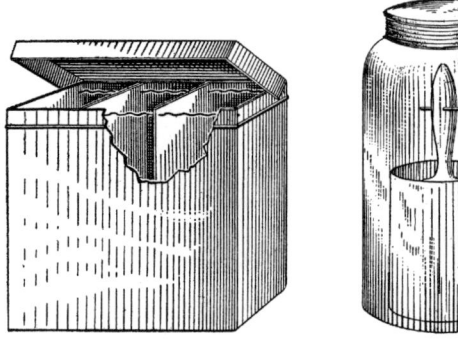

Brush Keeper Boxes
From the Hub July 1895

out of shape. If the paint doesn't want to come out next to the ferrule, put on protective gloves and gently work the bristles through your fingers to dislodge the paint or varnish. If there is a paint and varnish build up, only occasionally should stronger solvents be used, as they tend to be rather harsh to natural bristles, drying them out. Brushes used daily are sometimes laid out in a shallow pan filled with clean mineral spirits. They will be ready for use the next day. Many times old coach painters had a container filled with a solution and by using a hook or rod through the handle they suspended the brush in the container, making sure the bristles didn't touch the bottom. Solvent evaporation can be reduced by placing plastic wrap around the top or cutting a hole

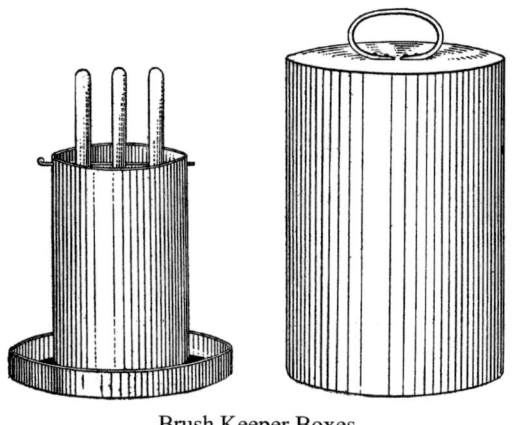

Brush Keeper Boxes
From the Hub July 1895

in a plastic lid for the handle and laying it over the top of the container. This will also prevent dust and dirt getting into the container. For storing brushes that are not going to be used for a while, first dry them (do not place them near excessive heat or you will shrink the wood away from the ferrule) and then wipe the bristles with oil that does not contain any detergents or cleaners. Some people use mineral oil, Neatsfoot oil or specialty oil preparations just for brushes that are made by specialty brush manufacturers. Shape the bristles and wrap the brush in a piece of construction paper or a paper towel. Secure it with masking tape or a rubber band. Store the brush in a safe place, such as a drawer or a sealed tuperware box (natural bristles can be eaten by moths). Most brushes also have a hole in the handle so that you can hang them on the wall. With the wrapper on it, it will stay clean and you will have a brush that is ready to use next time, rather than trying to shop for and break in a new brush. Quality brushes are not available at most stores but can be ordered from catalogs of specialty brush manufacturers. Art supply stores might carry some.

After taking the brush out of the wrapper, presoak it in the appropriate solvent to rinse out the oil and to "Load the Reservoir". The brush reservoir is the space below the wooden handle which is partly surrounded by the metal ferrule. Getting solvent into this area helps to act as a buffer between the paint and the brush. When working, the paint is never loaded on the brush that high. The higher up the paint tends to get on the brush the more it is apt to dry out, since you are only using the to ½ of the bottom of the brush for brushing. Without the reservoir of solvent to keep the paint from drying out on the top half of the brush, you might accidentally get dry flakes or semi dry paint deposits into your brush work. Presoaking allows for easier cleanup when you are finished with your paint job for the day, since it helps to prevent paint from depositing in the hard-to-reach places of the ferrule. For coach and carriage painting you will need to invest in a selection of good brushes. These include wide flat brushes for panels, narrower brushes to go around spokes, and small soft brushes for wiping the excess varnish from molding, corners and around the edges of nuts.

Primer Coats

For your program of carriage painting you should follow through with the coats of sanding sealer, paste wood filler, primer, color coats and varnish being oil-base or alkyds modified oil resins. This way you keep everything compatible, as some very hard finishes will lift the paint when applied over softer finishes. For priming you will need a high quality primer or undercoat that dries well, is elastic, and gap filling. Many household primers don't dry well enough for sanding, so if you are picking out a primer for the first time you might want to try a small area first to make sure that it dries sandable (doesn't gum up the sandpaper) in a day or two. Mixing a little Japan Drier[1] with the paint can speed up the drying time. Using Japan Drier is a very delicate situation and you can upset the balance very easily. It would require experience and experimenting to know when you have gotten it just right. Too much drier will cause the finish to dry hard and brittle. Recommend are any high quality marine undercoat or primer that is suitable for oil paints. These are designed with all sorts of tough requirements in mind and hold up well. The higher quality primers usually have a greater amount of titanium dioxide and calcium carbonate. Titanium dioxide is an excellent material but it is expensive and used only in the better primers and paints. Mr. Hillick remarked in 1898 that *"First-class paint and varnish stock is more handily worked and will cover more surface than inferior stock, and judged from any point of view one may elect it is the most economical material to buy."* In selecting a paint it is a certainty that the higher the price the better the paint. Higher priced paints contain more costly ingredients that give better working qualities, coverage, and long-term performance. Once it is determined what it is that you want your paint to do, it is economical in the long run to buy the best grade. Some products recommended by carriage members are Pettit's White Yacht Undercoater #6165®, Hi Hide® made by the Zar Varnish Company, and Enamel Undercoater California Brand®, primer/filler made by California Products Corp., Cambridge, MA.

If you have a really good sandable primer, some carriage members apply four to five coats of primer with only a light sanding between coats, allowing each coat to dry sufficiently in between before brushing on another coat. Other members like to sand with greater care in between coats, depending on which way suits you. It is helpful when sanding to have a guide coat and this can be done by making the last coat of primer a different color. Lampblack or dark universal tint can be added to some of the primer poured off in a can or purchase two quarts and add color to one quart. Sanding away the guide coat (top color) allows you to see instantly when the surface is smooth. It is important to sand down the surface until it is smooth as glass, using #200 to #320 sandpaper, with or without water as a lubricant. Otherwise any imperfections will be magnified in the color coats and varnish. (from Tim Ragle)

Color

To successfully brush paint, it is necessary to use a paint that has been formulated for brush work. While it is possible to add reducers to make a suitable brushing enamel, it is not possible to modify a spraying paint so that it can be successfully applied by brush. For carriage painting use an oil-base alkyd enamel, such as is made by several paint manufacturers. Recommended by carriage members are Pettit of New Jersey, Benjamin Moore, California Products Larcoloid High Gloss Enamel of Cambridge, MA., and Pratt and Lambert. These paints can be made either long oil or short oil. Long oil means that it is made with a higher percentage of oil. Traditionally coach painters used long oil varnishes and paints because they discovered that varnishes made with a high percentage of oil were more elastic and better wearing for coach painting. A good paint store owner should have the specification sheets for the different paints that are sold or he can call the manufacturer and find out whether it is short or long oil. It is all very frustrating, shopping for a paint that is going to work well for carriage painting, because when you do find something that works

---

[1] Japan driers or metallic driers are heavy metal salts or soaps added to drying oils in order to speed up the cure. Their action is a true catalytic one. They initiate or speed polymerization without changing chemically or becoming part of the molecule. The metals remain trapped in the matrix of the dried film. From *The Woodfinishing Book* by Michael Dresdner

well for you, the ingredients can change the next time you go to buy the same paint. In the United States the way paint is made is influenced by two major things: 1. The Environmental Protection Agency, which is putting pressure on paint manufacturers to change their ingredients to less toxic substances and to convert to water base paints. 2. Large paint companies that have established a good name are being bought up by other companies and the ingredients may change if a more cost effective product can be made. It is recommended that if you want a quality paint you shop at a good paint store rather than the discount department stores. Quality paints are going to be the more expensive paints because they use the more expensive ingredients.

Recommended is to apply 4 to 5 coats of color, with a light sanding in between. This way you don't run the risk of sanding through the color and having it too thin in spots on the final sanding (with #320 to #400 grit sandpaper). Once you have stirred the paint it is a good idea to have extra paint strainers and containers to pour and strain off from the can only what you are going to use at a time. Once the can is open it can start to be contaminated from the air and if you are constantly dipping your brush in and out this adds to containments, so that when you seal the can up at the end of the day it isn't as fresh as when you started. When you are able to sand down each coat with the wet-or-dry paper and the paint particles wash cleanly off the paper you know it is dry and you can continue. Apply each coat with great care as any errors such as drips will be made worse by further painting. Large drips can be removed easily and cleanly with a sharp chisel if the coat underneath is dry. After the fourth coat has been applied, allow the paint four or five days drying time. Then proceed to sand the work carefully with #320 grit paper. If you are afraid of cutting through the paint, use #400 paper instead and be very careful on sharp edges or corners which might cut through to the primer with little more than one hard rubbing.

Painting Wheels

To facilitate painting wheels you will need to have your wheels arranged so that they can be rotated and reached from both sides. One method is to insert a piece of pipe about 5 or 6 ft. through the boxing and place it between two saw horses. You will need to anchor the ends of pipe on the saw horses so that they don't roll off. Cut a notch in the top of the saw horses for the pipe to fit part way into or tack a nail on each side of the pipe or small boards and nails. Start by painting a face and side of a spoke. Brush it down to the hub bands. Turn the wheel until the back of the spoke is visible and paint the other face and side. In this manner a portion of the hub and the spoke are done simultaneously and you are able to brush out all drips as you go. For fast work you can do the same step to two or three spokes at a time before painting the back-sides. After six or seven spokes have been painted give the wheel a good spin. The centrifugal force will make the paint spread evenly and eliminate brush marks. Repeat as required. Next, paint the inside of the hubs and then finish the job by painting the felloes. There are a lot of ways of painting wheels, find the one that works best for you. (From Tim Ragle)

Varnish

Traditionally carriage painting included coats of varnish over the coats of color, giving the paint a depth and sheen not seen in any other process. Varnish coats with transparent pigments in them called glaze coats were sometimes used before the final clear coats of varnish. Using glazed coats gave the finish an additional depth mirroring the color coats underneath. Varnish for coach and carriage painting originally had four main ingredients : oil (linseed oil), resin (copal), solvent (turpentine), and metallic driers (lead and others) . Copal was a fossilized sap(resin) from trees that grew largely in Africa millions of years ago. The resin was imported melted and mixed with the other ingredients for various types of varnishes : rubbing, wearing, elastic wearing, body varnish etc. Even back when carriages were being made, copal was an expensive resin for varnish and only the best carriages were painted with the most expensive grades of varnish. Chemists of the early twentieth century begin developing synthetic resins which are more consistent in quality, availability and affordability. Phenolic resin (a combination of phenol and formaldehyde) was the first. Second was alkyd-resin (oils modified by ALCohol and an acID, hence the name AlCID, or more phonetically ALKYD) varnish, developed around the 1920's. This resin was cheaper and has become widely used in various types of finishes other than just varnish. A third varnish resin called polyurethane (derived from petroleum) was developed by chemist around the 1930's. Polyurethane is the toughest of the varnishes and the most scratch-resistant. Pure polyurethane finishes are sold in two parts that can be mixed together. Another variety is alkyd varnish modified with polyurethane resin, an uralkyd. The making of varnish has seen a change in the oils used from linseed oil that has a tendency to yellow, to the use of tung oil (processed from the seeds or nuts from the subtropical tung tree) that is less yellowing. Later oils were developed from soybean (soya) oil and safflower which are less yellowing than tung oil and cheaper to produce. Once the resin and oil are mixed and melted together they require a drier and traditionally this was lead metallics which offered great wearing properties to finishes. Warnings were published about the hazards of lead in paint for coach and carriage painters, but there didn't seem to be any substitute for the durability that lead offered to finishes. Finally the Food and Drug Administration (FDA) ruled against the use of lead in certain classes of paint that are used around the house. Present day driers for varnishes include cobalt, manganese, zinc, and zirconium.

The solvent used for making coach and carriage varnish was turpentine, a steam-distilled product from the sap of pine trees, largely produced in the Carolinas. This was found to be the most perfect solvent available at the time, and during the Civil War when turpentine could not be obtained, chemists put a great deal of effort into trying to find a substitute but nothing could be found that was as good as turpentine and some painters still prefer it today. **Never leave turpentine soaked rags laying around the shop as they will spontaneously combust.** Turpentine was thought to be the cause of many carriage factory fires. The modern day substitute for turpentine is mineral spirits or naphtha which are solvents distilled from petroleum. Naphtha evaporates more quickly than mineral spirits and is less oily. Naphtha used as solvent would cause the paint or varnish to dry quicker, and give you less time to work the finish with the brush.

There are two main divisions of varnish determined by the ratio of oil to resin. *Long-oil* varnish has a greater ratio of oil in it making it more flexible and softer when cured, and this type is generally sold as "spar" and "marine" varnish. *Short-oil* or *Medium-oil* varnish has a low percentage of oil and this varnish is usually sold as an interior varnish where the wood has less movement and a harder finish is desirable. The mixture of different resins and oils can affect the characteristics of varnish as : Phenolic resin often combined with a high percentage of tung oil is a spar varnish for outdoor use that is water-resistant and flexible and yellows significantly. Phenolic resin combined with a low percentage of tung oil is a hard rubbing varnish for tabletops, that can be rubbed to a high finish. Alkyd resin is not as tough as phenolic resin, but it doesn't yellow as much and is cheaper. Alkyd resin combined with polyurethane resin is the toughest of the varnishes, but it has the disadvantage of not bonding well with other finishes, it doesn't hold up well in sunlight and it has a slightly cloudy appearance. What makes varnish such a good finish is its excellent resistance to heat, wear, solvents, acids, water-vapor, and water. It is slow drying making it easy to brush without getting tacky and dragging. The paradox is that the long curing time associated with varnish is also a disadvantage, because dust can easily get on the finish.

Some of the varnishes that have been used by modern carriage painters are V62 Extra Pale Varnish manufacturered by Mason Paints, England, and varnish made by Pettit of Rockaway, NJ., and McCloskey. Shop at a quality paint store and have patience until you find the varnish that works best for you. Modern varnishes that are readily available tend to be somewhat amber in color, (all varnishes yellow with age) and this needs to be taken into consideration when varnishing over colors, as the color can become somewhat off from the original shade. The modern varnishes that come closest to the old varnish are long oil varnishes with alkyd resin. Carriage and coach painting was no less fustrating in the horse-drawn vehicle era. There were several books and numerous articles on the subject of painting and varnishing. In 1898 there were 13 varnish makers, each having 12-20 different kinds in their product line, all claiming to have the perfect varnish for carriage painting. There was no one secret reference book or varnish that was the answer. Master carriage painters learned from years of experience and practice.

Applying Varnish

Generally speaking, coach and carriage varnishes needed to be elastic, and this meant long-oil varnishes were used that took a longer time to dry. They were flowed on wet with a brush and brushed lightly again over the top with a soft brush this eliminated brush marks, runs, sags, excess varnish, and build up in the corners. There doesn't seem to be any way of applying varnish that is more correct than another. It is mostly a matter of practice and finding the way that is right for you.. Some people find foam brushes satisfactory while other prefer a good natural bristle brush.

The following directions on how to varnish a brougham come from the "Coach-Makers' Illustrated Hand-Book" published in 1875 that might be used as a guide.

The beauty of the finishing coat depends almost entirely on the perfection to which the rubbing or leveling coats are brought up. We will now endeavor to explain the points assumed, first directing our remarks to the use of rubbing varnish.[Varnish is a finish that does not bond well to itself, so a mechanical bond needs to be established between coats by sanding}.

1st. *The varnish should not be patched on.*

By this we mean, that the varnish, when applied to any part of the surface of a body, should be brushed over a certain part, previously decided on, which will, when completed, form a connecting whole, without laps, and not, as is the practice with many painters, lay on the varnish only the width of the brush at a time, and that so lightly that when a fault appears the varnish is found to be set too much to be worked and blended together. The attempt to rebrush the defective part, be it a run or heavy lap, will be found of no avail. The unsightly joint, if such it may be called, will not unite with the rest of the varnish, and nothing but the strong arm and skill of the rubber will remove it. Just here we would say, that a first-class varnish rubber is one of the most important hands in a body room.

2d. *On all large connecting surfaces more varnish should be applied than it is intended to leave on.*

We will take, for example, the upper back panels of a coach. The back light, or window, and the drip molding over it, divide the surface into what we might term four spaces; two vertical portions, and two which are horizontal. To lay a level coat over this portion of a body, the varnish should be put on quite heavy. No attempt should be made to level the varnish until a sufficient quantity has been put on over the whole surface to insure against its setting. Having applied it as stated, run through it quickly with the large brush, and with a smaller one carry a portion of the varnish upon and underneath the drip molding.

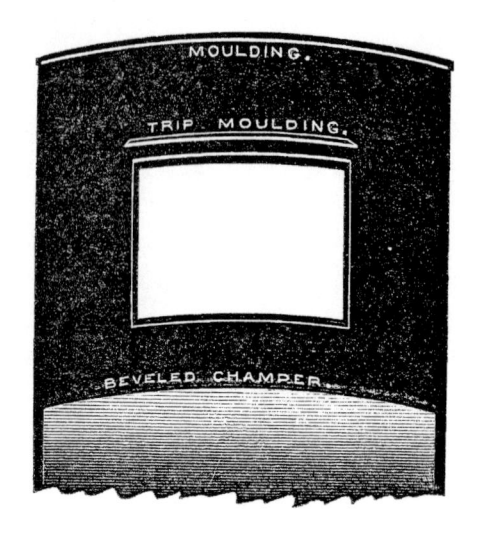

This first laying off of the varnish is designed to connect it over the whole surface; and while the skillful varnisher will spread it with a view to having about an equal quantity over every part, he will not care so much for that as to be certain that he has a sufficient quantity applied to insure it against setting before he has properly manipulated it.

The next care will be to remove a portion of the varnish above and beneath the drip molding, and around the back light, to prevent it from sagging, after which he again addresses himself to the panels, this time with a view to the proper leveling of the whole. His quick eye detects those portions where the varnish is heaviest, and by up and down or by cross brushing, as it may require, the varnish is leveled off. Again the tool (small varnish brush) is passed around, or under the moldings, and then the panels are brushed horizontally over every part, and finished by vertical strokes.

During this whole operation the painter must work quickly, and aim to finish the portion in hand before the varnish sets, so as to allow it to "flow out." In the process of leveling off the brush should be occasionally cleaned out, by wiping it on the wiping cup; for, as we stated before, more varnish has been applied than it is designed to leave on.

Varnish laid on in this manner will show no laps; for, having been finished together over the panel, it will flow out together, and appear as one undivided whole.

3d. *When a narrow space connects with a large panel, the whole should be completed together.*

We mention this separately from the second proposition, because it is the practice with some varnishers to finish each part separately, thus giving a broken connection, as where the head rail space joins the back quarter. As the remedy has been laid down in the plan of varnishing the upper back panels, it will need no further explanation here.

4th. *The varnish should be brushed "up and down."*

That is, it is to be brushed vertically, "Up and down" is the language of the shop, and, of course, it is natural to use it. Now, a panel an inch or two wide, a narrow belt, or space, cannot be so brushed; but experience has proven that larger panels require to be laid off in this manner. The advantages are, that a greater quantity of varnish can be laid on with less liability to run or sag; the varnish flows better, and the result is, better work is produced.

5th. *In rubbing, or leveling, all brush marks and faults must be corrected.*

When the first coat of varnish is being rubbed, it is necessary to merely remove the gloss, as in the attempt to remove grit, etc., the color might be disturbed. The second and third coats will bear to be well rubbed. The second coat will hide the defects of the first coat, and the third improve on the second, thus preparing the surface for the season of anxiety - the preparation for, and the applying successfully of the finishing coat.

Brush Painting

Before this interesting period in the history of every carriage has been reached, much hard labor of body and mind must be endured. Runs, bruises and burns may have to be corrected. Runs on the second coats are more easily corrected than when they appear on the third, as they get two coats, which is also true in regard to other defects. If, after a job is varnished, a run is discovered which cannot be corrected with the brush, it (the run) should be rubbed over as soon as the varnish is hard enough to bear it, allowing it to dry until the body is rubbed for the next coat. By this means half the run is destroyed, and the next rubbing will remove it entirely. If this course is not pursued, the run will be softer than the level portions of the surface, and will not come down under the leveling block.

In leveling the coats of varnish, use pieces of cork, wood or lump pumice stone, cut to suit the various spaces, and covered with two thicknesses of cloth. Block down both small and large spaces, using a somewhat coarse, though even grade, of ground pumice, rubbing across the brush marks. Pumice stone should be used freely, and the strength of the arms and shoulders laid out of the work. Brush marks, and other defects, must be rubbed out. To do this it is not necessary to draw the finger over the panel every moment to look at something you know not what. The wet panel will show the ridges far better than the part dried off by the finger. By drawing the rubbing block across the ridges, they will show whether they are rubbed enough or not. If you have laid on a proper second coat, you need not be afraid to lay out your strength on it. Cut it down well, slighting no part. To rub close up to the moldings, and in sharp corners, have a stick of hard wood cut at one end in the form of a knife blade, and place the cloth over it (one thickness) placing the sharp edge up to the molding, which will, by a few strokes, remove the grit that may be there. The coarse pumice will grow finer in the process of rubbing, which will answer to finish with. Or a fine grade may be used, kept for the purpose. No pumice should be allowed to dry anywhere in the corners.

Rub next to the moldings last, for there is more danger of rubbing through, as there is less varnish here than out on the panel. Having slighted no part, wash off clean, touch up where any sharp edges have been cut through, and apply the third coat, which should be as carefully handled as the finishing one. When this has stood a few days, give it a light rubbing, and let it stand until ready for the finish. It will then be well dried and cut down nicely; the grit, if any, will not tear out. If the third coat has been laid on properly, it will not require so much rubbing as the second. The pumice should be fine and even, so as to avoid scratching. The sharp edges should not be rubbed off bare, for it is preferable to slight them in the rubbing rather than to be compelled to touch them up. The practice of having to touch up the edges all over a body, previous to laying on a coat of varnish, is a very foolish one, and may be avoided in a great measure by rounding them slightly when the body first comes from the wood shop.

The after coatings will sharpen them sufficiently not to be detected; but where this precaution has not been taken, slight them in rubbing, as the third coat should be well nigh as perfect as the last or finishing. The experienced rubber will look carefully over each panel before putting on any pumice; and where there may be grit, or any slight defect, he will give these his especial attention.

Having leveled the surface, less pumice should be used, and finally scarcely any. The panels should be finished off by passing the rub cloth throughout their length, bringing them to a polish. A body that has passed through the hands of a first-class rubber will, when washed clean and dried off, present a beautiful appearance. The finisher, as he surveys it, will feel a sense of pleasure, and at once decide to spare no pains in the effort to complete the job. In our largest and best regulated shops the finisher is not a man of all work - one day with a pot of lead in his hand, the next coloring; now in the body room, and then in the gearing room. Oh, no, nothing of the kind. He is a finisher in the truest sense, and is not even required to rub varnish. Still further, he does not varnish the roof, arch and the inside edges of the body. He has help in the finishing room, which varnish all except the panels. These he attends to, and through his skill, attained by daily practice, the finishing coat is put on so nearly perfect that, to painters who have never had like advantages, surprise and mortification will be mingled as they gaze at the beautiful work, and remember their own wavy and dirty jobs.

The method adopted in laying the finishing coat is similar to that in the use of rubbing varnish. The varnish is applied heavily, leveled by repeated brushing, and carefully examined during the operation to detect any foreign particles that may appear.

A picker is used, made of whalebone, sharpened to a point, or any other device that will remove the particles of dirt or gum. Having brushed the varnish throughout a given surface, let it stand a few moments, when the bubbles will evaporate, thus leaving the hard particles remaining, which must be removed. The finishing strokes are given lightly. As it is beyond the power of words to give a perfect description of the manner of laying off this last coat, we will have to leave the inexperienced to gather whatever may be of value from the foregoing, and by care, good taste, and an unbending purpose, supplement our hints by practice.

In conclusion we would remark, that to secure a perfectly clean piece of work, the room, body, cups and brushes, and the clothing of the varnisher himself, must be scrupulously clean; for, without these precautions, it will be madness to make the attempt." from Coach-Maker's Illustrated Hand-Book.

Rack for holding window frames for varnishing.
Carriage Monthly Nov. 1877

Rack for holding doors for varnishing.
Carriage Monthly Nov. 1877

Glaze Coats
Glaze coats of varnish were usually the first coat of varnish after the color coats, although some varnishers thought that they were less difficult to work if applied after one coat of thin varnish. To make a glaze coat, finely ground transparent colors were mixed into the varnish. Striping, lettering, ornamenting and scrolling were applied to the varnish coats just before the last coat of varnish.

Getting Ready to Varnish:
The carriage or coach is usually varnished apart in sections : wheels, window frames, body, undercarriage (divided into two sections without perch).
1. You need to have a clean room free of dust and the ideal situation is to have a separate finishing room or paint room. If this is not the case you should clean the area to be used for painting as clean as possible from dust and dirt.

B. MILLER'S
Adjustable Jack.
Indispensable in the Paint Shop, for Bodies, Wheels, Seats, &c.
For sale by all dealers in Carriage Goods.
Send for Circular and Prices to
B. MILLER, Paola, Kansas.
From Carriage Monthly Oct. 1885

Using a garden sprayer you can mist the area around the project to settle the dust particles. Mop the floor with water and leave it wet while you are varnishing, this way as you are walking around to varnish you don't stir up the dust from the floor. If you have a large open building with a high ceiling and there isn't any way of controlling the dust you might consider using some plastic drop cloths and drape them around and over the surrounding area of your project.

2. Environment of the finishing-room -Varnish works best if the temperature is about 75 degrees F. Some oil varnishes can work as low as 45 degrees F., but you must expect it is going to take them considerably longer to cure. It is not advisable to work varnish when it is over 90 degrees F. as bubbling of the surface may occur. Of the different finishes used by wood finishers, modern varnish seems to be the least affected by humidity, as opposed to the belief of old coach painters that the humidity had a tremendous effect on the varnish. It is important to have good ventilation with fresh air coming in and bad air moving out, for the varnish to dry properly and for the person working to have clean air to breath. Some people are more affected by different solvents than others, so if you experience dizziness you should get to fresh air and get a different ventilation system set up. There also isn't any safety in thinking that because the solvents do not bother you today that there isn't going to be a long term effect in the future, if you are going to be doing a lot of refinishing.

3. Next make sure the lighting is adequate when you start varnishing. A reflected light source is the most helpful.

4. The varnisher's clothes should be clean of dust, grease and dirt, so if you should rub up against the surface of your project you won't contaminate the surface with unwanted dirt, dust, or grease spot.

5. When you open the varnish can, gently stir the varnish to mix it. Excessive stirring will cause undesirable air bubbles in varnish. Pour off the amount of varnish you think you will be using by straining it thorough a paint strainer into a clean empty can, and seal up the unused varnish. If air bubbles have formed you might have to allow the varnish to sit awhile until they disperse. Once you get started you will need another can in which to brush off the excessive varnish.

6. Be sure your brush is clean and free of loose bristles, and has been presoaked in solvent.

7. While you are waiting for the air bubbles to disperse in the varnish, wipe your project one last time with a tack cloth to make sure it is free of lint and dust.

8. Before starting the body, the varnisher must decide on a plan of attack, dividing the work into clearly defined areas, each area small enough to be varnished and brushed out before the varnish becomes too tacky, and bounded by moldings or corners so that there is no problem of overlapping and leaving brush marks. Big panels are the hardest part, and the procedure is to lay the varnish on up and down first, then side to side, then diagonally both ways. As before, a full coat is laid on, then picked up as before - up and down, side to side, diagonally - finishing with long, even hard strokes down, taking care to pick up all the excess from the bottom molding. Before moving to another section, the work must be looked over for any brush bristles which can be picked up carefully with the corner of the brush.

9. Flow the varnish on wet if you are using a heavy varnish and then tip it off removing the excess, and brush marks. If you are varnishing on natural wood when you tip off the varnish you should brush in the direction of the grain. Coat one area or section at a time.

10. Allow the varnish to dry from 1 to 5 days depending on the normal drying properties of the varnish, and if it is cooler temperatures it is going to take longer to dry. Varnish being a reactive finish dries from the top down, so although it appears dry on the top it may take days before it is dry enough to be rubbed or sanded.

11. Coats of varnish are either sanded with wet/dry or dry sandpaper of 320 grit or more.

Some people prefer to rub the coats with fine steel wool, (but this can leave small particles), or a synthetic abrasive scuffing pad. Pumice is good, but time consuming, and was one of the original choices of carriage and coach painters. If you want a perfectly level surface you will need to sand out the brush marks between each coat. The high parts (ridges) of the brush marks will become dull in appearance as you sand and the low parts (valleys) will appear glossy or shiny. Once the entire surface starts to appear dull it is time to quit sanding and clean your work.

12. Next, start everything all over again.

Some Problems of Varnish:

Cracking: May occur if a layer of finish was not dry enough before applying another layer. This would be especially true if the most recent coat is of a different makeup or dries at a more rapid rate. One fail-safe method of ascertaining whether the finish is dry enough for a re-coating is to gently sand the work with wet or dry paper and water. If it sands cleanly and does not clog the paper, the finish is dry enough.

Blistering: Blistering generally occurs if there is any moisture trapped in the woodwork, either from improper seasoning of the wood if the carriage is new, or perhaps from sanding the primer coats with water and not allowing enough time to be sure that no moisture has seeped into the woodwork before painting. At a later date, when the carriage is completed, and you have a particularly hot and sunny day, this moisture will be drawn through the primer coats to the paint coat and cause blisters. Likewise, if you use linseed oil to moisten and revitalize the old woodwork, be sure that you allow two weeks before covering your primer coats or the same problem may occur.

Air bubbles: Air bubbles appearing in the varnish as you are brushing it and then drying in the finish, may be caused by the friction of the brush against the surface. Sand out the coat of varnish and then try using a softer brush on the next coat or another solution might be to thin the varnish with a 10 to 20 percent mineral spirits. Thinning the varnish gives it a longer curing time and gives the air bubbles a chance to pop out.

Crawls: When the varnish crawls into ridges after you apply a second coat, this may be contaminants on the surface such as silicone or oil. If the varnish appears to be doing this you may have time to wipe it off with a rag soaked in mineral spirits. A paint additive called fish-eye eliminator that can be added to the varnish may help to solve the problem. If the fish-eye eliminator does not work you will have to strip the project and start over.

Doesn't dry: Varnish that doesn't dry can be quite troublesome, and it may be caused by temperature being too cool, or uncured previous finishes, such as linseed oil. Allow more drying time and if it still doesn't dry you will have to strip the finish and start over.

Bibliography and additional references :

Dresdner, Michael. The Woodfinishing Book. Newtown, CT : Tauntom Press, 1992.

Flexner, Bob. Understanding Wood Finishing. Emmaus, PA : Rodale Press, 1994.

Isles, George L. The Restoration of Carriages. London, England : J. A. Allen & Co., 1981.

Ragle, Tim. "Authentic Carriage Restoration." Carriage Journal. Vol. 26 No. 4 (Spring 1989), pp. 161-167.

Ragle, Tim. "Authentic Carriage Restoration Part 2. " Carriage Journal. Vol.27 No.1 (Summer 1989), pp. 32-34.

Ragle, Tim. "Problem Of Cracking Or Honeycombing Of Paint Finishes." Carriage Journal. Vol. 29 No. 1 (Summer 1991), p. 16.

Brush Painting

The Carriage Museum of America wishes to acknowledge and thank the following for information used from their publications.
Some information reprinted from Understanding Wood Finishing, copyright 1994 by Bob Flexner. Permission granted by Rodale Press, Inc., Emmaus, PA 18098-0099
Some information excerpted with permission from The Woodfinishing Book by Michael Dresdner copyright 1992 by The Taunton Press, Inc. All rights reserved.

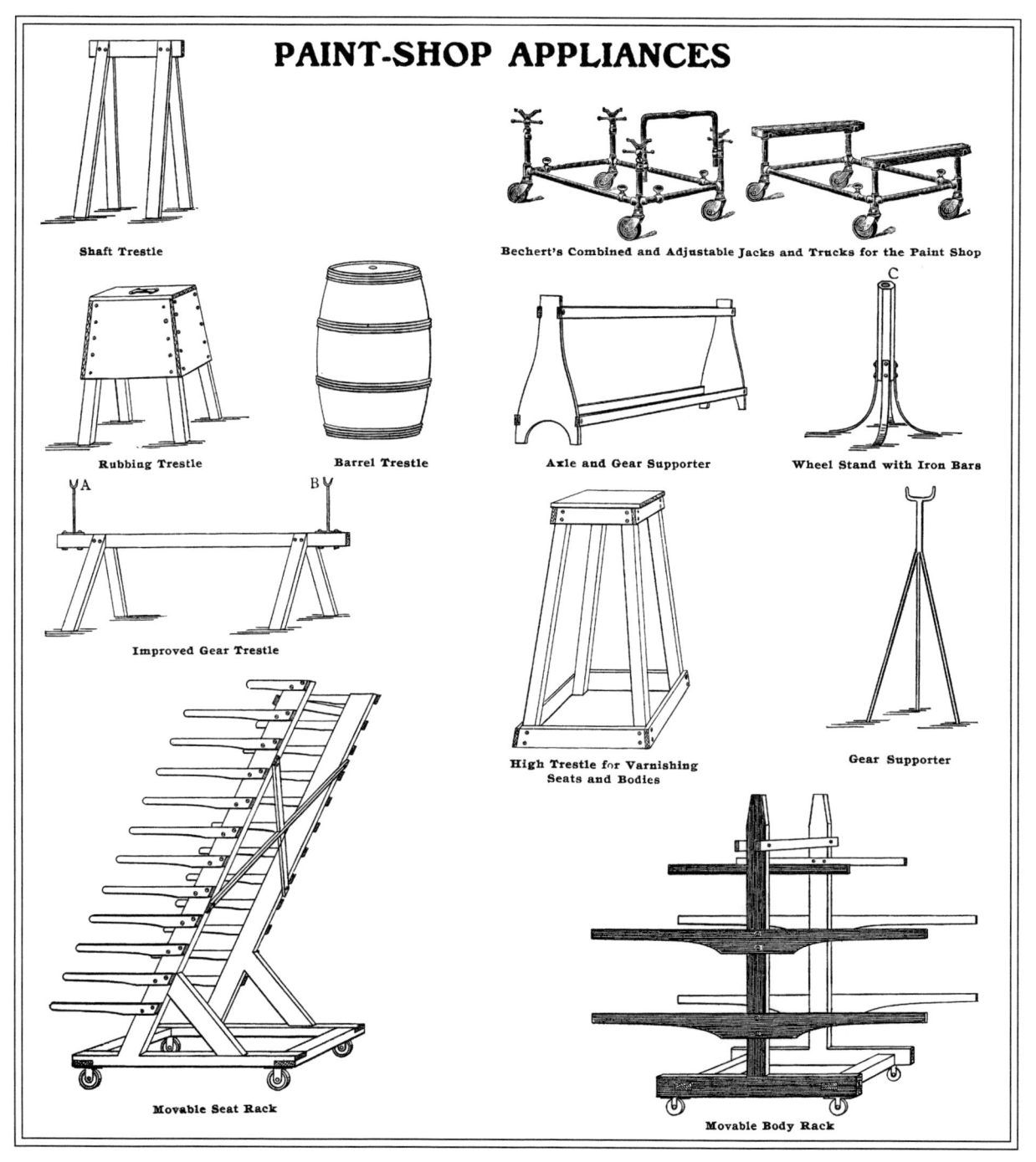

PAINT-SHOP APPLIANCES

Shaft Trestle

Bechert's Combined and Adjustable Jacks and Trucks for the Paint Shop

Rubbing Trestle

Barrel Trestle

Axle and Gear Supporter

Wheel Stand with Iron Bars

Improved Gear Trestle

High Trestle for Varnishing Seats and Bodies

Gear Supporter

Movable Seat Rack

Movable Body Rack

Fom the CARRIAGE MONTHLY February 1903

127

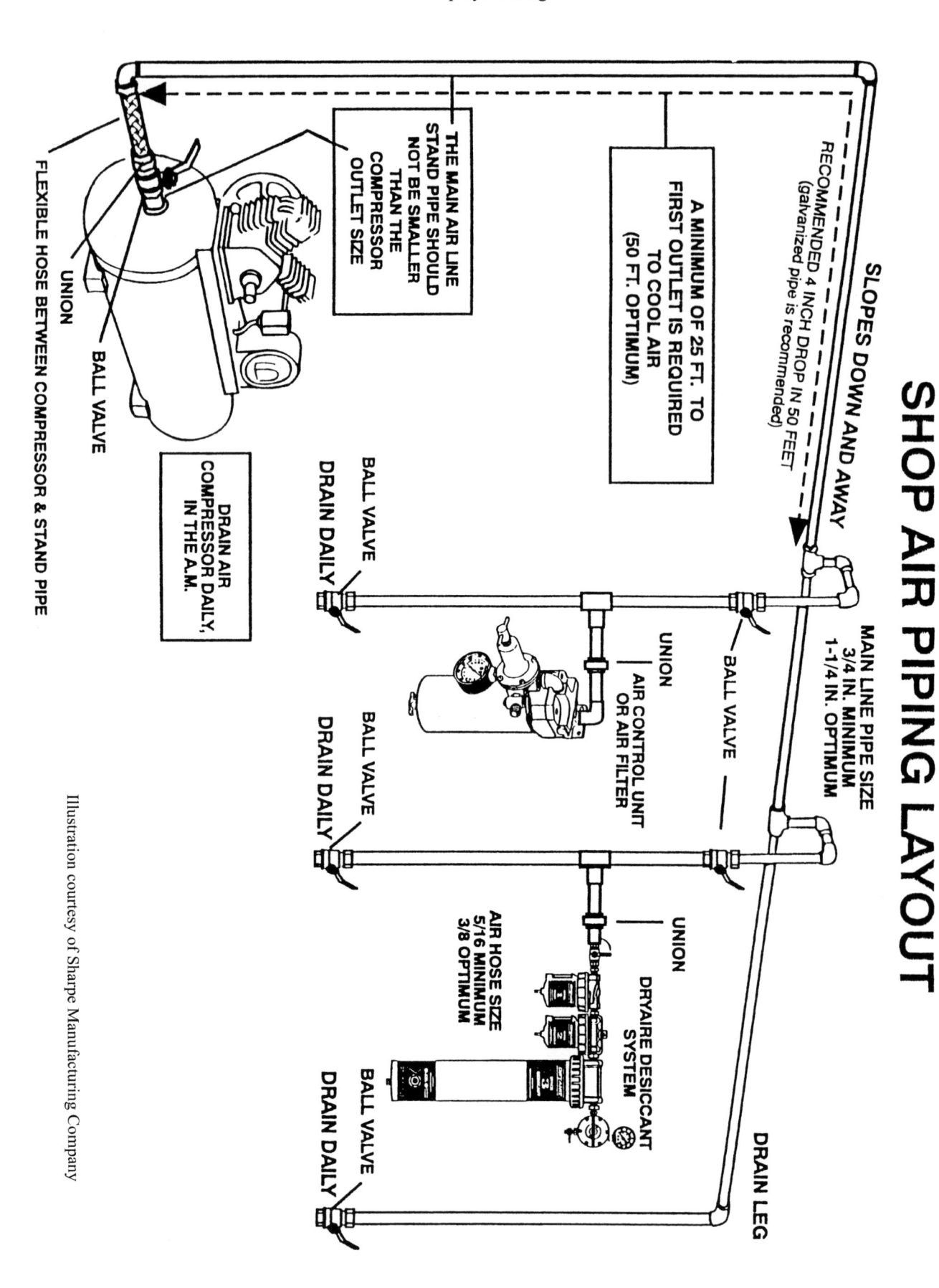

Spray Painting

SHOP AIR PIPING LAYOUT

CHAPTER 12

SPRAY PAINTING
by Darell Shannon

Like all other aspects of carriage restoration, a good understanding of preparation methods and materials is essential for a proper job of spray painting. The objective of any restoration is to produce a high gloss finish that will last many years and not crack or chip under normal use. If done properly this objective can be accomplished using modern automotive paints.

Some people are of the opinion that modern day automotive enamels are not elastic enough to be used on wood; however, if applied on properly prepared wood surfaces it works as well as any other method of painting. While metal surfaces are not affected by moisture and humidity as wood is, it contracts and expands as much as wood with extreme temperature changes. Whatever method of application or type of paint used, if the surface is not prepared correctly and paint applied correctly the finished product will not look good or have the durability required for top class work. Most of the poor restorations can be attributed to a lack of proper preparation. There is a tendency to get the job finished and paint is often applied too soon, and no amount of paint can cover up a poorly prepared surface.

Equipment Needed

The first piece of equipment needed for spray painting is an air compressor. Compressors come in several sizes ranging from a small portable size to large stationary types. A compressor that will produce 7 SCFM at 90 PSI will be sufficient for most painting needs and will also run most air tools such as sanders and drills that would be used by the carriage restorer. Compressor air delivery is measured by standard cubic feet per minute (SCFM) at pounds per square inch (PSI). A higher SCFM allows more paint to be sprayed in a given time and increases the number of tools that can be operated by the compressor. Higher PSI allows a heavier body paint to be sprayed and more effective operation of air tools.

The next item needed is a paint gun The two types of guns most commonly used are the siphon fed and the high volume low pressure (HVLP). The siphon fed is the most often used gun and is well suited for carriage restoration. This is also the least expensive. The second type of spray gun and one that is relatively new but gaining in popularity is the (HVLP) high volume low pressure gun. This type of gun has a lower nozzle pressure than the siphon fed guns and offers several benefits such as:

(1) Less fogging which makes the gun safer for the operator

(2) Less over spraying which means less wasted paint. The HVLP gun has about 10PSI or lower at the nozzle. With the HVLP gun about 80 per cent of the paint reaches the surface compared to about 50 per cent of a siphon fed high pressure gun.

(3) Health and environment benefit because less paint and harmful fumes are going into the lungs of the operator and into the environment. California already requires low pressure spray painting with a transfer efficiency of 65 percent or higher. Other states are considering similar laws. While these regulations may not reach the small buggy shop or hobbyist the HVLP guns offer advantages to the restorer.

Figure I is a drawing of a compressor and air line layout for a well planned paint room and shop. In order to produce quality paint jobs you will need a system similar to this, although it does not have to be as large. Unless you have a large stationary air compressor you can eliminate portions of this layout. Portable air compressors usually have a regulator that controls the air pressure to the paint gun. This type of pressure control works well but you will need to add a filter to prevent moisture in the line and the air tank needs to be drained often. On a hot and humid day the tank will need to be drained at least once each day. Moisture in the air lines must be avoided or water will enter the paint gun . To prevent moisture in the lines at least one drain is needed, this should be located near where the air hose connects to the metal line and must be lower than the metal line. A filter should also be located in the metal line. Paper filters are more expensive but are well worth the extra cost. Automotive stores that sell paint usually carry this type of filter.

When using the spray painting method of application, there are some safety precautions that must be followed. Whatever is used as a paint room must be ventilated well enough that it carries over spray and paint fumes out of the area. When using automotive paint, a good respirator must be used at all times. This should be the type that has replaceable filters and the filters should be changed often. Always keep paint and cleaning materials away from any open flame.

Preparation

Before the start of dismantling you should always make an evaluation as to the soundness of the vehicle. If old paint and fabric are intact, conservation might be a better alternative. We are losing far too many of our original condition vehicles, so don't be too quick to start dismantling and stripping if it is possible to keep the vehicle original.

The first step in any restoration project is to take several pictures from different angles and close ups of any special or unusual feature and of any original striping and paint. Pictures are invaluable in reassembling the vehicle and they should always remain with the vehicle as proof of the original condition and colors. A written record should also be made during restoration. This should include information such as replacement parts used, original striping, color and type of paint used. If any original top material or fabric is on the vehicle a portion of this should be saved and kept with the vehicle. Mention should be made of any apparent previous work and all known previous history of the vehicle. We owe future generations as much history of the carriages as we can pass on. What might seem insignificant today could be a tremendous asset to future owners of the vehicle.

Since stripping and cleaning of the wood and metal are discussed in other sections of this book, I will skip that and go directly to the preparation. After the wood and metal parts have been cleaned of old paint, it is time to start filling cracks and imperfections. The best product to use for this is an automotive epoxy filler. There are several brands of this type filler. The one most recognized is bondo; however, most automotive stores carry this as well as other brands and they all work about equally well. These epoxies bond to wood and metal exceptionally well. I have dipped bodies and wheels in a strip tank that contained these epoxies and they remained intact. Some of the epoxies contain fiberglass and do not work well for carriage restorers as they were developed for covering large rust areas on cars and are harder to work smooth on the smaller cracks of carriages. Any imperfection larger than a pin head should be filled with epoxy. These epoxies come with a cream hardener and you should experiment with mixing them if you have not used them before. Too little hardener and it will take too long to harden and too much and it will harden before you can apply it. Even with the correct mix you will only have about five minutes to apply the mixture, so mix it in small amounts only. Do not apply any more than is necessary as this will cause a lot of extra sanding. Be careful when applying this material around molding and corners and do not cover up or interfere with any of the natural lines and joints. It takes a lot of filling and sanding to cover all imperfections and don't expect to cover them all the first time. Don't be in a big hurry to get primer on because it is best to get as many imperfections as possible filled before applying primer. If rotted or spongy wood is present, it is best to replace it with new wood of the same type. If only a small amount of this rotted wood is present there are two products that work well to restore it. One is called liquidwood and can be purchased from Abatron, Inc. If a carriage has been reupholstered several times the area where tacks were located sometimes becomes too soft to hold new tacks. Liquidwood can be applied in this area and new tacks will then hold. Liquidwood is a two part product consisting of two components (a) resin and (b) hardener. When the two parts are mixed they remain a thin clear liquid designed to impregnate wood and to harden after penetrating. It will restore strength, stiffness and hardness to the wood. After the liquidwood has hardened, at least twenty four hours, it can be sanded and primed and paint can then be applied. If small pieces of wood are missing, Abatron also sells another product called Woodepox which is a non shrinking, lightweight, adhesive paste that is designed to adhere permanently to wood as a filler or substitute for missing parts of wood. Woodepox and liquidwood are entirely different in consistency, appearance and method of application. They can be used independently of each other; yet, they complement each other. Tacks or screws will hold much better after applying one or both of these products.

Once you have filled as many imperfections as possible it is time to put the first coat of primer on. For this first coat a very hard primer should be used as this is the most important coat you will apply. Make sure any grease or oil is cleaned before applying this first coat of primer. This can best be accomplished by rubbing a clean rag soaked with lacquer thinner lightly over the area to be primed. This should also be done after the final coat of primer has been applied, but remember to use enamel reducer for this coat as enamel paint will be used next. If this first coat of primer does not bond well to the wood, it will cause peeling after the paint is applied. Apply this to both the wood and metal as a first coat. Each leaf of the springs should receive this primer and one coat of color before they are reassembled. This First coat should be a different color than the following coats of primer and you should avoid sanding through this first coat to the wood or metal. Most primers come in either gray or red. The color of the primer does not matter as both red and gray are equal. When sanding additional coats of another color primer, stop when you reach this first coat. One primer I have found that works well for this first coat is made by the Acme Paint Company. The primer is 158, the hardener is # 150 and you should use # 160 as a thinner. Don't try to build up cracks and imperfections with primer alone as this will make it too thick and lead to peeling and cracking. Always make sure at least one coat of primer covers any epoxy or putty or it will be harder to cover with paint.

After the first coat of hard primer all subsequent coats should be of a high fill type primer. DuPont makes a primer called Sand and Fill and other companies offer similar primers. This type of primer works better on wood and although it costs more per gallon it is actually cheaper in the long run because it takes fewer coats. Mixing these fill and sand primers will require about three parts thinner to one part primer or it will not go through the paint gun and they must be stirred often or the heavier primer will settle to the bottom of the gun. Use as many coats of primer as is necessary to get a glass smooth finish. Sand each coat lightly with # 320 or # 400 sand paper and by your second or third coat you should have most of the larger imperfections filled with epoxy. It is okay to use epoxy over primer but once the larger imperfections are filled you should then switch to body putty to fill in the smaller ones. Body putty usually comes in squeeze tubes and is applied as it comes out of the tube. The putty takes longer to dry than the epoxy and it will also shrink so be sure to let it dry at least thirty minutes or more before sanding or applying any primer over it. Some companies are now producing a two part putty that consists of the putty and a hardening agent. This type works well on wood or metal and does not shrink as much as the putty that comes in a tube. Since they require mixing they take longer to apply. This type putty will fill larger imperfections, but should only be used on small imperfections as they are not intended as a replacement for the epoxies. Both the epoxy and the putty should be applied with plastic applicators than can be purchased anywhere the epoxy and putty can be purchased.

Remember an old painter's advice, "what you see is what you get." In other words if you see an imperfection before you start applying paint, you will also see it after the final coat.

Choice Of Paints

Lacquer paints do not have the elasticity to expand with the wood so they should never be used on carriages. Most of the automotive industry has now switched to enamels as they are much more durable and elastic than lacquer. There are several types of enamel that have clear coats and these also should be avoided. A clear coat over the enamel gives the paint job a very shiny finish; however, it is not the deep shine that duplicates the old carriage finishes. Since a lot of carriages have panels painted one color and the molding another this requires a different approach than a body that is painted one color. It doesn't matter if you paint the panels or the molding first, but whichever is painted first will need to be masked off in order to paint the other. Masking tape should always be purchased from an automotive store as automotive masking tape is thicker and can be removed much easier without damaging the new paint. Most masking tape sold at other stores is not the correct type for carriage painting. After the molding or panels have been painted the paint must be allowed to cure at least three or four days before applying masking tape to the new paint. Most enamel paints have a hardener that can be added and these hardeners can be used in the first paint applied and this will help to keep the masking tape from pulling any paint off thus leaving marks in the paint.

There are several companies that make enamel automotive paint and they are all similar and work well for carriages. It is not advisable to mix different brands of paint with other brands of reducers. It is best to use one brand of paint and stay with it. In this way you become familiar with that brand and the different agents than can be used with it. It is best to use the brand that is most readily available in your area. It is okay to use one company's primer while using another brand of paint. Remember that most primers require lacquer thinner and if you use the same gun to prime and to paint with, be sure to clean it well as only a drop of lacquer thinner can cause problems if accidentally mixed with enamel paint. If lacquer thinner is used to clean the paint gun be sure to spray at least a small amount of enamel reducer through it before you add the paint. This will help make sure there is no contamination from the lacquer thinner. A thinning agent for lacquer is referred to as thinner while a thinning agent for enamel is referred to as a reducer.

Paint does not always react the same on wood as it does on metal. Unless it is extremely cold (below 65 degrees) in your paint area you should use a much slower drying reducer on wood than you would on metal. DuPont # 8093 or # 80% works quite well. Automotive store personnel are usually not familiar with painting wood surfaces and will usually advise a faster drying reducer than is needed for carriage restoration.

Use Of Spray Gun

Whether a siphon fed or HVLP gun is used the procedure is the same. If you have already been using a siphon fed gun and switch to the HVLP it is best to practice with it first before your spraying your carriage. There is a tendency to apply too much paint until you have adjusted yourself to more paint being applied with each pass of the gun. Before applying the first coat of paint, double check for any imperfections and correct them before painting. This is one disadvantage of spray painting opposed to brush painting. With brush painting, it is easier to cover small imperfections.

SPRAY GUN TEST PATTERNS

CONDITION	CAUSE	CORRECTION
RIGHT	Correct Normal Pattern.	No Correction Necessary
WRONG — Heavy Top Or Bottom Pattern	1. Dirty or damaged air cap. 2. Dirty or damaged fluid tip.	1. Rotate air cap 180°. A. If pattern follows air cap, problem is in air cap. Clean and inspect. If pattern is not corrected, replacement is necessary. B. If pattern does not follow the air cap, the problem is in the fluid tip. Clean and inspect the tip for dried paint, dirt or damage. If the pattern is not corrected, replacement is necessary.
WRONG — Split Pattern	1. Air pressure too high for material viscosity being sprayed.	1. Reduce air pressure. 2. Increase material viscosity. 3. Pattern may also be corrected by narrowing fan size with spray width adjuster control knob.
WRONG	1. Dirty or distorted air horn holes. 2. Complete blockage of one air horn hole.	1. Rotate air cap 180°. A. If pattern follows air cap, clean and inspect the air horn holes. If horn holes are distorted replacement is necessary.
WRONG — Gun Spitting	1. Air getting into paint stream somewhere. *EXAMPLE*: Same symptoms as a siphon cup running out of paint.	1. Check and tighten fluid needle packing nut. 2. Tighten fluid tip. 3. Check fluid tip seat for damage. 4. Check siphon tube for crack. 5. Check for poor gun to cup seating.
Air Back Pressuring Into Cup	Excessive Air Blowing Back Into Cup.	1. Tighten fluid tip. 2. Check fluid tip seat. 3. Check for damaged fluid seat on tip or seat in gun head.

Illustration courtesy of Sharpe Manufacturing Company

Spray Painting

Most automotive paints will dry to the touch in about thirty minutes. This is an advantage over brush painting as dust is less of a problem with the faster drying paint; however, this does not mean the dust problem is eliminated. All possible effort must be made to prevent dust in the paint area. The floor and walls are where most dust comes from. If possible they should be hosed down just before painting. If this is not possible a large sponge or mop can be used to clean the dust. The clothing of the painter is another source of lint and dust. Just before painting a tack rag should be rubbed over the vehicle to be painted and should also be rubbed over the painter's clothing.

Most paints should be mixed one part paint to one part reducer. Air pressure at the gun should be between 35 and 45 PSI. If new to spray painting you should practice using the gun before starting to apply paint to your carriage. A lot of the problems with spray painting are caused by improper adjustment of the gun. Figures 2 and 3 show the more common problems and how to correct them. Enamel paint must be sprayed on with a wet tool If dry spots appear as the paint is applied they will also show after the paint has dried. Dry spots can be caused by too much air pressure, using a too fast drying reducer or they can be caused by trying to paint small areas that have already been painted. It is very difficult to spot paint only a portion of an area. Learn to cover all areas with an even movement of the gun without overlapping previous passes. This helps prevent runs and assures an even coat of paint on all parts of the carriage.

When applying paint the hard to reach areas should be painted first. This is especially true of the under carriage. There is a tendency to apply too much paint to these areas and this is one of the causes of runs in the paint. Paint should be applied in several thin coats rather than one or two heavy coats. There is no rule as to how many coats should be applied, but for a top class job it takes at least four or more.

Wheels are especially hard to paint without getting runs. You will need to mount the wheels on some type of rack so they can be rotated as you paint. Standing in back and facing the left half of the wheel, paint the face and top of each spoke as the wheel rotates counter clockwise. Then while still standing in back and facing the right half of the wheel continue to rotate counter clockwise and paint the other side of the spokes. While still in back of the wheel paint the rim and hub and then move to the front of the wheel and repeat the process. It is a common tendency to get too much paint on the spokes where they fit into the hub. To help prevent this, release the trigger of the gun three or four inches before the hub. Then paint the hub last.

It is best to start with smaller projects and progress to larger ones as experience is gained. Don't expect to be perfect the first time you attempt using a spray gun. As with all other aspects of carriage restoration, it takes practice and learning by trial and error. We have all had to wash paint off and repeat the process.

For additional help

For help with spray painting automotive finishes the Sherwin Williams Company offers training courses in five locations: Atlanta, Philadelphia, Dallas, Reno, and Chicago. There isn't any information offered on spray painting horse-drawn vehicles, so a person would have to be able to adapt the information to horse-drawn vehicles. Some spray equipment manufacturers offer instruction bulletins on spray painting that can be helpful in solving different problems.

CHAPTER 13

COLORS

Most horse-drawn vehicles that we would see now are from the last seventy five years of the carriage era. If one should have access to the old trade journals published for the professional carriages makers one would see that there were no set rules for color for vehicles over this seventy five year period. Because of the annual manufacturers trade shows a very opinionated attempt was made each year to state which were the most appropriate colors. In fact there was a difference of opinion from month to month and from one region to another. In 1898 an editorial in HUB commented that country people had their vehicles striped in rather poor taste with too much striping. There are now a number of restoration people and judges that are rather opinionated as to what a modern carriage paint job should look like, never mind that there were many thousands of different ways all the different styles of carriages were painted. It is important to take color photographs and document any original paint if you are going to restore a vehicle. If you are going to enter a restoration competition the photographs should be displayed in a binder to document why your vehicle is painted the way it is. Some people decide they do not like the original color and others sometimes have a new vehicle or a rebuilt vehicle that did not have any paint left.

Some general guidelines for painting vehicles were found in the *Carriage Journal* Vol. 1 No.2 (Oct. 1963). This is not an original source document but a summary of what an old carriage painter had concluded in his lifetime. "We might state that very few carriages other than those used by undertakers were completely painted black.

We are most certainly not attempting to dictate fashion and we see no reason why you should not paint your carriages according to your own notions,[Some wealthy carriage owners had their carriages painted in their own particular color]. however, we do want you to know what was commonly done during the carriage era.

CORNING TYPE TOP WAGON which was a variety of Buggy. The body is black. The gear, that is, axles, springs, reach, wheels and all other parts of the under works is colored. On this type of carriage the color areas might have been painted subdued or in somewhat lively colors according to the taste of the owner. We, ourselves, would enjoy seeing a deep cherry red or forest green. This is not really a sporty carriage and thus conservative colors would seem to be desirable. If cherry red were chosen, the striping might be bright red or black. In all vehicles of this type, the striping would be narrow. The inner and outer hub bands would habitually be black with no stripe. These suggestions apply to any Buggy, Surrey or Phaeton.

Elliptic Spring Corning Buggy, made by Cortland Wagon Co. From the Hub Sept. 1891.
Painting.--Body & moldings, black; seat, dark blue. Gearing, carmine, striped with two fine lines of black. Trimming.--Dark blue cloth; mountings, silver.

CABRIOLET OR PANEL BOOT VICTORIA. The body moldings and front boot should be black. While the vehicle is not as formal as a Victoria proper, it nevertheless rates conservative treatment. Maroon, dark blue, dark green, dark brown or other dark color. Usually the gear would be painted the same color as the panels. Appropriate striping on maroon could be carmine or another shade of red not too contrasting. On dark blue, dark red or buff. On dark green, a somewhat lighter green, black, dark red or deep buff. On dark brown, brick color red, cafe au lait, deep burnt orange, corn color, buff or a lighter brown, but never anything flashy. Narrow striping could be used on the inner edges of the moldings. This painting applies equally to Coaches and Rockaways although on light Rockaways a little more latitude would have been permitted.

BROUGHAM. The same colors and striping as recommended for the Cabriolet would be appropriate.

LANDAU. The same treatment as the Cabriolet and Brougham would be desirable as all three of these vehicles are of the same level of caste.

Cabriolet
From the Hub Oct. 1889
Painting.--Seat quarters and lower panels, dark green; boot and moldings, black; moldings, striped with fine line of imitation old gold. Gearing, green, a shade lighter than panels, striped with two fine and one broad line of imitation gold.
Trimming.--Green cloth is used throughout, mountings silver.

Straight-Front Brougham
From the Hub Aug. 1894.
Painting.--Door panels, lower quarter panels and back panel, deep blue; boot and upper quarter panels, black; molding, black, striped with orange; gear, deep blue striped with ¼ inch line of light blue edged with two fine liens of light blue.
Trimming.--Blue cloth.

Five-Glass Landau French System
From the Hub July 1889
Painting.--Quarter and door panels, maroon. Boot and moldings, black; moldings striped with fine line of carmine. Gearing, maroon, a shade lighter than panels, striped with two fine lines of black.
Trimming.--Maroon cloth throughout. Plain maroon carpet. Mountings, gold.

SURREY. Colors for this carriage might be the same as for a Brougham but possibly a bit gayer, but always with black moldings. Remember this is not a sporting Trap.

Surrey made by Cortland Wagon Co., Cortland, NY
From the Hub Sept. 1891.
Painting.--Body and moldings, black; with fine line of carmine. Gearing, carmine striped with two fine lines of black.
Trimming.--Dark blue cloth. Mountings, silver.

Colors

RUMBLE SEAT BASKET PHAETON. Same treatment as surrey but as this is a ladies' carriage, conservatism would be in good taste. The basket work should, to look its best, have a thin coat of oil stain under the varnish.

DOG CART. This particular type was called a Going To Cover Cart. Here at last you may let yourself go as to color as this is a true sporting vehicle. These carts were all originally painted white on the carved imitation basket work panels, not a chalky white, but just the very slightest tint towards creamy buff. They had bright red gear and the louvers or shutters were also painted in this color. All moldings were black, the striping was black about 3/8" in width. The lower edges of the louvers might be striped, and if desired, a very narrow stripe on the moldings. Any other bright color might be substituted for the red, but white always seemed smarter on the panels.

WAGONETTE BREAK. Here bright colors might be used. The color of the gear should be applied to the top bottom of the toe board and seat risers. The body panels should be a pleasing contrast to the gear which is vermilion or yellow, might be done in dark blue. It is also desirable to use a darker color on the body panels than on the gear. The moldings and seat rails should go black. Black striping is best on any sporting trap. In this case it should be ½ " in width". end Carriage Journal article

PRIVATE COACH OR PARK DRAG. Besides the upper quarter panels, front and hind boots always being painted black these vehicles can be made up of two other colors. The seat risers and the under side of the toe-board, are usually painted the same color as the gear. The lower body panels and the door panel for the rear boot can be of a different color then the gear. The gear color for these vehicles range from yellow and bright red to more conservative colors such as dark blue, darker reds, dark greens.

Rumble-Seat Basket Phaeton
From the Carriage Monthly Feb. 1904.
Painting.--Body, black, basket cane natural color; gearing, deep green, striped two fine lines of yellow.
Trimming.--Cream-colored corduroy for main sat and green cloth for rumble; Sprague-style umbrella top, and rug to match. Finish.--Square, silver-plated lamps.

Dog Cart or Tandem Cart made by Horace Ervein, Ogontz, Pennsylvania
From the Carriage Monthly June 1894.
Painting.--Body, black; slates, carmine; gear, carmine, striped black.
Trimming.--Deep green imported English corduroy cloth.
Finish.--Latest style of sliver plated lamps, and carpet front to match. All iron rails painted black.

Body or Wagonette Break
From the chart of Carriage Association of America

Coach made by Holland & Holland, London, England.
From the Hub June 1891, no description.

Colors

There is also a wide range of striping patterns from no striping to a bold stripe with two fine lines. It is generally accepted that if there is striping on the body it should be a fine line on the moldings around the panels and not on the panels. Coaches and other vehicles with brass moldings around the body panels should have these painted black rather than polished brass. Brass moldings around leather seat valances and leather top valances are usually polished.

Black Parts

For all carriages generally parts of the gear that were subject to wear were painted black; steps, hub bands, roller bolts, shafts tips and the like places that would show wear. These pieces could then be easily touched up. Parts of the body, if not plated, that would generally be painted black would be lamp brackets, rein and hand rails.

For other sources of paint and upholstery colors.

Berkebile, Don. Carriage Terminology : An Historical Dictionary. Washington, DC : Smithsonian Institution Press, 1978 +. *Fashion plates from the HUB and CARRIAGE MONTHLY.*
Berkebile, Don H. Horse-Drawn Commercial Vehicles. Mineola, NY : Dover Publications, 1989.
Berkebile, Don. American Carriages, Sleighs, Sulkies and Carts. New York, NY : Dover Publications, 1977.
Horse-Drawn Vehicles: Colored Plates from the Hub November 1882-January 1892. Bird-In-Hand, PA : Carriage Museum of America, 1999.
Green, Susan. Horse Drawn Sleighs. Mendham, NJ : Astragal Press, 1995.
Two-Wheeled Vehicles for Equine. Bird-In-Hand, PA : Carriage Museum of America, 2000.

Natural Wood Carriages

Carriages in "NATURAL WOOD" finish came into fashion between about 1885 and 1900's. Generally carriages finished in natural wood were thought to be for the country or driving at summer resorts. A natural wood finished vehicle that gained great popularity was the modern buckboard made by the Glens Falls companies. The Brewster Co. of New York had a full line of natural wood finished vehicles runabouts, broughams, town coaches and vis-a-vis. Vehicles that had a natural wood finish, usually had woods specially selected and sawed to show off the grain of the wood when varnished. Woods used by American builders were ash, oak, hard elm, button wood, maple, and butternut. Mahogany and walnut, a wood used by European builders for painted coach and carriage panels, could also be finished natural. Another way that a natural wood grain finish can be achieved is to grain paint. This can result in quite a spectacular finish if done by a skilled professional wood grainer. Wood graining was sometimes used in combination with a painted finish to achieve all kinds of different effects. The inside dash board of a sleigh might be grain painted or the side panels of a runabout and the rest of the vehicle painted in solid colors. The ironwork on natural wood carriages can be finished in black and was commonly done that way. Natural wood carriages exhibited at the 1893 World's Fair

Three-Spring Pleasure Wagon with Canopy Top made by the Cortland Wagon Co., Cortland, NY
(finished in natural wood)
From the Hub June 1891
Painting.--Ironwork painted to match woodwork.
Trimming.--Drab corduroy.

138

were reported to have the iron work painted a silver bronze color. In order to paint the gear silver bronze the following directions are given from Practical Carriage and Wagon Painting by M. C. Hillick. "Bring the work up to the point of the foundation color for the bronze very carefully, using no lampblack in the priming and first lead coats to throw them to a slate color. The foundation coat should be pure white, mixed to dry without gloss and applied with a camel's-hair brush. Over this coat flow on a coat of rubbing varnish, and when the right "tack" is reached apply the bronze with a soft, clean camel's hair brush. The wiping off and the delicate burnish may be given with a soft piece of chamois skin. Stripe with some color that harmonizes nicely with the bronze, and use no varnish over it. Varnish destroys the richness of the bronze."

The Ferd. F. French & Co., of Boston catalog states that their natural wood vehicles come "with ironwork grained to match." Another option would be to paint the ironwork brown. Striping was not common on natural wood vehicles, but we have seen a fine red line on a natural wood buckboard from Bar Harbor, Maine and a bold black strip with fine yellow lines on a natural wood French wagonette.

Books for additional help with natural wood finishing and graining are:

Marx, Ina Brosseau, Allen Marx, and Robert Marx. Professional Painted Finishes. New York, NY : Watson-Guptill Publications. 1991 - *Chapter on Graining includes: Macassar Ebony - Zebrawood - English Brown Oak - Orientalwood - English Harewood - American Sycamore - Bird's Eye Maple - American Oak - Brazilian Rosewood - Burl - Mahogany - Satinwood - Country Graining.*

Dresdner, Michael. The Woodfinishing Book. Newtown, CT : Tauntom Press, 1992. *Excellent help with staining, filling and finishing natural wood.*

Flexner, Bob. Understanding Wood Finishing. Emmaus, PA : Rodale Press, 1994. - *Excellent help with staining, filling and finishing natural wood.*

Three Spring Wagon.
From the Carriage Monthly September 1894.
Painting.--Lower part of body: deep blue; studs and rails, black; belt, cream white; lettering, black, shaded gold. Carriage part: blue, striped cream.

Colors
PAINT COLOR LIST

John W. MASURY & Son circa 1895	Dupont Spectra Master SolidColor Library M482	RM Fleet Color Book	RM Automotive Color Book
French Chrome Yellow	YS300	3069	1980 Buick A-1143V
Merrimac Green L.	GS184	3238	
Sap Green	GS088 or GS057		
9524[red]		3101R	1980 Buick A-11419V
Milori Green L.	GS173		
Cardinal Red	RS901	3114R	
English Vermillion D.	RS627	3101	1979 Chevrolet A9388F
Brewster Green L.	DS120	3238	
Turquoise Blue		3213	
Ohio Brown D.	DS011		
Car Body Color		3068	
Garnet	DS072	3050	1978 Lincoln A926D
Persian Green	YS576		
9504[burgundy]			1977 Chevrolet A-8705F
American Vermillion L	RS675		
Cobalt Blue		3172	1978 Lincoln A8732,E8732
9528[very dark brown]			
9501[burgundy]		3124M	1980 Chevrolet A989OF E989OF
Cerulean Blue	BS205		1980 Chevrolet A11500,E11500
9509[bright blue]	BS904	3164	
Perfect Blue	DS016		
9527[dark red]		3120	
One Coat Claret	RS660	3126	
9529[very dark wine]	DS072		1978Lincoln A9287F,E9287F
Chrome Yellow O	YS113	3091	
9513[dark blue]			
Golden Ochre	YS242	3094	
Albion Drab	YS257		
9530[dark burgundy]	RS472		
Quaker Green M.	YS456		
Very Deep Green			
Chrome Yellow L. L.	YS912	3068	
One Coat Scarlet	RS660		
Carriage Part Lake	RS388		
Brilliant Green	GS170		
Coach Painters' Green L.	GS274	3218	
Citron Yellow	YS374		
Coach Painters' Brown D.			1978 Lincoln A9296D
9507[bright green]		3217	
9533[dark red brown]			1979 Mercury A1941F/E1941F

Colors

Color Name	Code 1	Code 2	Reference
Primrose Yellow		3067	
Perfect Purple[Lake]			
Chrome Yellow D. O.		3089	
Western Red		3097	
9526[dark red]			
Russian Green	YS560		
Quaker Green D.	YS352	3237	
Brewster Green D.			
Corsican Brown			1978 Lincoln A9296D
Azure Blue		3157	
9511[dark blue]			1978 Lincoln A9299
Chrome Yellow L.	YS300	3075	
9514[dark green]	GS072		
9523[bright red]		3102R	
9536[peach]			
9532[dark tan]			1979 AM&Jeep A-2986F
9535[rose color tan]			
Tuscan Red D.	RS660		
Wine Color			1982 Ford Truck 11444V 2L
Carmine No. 40 L.	RS472		
9518[dark blue]	BS204		1980 Chevrolet A9153,E9153
Ultramarine Blue	BS376		1978 Lincoln A8732,E8732
English Purple Lake	DS010		
Road Cart Red			1978 Cadillac A9392R 80
Imitation Carmine		3124M	
		3125M	
Munich Lake B.			1978 Lincoln A9287F,E9287F
Coach Painters' Green L. L.	GS084	3029	
Brilliant Lake B.			1986 GM 16019 78
Aurora Red L.			1976 Buick A2648F 72
English Vermillion L.	RS674	3094	
Pullman Standard Car Color	YS260		
9516[very dark green]	YS552		
Imitation Gold	YS206		
Indian Red L.	RS664		
9502[dark red&brown]			1977&1978 Chevrolet & GMC 9160 76
Invincible Green	YS354	3232	
Aurora Red D.		3120R	
Mazarine Blue			1981 Chrysler 9850G - Sc9,DT - 8804
American Vermillion D.		3102R	
9508[bright red]	RS910	3117R	
Carmine Red[Lake]		3124M	
Milori Green M.	GS170		
Coach Painters' Green M.	GS275	3215	
Blue Green	GS472		1978 Lincoln A9532G,E9532G

Colors

Name	Code 1	Code 2	Notes
Indian Red D.	RS668		
9506[bright green]			
Royal Green L.	GS184		
Colonial Yellow		3065	
9515[dark olive green]	YS450		
Perfect Yellow	YS380		
Naples Yellow L.			1974-75 Dodge Truck DT2245 A4436, E-4436
Russet L.	YS247		
Russet D.	YS165		
Coach Painters' Brown L.		3048	
Ohio Brown L.		3049	
Baldwin Brown		3050	
9519[dark blue]	BS448		
Oriental Yellow	YS169	3084	
9510[dark brown]	DS011		
9505[bright red]		3114R	
9517[olive green]	YS553		
Eureka Vermillion	RS675	3101E	
9521[olive yellow]			
Masury's Green D.	GS372	3215	
Coach Painters' Green D.	GS480	3231	
9534[red&brown]			
English Scarlet Lake A.		3125M	
Carmine no. 40 D.	RS468	3127M	
9512[dark blue]			
9525[red & orange]		3098	
Milori Green D.	GS284	3215	
9531[red & brown]	RS651		
9522[bright green]			
Red Lake B.		3126M	
9520[dirty yellow]	YS384	3065	
Moss Green	YS460		
Imperial Brown	DS011		
Tuscan Red L.		3124M	
1894 Red		3112R	
Royal Green ?		3237	
9503[dark plum]	RS560	3127M	
Plum Color			1978 Lincoln A9296D 5L
------------------			1978 Lincoln A9532G,E9532C 72
Permanent Red	RS910	3117R	1980 Cadillac A9390F
N. V. Green	GS252		
Sagamore Red M.		3119R1	980 Chevrolet A9889F,E9889F
Jasper Red	RS564	3120R	
Victoria Lake	RS392		
Cinnabar Red L.		3101R	
Tonneau Red		3119R	

Colors

Autumn Brown L.			
Autumn Brown D.			1981 InternationalHar 12447 1625
Cinnabar Red D.	RS904	3111R	1979 AM A2986F
Sagamore Red L.	RS915	3117R	
Sagamore Red D.		3125M	
Royal Blue			1978 Lincoln A8732-E8732 31
Auto Gray	LS128	3262	
Delft Blue LL.[dark blue]	BS536	3172	
Delft Blue L.[dark blue]			
Delft Blue M.[dark blue]			
Delft Blue D.[dark blue]			

These colors may not be an absolute match. Colors that are listed as lakes would not have an absolute match, because lake refers to a process not a solid color. A transparent pigment known as lake sometimes was suspended in the varnish coat and applied over solid colors. This varnish coat called a glaze coat would then mirror the coats of paint underneath. The John W. Masury and Son color book from the collection of Jack Day is only a few of the many hundreds of different colors for painting horse-drawn vehicles. Most colors such as carmine came in a range of about 6 to 10 different shades from bright red to red-brown (almost black).

Driving Trap
From the Hub June 1896

Painting.--Body, imitation canework, painted white, with large medallion in center painted vermilion. Moldings, black. Seat, toe-board bottom and back panel, vermilion. Gear, vermilion, striped with a broad line of black.

Trimming.--Front seat, one long cushion, driving cushion and fall, light Bedford cord. Back plain. Back cushion made in seat. Finish, black.

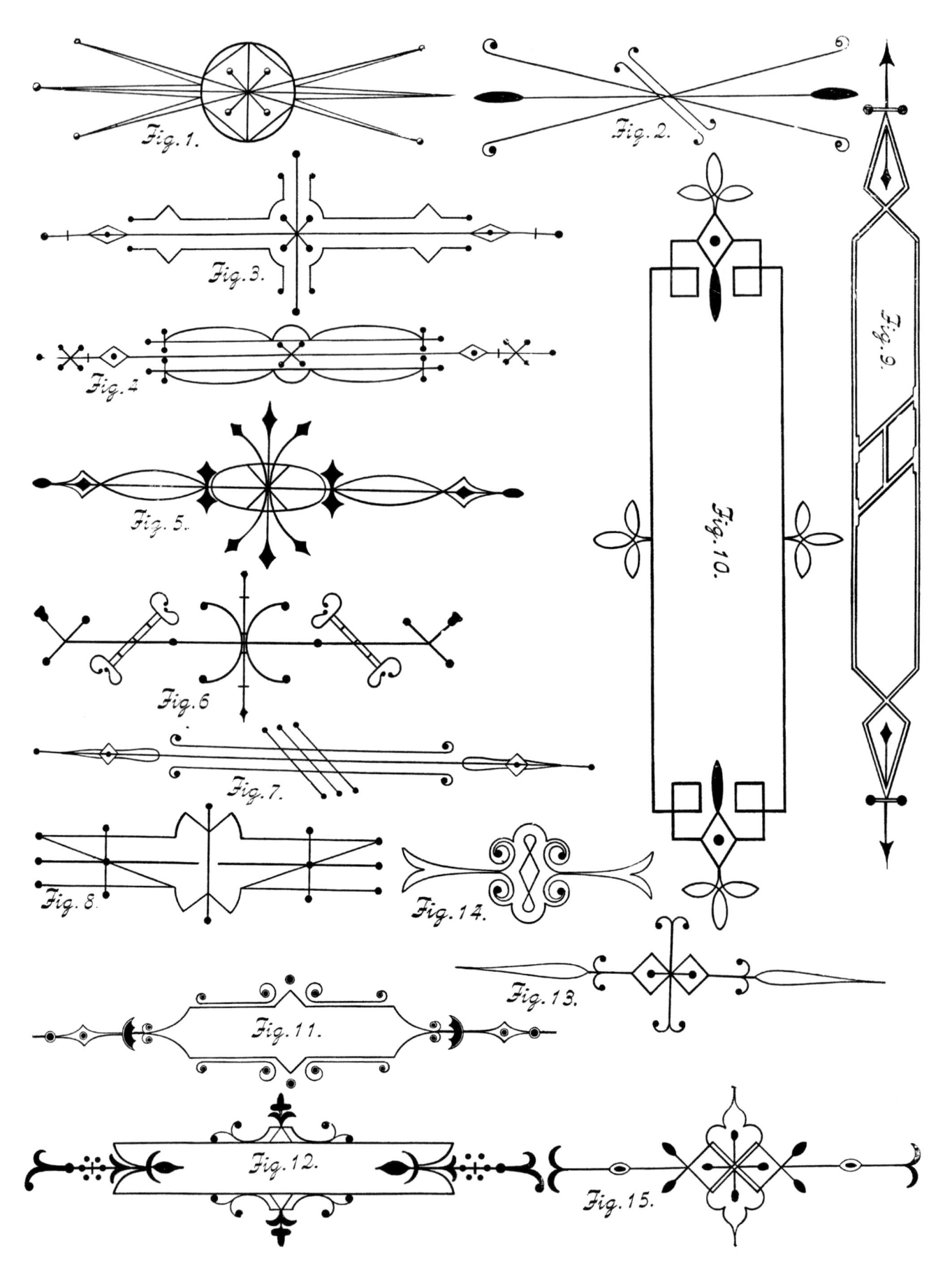

Striping and Ornamenting

CHAPTER 14

STRIPING, SCROLLING AND ORNAMENTING

*Ornamenter's box of tools
Painters' Encyclopedia, 1887*

"The striping is the main ornamentation given all vehicles that are ornamented at all and frequently consists exclusively of that. It is really the most difficult of all the rest for if it is not well done, it will show at a glance by the unevenness of its lines, while mere ornament may look fairly well even when the lines are not perfectly true. It is therefore of the greatest importance that the operator should have had some practice in order that he may have enough confidence to enable him to produce perfect lines."[1]

Vehicles such as farm wagons, commercial vehicles, and Albany sleighs, had very elaborate scrolling. The artists that performed this final art work to the vehicle would not necessarily have to be proficient in both scrolling and striping. In a large factory typically there were separate skilled artisans just for striping, scrolling, crest painting, varnishing, rubbing, body painters, and painters for the undercarriage.

From the Carriage Journal Vol.1 No.3

Styles in striping changed with the times and also varied with the type of carriage in hand. What was good style on a Brougham in 1850 was not necessarily so in 1900. And what was appropriate for a Victoria was surely not appropriate for a Dog Cart. Inasmuch, however as we are dealing with the restoration of carriages, we may presume that some vestige of the

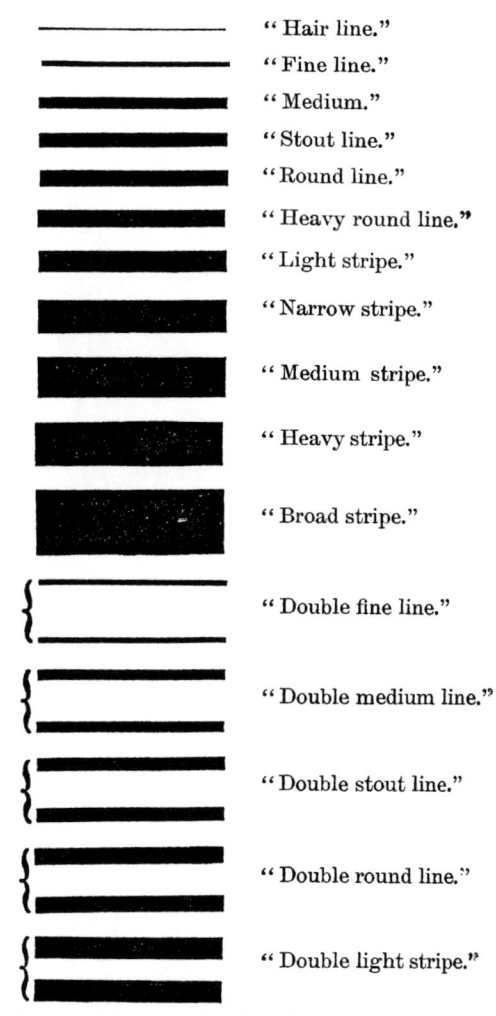

"Hair line."
"Fine line."
"Medium."
"Stout line."
"Round line."
"Heavy round line."
"Light stripe."
"Narrow stripe."
"Medium stripe."
"Heavy stripe."
"Broad stripe."
"Double fine line."
"Double medium line."
"Double stout line."
"Double round line."
"Double light stripe."

Lines are less than ⅛ inch and stripes exceed ⅛ inch.
Complete Carriage and Wagon Painter, 1891.

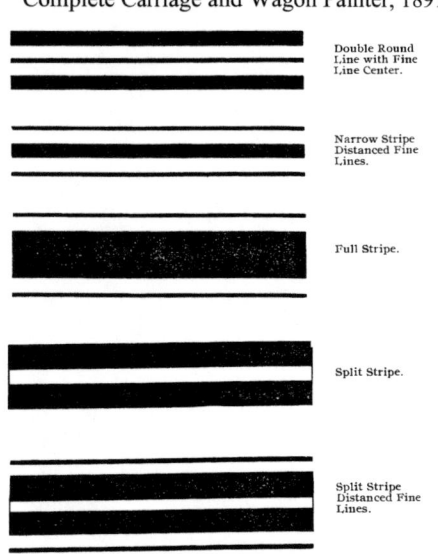

Double Round Line with Fine Line Center.
Narrow Stripe Distanced Fine Lines.
Full Stripe.
Split Stripe.
Split Stripe Distanced Fine Lines.

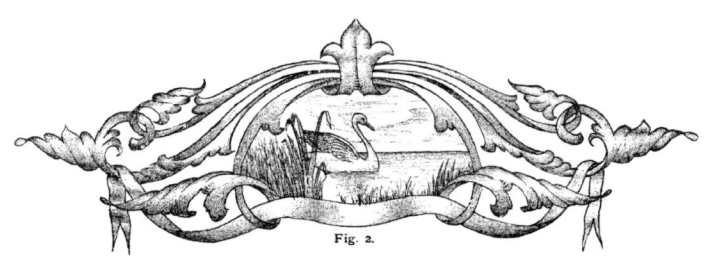

Design for pleasure sleigh, done in gold with scarf glazed with some nice transparent color. First, lay the gold, and shade it with asphaltum, scarf and all, when the shading is quite dry, apply the glazing to the scarf. If desired, the scarf can be glazed with two colors, for instance, the front carmine, and the reverse side, verdigris.

From the Hub Aug. 1888

From the Hub June 1895.

Striping and Ornamenting

original striping is on some part still extant and as has been previously recommended, all such clues should be recorded prior to the removal of the old paint. In restriping it would be well to follow as closely as possible what was initially done, for it would be hard indeed to improve on the old craftsman's work.

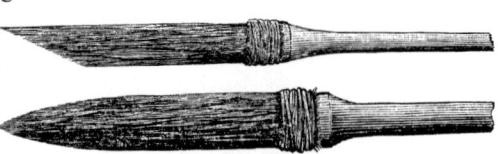

Sword striping brushes
From the Carriage Monthly May 1885

STRIPING

Striping brushes, or pencils as they were called, generally came in two forms, each in various widths. One form had all of the hairs about two inches long, which were usually set round in a quill. The hairs of the other form were graduated in length and were generally attached to a small wooden handle. These were called sword or dagger pencils. Many professional stripers, especially in the old days, made their own striping pencils. Both kinds are still obtainable from art supply stores, art supply catalogs and speciality brush manufacturers.

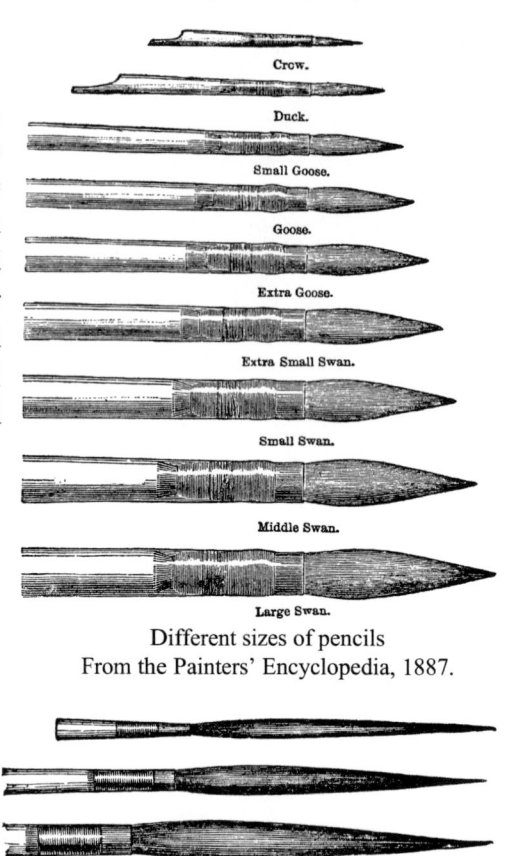

Different sizes of pencils
From the Painters' Encyclopedia, 1887.

Position of the hand in striping the rim of a wheel
From the Painters' Encyclopedia, 1887.

Striping pencils
From the Painters' Encyclopedia 1887

For striping over rubbing varnish in the old conventional manner, Japan color in tubes is best. It should be thinned to a consistency which will run out of the pencil without spreading or remaining in a ridge, with a small amount of rubbing varnish and turpentine.

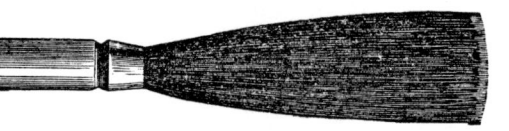

Broad striping pencil
From the Painters' Encyclopedia, 1887

On more modern paint surfaces, professional sign painters use a paint called "1 Shot" It is specially made for sign painters and contains lead. The content of lead causes the paint to act like it has microscopic roller bearings in it and it flows and adheres better than other paints without lead. 1 Shot is available at most artist supply stores or through an art supply catalog.

A small amount of the Japan color should be squeezed out on the palate and thinned to the desired consistency with the pencil being alternately dipped into the varnish and turps, then worked into the color in such a

Ornament or Scroll for commercial vehicle or Albany sleigh. Scroll in gold shaded with asphaltum, than shaded with thinner asphaltum, and pick out with lemon chrome.

From the Carriage Monthly June 1883.

146

way that all of the hairs are filled right up to the handle. The pencil is then held between the thumb and forefinger and the hairs laid down on the end of the surface over which the stripe is to be pulled now without hesitation and with confidence, pull the stripe its full length, using the ring and little finger as a guide. Do not be overly concerned if the stripe is a little irregular at the ends as one may carefully wipe it off sharp with a thin rag tightly pulled over one finger. Better still take a clean pencil dipped into linseed oil and draw it over the irregular end. The exposed Japan color stripe will dry long before the oil which may then be wiped off, together with the unwanted still soft color underneath.

The style of pencil is largely a matter of preference. Stripes of over one eighth of an inch wide, however, are best done with the round pencil. The diameter or width of the pencil determines the width of the resultant stripe. Therefore it is necessary to have a variety of sizes in order to pull stripes of various widths. Tapering stripes or those terminating in points, as on the face of spokes, are best done with the dagger pencil.

Most stripers use a sheet of glass about eight by ten inches for a palate, as after use it is readily cleaned. To the palate should be attached, with masking tape, two small cut-down paper cups or two artist's clip-on tin cups one for varnish and one for turpentine. Professional stripers made their own cups by folding up a piece of paper.

The pencils should be thoroughly cleaned with turpentine after use, treating them carefully as the soft hair is easily damaged. When clean they may be preserved soft by working Vaseline in the hair, [others use neatsfoot oil, sweet oil and specially prepared solutions by brush manufacturers] which should be gently pulled straight between the thumb and forefinger. A tin lead pencil box makes a good keeper. (End of Carriage Journal article.)

For people wishing to do a small amount of striping and they do not have time to master the hand painted method, striping tools are available. These tools apply the color by means of wheels in a range of widths, some even make double stripes. The Beugler Manufacturing Company makes the most versatile striping tool. It has the paint fed into the wheel by pressure, enabling the user to hold it at any angle, plus an assortment of different wheels. Wheel heads are available in widths from a hair line to a broad stripe ½ inch in width, with varying combinations of double wheel heads.

Typical designs for monograms found on seat risers, and the crest panel of doors.

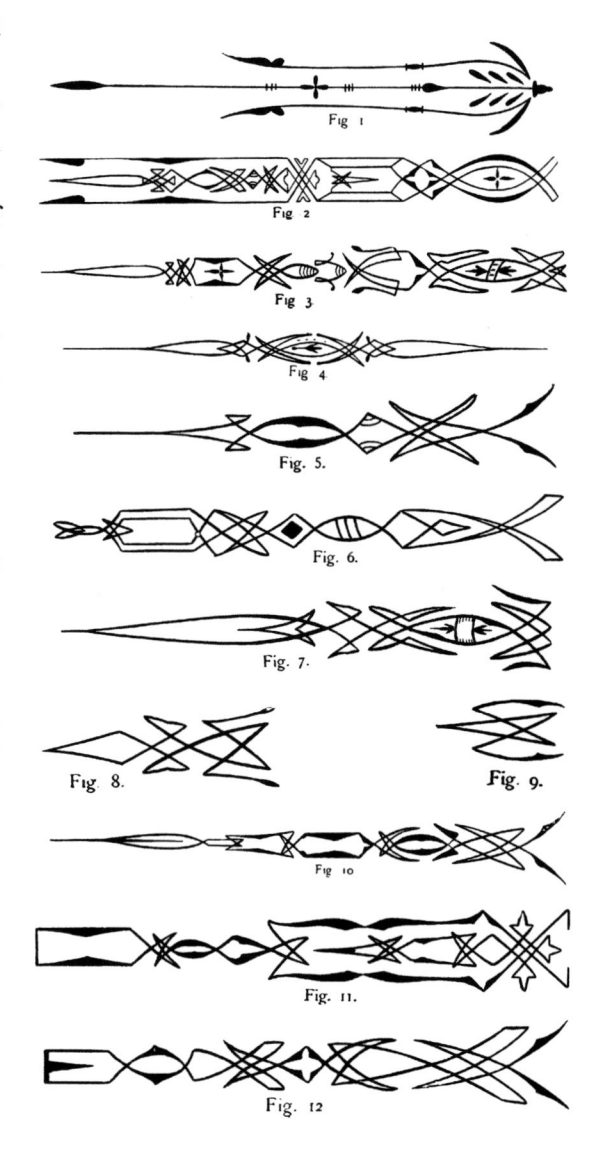

Designs for striping heavy business wagons
From the Hub Jan. 1892

Striping and Ornamenting

A striping tools should be used with a guide as it is difficult to make a perfectly straight line freehand. For straight lines a guide strip should be clamped or secured to the work. For work on steel or iron surfaces the art supply store can supply a magnetic guide strip. Adjustable guides can than be fitted to the tool to follow a guide strip. For striping on felloes, a guide may be used to work against the tire or tire channel.

If someone would like to learn striping, there is an excellent step by step instruction book by John Hannukaine called Pinstriping and Vehicle Graphics, in which he gives product information and tips on striping. It is an art that has seen a revival, not specifically for horse drawn vehicles but for customizing motorized vehicles and sign painting. Many ideas for designs on motorized vehicles came from the horse-drawn vehicle era. If there is not a striper in your area that has worked on horse drawn vehicles it will be your responsibility to provide research for the sign painter or striper as to what is needed for your vehicle, either photographs and tracings of the original layout or copies of patterns from old trade journals, or photographs of other similar vehicles. The easiest way to have a vehicle striped is to have it apart in sections. Have a stand on which to turn the wheels for easy striping. Give some thought to how your vehicle is going to look when it is together. You would not want to have an elaborate ornamental design on a wagon box only to have the design hidden when the wagon box sets on the undercarriage.

Aids for laying out patterns are the use of a chalk line for straight lines and china markers or wax pencils for curve lines. Wipe off the marks with mineral spirits when all the paint is dried. A traditional method used by carriage painters to lay out a pattern was called pricking and pouncing for complicated scroll designs. In pricking the pattern is traced onto a piece of paper and then a tool with a wheel of sharp points is used to make pin holes along the various lines of the pattern. The pattern is lightly sanded and then placed up against the vehicle. Then a pounce bag is used to dust chalk over the pattern leaving little dots of chalk on the vehicle. In looking through art supply catalogs

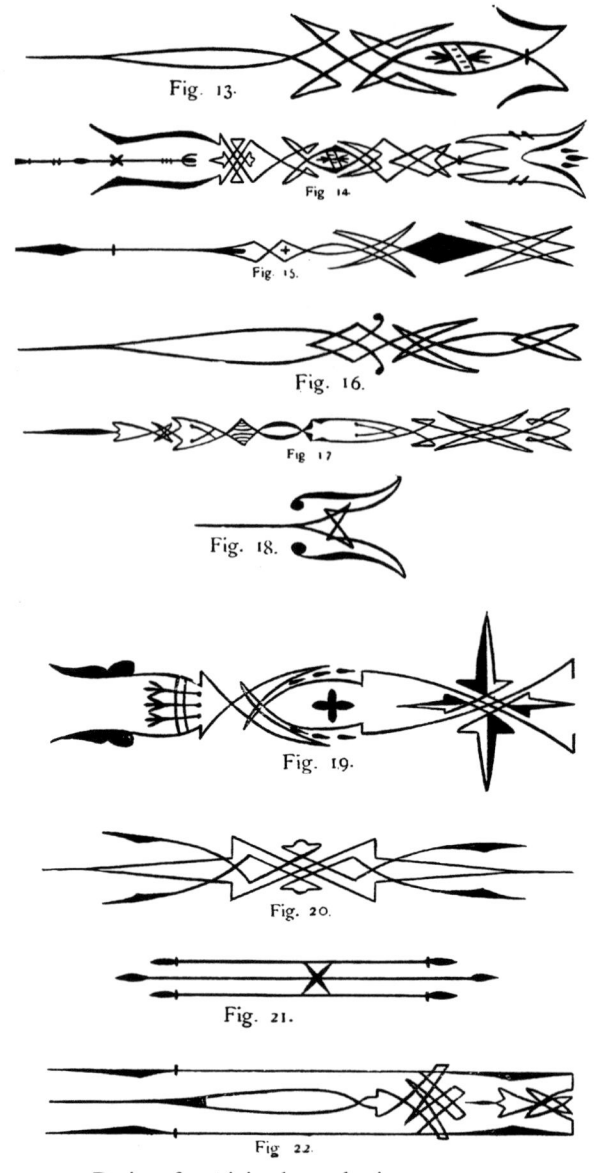

Designs for striping heavy business wagons
From the Hub Jan. 1892

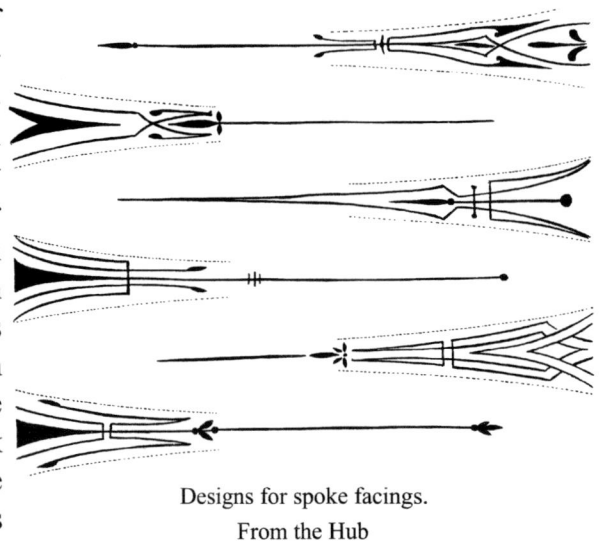

Designs for spoke facings.
From the Hub

you will find some sophisticated help aids nowadays for pouncing: pounce wheels, electro pounce, pounce powder, pounce pads, and brown kraft paper for pattern making.

An alternative to applying striping freehand is the use of some help aids such as tape. There are specially designed striping stencil tapes that are flexible and will go around curves and once the tape is applied the paint is brushed in. The tape is pulled off while the paint is still wet making a uniform line. Narrow 3M tape will also work to go around a wheel rim. Masking tape does not work because it is porous and the paint seeps underneath making a ragged edge.

Besides the highly skilled artist work of the striper and ornamenter using meticulous hand methods, other methods of decoration to the paint work of vehicles were stenciling and transfer ornaments. Stripers and ornamenters originally applied their art work to horse-drawn vehicles before the last coat of varnish, and once all the art work was finished the final coat of varnish was applied.

TRANSFERS

Transfer ornaments are similar to what we now know as decals, except that they reflected the design and taste of the horse-drawn era and they were not self adhesive. During the carriage era about four to six different

Designs for buggy panels and risers, practiced by Western wholesale carriage manufacturers. From the Carriage Monthly May 1905.

companies advertised in the old trade journals transfer ornaments for carriage, wagon and sleigh builders. Transfer ornaments were fashionable for vehicle decoration as early as the 1860's and they advertised them up to the 1900's. Transfer ornaments became less popular on many different types of vehicles late in the carriage era. The following description was found in the *Carriage Monthly* of May 1873 for "The Making and Using of Transfers." "The first step in the process after making the design is to take an outline drawing. This drawing is then transferred to as many stones as there are to be colors in the ornament or picture: each color or shade requiring a separate stone. Before the stone receives the outline, it must be polished to a glassy smoothness with pumice stone. The best work requires from twelve to twenty stones, costing about $80 each. The only stone that can be used successfully is found in and around Bavaria in Germany. Crayon is now covered over such portions of the stone as are to receive a certain color - the brown shading of a scroll it maybe, or the blue sky of a landscape - which, when the stone has been placed under acid, are the only portions of its surface that will receive, or transfer to paper, any color whatever. The next stone is prepared in the same way, and so on until the stones are ready. The first stone is then placed upon the bed of the press, which is the last in a chromo-lithograph, being transposed that the ornament may show perfectly when transferred.

The color having been spread over it with a roller, as in type printing, the sheets of prepared paper, upon which the picture is to be printed, are placed upon it, one by one, and an impression taken. When the whole edition has received the first color, the second stone takes the place of the first, and the same sheets are run through the press again and the second color received. The second stone is then replaced by the third, and this in turn by the fourth, and so on until the picture is finished. The paper is prepared with a coating of gum that can easily be dissolved by water.

Directions for Using the Designs Cover the face of the ornament entirely with a slight coat of fixing varnish or cement. Leave it a few minutes to set, then put it on the object to be ornamented, gilt side down, and press it with a knife, pencil, or any hard, smooth object, to make it adhere well, Then wet the back of the paper thoroughly with water, pressing it down at the same time. After the paper is thoroughly wet, pull it off, slowly raising one corner first.

The ornament, when freed from the paper, must be rinsed with clean water and dried, which prevents cracking. Several hours should elapse before the varnish for finishing is applied, that the Cement may get perfectly dry.

To clean the edges or remove a design, use spirits or turpentine or alcohol.

In transferring, the water softens the gummy substance between the design and paper, which causes their separation, while the cement fastens the design to the surface. Quick-drying varnish, or gold size, is often used by painters instead of cement."

No. 1047

Page of transfer patterns from the 1876 Sample Book of Chas. Palm & Co.

Modern Transfer Ornaments

Anyone wishing to reproduce transfer ornaments should inquire at the sign shops in your area. They are doing remarkable things with computers now in the sign maker's industry, which makes it quite possible to reproduce some old transfer ornaments. These transfers no longer have to be applied to wet varnish, but are prepared with their own adhesive and can be rubbed on any smooth surface.

Striping and Ornamenting

STENCILING

Stenciling can be seen on farm wagons where the manufacturer often stenciled their name on the side of the wagon box or on the axle bed. Other uses of stencils were for some designs on the face of the spoke. Materials for stenciling can be found in most craft stores nowadays and more sophisticated supplies can be found in the art supply catalogs or art stores for making custom stencils, along with special brushes made for stenciling.

Brush used for stenciling
From Painters' Encyclopedia, 1887.

Stencil designs
From the Painters' Encyclopedia, 1887.

GILDING

Gilding is mostly thought of in connection with state carriages, with some state carriages having their entire surface gilded. Other vehicles might have gilding as part of their art work as commercial vehicles and swell body sleighs with sign lettering, scrolling and ornamenting. Gilding is the art of laying on very thin sheets of metal to a tacky surface. Most often gold is the metal being used. Gold with an additive is one of the most ductile of the metals and it can be beaten into very thin sheets. It needs to be beaten extremely thin so that the joints are hidden when the pieces are laid together. It is possible to beat the gold so thin that it would take 350,000 sheets placed one upon another to make a pile of them one inch in height and one ounce of gold will beat out into 2,500 leaves 3 1/4 inches square. Today gold leaf comes in books containing 25 leaves 3 3/8 inches square (the thin sheets of gold are laid out between sheets of paper called a book) and a pack contains 20 books. 1 book containing 25 leaves covers an area about 1 ½ square feet. Gold leaf is sold in three main types. Surface gold is used on surfaces that will be exposed to weather or handling; Glass Gold is for inside surfaces such as windows or glass doors: Patent gold is attached to a carrier sheet so it can be handled easily and is used where there is too much wind for glass or surface gold. Besides the 3 3/8 inch square sheets the art supply catalog has available gold in 67 foot long rolls in widths of 1/4, ½ and 3/4 inches.

The tacky surface called sizing is applied only where the gold leaf is wanted, and some old instructions we found recommended that first a release agent should be put on the area where the sizing is not going to be applied. It might take days or weeks for a coat of varnish to cure completely and to prevent the gold from accidentally sticking to some place it isn't wanted, the area surrounding the intended gilding surface should be coated with pounce powder or the whiting of a potato. There are specially made preparations for sizing to get the right adhesion and working time, anywhere from ready to gild in 2 minutes to 12-15 hours. The very thin sheets of metal are laid on the tacky surface

Gilders' cushion or palette
From the Painters' Encyclopedia, 1887.

at just the right time with a gilder's tip, (a brush about 4 inches wide with very soft hair from a camel or squirrel, about 2 inches long). It is an art that restorers of fine furniture, picture frame restorers, house restorers, and sign painters still practice.

Books for instructions and pattern designs:

Antique Auto Body Decoration for the Restorer. Lockport, NY: Lincoln Publishing, 1994. (This book contains much of the information from Fritz Schriber book Complete Carriage and Wagon Painter 1907)

Carriage Monthly. Philadelphia, PA: Ware Publishing Co., 1865-1916.

Hannukaine, John, Pinstriping and Vehicle Graphics. Fort Myers, FL: Sign Craft Publishing Company, 1992.

Hillick, M. C. Practical Carriage and Wagon Painting : A Treatise On The Painting of Carriages, Wagons and Sleighs Embracing Full and Explicit Directions For Executing All Classes of Work, ... Mendham, NJ : Astragal Press, 1997. (Reprinted of the 1898 edition.)

Hub. New York, NY: Hub Publishing Co. 1858-1919.

LeBlanc, R. J. Gold Leaf Techniques.

SignCraft Magazine. Fort Myers, FL: (current publication).

Ware, I. D. Coachmakers' Illustrated Handbook. Mendham, NJ: Astragal Press, 1995. (reprint of the 1875 edition).

Endnote

[1]. Maire, R. Carriage Painting, Chicago, IL. 1911.

American Roll Gold Leaf Co.

Patented by the America Roll Gold Leaf Co., Providence, R. I.
From the Carriage Monthly April 1914

Trimming Materials

CHAPTER 15

CARRIAGE TRIMMING MATERIALS

Tools

In 1796 William Felton defined trimming as "the covering with cloth, leather, etc., the inside and outside of a carriage." The trimmer therefore requires tools for leather working as well as tools for upholstery work. The following is a list of the basic tools needed. They can be obtained from suppliers of upholsterers' materials and leather craft suppliers. If there is not a retail store in your area there are a number of mail order catalogs. A list of tools includes some of the following: claw-tool or tack-lifter, trimmers's hammer, square-pointed knife, mallet, needles, sewing needles bent and tufting, nippers or pincers, pliers, spools of heavy waxed thread, rule and tape measure, shears, straining fork for stretching webbing, thimble pad, awl, tufting twine, buttons, and tailors chalk.

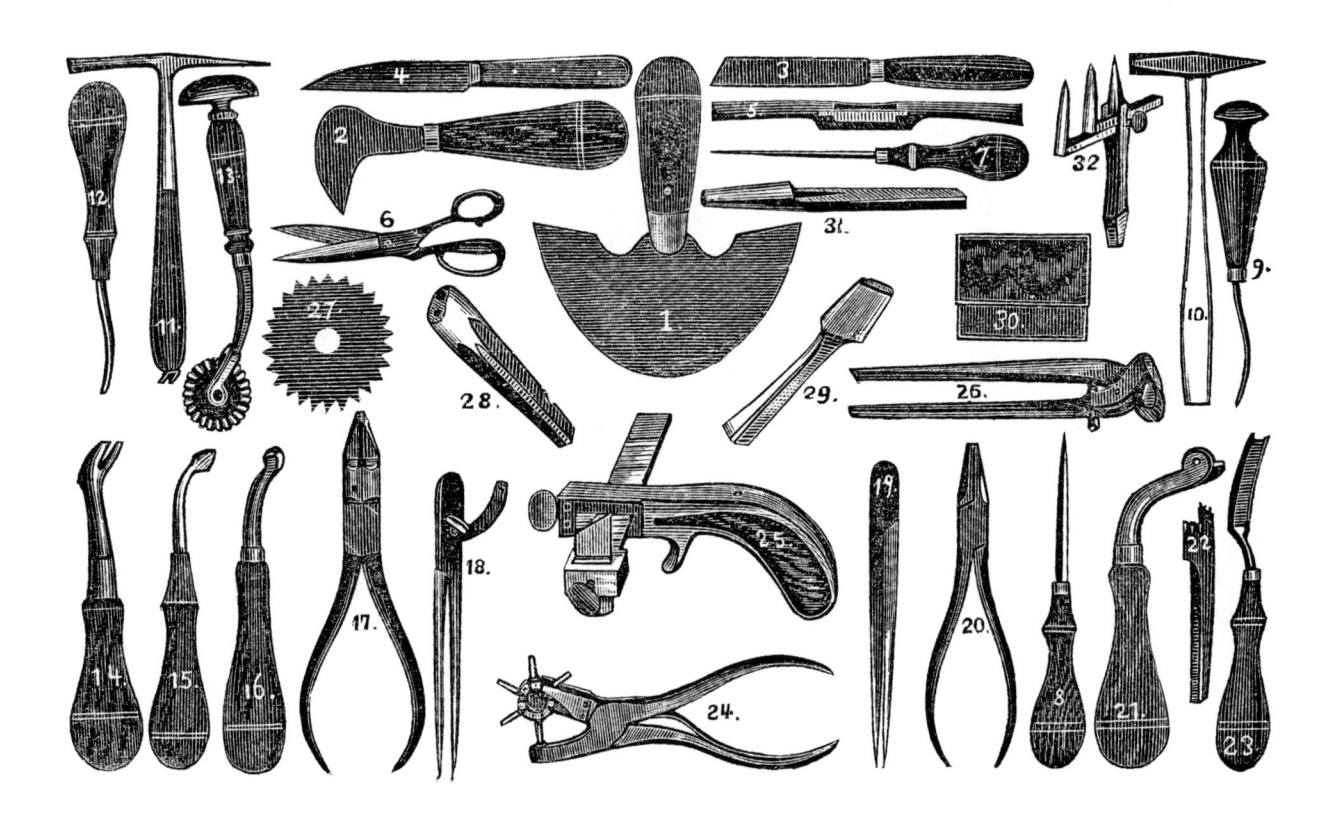

Trimmers' Tools
1. Round knife, 2. Head knife, 3. Square-point knife, 4. Sharp-point knife, 5. Spoke shave, 6. Shears, 9-inch, 7. Seat awl, 8. Square awl, 9. Lacing awl, 10. Riveting hammer, 11. Trimmer's hammer, claw on handle, 12. Patent leather tool, 13. Scalloping carriage, 14. Claw, 15. Single tickler, 16. Single edge creaser, 17. Side cutting plyers, 18. Patent leather compass, 19. Common compass, 20. Pincer plyers, 21. Pricking carriage, 22. Round pinking iron, 23. Edge tool, 24. Revolving punch, 25. Draw gauge, 26. Cutting nippers, 27. Prick wheel, 28. Rivet set, 29. Oval punch, 30. Glass slicker, 31. Round punch, 32. Washer cutter, three foot rule, wrench, stuffing sticks, loop sticks, needles, tufting needles. From the Carriage Trimmers' Manual, 1881.

Sewing Machine

The most expensive set up cost is going to be a good upholstery sewing machine. Although it might be possible to struggle by with a home sewing machine or hand sewing for some jobs, the work will go along so much more pleasantly if you have an upholstery sewing machine with a walking foot to help feed heavy and bulky layers of fabrics in unison. A normal sewing machine has feed dogs on the bed of the sewing machine to help feed the bottom layer of fabric through. Having an upholstery sewing machine with a walking foot means that while the feed dogs are feeding the fabric through on the bottom layer the walking foot is also helping to feed the fabric through the sewing machine on the top layer.

Materials

The materials used in trimming carriages were numerous and they went through many style changes over the course of the horse-drawn vehicle era. Early state carriages were upholstered with silk brocades and similar rich fabrics. Later carriages that were for the general public and would get a lot of use were upholstered with more practical fabrics or leathers. English woolen broadcloth (simply called cloth in the trade) and leather seemed to be the two most common types of materials used on later horse-drawn vehicles. There were various grades of English woolen broadcloth. A fabric known as union cloth was made with a cotton ground and once the woolen surface wore away the upholstery became rather worn looking. The best grade of **English woolen broadcloth** is 100% wool and when finished has the woven threads concealed by a fine nap. A fabric with a nap means that when you run your hand in one direction of the cloth it is going to be smoother than running your hand in the other direction. When laying and cutting out this type of fabric care should be taken that the nap runs down all in one direction. A fabric with a nap causes the light to reflect differently, causing one part of the fabric to look darker or lighter than the other if the nap is not running in the same direction. This type of fabric was something that was carried over into earlier automobiles and this has helped to make this fabric readily available today through upholstery dealers for antique cars. It comes in widths from 54 inches to 60 inches wide, a light weight fabric of 22 oz. to a heavy grade of 34 oz. The weight in ounces refers to how much the fabric weighs per square meter since it is English cloth, if it is American cloth it would be the ounces per square yard. The best of this cloth is made in England and can be purchased through distributors in the United States. When you are able to match the different weights, it is recommended that the light weight fabric be used for the head liner. Woolen broadcloth was used on just about every type of vehicle, a high grade for more expensive vehicles and possibly a lower grade of cloth for cheaper vehicles. We have seen landaus upholstered in anything from an off white color to a dark blue. The color of the upholstery seemed to change with the new styles and fashions, so we really couldn't recommend any particular colors, other than you should always try to do what was original to your vehicle, and if you don't have any original upholstery left in your vehicle, try and do as much research as possible to similar vehicles in museums or the fashion plates in the old trade journals.

Wide and narrow ribbed Bedford cord
From the Hub Jan. 1895

Bedford Cord is a woven fabric with ribs woven into it. This fabric comes in various fiber contents, the best having mostly wool, and from 28 oz. to 30 oz. weight, and various widths of ribs. This fabric was mostly used for sporting vehicles, the outside cushions of road and park coaches, breaks, traps and it looks quit attractive when leather is used for the binding of the cushions. It comes in widths of 55 inches or 62 inches.

Trimming Materials

*Fine and narrow ribbed whip cord
From the Hub Jan. 1895*

Whip Cord is made with hard twisted yarn woven to show diagonal cords. The ridges are very fine as opposed to the ribs of Bedford cord. This cloth is not always easy to find and the best place to start looking would probably be a very high class interior decorators distribution center. This fabric would be quite appropriate on smaller class sporting vehicles, traps, spider phaetons including the head liner, some runabouts, ladies wicker phaetons and any semi- sporting vehicles.

Plush in America was largely a traditional upholstery for the Albany sleighs or swell body sleighs, it has occasionally been seen on some Portland cutters. Portland cutters were more traditionally upholstered with whip cord and woolen broadcloth or similar fabrics. For a number of years plush with a floral designs was quite popular for Albany sleighs. Other things we have seen that we might think of being out of place nowadays was plush that was a very brilliant purple color. Modern taste seems to lean toward plush of different shades of reds, (which some of these sleighs were traditionally). Plush or Silk Plush were the terms applied to long cut pile fabrics with a long and shaggy pile and not being evenly shorn. Mohair plush was the term applied to close, even, relatively low stiff pile. Mohair plush in solid colors is presently available from the antique automobile upholstery supplier or the interior decorators. It does not match in quality to some of the original plushes found on sleighs that had a longer cut pile, or plushes with a floral design. We do not know of any plushes presently available that have the floral design, so it would be important to preserve this type of original fabric when possible. If you needed to display your sleigh and the original fabric is pretty bad you could always throw a sleigh robe over the seat to hide the ugly spots, but as more people get educated they might enjoy seeing the original fabric, as this fabric is no longer made in this high tech world.

Part of the loop cut on the left, uncut loop on right.

Pile or plush weaving is of two kinds, loop pile and cut pile. The way in which this is produced is by having, in addition to the usual warp and weft threads, a third thread, which is introduced as warp, and woven into the ground, and formed into loops on the surface of the cloth, by being woven over wires the breadth of the cloth. In the case of a loop pile the wires are simply drawn out, but in the case of a cut pile the wires are cut out by passing a sharp knife along a groove in their upper surface, or by having a sharp knife affixed to the end of the wire, which cuts its way as the wires are drawn out. [1]

Tapestry cloth as it was called by the Brewster & Co. of New York was a fabric with a loop pile or cut pile with a small geometric pattern throughout, of browns and blacks. (In the traditional sense of textile terminology this would not be called a tapestry cloth). This fabric was used for the outside cushions of coaches, breaks and bronson wagons. Presently this fabric is produced commercially for interior decorators mostly in solid colors, and fabric matching the original would have to be custom made.

Tapestry cloth with a loop pile and small geometric figure

155

Camels Hair Cloth

Camels Hair is an upholstery fabric that was found on a line of natural wood or country style vehicles made by Brewster & Co. of New York. It was a plain woven fabric of a tan color or light brown color and it is believed that there were different types. Some was made using wool and some carriages were upholstered with a fabric made of cotton.

Damask in the head liner of a stagecoach.

Luxury Fabrics were used frequently up to about the 1860's for trimming the interiors of closed carriages. The most usual material was tabarette, made with a cotton back faced with silk. Plain colored satin was sometimes used for the inside trimming of broughams or coupes. Other luxury fabrics for carriages were figured damask or brocade. Traditionally Damask upholstery was a solid-colored silk or worsted fabric whose pattern was created by contrasts in light reflected off its warp-faced satin weave figure, set against its weft-faced satin weave ground. Its complex woven pattern was usually flowers or foliage, but might include all sorts of other decorative elements...

Brocade in the late 19th century was a term applied to many types of fabrics, whose only connection seemed to be the presence of a pattern. To brocade is to weave a supplementary pattern weft into the ground weave of a fabric, inserting it only where a figure is desired. Brocading wefts are not thrown across the full width of the cloth; they can usually be recognized as long floats on the reverse side that mark the outer edges of each brocaded motif.[2] These types of fabrics have been seen in the head liners of stagecoaches or the lining of parasol tops for carriages, either a solid color or a multi color.

Solid color silk was used for shades with rollers. This fabric was usually in narrow widths with the selvage edges used as the side hems. It is possible to find this silk at fabric stores for high quality dressmakers, but the side hems would either have to have a stitched hem or an anti-fray glue used on the edges. An anti-fray glue can be used to make a fake selvage by running a piece of about " from the edge and then applying the glue. In storing carriages with silk fabric, keep in mind that silk is destroyed if it is exposed to sunlight for a lengthy period. Luxury fabrics can be found at interior decorators' stores, and some of these fabrics can also be found at fabric stores for dressmakers.

Leather of a fine quality, such as Morocco, later replaced the use of luxury fabrics in closed carriages. True Morocco is made from goat skins with a special grain called Morocco grain. It is tanned with an infusion of the leaves of a variety of sumac. Being made from goat skins makes for small leather hides, therefore requiring great skill in matching and cutting. Morocco leather is expensive, but it is still available through suppliers for bookbinders. It may be also possible to get some imitation Morocco leather made from larger hides that are grained to look like Morocco grain.

Trimming Materials

The most common types of American carriages such as buggies, surreys and driving wagons were often trimmed with leather, usually split cow or ox-hide. Besides the traditionally popular black color we have found years in the old trade catalogs in which reds, and blues were popular. A range of upholstery leather is still being made for the automobile and furniture trade and it is supplied in full hides, 40 to 45 square feet, or half-hides 20 to 23 square feet. There is a large selection to choose from with some leathers being soft and supple and other hides being more stiff. It is important to consider what the job is and what kind of look and feel you are trying to achieve.

Tanning Methods: there are two methods of tanning. One is known as Chrome Tanning and the other is Vegetable Tanning also called Oak Tanning. Chrome Tanning involves the use of chemicals usually compounds of the metal chromium, hence the name, "Chrome Tanning." Leathers tanned in this manner are usually water resistant (not waterproof). Leather being a "skin" has pore holes and after a time allows water to penetrate. The advantage of Chrome Tanning is that the fibers of the leather are tightened and thus it is given more tensile strength. In Vegetable Tanning, the extracts from tree bark, Quebracho, Oak and others, are used. Most of this tanning material is imported from South America. This process of tanning is long and costly and often requires one hundred days or more.[3] Vegetable tan leather has the ability to absorb water immediately and if it has a finished surface it can be made wet from the back for shaping and molding. For carriage trimming vegetable tan leather has a better character when being used for straps, covering dashes and fenders, shafts and pole coverings and top work. Upholstery leather may be of either chrome tan or vegetable tan leather depending on your personal taste.

Patent leather is leather with a very shining surface applied to it. It comes in various thicknesses to be used for dash and fender covering, shaft and pole coverings and heavy weight for seat and top valances. There are about three or four places that have a special model 67-1 Singer sewing machine in operation so that they can still sew dashes and fenders by machine. It is also possible to recover your own dash and fenders by hand stitching with an awl. The stitching holes need to be first marked off with a prick wheel. Available for dash and fender covering is also imitation patent leather which might be easier for some people to work with when hand stitching. There are some very good looking grades of imitation patent leather and some cheap grades, so it might be necessary to shop around.

Gum drill (coated with varnish) **or Macintosh cloth** (coated with a rubber mixture) was a waterproof cloth that was largely used for the underside of cushions, rain aprons, underside of the cushion fall, folding tops of buggies and surreys and rain covers for the vehicle. Variations of this cloth have been seen glued to roofs of broughams, standing surrey tops and similar roof tops. Other names for this waterproof cloth used on buggy tops, etc. was American Leather Cloth, Enameled or Oil Cloth. There are two very excellent substitutes sold now for these purposes. One is a vinyl coated nylon topping material that works well for the bottom of seat cushions where you have to hand sew them closed. This fabric is very strong for stretching and pulling and stitching and it is soft enough to mold ever so slightly to seat brackets that might be under the cushion. The other is a vinyl coating on a cotton canvas which is stiffer and harder to sew by hand and this works well for gluing on roof tops and making buggy tops, and for the use of the underside of cushion falls. We have seen people make the mistake of using vinyl upholstery fabric or real leather that is soft and pliable intended for upholstery for the folding top. These materials are too soft and flexible and they do not create a nice crisp look, as if the proper materials were used for tops. The material for the top needs to be stiffer so that it does not sag and lose its crisp shape.

Artificial leather

Also available in a much greater range is upholstery vinyl with imitation leather grain. This artificial material is durable and in some respects superior to leather, being uniform in strength, and less waste in cutting. Artificial leathers were on the market in the latter part of the 1850's and were made of fabric coated with some kind of rubber compound.

Ralph Lane has supplied the following information on modern artificial leather.

Naugahyde

Naugahyde is a trade name that one hears quite often, and applies to a vinyl leather-look-alike. However this does not mean much, except to say that it is quality replacement for the real thing. There are many other makers of "vinyls" in a thousand hues and finishes. Most are durable quality and faithfully represent the leather look of old. It is probably the look of real leather that is most desirable for our needs on a buggy seat, but we must consider some other very necessary qualities if we want our seat to provide lasting comfort under a wide range of conditions. Marine seating is subjected to more abuse from physical use and the elements than most other seats; given the fact that they are stood upon as much as sat upon, as well as usually being left to dry in the hot sun after absorbing water as well as the sometimes violent shocks transmitted through the hull of a fast boat. Manufacturers have addressed these factors by introducing many new supported vinyl fabrics suitable for this type of use, and I find them to be a good choice for other forms of recreational outdoor seating. These products are sold under a variety of different names or brands, such as Naugahyde, but just make sure that whatever you buy is classified as being suitable for outdoor use. I like to use a product called Windsurfer by Boltaflex, that is by weight, 26.4 ounces per lineal yard and has a Polyester non-woven backing. It is also not as slippery as some of the other

Advertisement from the Hub Aug. 1891.

vinyls, which I believe to be used on seats where the operator is not strapped in, as in a motor vehicle. This product is also ultra-violet ray resistant to reduce fading, as well as being mildew resistant and hard wearing. Coated at the factory with PreFixx this vinyl is designed to be cleaned easily over and over without premature wear. Whatever you choose to buy is up to you, but try to avoid the cheaper grades of unsuitable, sometimes diamond quilted goods that are carried in a lot of the larger "Do It Yourself" stores.

The thread used in the manufacture of outdoor seating ought to be of the kind that will resist the effect of ultra violet rays as well as moisture. The best is Dacron and failing that, a polyester cotton blend is a good choice. Both types will fill the needle holes as long as the correct size of needle for the thread size that will accept the thread being used is chosen. A good rule of thumb is to use the finest needle size that will accept the thread and lay a nicely formed stitch. Round-point needles are suitable for vinyls and upholstery-weight leather. Triangular points are only needed where a distinctive diagonally formed stitch is desired on the heavier leathers.

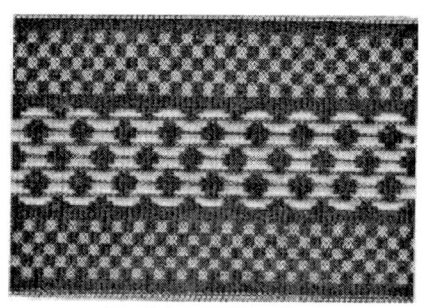

Coach lace or Broadlace
From the Carriage Monthly Dec. 1901

Carriage Lace - The better carriages trimmed in wool broadcloth, leather or luxury fabrics usually had seat falls, door pockets etc., finished with carriage lace. This lace was woven in a wide range of patterns and textile fibers. Being most like Brussels carpet weaving the ground warp was usually linen or cotton with the face warp being wool or silk. Depending on the current fashions the designs were elaborate and bold for some years and more subdued in color and design for other years. The different kinds of carriage lace are broad lace or coach lace, made from 2 ½ to 3 ½ or more inches wide. Seaming lace was a narrow lace with two selvage edges used for cushion edges with a cord sewn in it. Pasting lace is the narrowest of the laces made in widths of ½ or 3/4 inch and this was used to cover tacks or nail heads, or where other parts of trimming are joined. Carriage lace is still made in a limited range of patterns and colors, but it is can be quit expensive. An enclosed coach body can take up to 100 yards of seaming and pasting lace.

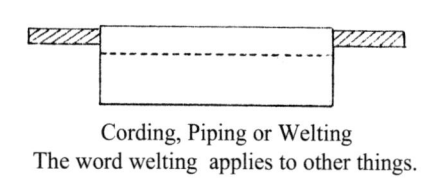

Cording, Piping or Welting
The word welting applies to other things.

Made-up edge welts and piping or welting (formerly called seaming lace) for trimming can be obtained ready made or you can make your own. Piping and welting have generally come to mean the same and refer to a strip of material folded over a cord of cotton, vinyl or other synthetic filler. The strip of material is stitched closed over the cord using a welting foot or zipper foot on the sewing machine. The welting is then stitched between the seams of cushions to give the seam greater strength or tacked along the edges of squabs to give it a finished look with an edging of coach lace or pasting lace. When stitching welting between the seams of a cushion care must be used so that the stitching does not show from the welting. Leather already cut to the appropriate width for making welting can be bought in rolls from the car upholstery supplier or sometimes can be bought with the cord already sewn in. Leather welting was used by some carriage makers, because it was thought to wear better as well as being attractive. When making your own welting out of the fabric to match there does not seem to be any set rule as to the direction in which carriage makers cut the welting out of the fabric. We have seen Bedford Cord with the welting having the ribs running in both directions and occasionally have seen it running in the direction of the bias. Any good dress maker would tell you that welting should be cut on the bias so that it can stretch around the curves, but this also takes more fabric.

Trimming Materials

Stuffing materials the materials used for stuffing carriage cushions etc. included flock, hair, cotton waste, Spanish moss, bass or whalebone shavings, waste hemp or jute, pulu, a variety of seaweed and coconut fiber. For seat cushions unquestionably the best stuffing material was curled horse hair, because it maintains its body and elasticity. In fact old cushions stuffed with horse hair are still good today if proper care was taken of them. The only problem with horsehair is that it is eaten by moths. The other stuffing materials tried from plant fibers, would not be eaten by moths, but they were found to deteriorate with age and turn dusty. A company that originally supplied horsehair to the carriage industry is still in business in Philadelphia and if you are looking for a traditional carriage upholstery job this would be the best stuffing. Horse hair and hog hair is supplied in different grades in 50 lb. bales.

Most commercial jobs for carriages now use **Polyurethane foam** and polyester batting is substituted for cotton batting. In most cases it is detectable when foam is used as it has a slightly square shape on the corners rather than a soft rounded look. Part of the square look can be taken off by rounding the corners with a knife.

Facts On Foam from Pacific Fiber Products

Polyurethane foam has become one of the most widely used products in upholstered furniture. Unfortunately, for the reupholsterer, it is also one of the least understood.

Over the years, cushion complaints have been the #1 problem faced by manufacturers. This is why, in recent years, the furniture industry has been upgrading the quality of the foams that they use, particularly for seating. Reupholsterers can eliminate a lot of seating problems by following this trend.

There is also a lot of misunderstanding of the terms used to describe foam. Here are a few of them:

DENSITY-this is a measure of the weight of foam, not the firmness. It is measured in pounds per cubic foot.

ILD(Compression)-this is the measure of the firmness of foam. Using a piece of foam 4" thick x 19" x 19", a machine measures the force needed to compress the entire piece from 4" down to 3". This is also measured in pounds.

Many foam producers use a 4 number system to identify their foam types: (for example) 1835-first 2 numbers are the density, or 1.8 lbs. per cubic foot. Second 2 numbers are the ILD - 35 lbs: 2860 - this would be a 2.8 lb. density and a 60 lb. ILD.

Some foamers may use other names or numbering systems, but the foams are still measured this way.

Quality: With the exception of loaded foams, the higher the density, the better the quality and the more expensive the foam will be. So if you are comparing prices, be sure you are also comparing the same densities.

Loaded Foam - also sometimes called filled foam. This type of foam achieves a high density (heavy weight) by means of an added filler material. In other words a 3.0 lb. loaded foam might be 1.5 lbs. per cubic foot of filler weight. This achieves the desired effect of making cushions feel heavy, but unfortunately does nothing for the foam quality.

Summary- When comparing foams, the higher the density (excluding the loaded foams) the better the quality. The higher the compression number, the harder the foam. The right compression for you is a matter of personal preference.

Trimming Materials

Floor coverings

Floor covering for carriages can be **oil cloth** that is solid in color or has a small printed pattern on it. It is similar to what we now call linoleum, only modern linoleum is not made on a canvas fabric. A type of linoleum, now available in solid colors, called battleship linoleum with a burlap backing is very much like some of the original. To find linoleum with a small printed pattern might be a more difficult task.[4] Oil cloth was used on the flooring of all types of carriages. It was often used on the flooring for the inside of coaches to be used in muddy and rainy weather. In fair weather a piece of carpet with a binding that matched the seaming lace of the upholstery was laid over the linoleum to be used in sunny weather.

Printed linoleum

Battleship linoleum on the top of a coach would be bound with leather binding except where it butted against the frame, and tacked fast to the carriage with small brass brads. Other ways we have seen this linoleum finished is to burnish the edges and mark a crease along the edge the same as finishing the edge of a leather strap.

Wilton carpet is a carpet with a cut pile, still available from the antique automobile upholstery suppliers. Originally some Wilton carpets had a small geometric pattern. A carpet with a looped pile is known as a **Brussels carpet** and was used on some carriages. Other floor coverings used on carriages would have been **rubber mats**, they came in various designs some were rather thick mats with a filigree design, and we have seen in manufacturers catalogs that some companies supplied thinner rubber mats with their name embossed on the mat.

Two designs for Brussels carpeting
Carriage Builders' & Harness Makers' Art Journal, 1859

Endnotes

[1]. [Ashenhurst, Thos. R.] Weaving and Designing of Textiles Fabrics. [s.l.]; [19?].

[2]. Adrosko, Rita. "Identifying Late 19th-Century Upholstery Fabrics." Upholstery Conservation Preprints of a Symposium held at Colonial Williamsburg Feb. 2-4, 1990. Fremont, NH : American Conservation Consortium, Ltd., 1990.

[3]. Tandy, Dave L. "Leather Knowledge." Forth Worth, TX : Tandy Leather Company, 1988.

[4]. Fred E. Hollaender of Holland has put together a documentation of how this linoleum was made.

Rubber Mats and Matting in many designs and styles for the Carriage and Automobile Trade in black, white and red, with and without special design name plates.

Carriage Monthly September 1909

The Victor Rubber Co.

SPRINGFIELD, - OHIO

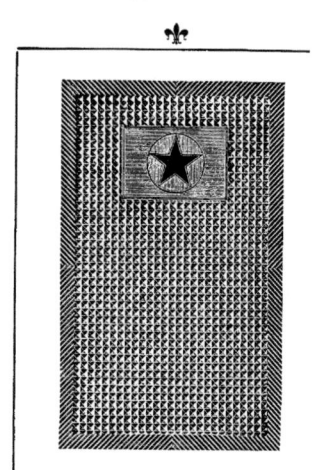

161

Trimming Materials

Material for Trimming Top Side-Bar Wagon

Width on Seat, 30 inches: Spread of Top, 3 feet 6 inches; 3 Bows

65 feet top leather
6 feet soft leather
7 feet railing
8 feet grain dash
1½ yards body cloth
3⅝ yds. head lining
⅞ yds. enamel cloth
2 yds. rubber
1⅝ yd. velvet carpet
2¼ yds. buckram
8 ½ lbs. curled hair
½ lb. wadding
78 buttons
72 nails

31 screws
24 knobs
2 papers tacks
¼ lb. cord and twine
1 oz. thread
3 bows
1 set joints and props
12 rivets and nuts
1 whip socket and fasteners
1 set slat irons
½ lb. paste
4 buckles and billets
1 back

2½ yds. webbing
5 yds. carpet binding
1 back light
13 feet risers
20 straps
4½ yds. muslin
¾ yds. patent cloth
4 carpet loops
2 steel back straps
6½ in. rubber for prop blocks
4 prop washers
1 pair lamps

Material for Trimming Landau, Leather Top

Width on Back Seat, 52 inches; 6 Bows

120 feet top leather
20 ft. Japan trimming
6 ft. skirting
36 ft. enamel leather
17 lbs. harness leather
14 goatskins
7½ yards body cloth
2 yards doeskin
10 yards cotton
1½ yards bulaps
2 yds. enameled cloth
24 yds. broad lace
100 yds. Narrow lace
2 yds. oil carpet
2½ yds. velvet carpet
5 yds. buckram
½ yd. plush
2 pairs gimps
2 pairs frogs
3 paris of triggers

15 lbs. curled hair
8 lbs. wadding
3 gross tufts
1½ gross nails
2 gross screws
4 knobs
3 paper tacks
½ lb. cord and twine
2 balls thread
7 large tassels
4 spring barrels
9 yards molding
3 ½ yards silk
6 bows
2 pairs joints & props
4 rivets & 8 nuts
2 glass
3 glass string slides
1 whip socket
1 pair lamps
1 looking glass

1 card case
2 pairs slat irons
10 lbs. paste
6 buckles & billets
1 pair cross straps
1 pair pole straps
4 silver buckles
2 backstrap loops
2 slides
5 yards webbing
12 springs
2 curtain lights
1 pair silk frogs
2 lbs. risers
1 set cushion straps
1 speaking tube
1 bell pull-to handles
2 inside handles
1 bell
1 pair door handles
1 pair dickey seat handles

Material for Trimming Vis-a-Vis

Width on Back Seat, 40 inches; Spread of Top, 49 inches; 3 Bows

75 feet top leather
26 ft. Japan trimming leather
50ft. colored leather or 4yds. body cloth
9 feet hard splits
6 feet soft splits
13 feet railing
4¾ yds. headlining
3 yards cotton
6 yards burlap
4 yards cambric
7 yds. enamel cloth
2¾ yards rubber
8½ yards broad lace
32 yards narrow lace
1¾ yds. oil carpet

3¾ yards carpet
15 lbs. curled hair
5 lbs. pig hair
1 gross tufts
3 yards wadding
4 doz. buttons
3 gross nails
⅔ doz. screws
3½ doz. knobs
3½ lbs. tacks
1 lb. cord & twine
¼ lb. thread
7 feet molding
3 bows
4 each joints & props.
4 rivets
8 nuts
1 set slat irons

6 lbs. paste
8 each buckles&billets
1 pair cross straps
4 silver buckles
1 card case
5 yards webbing
8 springs
8 pressed loops
1 back light
1 storm curtain light
½ sheet straw board
1½ lbs. risers
1 pair roll-up straps
1 pair apron straps
1 whip socket
1 pair spring-lock handles
1 pair pull handles
4 silver dash hooks

Material for Trimming Albany Cutter

Width on Seat, 38 inches

7 ft. soft russet leather
1¾ yds. body cloth
3 yards cotton
¾ yds. enamel cloth
1½ yards broad lace
19 yards narrow lace
2½ yds. velvet carpet
2 yards buckram
2 lbs. curled hair

2 lbs. moss
6 dozen buttons
1 dozen nails
3 papers tacks
3 oz. thread
1 pint paste
1 pair safety straps
1 whip socket
¼ lb. cord & twine

Material for Trimming Portland Sleigh

Width on Seat, 30 inches

2½ yards plush
1 yd. enamel cloth
1 lb. harness leather
2½ yards broad lace
8 yards narrow lace

1 yard velvet carpet
2 yards buckram
1½ lbs. curled hair
1 lb. moss
3½ dozen buttons

2 dozen nails
3 papers tacks
¼ lb. cord & twine
3 oz. thread
1 pint paste

Trimming Materials

Material for Trimming Brougham
Width on Back Seat, 42 inches

26 ft. Japan trimming
2½ feet skirting
5 feet hard splits
3 feet sort splits
6 feet railing
14½ feet grain dash
7 goatskins
5¼ yds. body cloth
⅞ yds. black cloth
2½ yds. cotton duck
6½ yd. cotton drilling
2 yards burlaps
4 yards cambric
1 yard enamel cloth
2⅞ yard rubber
16 yards broad lace
60 yards narrow lace
2 yards oil cloth
4 yards Wilton carpet
2 yards braid
1 whip socket
1 pair shaft tips

1 set shaft straps
1 pair apron straps
1 pair pole straps
18 lbs. curled hair
1 lb. wadding
21 buttons
183 tufts
1 gross nails covered
½ gross screws
2 knobs
1½ lbs. tacks
¾ lbs. Cord & twine
1 pair silver eyelets
1 oz. thread
4 holder tassels
3 curtain tassels
6 acorn tassels
3 spring barrels
5 feet molding
3 yards silk
8 yards silk cord

1 looking glass
4 French plate glass
1 check cord
½ dz. finishing screws
1½ dz. silver finishing screws
1 set dash hooks
4 lbs. paste
2 each buckles & billets
1 pair silver buckles
3 bone slides
3 yards webbing
22 springs
1 back light
2 side lights
1 lb. risers
1 set cushion straps
1 pair frogs, silk
1 pair frogs ivory
1 card case
1 pair lever handles
1 pair door handles

Material for Trimming Dog Cart
Two-Wheeler; Width on seat, 35 inches

3 ft. Japan trimming
20 ft. hard & soft splits
7 ft. railing
1⅜ yds. body cloth
3 yds. cotton
1 yd. enamel cloth
2 yds. rubber
1¼ yds. oil carpet
1¼ velvet carpet

1½ yds. buckram
5 lbs. curled hair
3 lbs. pig hair
½ lb. wadding
2½ gross buttons
8 screws
2 knobs
½ lb. Tacks
⅛ lb. cord & twine

1 oz. thread
1½ lbs. Paste
2 buckles
2 silver buckles
3 silver dash hooks
1 pair shaft straps
1 pair cushion straps
1 pair apron straps
3 dash straps

from the Carriage Trimmers Manual by William FitzGerald, 1881.

164

FESTOONS, CLOTH VALANCES AND FRINGE FOR CARRIAGE TOPS

The earliest use of fringe for carriage tops was what was known as festoons. William Felton describes these in 1796 as, "The festoon curtain: a silk curtain trimmed with silk fringe; mostly intended for ornament only, being found inconvenient for use; they are fixed over the lights or windows of the doors as represented, and are sometimes made to hang in a drapery form on the sides, but mostly are used for the top only. They furnish very much the inside of a carriage, but are of no utility other ways." This first use of fringe for tops is a narrow plain fringe used for the interior trimming of the valance or, as Felton called it, the festoon around the sides of the head liner. This trimming is seen as being fashionable in the illustration of an 1860s surrey and in the Abbot and Downing coach.

Other ways in which carriage tops could be finished is with cut work. Using good quality woolen broadcloth, a design could be cut by using sharp chisels formed to various designs.

Cloth Valances from the Hub Dec. 1872

From the G. & D. Cook catalog circa 1860

Festoon on an Abbot & Downing Coach made in 1882
From the collection of Jack Day

Cloth Valances for Open Tops
From the Hub Dec. 1872

No. I shows a pattern made up of two different designs, which if desired could be used separately. The size is in full, but on the top we have cut off the seam which would be necessary in sewing on.

No. II shows a running pattern, and in the carriage where we saw it used it was arranged so that the form was made to incline backward; but we prefer that it should incline front. In other words, we think that, in the way our cut is printed, it should be used in a carriage heading from left to right.

No. III shows a small pattern, and is therefore best adapted for a light top wagon or a pony phaeton. This is an original design with us, and we think it pleasing.

No. IV is a pattern well adapted for four or six-seat phaetons with five bow tops, on account of its size.

Trimming Materials

The first appearance of fringes on stationary tops, as what we know as the surrey today, was not until about 1875, and it wasn't until about the 1880s that it became a common occurrence.

Canopy Top surrey
Hub July 1901

Linthicum Scholsser Carriage Co., Defiance, Ohio
Carriage Monthly April 1892

M. M. Dennett, Amesbury, Massachusetts
Carriage and Harness Retail February 1893

Studebaker Bros. Manufacturing Co., South Bend, Indiana
Carriage Monthly October 1883

Keystone Wagon Works, Reading, Pennsylvania
Vehicle Dealer February 1903

Safety Buggy Company, Lancaster, Pennsylvania
Vehicle Dealer April 15, 1902

Trimming Materials

The first instruction on fringe making that we found was from *Recueil de Planches, sur Les Sciences, Les Arts Liberaux, et Les Arts Mechaniques, Avec Leur Explication* in 1762, being made by hand. The Horstmann Co. of Philadelphia, was the first company in America to employ automated plaiting and braiding machinery for fringe making in the 1840s. This company was one of the first supply houses for trimming materials for the carriage trade.

Other companies that supplied fringe for carriage trimmers were: Charles H. Albrecht & Co., Cincinnati, Ohio; W. H. Hutchiuson, Genesee Upholstery Trimming Works, and Schelegel Manufacturing Company, all three of Rochester, New York; C. Cowles & Company, New Haven, Connecticut.

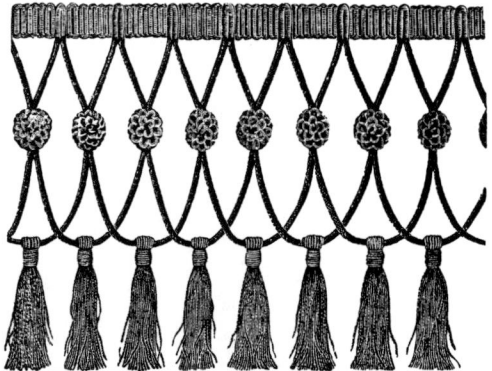

W. H. Hutchiuson, Rochester, New York
Hub February 1896

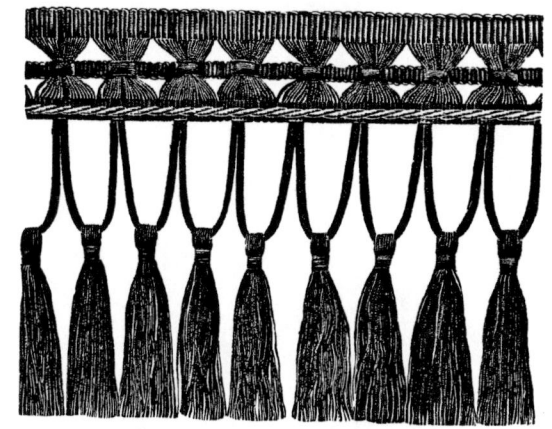

Carriage Monthly January 1896

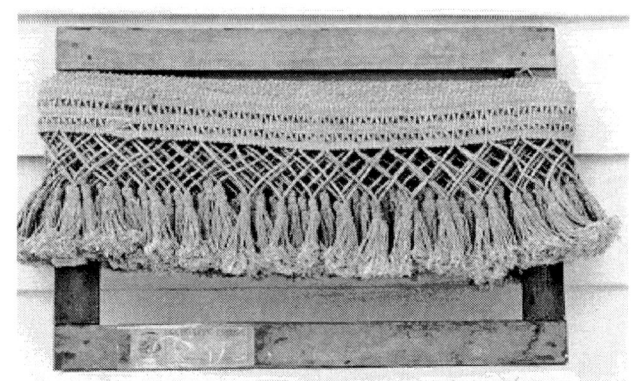

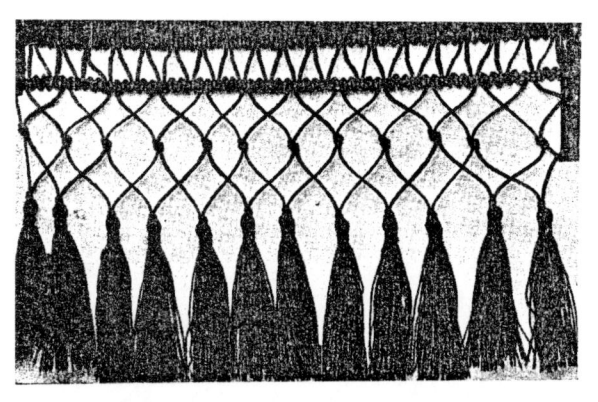

11 yards of original Gennape Fringe for carriage tops made by Wm. Horstmann Co., Philadelphia, Pennsylvania

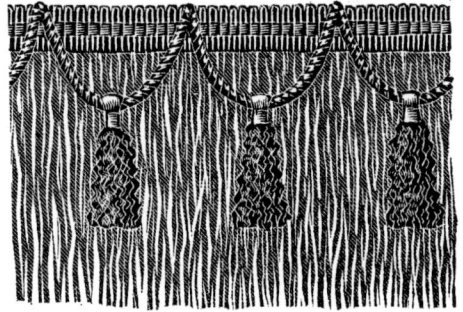

Schelgel Manufacturing Co., Rochester, New York
Hub April 1901

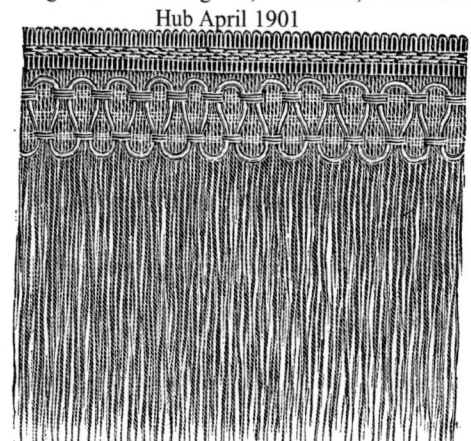

C. Cowles & Company,
New Haven, Connecticut
Carriage Monthly March 1891

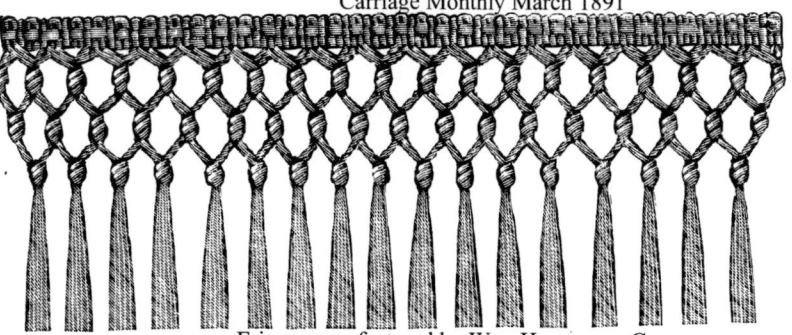

Fringe manufactured by Wm. Horstmann Company, Philadelphia, Pennsylvania
Carriage Monthly December 1901

C. Cowles & Comapny, Carriage Monthly June 1902

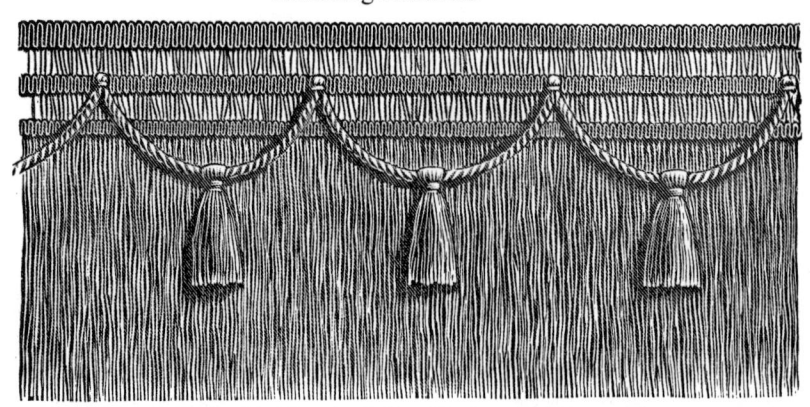

Trimming Materials

Charles H. Albrecht & Co., Cincinnati, Ohio
Hub July 1893

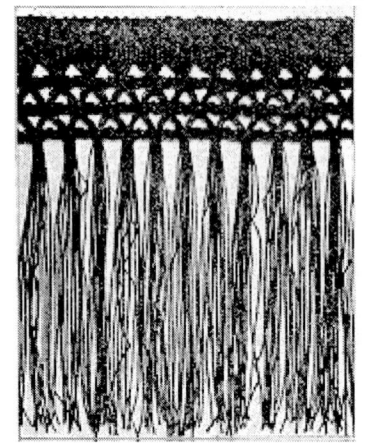

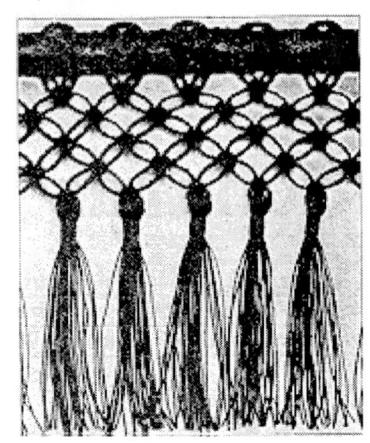

Genesee Upholstery Trimming Works, Rochester, New York
Carriage Monthly January 1895

Fringe on Surrey Top collection of George Taylor

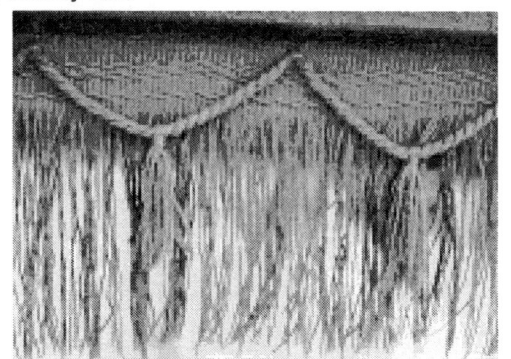

Surrey made by Noyes Carriage Co., Elkart, Indiana
collection of the Sowles Foundation

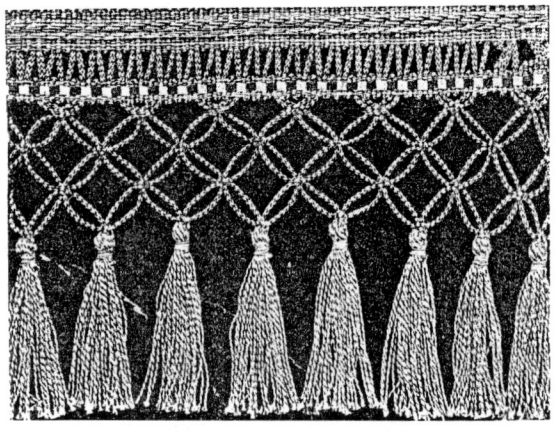

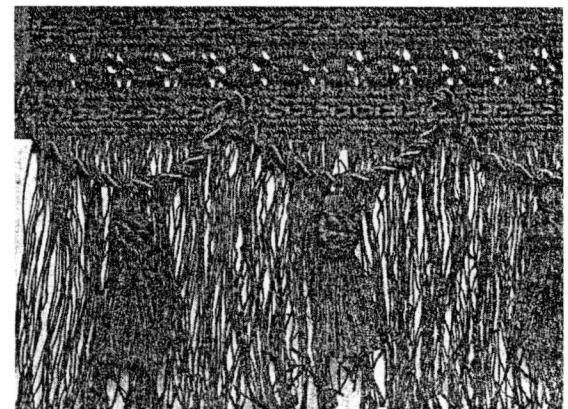

Schelgel Manufacturing Co., Rochester, New York
Hub April 1901

Trimming

CHAPTER 16

UPHOLSTERY

Upholstery for carriages was usually made up in three classes;
  First, upholstery that had no fullness between the tufts(buttons).
  Second, where allowance is made for quilting (¼ of inch to ¾ of inch).
  Third, where allowance is made both horizontally and vertically, and where the
    fullness is achieved by pleats, regularly distributed.(This may range from
  ¾ inch to 1 ½ inch fullness being added between rows of buttons.)

You should always conserve the old upholstery when possible, especially when it is material that is no longer available, such as some styles of broadlace and floral printed plush fabrics. When the old upholstery is removed you will need to save it as carefully as possible for a guide for laying out the new upholstery. We would suggest that you use the old upholstery only as a guide and not as an exact pattern and when you lay out the new upholstery you lay it out so it is mathematically correct and divided evenly. The old fabric was probably stretched and pulled so that it is no longer the true shape that it once started out. Other considerations are that an extra inch or so is needed around the edges sometimes for tacking. This allows for having something firm to hold unto when stretching the fabric in place. Big oversize tacks can be used to temporarily hold the fabric in place till everything is in position. Position the entire seat back or side panel of upholstery in place, driving the tacks part way in, then go back and take out any oversize tacks once it looks like the job is in place correctly. Drive the smaller tacks all the way home and trim off the excess with a sharp razor blade or similar instrument. Some people might want to learn how to do their own upholstery. It will take a lot of patience for the beginner and we might suggest that it is easier to start with a cloth upholstery rather then a leather upholstery. With fabric you have the option of going back and ripping out stitching and tacks, while with leather once you make a hole it is going to

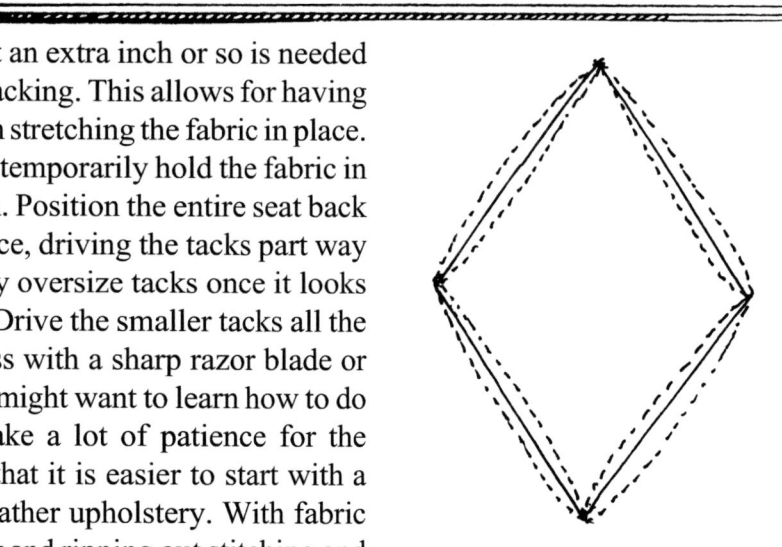

BASE PATTERN FOR SEAT CUSHION

MAXIMUM FULLNESS ADDED FOR UPHOLSTERY FABRIC FOR SEAT CUSHION

Once you have marked off the fold lines, stictch along the lines with an 1/8 inch dart. This will help the folds to lay in place easily.

169

Trimming

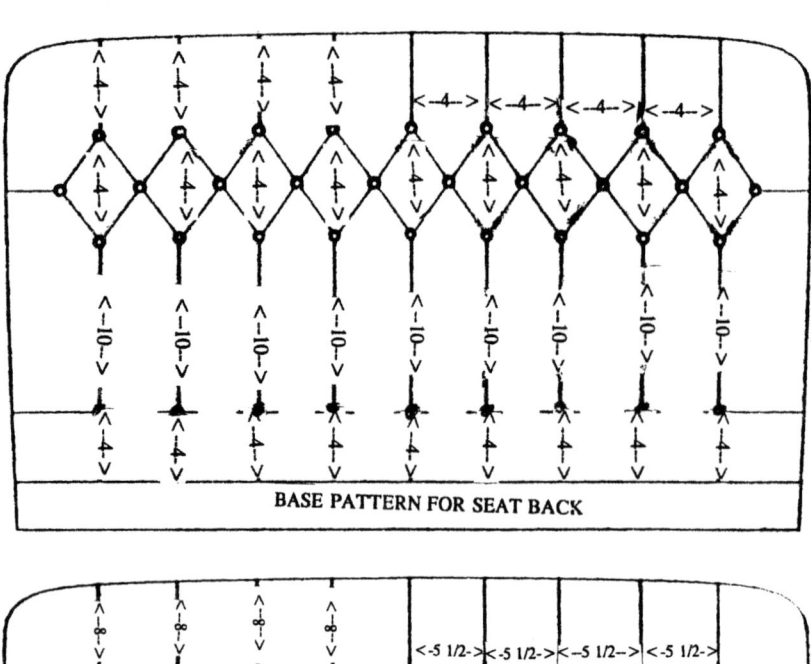

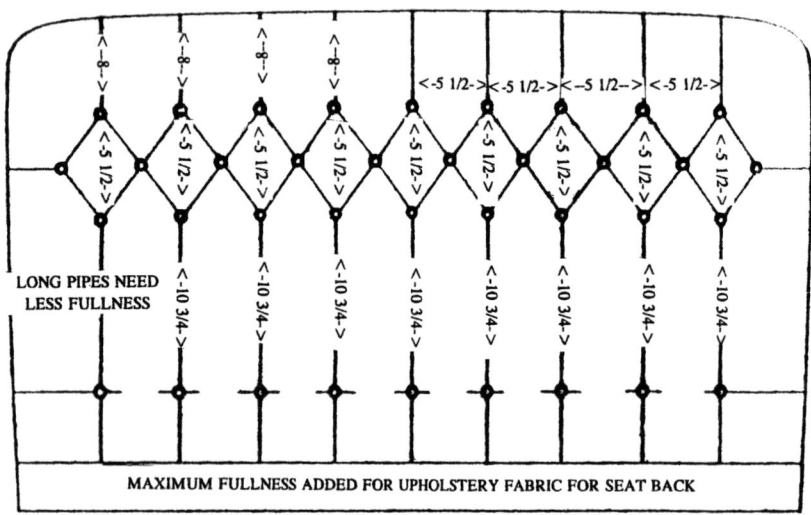

BASE PATTERN FOR SEAT BACK

MAXIMUM FULLNESS ADDED FOR UPHOLSTERY FABRIC FOR SEAT BACK

LONG PIPES NEED LESS FULLNESS

show. There are some books available on tufting that people who want to learn tufting can study. When you take the old upholstery out of the carriage and take it apart you can see how it was made and begin to understand how things were done. Generally the different sections of the upholstery were made up in what was called squabs. A piece of canvas was marked off for the bottom of the cushion, seat back or side panel, this stretched out on a frame or tacked to the work bench. The upholstery fabric was then marked off with appropriate fullness. The stuffing was laid out on the canvas and a piece of cotton batting was laid over the stuffing before the upholstery was placed on. The buttons were loosely tied and using a regulator the stuffing was pushed around in place till the squab was properly stuffed. There are hundreds of variations to this. Sometimes the canvas back needed to be very stiff and layers were glued together. Sometimes a cushion was made up with a lining and the upholstery fabric was than laid over the cushion that was already mostly made up.

For additional information on tufting carriage seats:
Butler, Herbert. Antique Auto Body Leather Work For the Restorer. Lockport, NY : Lincoln Publishing. *Has different patterns for seats and door panels, etc. along with dimensions.*

SEAT FALLS

The Carriage Monthly - December, 1901

The styles of falls are various and depend upon whether they are used on light, medium or heavy work. For buggies scarcely any change is noticeable. In some cases the falls are perfectly plain, bound with black leather, cloth or with tan colored leather around the edges. Novelties are seldom introduced on this kind of work and the general finish consists of flat raisers near the edges of the fall, ¾ or ⅞ inch wide, which are about ⅜ inch away from the edges.

There have been noteworthy changes in cushions, however. Lace fronts have been fashionable, and are likely to be for the next year. Welts on cushion fronts do not appear to be taking. Plain fronts seem to be preferred. For medium and heavy work lace-edged falls and lace cushion fronts are considerably used, both for low-priced and high-priced work.

A few illustrations will serve to show the styles at present in vogue. Fig. 1 is often seen on all kinds of vehicles, when the edges are bound with cloth and the ⅞ inch wide raisers are ½ off the edges of the fall. The shape of the raisers is generally flat, but flat-round are also seen frequently. Many are also used with raisers close to the binding.

Fig. 2 is a fall used on driving seats of broughams, coaches and landaus. They have been made in exactly this style for a number of years. The shape varies to suit the conditions of the boot. They are generally bound with cloth, and have ⅞ inch raisers.

Fig. 3 is often seen on phaetons and traps. The edges are bound with cloth and a space of ⅜ inch is left between the binding and a ⅞ inch raiser. A similar space remains between the raiser and inside welts. This is about ¼ inch full round. These look well, but are not as often seen as are other styles.

Fig. 4 represents one of the low edged falls. The panel is perfectly plain, but in some cases is padded. The lace is mitred at the corners.

Fig. 5 is a style edged with broad lace with a bar in the center, thus forming two panels instead of one. These are used on heavy work.

From the date of the Paris Exposition in 1889, plaits or pipe falls have been somewhat in use, but have never become really popular. They add, however, greatly to the appearance of any vehicle on which they are used.

Fig. 6 represents a tapered plait. There are five with spaces between perfectly plain, while the edges of the rest of the fall are bound with the same material as the fall.

Fig. 7 shows four parallel pipes and the bottom edges are flat on the top. The edges are close together and the pipes as well as the rest of the fall are bound with the same material.

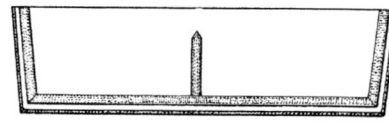

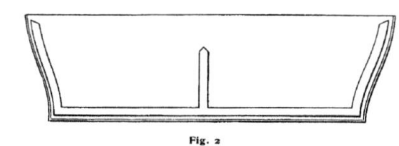

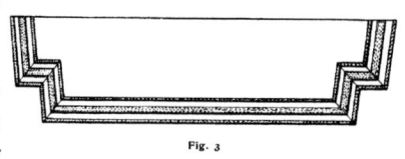

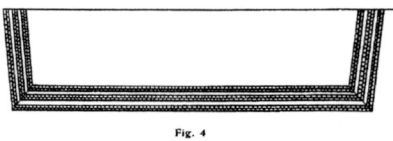

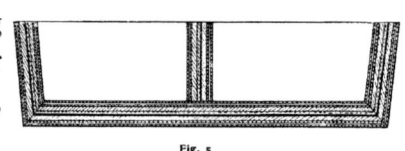

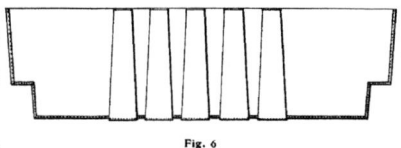

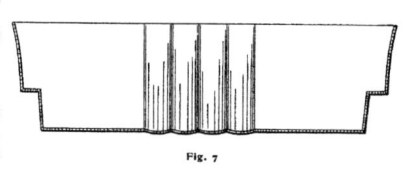

Trimming

Fig. 8 is a four-piped fall. The pipes are parallel with 2 inches between, flat-round on the top and full-round at the bottom. The edges are bound with cloth and there is a raiser close to the binding on each side of the pipes.

Fig. 9 illustrates a tapered lace edged fall. The pipes are flat-round on the top and full-round at the bottom for the sake of better retaining the shape. These are made for phaetons, broughams and landaus where the fall is set back of the cushion front.

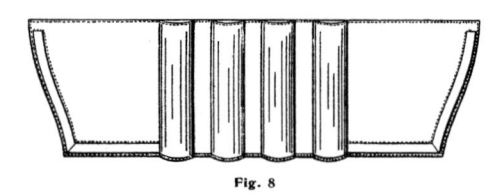

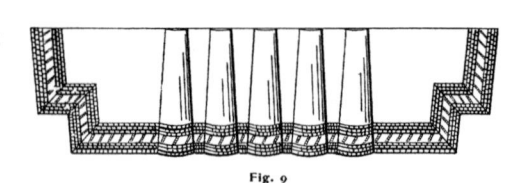

DOOR TRIMMING
Carriage Monthly - December, 1901

Herewith we present illustrations of a few of the many styles for trimming doors of depot wagons, rockaways, broughams and coaches.

Fig.1 represents one of the plainest doors now seen on depot wagons. The entire finish is in cloth welts, with a small mitered panel in the center and all the rest perfectly plain. In some instances these plain surfaces are padded to give them a raised appearance. This is an appropriate trimming for doors where the rest of to the work is in harmony with it. The division front is made up in the same style, the cushion fronts being bound with cloth and having no raisers but with a welt of the size to correspond with the doors in front. Its position is about ¾ inch from the edges.

Fig. 2 also represents a depot wagon, or rockaway door. It is bound with cloth or pasting and seaming lace around the edges. It has two flat, or flat-round, raisers, and can be made from ¾ inch to 1 ½ inches in width. To prevent excessive plainness the panels are creased from each corner and have buttons at the centers.

Figs. 3 and 4 represent styles of omnibus doors. Fig. 3 is edged with lace, the spaces between being plain, with a pocket at the tip of plain cloth. Such pockets are frequently seen on private omnibuses, and are really very useful.

Fig. 4 is edged with broad lace and bound with seaming lace around the outside edges, the lace running through the center, the lower part being plain and the upper part finished with blocks. There are 24 blocks and 15 buttons.

Fig 5 represents a brougham door which has lace around the edges, and plain square center with a small button at each corner. The miters are either sewed or creased, and each part has the same fullness.

Fig. 6 is edged with broad lace similar to that of Fig. 5. The inside square is made up of broad lace mitered in each corner. The spaces between are perfectly plain, and can be creased or padded if desired.

Fig. 7 is a brougham or coach style with pasting lace around the edges and also around the diamonds and the inside edges of the upper part with small panel between. The lower part is made up of diamonds with a slight fullness for each.

Fig. 8 is edged with broad lace, with pasting lace on the inside and outside and with twelve blocks and nine buttons for each. The blocks are generally made very full.

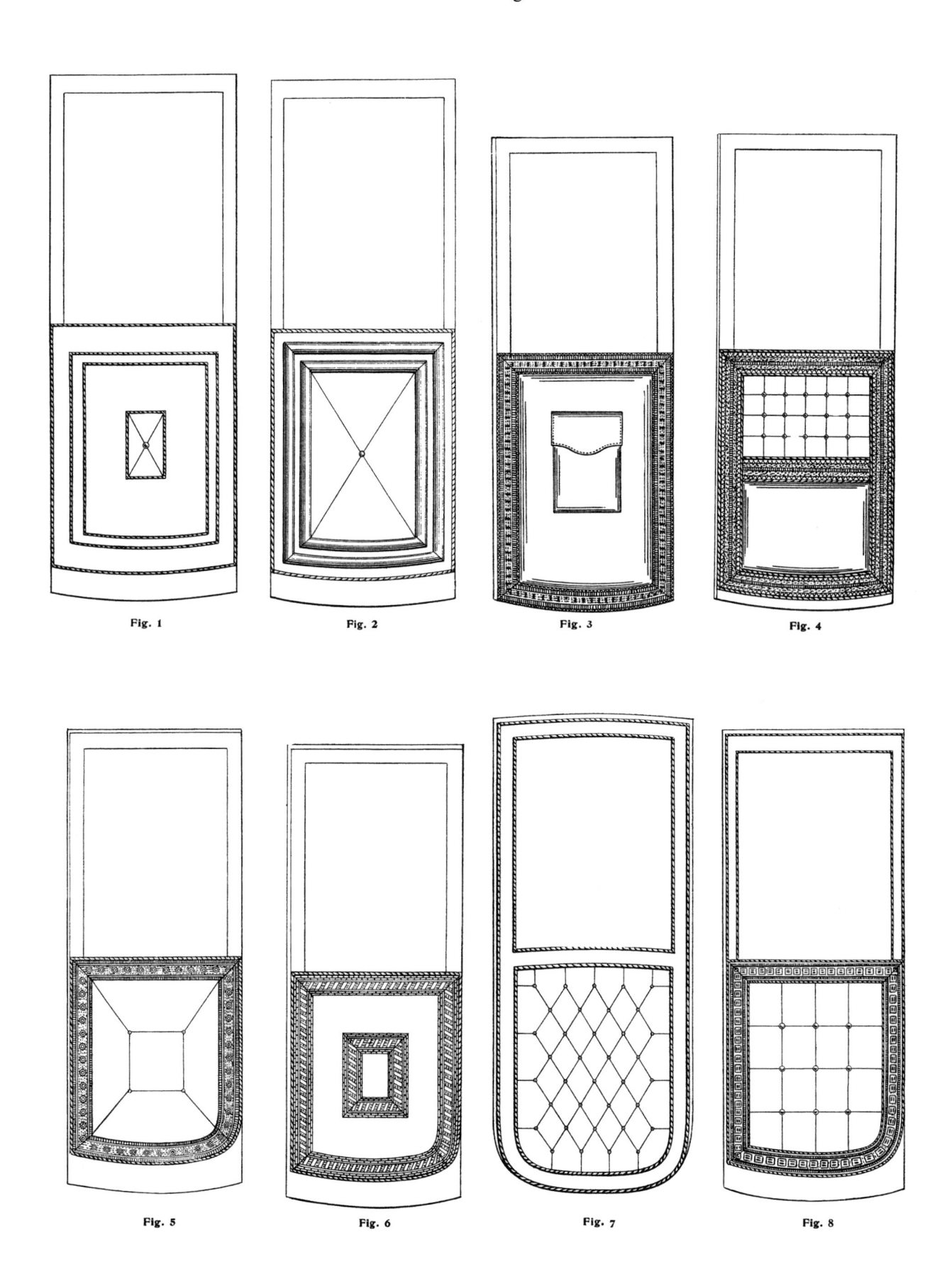

Trimming

Fig. 1 Fig. 2 Fig. 3 Fig. 4

Fig. 5 Fig. 6 Fig. 7 Fig. 8

SHAFTS
Trimming
Carriage Monthly-August 1885

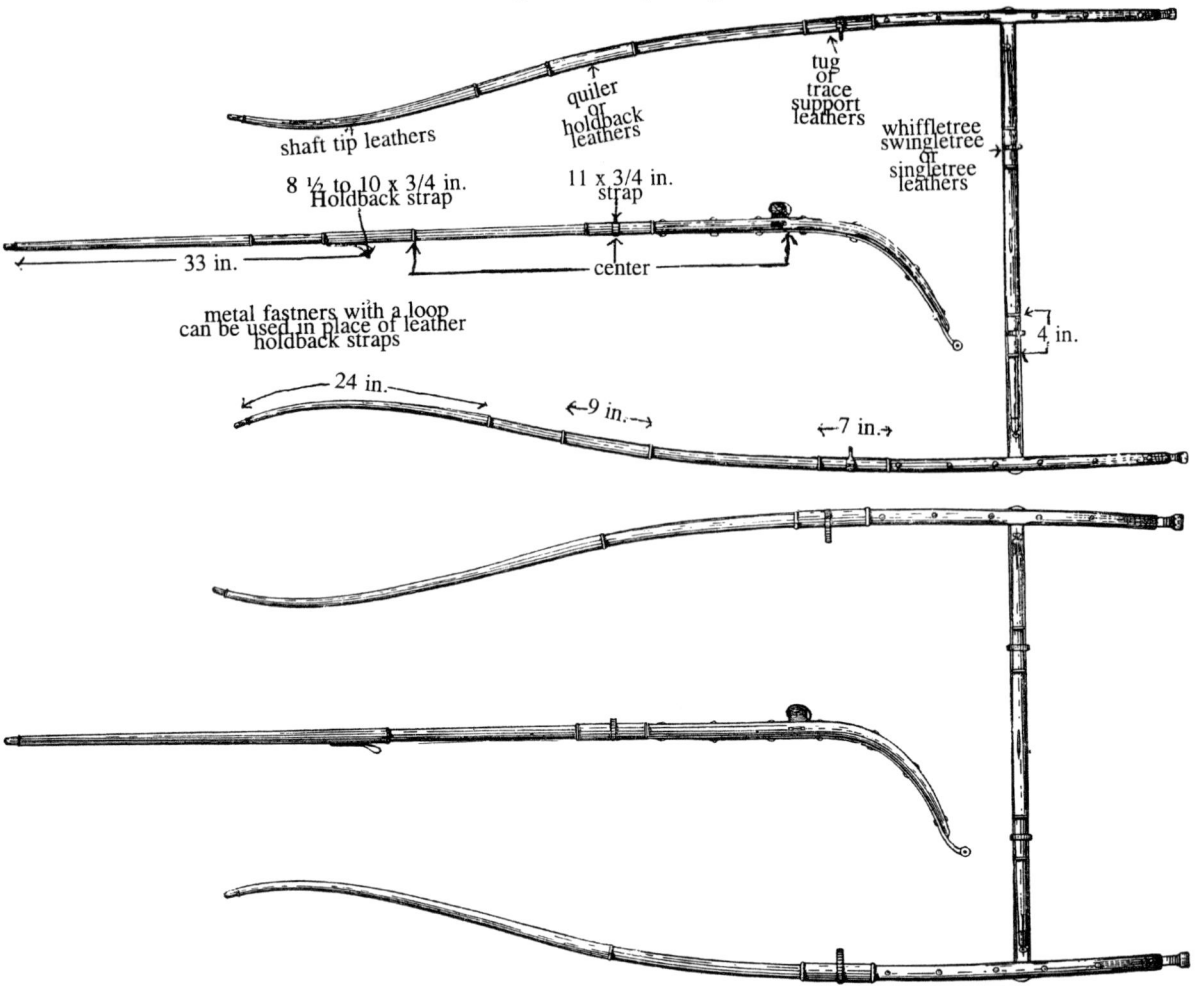

[Diagram labels:]
- shaft tip leathers
- quiler or holdback leathers
- tug or trace support leathers
- whiffletree, swingletree or singletree leathers
- 8 ½ to 10 x 3/4 in. Holdback strap
- 11 x 3/4 in. strap
- 33 in.
- center
- 4 in.
- metal fastners with a loop can be used in place of leather holdback straps
- 24 in.
- 9 in.
- 7 in.

A cheaper way of trimming shafts. The shaft tip leathers and the holdback leathers are all one piece. Hub August 1888.

The leathers are usually cut in the following lengths, namely: tip leathers, 24 to 26 inches; quiler leathers, 9 inches [some say 10 inches]; trace leathers, 6 inches [some say 7 inches], and swingletree leathers, 3 inches [some say 3 ½ and 4 inches]. The positions on a 6 foot shaft are as follows: The tip leathers on the ends of course; the quiler should be 3 ½ inches from center of quiler loop or "Hold back" to the front edge, [The hold-back straps are placed 33 inch from the end of the shaft to the folded end of the same. Feather edge and round the ends of the straps and fasten them on the shafts with two 12-oz. tacks, or a cup washer and screw.] and the trace leather, half way between the back edge of quiler leather and shaft bar: the swingletree leather is placed 1 inch out of the center (toward the ends).

There are various ways of finishing the ends of these leathers. The simplest and neatest, perhaps, is turning the edges under, but to do this it is necessary to use light leather, such as bow leather. Which of course soon wears out. Another way is to tack an extra welt around the edge; another, to bind the edges, but this is not at all durable. Another way is to prepare small strips of harness leather and butt up to the edges of the same; this mode, if properly done, will insure satisfaction. The strips of harness leather are about ¼ inch wide and blacked and creased. Perhaps the best way, were it not for its cheap appearance, is to leave the edges raw, and simply blacken them.

Trimming
Hub-August 1888

In tacking on the edges of the leather they should be butted together. To bind, take a strip of thin trimming-leather 1 inch wide; wet and fold the edges together and rub down; draw this carefully around the ends of the various pieces after they are tacked on, and tack underneath, with the exception of the front ends of the long pieces which of course finish against the shaft tips. For the very fines jobs, use a piece of harness leather cut ½ inch and skived along the edges. This should be dampened and raised in the center, which will allow the edges to rest down smoothly on the shaft. Tack pieces prepared in this way along the bottom where the edges meet.

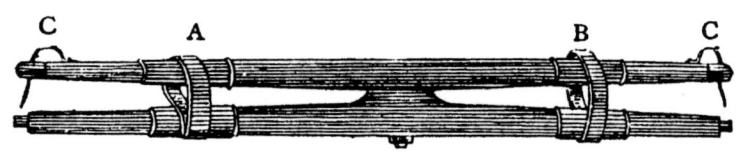

Two ways of fastening the whiffletree leathers.
From the Hub February 1885

The straps which support the tugs are cut 11 inch in length, and ¾ inch in width, and should be rounded for the best work, leaving them flat 1 inch at one end and 3 inch at the other, to tack to the shafts. The pieces which hold the whiffletree in place are cut 11 inch long, ¾ inch wide, and are rounded, leaving 1 inch flat at the end to tack to the cross-bar. [The length of the whiffletree strap should be long enough that the whiffletree moves freely.] The whiffletree is also provided with harness-leather keys to prevent the tugs from becoming unhooked.

Shaft leathers are usually tacked in place by using the smallest tack that will hold the job. After tacking paint over the tacks to prevent them from rusting. One restorer believes real leather is still the best for trimming shafts. As he has found that imitation patent leather tends to rot the wood within a years time when the vehicle is restored or built to use.

Real patent leather used for covering shafts can be made wet on the flesh side and this is a help in stretching the leather over shaft that have a great deal of curve. Vehicles with shafts that have a compound curve at the tip, usually have a metal strap running underneath the shaft. These shafts do not allow the leather to be tacked on and it therefore must be sewn on by hand stitching. There are two general ways in which this can be done. One way is to butt the edges together and using the cross stitch or the herring-bone stitch the edges together. This requires the greatest difficulty in shaping and molding the leather. Cut the shaft covers a little larger than needed to start with. Wet the back of the leather and shape it over the shafts. Using some cloth strips rolled up like bandages wrap these cloth strips around the leather shaft covers making sure the two edges overlap sufficiently. Let the leather dry and unwrap the cloth bandages. Mark out a center line underneath the shafts with a wax pencil and then precede to cut along the center line with a razor blade. The shaft covers can then been wrapped up partially if you find it helps to hold the leather in place while you are stitching.

Another way of stitching up shaft covers over metal is to use the double needle method or a stitching awl and sew the two edges together. Once again allow some extra leather, wet it and shape it over the shafts. This time instead of overlapping the two edges clamp the two edges together with clothespins or the like. Use a prick wheel and mark the stitching holes. Stitch the two edges together and once finished trim off the excess close to the stitching. Some believed the butted edges looks the neatest. While others believed stitching the two edges together in a seam will cause less wear on the stitching, because there is a leather edge to protect the stitching.

For additional information on Hand Sewing
Stohlman, Al. The Art of Hand Sewing Leather, 72 p., Tandy Leather Co., Fort Worth, TX.

Trimming
POLES
Hub-June 1888

Buggy Pole

We will begin with a buggy pole. The neck-yoke is trimmed as follows. The pole-straps are made up 3 ft. 7 ½ in. Over all, with two 1 ¼ in. Loops, one over and one under, with a good lap. As it is unnecessary to double and stitch for a job of this kind, heavy harness-leather should be used.

The center-piece is made from one medium and one light piece of harness-leather, long enough to extend around the yoke, and form the loop for the pole between these. An extra piece should be inserted, which will give five thicknesses for the wear of the pole. The light piece should be used for the outside, under which a riser, extending around the pole and over the yoke, should be inserted.

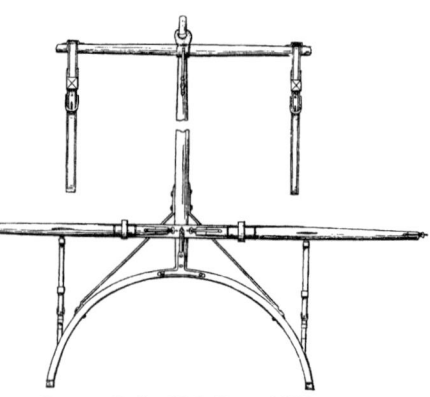

Buggy Pole. Hub June 1888

The yoke should also have a safety-strap, about 10 in. length, attached to the top of the yoke in the center by a screw, and punched at the end, extending backward in the form of a billet. This takes a buckle, attached to the pole by a buckle-piece by a single narrow loop. This will prevent the yoke from allowing the pole to drop down in case a tug should become accidentally unhooked.

The whiffletrees are provided with harness-leather keys, and also with a wear-piece of dash-leather, 4 ½ in. long, next to the pole, as shown in and around the center of this, and attached to the evener, is a ¾ in. strap, cut 11 in. long. Safety-straps are also attached to an eye, which is attached to the forging underneath the circle and on a line with the ends of the evener. These are made up with two loops, one under and the other over the buckle; and also with two slip-loops, one at either end. These straps should also be cut ¾ in.

Heavy Pole

A heavy pole has the trimming which is 33 in. in length, and extends from a point 26 in. back of the end of pole. It is put on as follows; Wet a quantity of straw sufficient to form the swell at the center, and cut the required length.[Some trimmers preferred pieces of carpet for padding]. Now, take a piece of duck canvas of sufficient width, and tack through the center to the top of the pole. Fill in one side with the straw, secure for five or six inches at the center, and then trim off the straw with a straight knife, giving it the right taper, and pull the edges of the canvas together on the under side. The cover, which should be of dash leather, is cut in the form shown. It is bound with binding-leather at the ends, and is tacked through the center at the top with japanned nails, at intervals of 2 ½ in. On the under side the edges are butted together; and a strip of harness-leather, cut ⅝ inches wide and skived down rather thin at the edges, is tacked the entire length, to cover the edges of the cover and form a smooth finish.

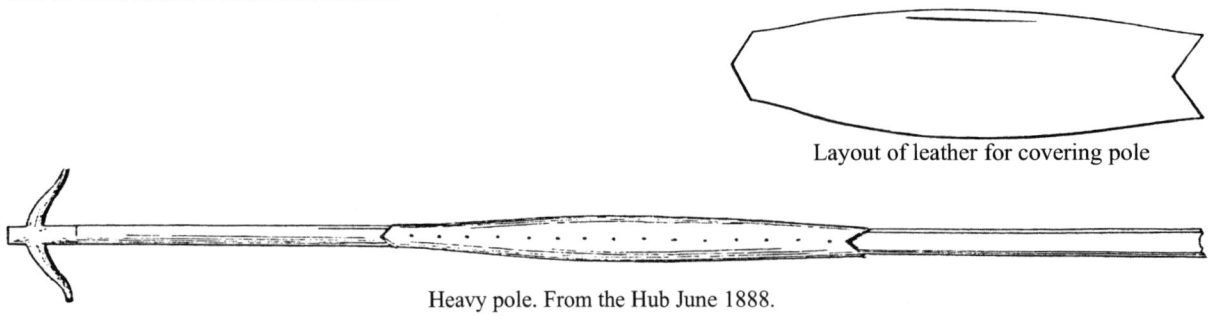

Layout of leather for covering pole

Heavy pole. From the Hub June 1888.

Trimming
Bibliography and additional references for shafts and poles

"A Few Hints About Trimming Poles." Hub. (June 1888) p. 192.
"Cock Eyes and Safety Straps." Carriage Monthly. (June 1886) p. 73.
"Coupe Shafts and Shifting Bar." New York Coach-Maker's Magazine. (April 1869) p.169-170.
"Hints on Trimming Shafts." Hub. (Aug. 1888) p. 350.
"How to Trim Shafts." Carriage Monthly. (Aug. 1885) p. 135.
"Lead Bars for Four-in-Hand Drag." Carriage Monthly. (Nov. 1873) p. 133-134.
"Neck Yoke Braces." Coach-Makers' International Journal. (June 1871) p. 132-133.
"Practical Instruction Pertaining to Carriage Parts and the Suspension of Carriages : Shafts, Poles, Yokes, Single and Double Trees." Carriage Monthly. (July 1887) p. 92-93.
"Shaft Leathers and Their Positions." Carriage Monthly. (May 1885) p. 43
"Trimming Poles." Carriage Monthly. (March 1888).

SPLINTER BARS
Coach Trimming by W. Farr & G. A. Thrupp, 1888

The roller bolts, caps, and ferrules have to be covered that the iron may not wear against the leather traces, and washers fixed on to the bar to prevent the traces wearing on to the wood-work. To make the caps take the size of caps with calipers and diameter of ferrules, and measure height of ferrules. Mark off the caps on the leather, which will need to be slightly larger than the exact measure (about ⅛ of an inch added to it), scribe a circle with the compass race, thus channeling out the sewing line. Outside this, at a

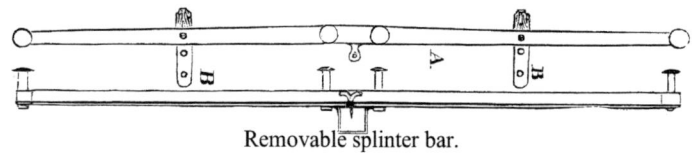

Removable splinter bar.
From the New York Coach-Maker's Magazine, April 1869.

distance of not more than ⅛ of an inch, scribe another circle, to which line, when the caps are sewn, you can pare off. On the oil leather for underneath the cap obtain a circle the size of ferrules, and, with the same radius, describe four other on leather for the washers, also making the outer circle of the washers at a suitable distance, just wide enough to be well supported by the bar, without going far beyond such support; or it will only serve them to flap loosely, and in an untidy manner. [Some trimmers sewed a metal washer in between to help keep their shape.] The washers may afterwards be cut with a washer-cutter. Then clean off the caps, and place them on the roller-bolts. For this purpose the underneath piece must be slit away in this manner, so that the cuts may be allowed to open sufficiently to insert top of roller-bolt. A little paste is rubbed on top of the roller-bolt before covering it with the cap. When thus covered, fixing all four complete, the cuts must be attended to. This is done by means of stitches with a single thread across each slit in the way shown. To place the washers round the ferrules, we slit them from the center to the outside. In opening the washer, and placing it round the ferrule, be careful that the edges of the cut fit; fix them with small pins close to the ferrule, so that its covering may hide them. The end roller-bolts often form treads [steps]. Covering these would be useless; but, to prevent the traces wearing against the iron, leather must be fixed beneath. The treads will have holes suitably placed, with a recessed channel connecting them. The cut should be arranged to come between two such holes; copper wire is then threaded through the tread to fix the leather.

Washer with slits

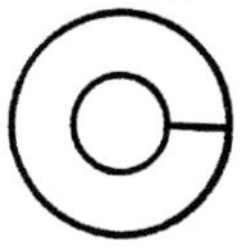

Washer with slit

Trimming

VALANCES FOR SEAT BORDERS

Seat-boards that do not otherwise have the edges covered up usually are protected and finished by means of a valance or border. Patent leather was used quite frequently although a wooden valance could also be used. The patent leather used needs to be a heavy weight leather. If you can not find heavy patent leather cut out a piece of heavy leather and glue a thinner piece of imitation or real patent leather on top with contact cement. In most cases the border is made to project about ¾ inch above the seat board, this forms a tray which helps to keep the cushions of such seats in place. The same amount of ¾ inch, is below, to make an even appearance. These two widths of ¾ plus the thickness of the seat board of about ¾ inch add up to a total width for the seat border of 2 ¼ inch. For the length of the valance measure the seat board where the valance is to be placed and add about ¾ in. for each. (Remember that the valance will shorten in turning round corners.) When the seat boards are rounded, the seat border may be made in one piece; if the seat has square corners, it will be necessary to miter a joint.

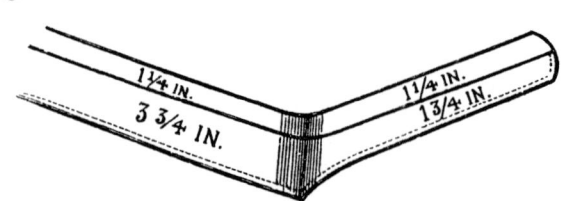

Flared valance for round-cornered dickey seat.
From the Hub Oct. 1892

Seat valances and top valances have their edges finished with a sewn-on binding of thin leather. In some cases this binding extends to the back side of the valance to make a lining that is tacked to the underside of the seat board. An easy way to sew on binding is to cut your binding material about an inch larger around the edges. Glue part of the binding around the edges on the back of the valance piece. Pull the extra binding material to the front side of the valance and then using a guide on the sewing machine stitch the binding material to the valance material around the edges. Then trim off the excess binding material close to the stitching being careful not to cut through to the valance material.

Seat valances are installed by nailing them to the seat edge, and the nail heads are then covered with a metal beading or molding. Traditionally this molding was a thin brass or silver plate strip that was rolled into a half-round tube and filled with lead, with pins fixed in the lead at about 3 inch This beading is no longer made, and a good imitation can be made by using half round solid brass. The ends can be shaped to a taper by grinding, and then polishing them off with increasingly fine sand paper. Next you will have to drill some oversize holes every three inches on the flat side of your brass rod using a stop in the drill press so that you do not drill all the way through to the front side. After the holes are drilled solder some small nails in the holes. When possible the old molding should be removed with great care and any broken pins replaced by soldering. When attaching this metal molding to new seat borders, it is best to mark the places for the pins and prick through the leather with an awl so that the pins will not bend when being driven in.

Valances for Folding Tops

Many carriages with a folding top usually have a valance attached to the front bow. This serves the purpose of hiding the edges of the top leather and head lining cloth where they have been tacked to the front bow. Head valances are about the same width as seat valances. These valances are made similar to seat valances with the same kind of heavy patent leather being used and binding stitched on the edges.

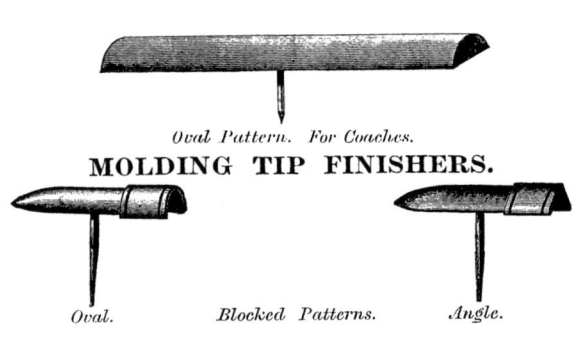

Oval Pattern. For Coaches.
MOLDING TIP FINISHERS.

Oval.   *Blocked Patterns.*   *Angle.*

From the S. D. Kimbark catalog, 1888.

178

Trimming

A top valance normally has a curved metal beading fixed along its center and this can cause some difficulty if you have to make up a new brass molding. A form will have to be made in which to bend the brass, bending around to get the desired curve. (See page 88) Warm the brass rod until it is anneal not red hot and bend it around the form for the curve.

This information on top and seat valances taken in part from "Coach Trimming" by W. Farr and G. A. Thrupp and for additional information refer to the same.

Some Suggestions for Clean-up and Repair of Old Folding Tops

Once old leather has become fragile and dry there is really no way of making it strong and flexible again. It will help however to keep it from deteriorating any further by using one of the leather dressings that has neutral PH such as Lexol. Before applying leather dressing the top should be cleaned, wiped with a damp rag and repaired. To repair small holes in the top you will need to find some top leather that comes close to matching the top leather of your vehicle.

2nd make a little tracing of the hole to be repaired.

3rd trace the outline of the hole on the leather to be used for patching and cut about half inch extra around the piece for the hole.

4th skive the finished side of the patch where the edges would come in contact with the old top leather.

5th with some good leather contact glue, glue the patch in place. For good leather glue we suggest you check with a shoe maker, harness maker, Tandy Leather Co., and the Leather Factory. You might want to make a test with different types of glue first, because not all glues are compatible with oils and finishes of some leathers. Like the paint industry glues are rapidly changing to meet new regulations and some glues that were known to work well are being taken out of the market.

After the holes are repaired the seams can be examined and stitching done where necessary. Tandy Leather Co., and the Leather Factory supply hand tools, thread and instruction booklets for hand sewing.

In caring for carriages it was recommended that carriages should have the tops in the relaxed position. If the tops have been left this way after many years and have not been oiled, they are most likely hard and brittle, and the surface area of the leather has shrunk. One way of returning them to position might be to lay a damp cotton sheet over them with a plastic drop cloth on top to hold in the moisture for awhile. After the top leather has become pliable again it can be put in the taut position. Most likely though when the leather dries it will shrink back to the former state and you will have to glue in an extension for it to remain in the taut position. After gluing in repairs and extensions the whole top can be dyed and a leather dressing put on. You may want to mask off the rest of your carriage with plastic drop cloths when using dye and leather dressing to avoid getting it on the rest of the carriage.

There are also liquid finishes supplied by automotive top finishers that can be used to restore leather and artifical leather top finishes.

For information on building and constructing folding tops

Butler, Herbert. Antique Auto Body Top Work For The Restorer. Lockport, NY : Lincoln Publishing.

LAMP COVERS
From the Hub, January 1904

The accompanying sketches illustrate two different designs for making lamp covers. Each of the covers will fit the same lamp, although they are cut and made entirely different. Each of the designs are cut in four pieces. Fig. 1 represents the shape that the four parts are to be cut. It also represents the back piece, with the reinforced piece to pass over the lamp socket. The pieces are cut to fit the lamps full with one-quarter inch seam: the four pieces are sewn together on the machine. The bottom edge is neatly bound with a piece of the same goods: the top part has a strong drawing thread worked around the edge: the parts are drawn close together and the thread made fast. A button or washer cut in circle out of landau top leather, about 1¼ inches in diameter; the edge of the washer is slightly skived off so as not to have the edge too thick; stitching holes are punched around the edge with a stitching awl, the washer placed over the drawing thread and stitched on with one needle and a good thread. A little must be used to keep the washer over the center of the cover. At the bottom of the sketch are small cross lines which indicate openings to work tape through to draw the cover around the shank of the lamp. Fig. 2 represents the cover in a finished state.

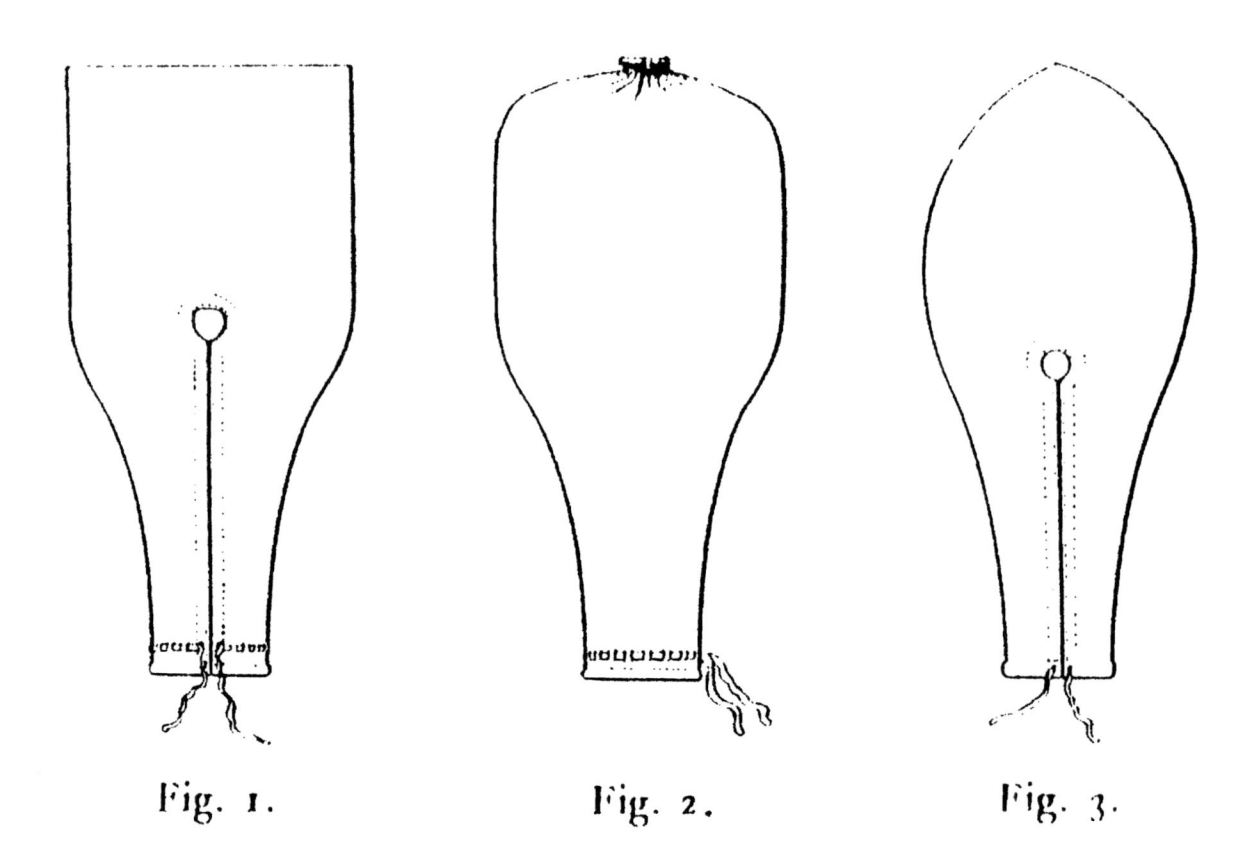

Fig. 1. Fig. 2. Fig. 3.

Fig. 3 illustrates another style for a lamp cover. It is more easily made than Fig. 1, and does not take any more material when a correct pattern is obtained than the other design. The pieces are cut full to the lamp, with one-quarter inch seam. After the four parts are sewn together the top of the cover is fastened with needle and thread. A hem is turned over at the bottom of the cover, wide enough for tape to pass through. The reinforced piece for the opening is cut from leather.

CHAPTER 17

CARRIAGE LAMP RESTORATION
by: Rick Bischoff of
The Luminary Shoppe,
Joliet, MT

Obtain the "Correct" Lamps

The restoration of a carriage is not complete until it is outfitted with the proper accouterments. On occasion, a carriage will have retained the original lamps provided at its manufacture. In such cases it is usually best to keep the original lamps with the carriage and conserve or restore them in a manner consistent with the work done on the carriage. In many instances, the lamps may have become separated from the carriage and be unavailable. This will then require consultation of the carriage maker's records, if available, to determine the appropriate style and size of lamps for the carriage. In the absence of maker's records, the research may be directed to other carriages of similar design, carriage restoration experts, or competition judges who have expertise with the particular class of vehicles to which the carriage may be assigned. Armed with the information so gathered, one may go about the search for that "just right" pair of lamps among the equine antique dealers, auctions, and purveyors of carriage accouterments.

Evaluating Lamps

When the appropriate lamps have been obtained, it is advisable to evaluate the lamps and determine what work needs to be done. A conservation or restoration plan can then be formulated. If the lamps are in reasonably good condition, basic cleaning, polishing and touch up techniques may be employed. However, if major damage, such as broken lights (glass), rusted body components, damaged reflectors or poor finish are present, a more in depth job will be in order. In this case, a restoration plan should be developed. The plan should identify all components to be repaired or replaced. Consideration of the order in which to complete each task or phase of the restoration will alleviate redoing work already accomplished. This process will also help determine whether or not the necessary skills, equipment, products and components are available to the owner, and identify the possible necessity of sending the lamps to a professional for restoration.

ELM CITY.   IMPERIAL FLANGE.   VENETIAN.   BRILLIANT.

C. Cowles & Co., advertisements from the Carriage Monthly January 1890.

Lamps

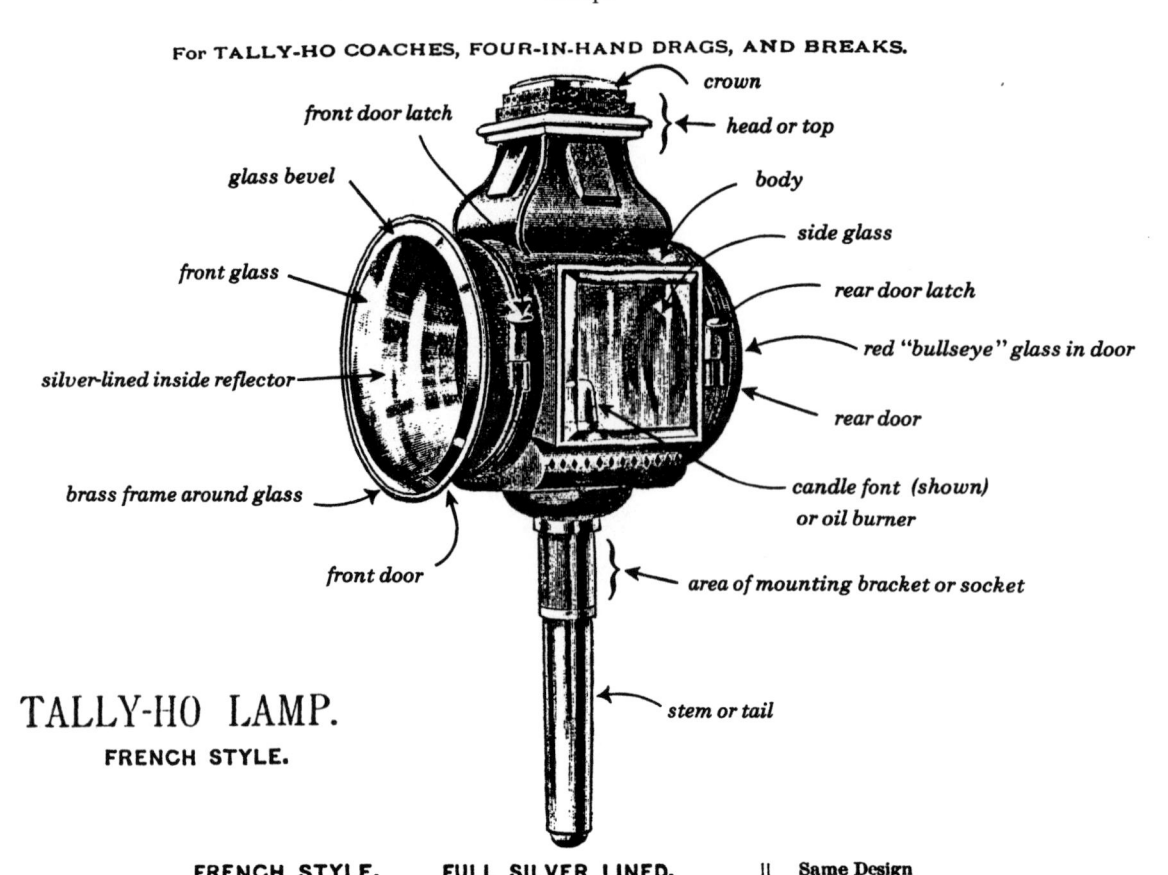

For TALLY-HO COACHES, FOUR-IN-HAND DRAGS, AND BREAKS.

Labeled parts of the lamp: crown; head or top; front door latch; glass bevel; body; side glass; front glass; rear door latch; red "bullseye" glass in door; silver-lined inside reflector; rear door; brass frame around glass; candle font (shown) or oil burner; front door; area of mounting bracket or socket; stem or tail.

TALLY-HO LAMP.
FRENCH STYLE.

No.	Diam. of Body.	Depth of Body.	Diam. of Glass.	Extreme Length.	FRENCH STYLE. FULL SILVER LINED. Price per pair.	Same Design finished English style. Part lined only. Price per pair.
1	9 in.	12¼ in.	11½ in.	26 in.	$52.00	$45.00
2	8 "	11½ "	10 "	25 "	46.00	36.00
3	7½ "	10 "	9 "	23 "	38.00	28.00
4	7 "	8½ "	8½ "	22 "	33.00	25.00

Large Wrought Sockets for Nos. 1 and 2, $2.50.
Regular Wrought Sockets for Nos. 3 and 4,   1.25.

The increasing demand for Tally-ho Coaches and vehicles of a similar character has induced us to present this magnificent lamp. Made in our best manner, finely finished, full lined, first-class in every respect. Nos. 1 and 2 are designed for Tally-Ho Coaches and Drags; Nos. 3 and 4 for Breaks and other large vehicles.

From an old catalog reprinted from the Driving Digest # 30, 1985/4.

Restoration Plan

A restoration plan may consist of a listing of the major phases of the restoration with sub-headings detailing each phase. A plan within the scope of the interests and abilities of the average carriage enthusiast might consist of:

1) Gross clean-up - Washing, removal of foreign material, e.g. insect nests, wax, oil, or dirt.
2) Operating components
    A. Clean and dress threaded parts (candle tails or wick holders)
    B. Tighten door hinges and adjust door latches
3) Polishing
    A. Liners (reflectors)
    B. Mounting (bright metal exterior trim)

4) Finish
- A. Buffing
- B. Touch up paint

Only the more experienced or adventurous will want to take on a restoration involving one or more of the following: Complete dismantling, requiring desoldering and consequently resoldering of major components, replacement of glass, polishing scratches out of glass, removal of rust-frozen operating parts, replacement of rusted through parts, repair or replacement of age-cracked or broken spun parts, replating liners and mounting, complete refinishing of paint. These tasks may best be left to the professional lamp restorer as they require resources not normally available to the average carriage enthusiast.

Accomplishing the Restoration

When the restoration plan is formulated, the work can begin. A good way to begin and end a restoration is with photographs. Additional photos during the course of restoration serve not only to document the process but also provide a reminder as to how to get the lamps back together in the case of a more involved project. Generally, the gross clean up phase can be accomplished with commonly available household detergents and plenty of hot water. Rinse constantly and rub lightly to avoid scratching the lamps. A razor blade scraper will remove hardened material from glass surfaces. Avoid using sand paper or pointed tools on or near the glass. Threaded parts frozen with rust, such as candle tails and caps or oil founts, can often be loosened by applying heat or penetrating lubricants. Once apart, the rust should be removed by wire brush or other means. Dry graphite applied to the threads will help to prevent future problems. Door hinges, latches, and other moving parts can be made operable by similar means. Cleaning and polishing of liners and mounting can be accomplished with non-abrasive products such as "Flitz" or "Peek" brand metal polishes. Multiple applications may be required depending on the degree of tarnishing. While the polishing products themselves are not abrasive, dirt and tarnish particles are abrasive. Therefore care should be employed to avoid dulling or scratching the bright metal surfaces. Often silver plating will be worn through due to repeated cleaning and polishing when the lamps were originally in use and/or due to recent clean up efforts. If this is minor it may be acceptable to simply polish the entire surface and use it as is. If it is desirable to restore minor worn areas in silver plate, a restorative silver plate and cleaner such as "Silversmith," made by EZ-way Chemical Co., POBox 525, Burlington, WA, 98233, may be used. Special care must be exercised in using silver plate products as they are usually cyanide-based and extremely poisonous. They should not be used near food or in food preparation areas, and appropriate personal protection, such as eye wear and rubber gloves, should be worn. Though these products are available to the amateur, silver plating and touch up may best be left to the professional. Minor touch up of the paint may be accomplished with model builders enamel and a small brush. If the paint is in reasonable condition an application of a good quality automotive wax such as "Polier" made by "Flitz," on both the painted and bright metal parts will lessen necessity and frequency of cleaning and polishing, and enhance the appearance of the lamps. Minor scratches and nicks on glass can often be diminished by applying wax-based polish to the glass surface. New paint should not be waxed or polished for at least 90 days to insure sufficient curing time. Currently, the preferred method of complete refinishing of carriage lamps is to use modern automotive products and techniques. Hand-brushed lacquers may be used, but the products and skills required to accomplish a first rate job are rare. At the other extreme, hardware store "rattle can" paints are used. These products generally lack the finish quality and durability desired, though an acceptable job may result with proper care and time invested in the preparation work

Hints

*Do preserve the maker's insignia, if present. It validates the historical value of the lamps and should not be polished out, painted or plated over in a way that makes it illegible.

*Do maintain all air supply and exhaust routes as the manufacturer intended for proper operation of the lamp.

*Do burn the proper fuel. Use lamp oil for wick holders, unless otherwise imprinted on the burner, and beeswax candles for candle lamps.

*Do not use abrasive tools or cleaner on reflectors and bright metal mounting.

*Do not apply open flame to lamps where lamp oil, candle wax or other flammable materials are present and may ignite.

*Do not pry up the bezel, or channel, around a light when replacing the glass. This will render the bezel unfit for later use.

*Do not use hot glue or other materials affected by heat for repairs.

*Do not use miracle metal, plastic steel or other epoxy type metal repair products. They seldom prove to be adequate in repairing old and rusted metal, and holding a finish.

*Do not polish and leave exposed more than one bright metal on the exterior. Makers often used several different metals in fabricating lamps, but usually only one was left exposed when the lamps were finished.

Use, Storage and Preservation

Upon the investment of time, talent, and resources required to restore a pair of carriage lamps, it would seem prudent to keep their preservation in mind when using, transporting and storing the lamps. The best way to preserve carriage lamps is to keep them clean and protected. Accumulated oil, candle wax and soot should be removed immediately. Beeswax candles are recommended as they do not drip, if trimmed and burned properly. Candle and oil wicks should be trimmed and adjusted properly to minimize soot buildup. Candles should not be left in the lamps when not in use, especially in warm climates or if the lamps are displayed with exposure to the sun. Due to the multi-layered construction of most carriage lamps, many blind pockets and areas that trap moisture are present. Great care should be taken in removing moisture after washing and cleaning. Soft, dry rags, paper towels and compressed air are useful, as well as placing the lamps in a warm, sunny, well-ventilated area until completely dry. Temperature and humidity changes may also be a factor in accumulating moisture in some areas and should be considered in planning for long term storage and display. Individual felt or heavy flannel bags and wood or metal carrying cases made specifically for individual lamps will help protect lamps during transport and storage.

Obtaining, conserving, restoring and preserving a pair of carriage lamps can be an interesting and rewarding project for the carriage enthusiast. Researching the vehicle and accouterments will lend a sense of historical validity to the project. Evaluating the lamps and planning the conservation or restoration process is often as enjoyable an activity as accomplishing the actual refurbishing. Providing for the proper storage and preservation of the lamps will insure the enjoyment of their historical significance, practical use, and elegant beauty for many years.

CHAPTER 18

WICKER AND CANE WORK

IMITATION CANE-WORK FOR PAINTED CARRIAGE PANELS

The fashion of decorating painted carriage panels to simulate woven cane-work is believed to have started sometime between the 1800-1850'. There were two main ways in which this was done, either by painting it directly to the surface or by using prepared sheets of imitation cane-work and glueing them to the panel. Each of these methods had several variations, among professional carriage builders searching for the most cost effective method and best quality job. Some methods that were tried were really not of good quality and they did not last very long in the market. The art of painting the cane-work directly to the surface was very tedious and difficult and especially difficult is the laying out the pattern on rounded and curved panels.

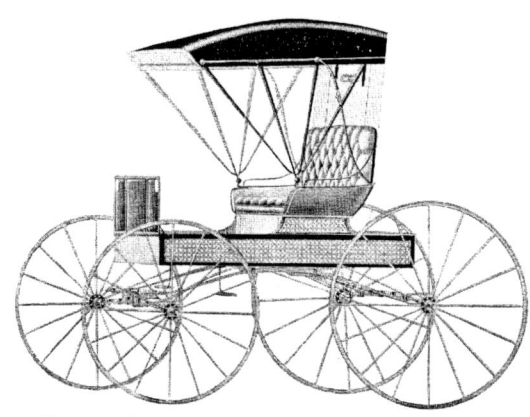

Cane-work was used on all classes of vehicles from buggies to landaus.
From the Carriage Monthly March, 1913.

Painting directly to the surface though seemed to be the most durable method and if the tube method was use called Sham-Caning with heavy paint this was the best quality work with good depth and relief. The other method of painting was to use paint of normal consistency and a regular striping pencil and this gave a flat appearance. Someone attempting to do this work for the first time on a rounded body panel should first start by practicing the layout of the pattern on a paper pattern cut to the curve of the panel. The top of the panel should be divided off into an equal amount of spaces as the bottom. The bottom is a shorter distance around and must have the spaces closer together.

Sham-Caning
The Hub - September 1877.

Sham-caning. The appliance necessary is a small bag made of sheep skin or bladder from the mouth of which is a small tube of tin or copper with a very fine hole for the paint to run out. Having filled the bag with cream-colored paint, mixed with japan principally, tie the bag and tube tightly together, and with a light pressure the paint may be made to exude from the end of the tube in the proper quantity to form the raised cane strings. The next thing necessary is the pattern. To prepare this, first take a piece of paper cut to fit the exact size of the panel to be caned, including the swell, and lay it

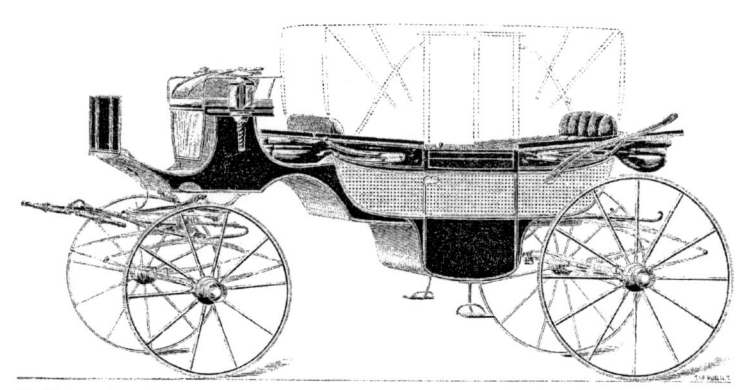

Full Leather-Top Landau: Painting--Lower part of door and pillars, bottle green. Moldings, black, with fine straw-color stripe; quarter panels and door panels between belt lines, imitations cane-work; upper part of door, bottle green, with all moldings black; boot, same shade of green; moldings, black. Gear, Nile green, striped black and straw-color. Trimming. Blue cloth, and lace to match throughout. Mountings, gold.
From the Hub March 1890.

out with dividers and pencil in lines as formed by real woven cane. When this has been done, the lines may be pricked off in the same manner as when doing an ornament. Then lay the paper pattern on the panel and keep it in place with a few tacks; pounce over it with a dust bag (a porous bag filled with finely powdered chalk) and, on removing the pattern, we will find the entire pattern laid out in white dots. With a straight edge we may draw the lines of paint, allowing one set of lines to get DRY before the cross lines are drawn.

The Hub - May 1881

Sir: Having been shown the other day your valuable paper, I saw some remarks about imitation cane-work, having worked at this for more than 25 years, I take the liberty of sending a little information on it.

In the first place you don't want so much filling up for the panels, and after being rubbed down it only wants one coat of black, one of japan, and a thin coat of varnish. I gained first prize for this work at the London Exhibition in 1851, and I did many carriages for my cousin the late Richard Andrews, celebrated coachbuilder of Southampton.

The way I have executed the work is to grind the white lead in gold-size, very fine, and tint it with stone ochre, to give it a cane colour. Make it thin enough to use without turps, as your lines would otherwise be apt to split or sink down in the middle. I use the striping tube, which flows much better than one squeezed out, because it comes out gradually, while squeezing out in the ordinary way you are liable to have more colour in one part than another.

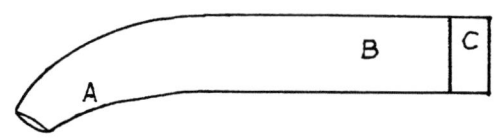

Striping Tube, made of tin or copper, oval shape. A-tapered end; B-vent hole; C-cork stopper.

Beginning your work, mark it well out with dividers, and do the longest lines first, because in crossing in squares you will not have the difficulty of getting over the short ones.

As for the leather or paper patterns pasted on, I would not recommend these. I have seen some, but they either peel off or blister. The best plan is as I describe, with the cane colour put direct on the panel.

The real cane does not last very long, as the wet and dirt get behind it and soon rot it away, while with the imitation you can wash the dirt off completely.

Now a few words as to the difficulty of round backs or round corners; draw your lines straight as far as you can, then draw your dividers around the corners, and get a piece of leather, about 3/4 inch wide, and sweep it round, and use it to guide your tube around to meet your other lines.

The pattern tube I send you will flow well with a vent-hole, as marked, so as to run gradually. Do not let this become stopped up or the colour will not flow.

Sandpaper off the edges of the straightedge or colour might flow under and spoil your lines. *James Warner.*

The Carriage Monthly - March 1913

Prepare the panel as usual up to the first coat of rubbing varnish, which is flattened by rubbing. The cane work is put on with a funnel with a short, flat neck. This funnel should be large enough to hold two pounds of paint, made of dry lead and orche, about the shade of rattan; mixed with japan and turpentine so to be sure to dry like putty or some painters use shellac, instead of japan(drying varnish), but where shellac is used, alcohol should be substituted for turpentine, as the latter will not work with shellac. Rules to be observed for raised cane work: Use a funnel with air-holes and the mouth hole the size needed for the size of the cane. Place the panel face upward, that is, in a horizontal position, to prevent the paint from running. Do not force the color in the funnel, but let it squeeze through by its own weight. The color must be such as to run slowly through the mouth. All the cane work must be outlined first with chalk, and to do this the lines must be equally divided, which is very difficult and tedious work.

Bibliography of painted cane-work.

"Imitation Cane for Buggies." The Carriage Monthly. (March, 1913).

"Specimens of Painting." The New York Coach-Maker's Magazine. (March, 1861), pp. 191-192.
   (Translated from the Mercure Universel)

"To Lay Out Imitation Cane Work." Coach-Makers' International Journal. (Oct. 1870), pp. 5-6.
   (Recommends the use of a ruler the width of the caning squares, and the lines are marked off on both sides of the ruler.)

Warner, James. "Application of Imitation Cane-Work." The Hub. (May, 1881), pp. 74-75.

IMITATION CANE-WORK GLUED ON

Mr. Whittingham of London, England is believed to be the first to come up with a method of gluing on imitation cane-work. The cane-work was first made on a piece of prepared canvas that had the surface prepared perfectly smooth with paint, usually black. The cane-work was then applied using the tube method of hand painting. In order to apply this canvas sheeting to the carriage a pattern was made of the panel and the canvas cut out to size and then glued to the panel with the cane-work. A final coat of varnish probably followed this application. Although this form of imitation cane-work along with later versions, made up in sheets, was a time saver there is the difficulty of trying to cut it out to look well on rounded body panels. As it was glued around a curve some of the squares of the cane-work would be cut in half. Mr. Whittingham is method of making sheets of cane-work still required much hand labor.

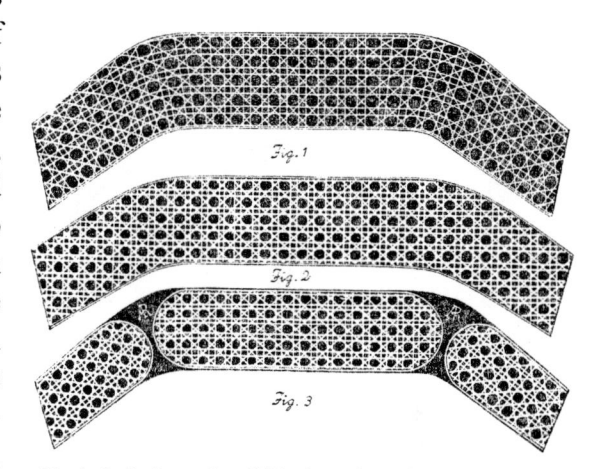

Fig.1 & 2 show the difficulty of cutting out sheets of prepared cane-work for round body panels. Fig. 1 has the squares and holes lined up on the bottom but they do not come out even on the top sides. Fig. 2 has the squares and holes even for the center back top & bottom, but the ends are uneven. Fig. 3 shows one solution to the problem.
From the Carriage Monthly Feb. 1900.

A later process invented by a French stationery maker by the name of Eugene Raud of Paris supplied imitation cane-work to the trade that was stamped and cut from, canvas.. In 1874 the Hub reported that it came very neatly prepared, by machinery, upon perforated canvas, and is sold in pieces 6 feet 6 inches long. It was available in varying widths and six different patterns. The cane-work was applied by preparing the carriage panel the same as sham caning. From the roll of cane-work cut out what is needed for the job and roll up the rest back in the powder that it was packed in. When the varnish is about half dry, and still tacky, put on the cane-work, which must be perfectly free from dampness. Press it down gently, but firmly, and if any difficulty be found in making it adhere, a little japan gold-size applied to the under surface will insure its sticking.

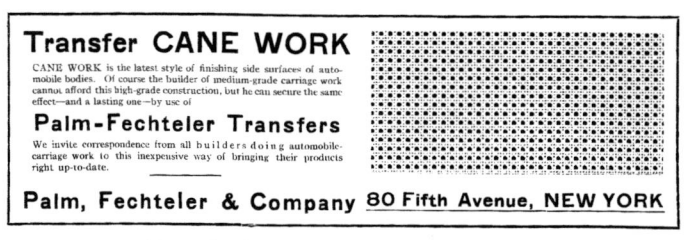

Transfer CANE WORK
CANE WORK is the latest style of finishing side surfaces of automobile bodies. Of course the builder of medium-grade carriage work cannot afford this high-grade construction, but he can secure the same effect—and a lasting one—by use of
Palm-Fechteler Transfers
We invite correspondence from all builders doing automobile-carriage work to this inexpensive way of bringing their products right up-to-date.

Palm, Fechteler & Company 80 Fifth Avenue, NEW YORK

From the Carriage Monthly March 1913.

Wicker and Cane Work

When dry a coat of varnish should be applied as usual. All the cane-work should be pressed down from the center outward.

Makers of transfer ornaments also marketed imitation cane-work in sheets to be transferred to carriage panels. This process was very neatly done with the shading of interwoven parts of the cane-work. The biggest objection to this was that it was perfectly flat.

Besides the traditional method of sham-caning the Brewster Co. of New York is reported to have employed another method of cane-work in which it was applied in sheets. "The paint (buff or straw colored) was placed on the board and worked into the pattern similar to the intaglio process of engraving, and the excess wiped off. The board was baked in an oven until the paint hardened and they would varnish the carriage body and affix this basketlike pattern over the tack varnish."[1] This method of making imitation cane-work seems to be consistent with a patent taken out by Peter Barry. His sheets of canework consisted solely of dried paint produced in a mold.

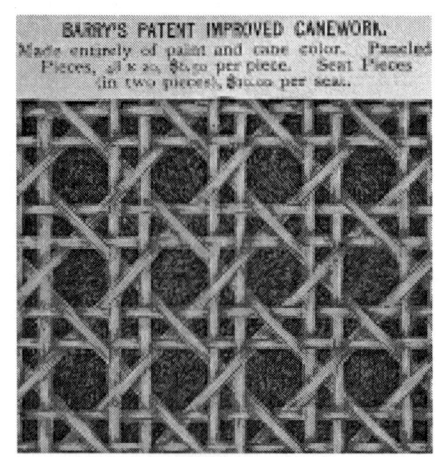

From the Hub Nov. 1885.

Although sheets of real cane-work were sometimes used most agreed it was the least desirable method. The back of the sheets are not smooth enough to adhere tightly to painted surfaces and water and dirt gets behind the work causing them to deteriorate. However some success has be achieved with this method using modern adhesives.

Bibliography of imitation cane-work.
"Cane Work for Round Cornered Phaeton Seats." The Carriage Monthly. (Feb. 1900), p. 377.
"Canework Finish." The Hub. (Oct. 1880), p. 315.
"Imitation Cane and Basket Work For Carriage Bodies." The Hub. (March 1884), p. 789.
"Imitation Cane-Work For Carriages. The Hub. (Oct. 1874), p.198.
"Real Cane, Imitation Cane, Imitation Basket Wood and Imitation Transfers." The Carriage Monthly. (May 1899), pp. 44-45.
Sherwood, A. S. "Dealer of Carriage Materials." The Hub. (Dec., 1885), p. 607.

Modern Method of Cane-Work
by Gerald A. Ralph - Carriage Journal vol.5 no.2

The mold consisted of a ½ inch plastic sheet into which the cane-work design was etched with a router. First cut the plastic sheet at least 3 inches larger than both the length and width of the space to be covered by the cane-work.

Place the plastic sheet on a work table and wedge it in place with a 6 in. strip of ½ inch fiberboard, completely surrounding the plastic sheet as this will be required for routing overrun. Be sure to nail on an outside edge so the router will not cut into nails.

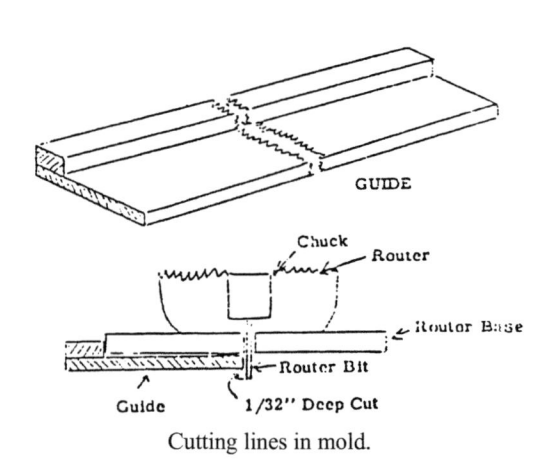

Cutting lines in mold.

---
[1] Howard, Francis Nunan. The Flying Lady, p.661.

Routing The Cane-Work Pattern

You will need the following tools:
1. Router 2. Three 1/6 in. router bits (they break easily) 3. A guide made as Fig. 2. 4. Compass with metal tips. 5. Two clamps for holding the guide in place while routing.

You are now set up to start routing. With the compass, scratch marks 5/8 inches apart along all four edges of plastic sheet matching the parallel side. Make a set of scratches 3/16 inch from the first set. (see Fig. 3)

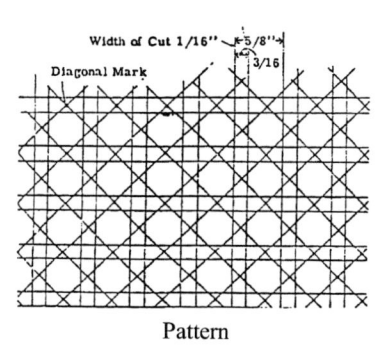

Line up the edge of the guide on scratched marks, clamp guides in place and route the line. Duplicate this process until all lines at right angles to the sides are cut. Depth of each cut should be approximately 1/32in. deep. After right lines are cut, mark the center of rectangle and cut diagonal lines (see pattern). Take a sample of real woven cane to a polyester resin supplier for assistance in mixing the color and appearance of real cane. You will need the following:

Polyester Resin (clear)-This is the same as the resin used in fiberglass products.
Curing Agent. Color Pigments. Flexicizer. Mold Release. (PVA-Poly Vinyl Acetate).
Roller--rolling pin will do.

The resin supplier will give you assistance on mixing the right formula of resin, pigment and flexicizer to re-create the cane. Enough flexicizer should be added to make the finished product pliable, yet not too elastic so as not to hold its shape. I would recommend making a small 6 x 6 inch sample mold to experiment on to work out problems and to develop a satisfactory material.

Procedure

Wash out the mold to remove any impurities. Let it dry thoroughly. Spray an even coat of PVA mold release onto the mold and onto one side of the acetate sheet. Be sure the entire area is covered as the polyester will stick to any uncovered area. Let dry thoroughly. Mix polyester resin solution--use as little curing agent as possible to ensure a slow cure. Pour into the center of mold; cover mold with an acetate sheet; and, with the roller and hands, work the excess resin out to the edges. The acetate sheet and high points of the mold must touch without the resin between. Note: the above work should be done at a room temperature of approximately 80 degrees F. After the resin cures, remove the acetate sheet. Use water sandpaper to remove thin membrane of the resin over the holes. Then remove the cane-work from the mold. Wash the cane-work and mold with water to remove mold release. After cane-work has dried, clean excess plastic and imperfections in it with a sharp exacto knife.

Cane-work is applied over a painted panel of the base color desired, which is usually black. Cut a paper pattern from butcher paper to the exact size of each space to be covered.

Cut the cane-work to the size of the paper pattern, using heavy scissors. Where two sections of cane-work come together, match the horizontal lines to maintain continuity of the pattern.

Wet sand the area to be covered by the cane-work. Spray a thin coat of clear enamel on the space to be covered and on the back of the cane-work. Wait until both become tacky (about 15 minutes), then bring together. Use a Formica roller (a hard rubber roller) to force adhesion. After allowing to dry for 48 hours, apply two thin coats of clear enamel over the entire caned area to seal the cane-work in clear enamel.

Wicker and Cane Work

WOVEN CANE WORK FOR SEATS

Woven cane work for carriages can be found on some sulky seats and on the seat frame underneath the passengers' cushion on many fine carriages. Cane is the outside part of rattan, a palm that grows in India, China, and the Malay Peninsula. All cane is glossy on one side. The glossy side is the top or outside. The cane is soaked in water to make it pliable and then is woven in and out of the round holes around the seat frame. Some furniture restorers can do this job, and there are more specialized people that just do seat weaving. It is not an extremely difficult task and many craft stores have supplies and

Woven cane-work for sulky seat

instruction books and very inexpensive pamphlets for seat weaving. There are a number of specialty shops that specialize in selling materials and instruction books for seat weaving and basket making. Natural cane - long select is 12 feet and up in lengths. For weaving seats, the size of cane required is determined by the diameter of the hole around the edge of the seat and the space from the center of one hole to the center of the next hole.

Cane size	Hole size	Center to Center
Carriage (1-1/2-1-3/4 mm)	1/8"	5/16" - 3/8"
Superfine (1-3/4-2mm)	1/8"	3/8"
Fine-Fine (2-1/4mm)	3/16"	7/16"-½"
Fine (2-1/2 mm)	3/16"	½"-9/16"
Narrow Medium (2-34mm)	1/4"	9/16"- 5/8"
Medium (3mm)	1/4"	5/8" - 3/4"
Common (3-1/2mm)	5/16"	3/4" - 7/8"

It is sold in hanks (approx. 1000 feet). One hank should do three to four average chairs. The seat board under a double passenger's cushion would equal two chairs and a half hank should be plenty.

WICKER WORK

Willow

There are two distinct kinds of wicker work and one should not be confused with the other when you are going to have repairs done. **Willow** work is typically stronger and more irregular in shape and has a smoother surface. It was used for making the bodies of country sleighs and often found painted. The ladies' wicker driving phaetons and park phaetons that we have seen made by the A. T. Demarest Co., New York, NY has typically used willow for the wicker work with a natural finish. Many carriage accessories such as umbrella baskets and picnic baskets typically used willow. People that work with willow are very few; and we only know of about three or four people. Willow for wicker work is a cultivated crop in which little shoots of willow are placed in the soil and they grow into a single shoot called osiers from about 3 to 8 feet when they are harvested. There were at one time large colonies of willow growers and willow weavers in the United States. The Amana Colonies, in Iowa is the only known colony left that still cultivates willow in the United States, only growing enough for their own use. The only retail sales of willow that we know of in the United States are osiers imported from England. They come in three types. For "Brown" the rods are dried with the bark on and they have a greenish-brown hue. For "White"

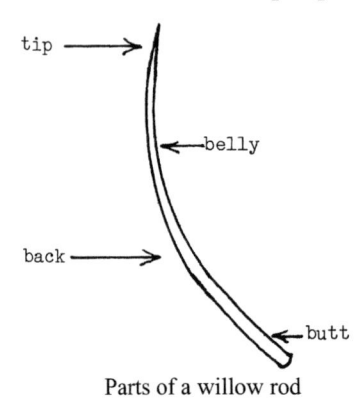

Parts of a willow rod

Basket Phaeton by A. T. Demarest & Co., New York, NY.
The willow work was finished natural.

A Basket Sleigh made in Pennsylvania, typically the willow work was painted.

the rods are peeled. For "Buff" the rods are dried with the bark on and then boiled in tanks for several hours. The subsequent peeling results in a beautiful red-brown colour. We have never found any instructions specifically for making bodies of carriages but many basket weaving instruction books can be well adapted if you should like to try weaving wicker carriage bodies.

The most noticeable thing about old willow work for carriages bodies is the tightness of the weave, so tight that the stakes are invisible and it looks water tight. To achieve such tightness, the rods are knocked down by a pounding iron as they are being woven with great skill and craftsmanship so that truly fine works of art are created, whether it be a sleigh body, a carriage or a simple umbrella basket.

Reed

Reed was maybe more commonly used on carriages, and it is put up in coils and can be gotten in diameters from 1/32 to 5/32 in. It is die cut from the core of rattan and is therefore more uniform in diameter than willow. Reed tends to be easier to work with, but has a coarser surface when trying to refinish it. Round reed is available in two grades: Premium (whiter, truer to size and virtually "hairless") and 1st Quality, a slightly lesser grade. They generally wove both types of wicker for carriage bodies over a metal frame or metal braces. These vehicles with wicker bodies often included a dashboard and wheel fenders that were also woven with wicker. Wicker sleighs generally did not have metal supporting frame work for the wicker work. Some carriage bodies that had wicker work with reed had some very artistic and ornate designs woven into them, giving the weaver many creative opportunities.

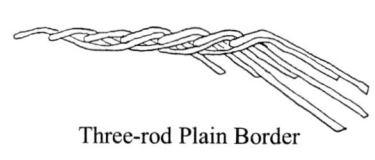

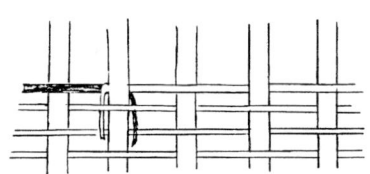

Three-rod Plain Border

Plaited or Madeira-type Border

Randing

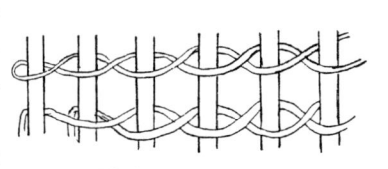

Slewing

Fitching or pairing

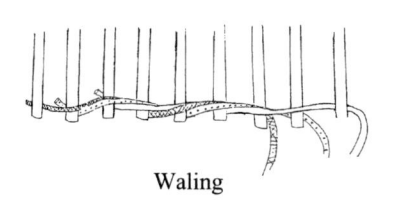

Waling

Museums
Books for additional information

Butcher, Mary. Willow Work.
Duncan. How to Buy and Restore Wicker Furniture.
Hartley. Care and Feeding of Baskets.
Knock, A. G. Fine Willow Basketry. Leicester, England : Dryad Press, 1946.
Lightner, Mary. "Remaking a Wicker Carriage Seat." Driving Digest. Issue 101 1997/3
Miller/Widess. Caner's Handbook.
Okey, Thomas. An Introduction to the Art of Basket-Making. London, England : Sir Isaac Pitman & Sons, 1912. (reprinted in 1986).
Rodgers, Fred. Willow Work. (6 hour Video).
Wright, Dorothy. Complete Book of Baskets and Basketry. North Pomfred, VT : David & Charles, 1983.

·ENTIRELY·NEW·

PATENT.

Rattan Wagons

OF EVERY DESCRIPTION.

BUGGIES, SURREYS, PHAETONS, Etc.

This is the prettiest, strongest, and most easy-riding carriage.

The framework of these bodies is made of steel. This surpasses the wooden framework, making the whole light, yet substantial in construction, the bottom of the body being the only portion gotten out of wood.

Parties wishing RATTAN WAGONS should furnish full particulars of style wanted. Bodies trimmed to order.

PATENTEE AND MANUFACTURER,
E. DEPERSENAIRE, 1665 BROADWAY, NEW-YORK.

Vehicle using both cane and reed. From the Hub August 1891.

Museums
CARRIAGE MUSEUM OF AMERICA-LIBRARY

The goal of the Carriage Museum of America Library is to serve as a source of historically accurate technical information on animal-drawn vehicles and related subjects. It is the only full time library dedicated exclusively to the Carriage Industry. Incorporated in 1978 as a non-profit educational institution, the Carriage Museum of America was headquartered in Salem, New Jersey at the offices of the *Carriage Journal*.

Thomas Ryder, a leading international expert on driving and carriages and former editor of The *Carriage Journal*, began the library collection. Major contributions have been made from the Paul Downing Collection and by Richard Harrington and Horace Sowles.

The library's collections have gained an international reputation attracting researchers from all over the world. it holds approximately 1200 books and trade catalogs on the subjects of carriages and wagons. Also housed in the library are books on stables and carriage houses, horse training, management, diseases, breeds and breeding as well as those on proper driving etiquette, whip and harness making, bridles, bits and horse shoeing. A number of histories of early travel and travel guides are also available.

Now located at Beechclale Farm in Bird-In-Hand, Pennsylvania, the library maintains collections of prints, photographs, drawings and blueprints of carriages. A collection of carriage making tools, donated in memory of Walter Leach, a former trustee can also be found among the historic pieces.

The Carriage Museum of America and its library are wonderful resources for carriage enthusiasts everywhere.

Available Publications

A Collection Of Essays On Horse-Drawn Carriages and Carriage Parts by Dr. Gordon S. Cantle. *This is the foremost technical book in print on the construction and engineering of carriage parts. $23.00*

A Treatise On Carriages by William Felton. *Reprinted from the 1794 and 1796 editions, It was the only book printed in English for this time period. An invaluable reference resource for people who want to study this time period and the history of carriages. $70.00*

Horse Drawn Sleighs by Susan Green for the Carriage Museum of America. *A compilation of sleigh designs in old trade journals, this is the only book ever published just about sleighs. $33.00*

The Royal Mews by Mary Stewart-Wilson, Photographs by David Cripps. *This book is illustrated in full color, showing the English state Carriages and stable. Outstanding photography of the harness and carriages. $28.00*

The Coson Carriage Collection At Beechdale. *This is about one of the premiere private carriage collections in the United States. It is illustrated with full color photographs and descriptions of the vehicles by Thomas Ryder. $33.00*

Wheelmaking : Wooden Wheel Design and Construction by Don Peloubet for the Carriage Museum of America. *It is a compilation of the technical articles on wheelmaking from the old trade journals, showing many designs of wheels.$33.00*

Working Drawings of Horse Drawn Vehicles. *100 engineering drawings for 20 different types of vehicles. The drawings come with a text page and dimensions. $55.00.*

Two-Wheeled Vehicles for Equine. *All different types of two-wheeled vehicles, plus comments on supension, old advertisements. Compiled from the Carriage Monthly and Hub. $43.00*

Horse-Drawn Vehicles: Colored Plates from the Hub Novmeber 1882-January 1892. *150 colored plates with text reprinted from the old trade journal the Hub. Very useful book if you have questions about what colors vehicles were painted. $105.00*

Manual of Coaching by Fairman Rogers. *Reprinted from the 1900 edition. It is the foremost book on driving and coaching. $70.00.*

Brewster Scrapbook. *Articles from the Carriage Monthly and Hub about the J. B. Brewster & Co., and Brewster & Co. Technical drawings of their vehicles and descriptions. Articles by John Britton, John Mosier, Franklin Gardner, John Gribbon of Brewster & Co. $80.00*

Research Services : The library staff is available to research carriage information. Please submit requests via mail including a clear photograph and the maker's name. All requests must be prepaid cash or check accepted. Research fees per question: $12.00 for members, $15.00 for non-members.

Post Office Box 417
Bird-In-Hand, Pennsylvania 17505 phone 717-656-7019

MUSEUMS

CALIFORNIA
Santa Ynez Valley Historical Society, Parks-Janeway Carriage House, Post Office Box 181, 3596 Sagunto St., Santa Ynez, CA 93460 phone 805-688-7889 The finest of its kind in the west, the Carriage House is dedicated to the late Tom Parks and Fred Bixby by Mrs. Betty Parks and Mrs. Elizabeth Bixby Janeway. This impressive building houses a collection of some 35 carriages, wagons and carts, as well as stagecoaches, buggies and other historical modes of transportation. Included are many vehicles used by the Los Rancheros Visitadores. Beautiful silver-mounted saddles, harnesses and other equipment are featured. Next to the carriage house is the blacksmith shop. Most of the tools, etc., on display are from local blacksmith shops that operated in the area. The Museum has many local history exhibits.

DISTRICT OF COLUMBIA
National Museum of American History, 14 th Street and Constitution Avenue N.W. Room 5010, MRC 628, Washington, DC, 20560 phone 202-357-2025. The collection includes 28 carriages, 14 wagons and 9 sleighs. Of these, 6 carriages, wagon, and one sleigh are displayed in the museum, which is open every day except December 25 from 10:00 to 5:30 p.m. An additional 3 carriages and one wagon are displayed in the Arts and Industries Building, which is open the same hours. The other horse-drawn vehicles are in storage and may be seen weekdays by appointment only by persons having a specific research or documentation interest in a specific vehicle. A library of horse-drawn vehicle books, journals, catalogs, files and photographs also is available weekdays by appointment only. Patrons may call 202-357-2025 to schedule an appointment, or they may write to the above address. Patrons may submit written inquiries to the above address; however, the museum does not conduct research or make copies, and most responses are limited to bibliographic assistance, photographic searches, and leads to other libraries, museums and organizations that may have materials the patron is seeking. The museum can provide limited information about vehicles in its collection. The museum does not have a carriage restoration program. Copies of horse-drawn vehicle drawings are sold by mail order, only ; a free price list is available.

ILLINOIS
Blackberry Historical Farm/Village, RR 3 Box 591, Barnes Road, Aurora, IL 60506-9125, phone 708-892-1550. All of the vehicles are of American origin. They have been gathered and restored to their original design to perpetuate the general theme of the Park. There are 43 carriages on display. The collection includes a wagonette, curtain rockaway, booby hut, Brewster Victoria & brougham, surreys, runabouts, delivery wagons, Cunningham hearse, Hooker c-spring brougham, spring wagons, beer barrel wagon, sleighs and carts.

Museums

INDIANA
Studebaker National Museum, 525 S. Main Street, South Bend, IN 46601, phone 219-235-9108. 1830 Conestoga wagon, 1857 Phaeton buggy, 1863 hearse, 1900 water wagon flusher, 1903 light delivery wagon, 1905 sleigh, 1905 fire hose cart, 1908 extension station wagon, 1909 & 1919 "Izzer" buggy, 1910 farm wagon, 1910 dump wagon, 1920 farm wagon, 1824 Lafayette's carriages, 1865 Lincoln's carriage, 1873 Grant's Landau carriage, 1876 Centennial wagon, 1889 McKinley's surrey, 1893 Columbian Exposition wagon, 1896 Harrison's brougham, 1917 U. S. Army ambulance, 1917 U. S. Army water cart, 1917 U.S. Army escort wagon, 1917 Army mountain wagon. The museum has an extensive advertising and photograph archives pertaining to Studebaker horse drawn vehicles.

KENTUCKY
International Museum of the Horse, 4089 Iron Works Road, Lexington, KY 40511, phone 606-233-4303 established at the Kentucky Horse Park is the largest and most comprehensive equestrian museum in the world. The museum is 52,000 square foot with a 2,000 volume research library and the William G. Kenton Jr. art gallery, which features both seasonal and permanent collections of equine art. The Museum's collection of horse-drawn vehicles is built around the thirty-four piece Pansy Yount Grant Spindletop Farm collection, donated by the University of Kentucky in 1977. Over the years, additional vehicles have been added. The collection consists of 37 horse-drawn vehicles: an 18th century French carousel sleigh, Albany cutter, Portland cutter, bob sleigh, Sicilian donkey cart, Concord stagecoach, victoria, rockaway, landau, and a hansom cab made by Studebaker.

MAINE
Owls Head Transportation Museum, Post Office Box 277, Owls Head, ME 04854, phone 207-594-4418, web site: WWW.OHTM.ORG, was established in 1974. The stated purpose of the museum is: "The Owls Head Transportation Museum is founded to collect, preserve and exhibit pioneer ground vehicles, aircraft and engines and related technology that is significant to the evolution of transportation or the state of Maine." The museum is 89,000 square feet on 111 acres, and the collection consists of 27 aircraft, 60 automobiles, 19 carriages, 8 motorcycles, 40 engines, 17 bicycles. Horse-drawn vehicles include 3 sleighs, Abbott & Downing stagecoach, Brewster Bronson wagon, Hansom Cab, surrey, Brewster roof-seat break, French & Co. brougham, Henry Hooker & Co. panel boot victoria, racing sulky and Brewster side bar runabout.

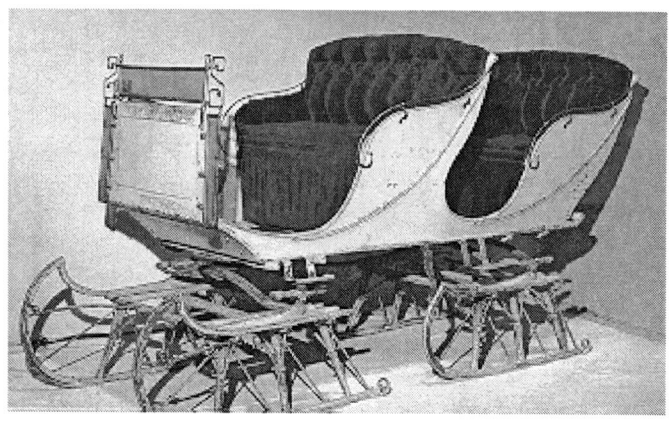

Museums

MARYLAND

Thrasher Carriage Museum, Allegany County Visitor's Bureau, Mechanic and Harrison Streets, Cumberland, MD 21502, phone 301-777-5905. The museum is a collection of carriages, wagons and sleighs spanning the carriage years of the mid 1800s to the early days of the twentieth century. There are over 100 pieces held by the museum with approximately one-half of these including sleighs, phaetons, delivery wagons, pleasure vehicles, assorted equipment used with carriages including whips, lap robes, saddles and harnesses on permanent display. Some of the more unusual pieces include Theodore Roosevelt's inaugural carriage, a Brewster Dog Cart, a private Park Drag, a funeral hearse, a Brewster Golf Cart, sleighs originally owned by the "Commodore", Cornelius Vanderbilt and several work wagons. Visitors should call ahead for updated hours and admission prices. The Thrasher Carriage Museum is located at 19 Depot Street in Frostburg, MD, phone 301-689-3380.

MICHIGAN

Henry Ford Museum and Greenfield Village, Dearborn, MI 48121, phone 313-271-1620, Bob Casey, Curator of Transportation. The museum's horse-drawn vehicle collection consists of over 100 carriages, wagons, and sleighs dating from the late 18th to the early 20th century. The wide range of horse-drawn vehicles represented includes coachman-driven carriages, excursion vehicles, owner-driven carriages, public transportation, commercial and freight vehicles, vehicles used to train and race horses, and agricultural vehicles. Highlights of the collection include a late-18th century coach, an early-19th century phaeton, a mid-19th century Albany sleigh, a Conestoga wagon, an 1870s barouche, a Road Coach and a Coupe-Dorsay exhibited at the Columbian Exposition in 1893, a Pan-American Exposition band wagon, a veterinary ambulance, a Concord coach, and a dray. Many vehicles retain their original finish and upholstery. Makers represented in the collection include Brewster of Broome St., Stivers & Tilton, James Cunningham & Sons, C. P. Kimball & Co., Studebaker Bros. Mfg. Co., Fish Bros. Wagon Co., Abbot, Downing Co., Crane & Breed Mfg., Co., and J. Goold & Co. Information about items in the collection is available through an in-house electronic database. Henry Ford Museum & Greenfield Village maintains a large reference library. Carriage related items include runs of *New York Coachmaker's Magazine, The Hub,* and *Carriage Monthly,* trade catalogs for makers of carriages and carriage equipment; and books.

NEW MEXICO

Museum of the Horse, Hwy 70 East, Post Office Box 40, Ruidoso Downs, NM 88346 phone 505-378-4142. The collection contains more than 10,000 horse-related items, most of them from the Anne C. Stradling collection. The roster of carriages and wagons runs to 65, with some 20 regularly rotated into the Museum's 60,000 square foot display area. Most of the vehicles are in original condition. The restorations which have been done have been undertaken under the most exacting supervision. Among the extensive collection are an English road coach, a fully refurbished fancy stage coach (pictured), a mountain coach, a children's hearse, and a J. B. Armstrong phaeton, to name but a few. Various sleds, sleighs, and other conveyances are also included in the collection.

Museums

NEW YORK
Long Island Museums of American Art, History and Carriages, 1208 Route25A, Stony Brook, New York 11790, contact Merri Ferrell, Carriage Curator, phone 516-751-0066, ext. 222. America's premier carriage collection of 250 horse-drawn vehicles, most in original condition, representing the best of their type; over 100 on view in engaging interpretive exhibitions. Over 10,000 related artifacts, accouterments, accessories, tools, costumes. Outstanding collection of rare books, drawings, prints, archives, trade catalogs and periodicals in the Gerstenberg Carriage Reference Library. The Carriage Museum open year round.

NEW YORK
American Museum of Fire Fighting, Firemen's Home, 125 Harry Howard Avenue, Hudson, New York 12534 phone 518-828-7695 contact Karen Del Principe, Curator's Assistant. The museum has 66 engines on display. There are 43 hand pulled, 2 horse drawn, 5 steam, and 16 automotive engines. Three of the hand pulled steam engines, 1 piano style hand engine and 1 hand pulled ladder truck were converted later on to horse drawn. The three authentic horse drawn engines are: 1. An 1882 steam engine manufactured by American La France Fire Engine Company, Elmira, New York. 2. 1911 Hose Wagon built by Charles F. Mayer of solid oak. 3. 1902 LaFrance/Hayes Aerial Ladder truck. Invented & patented by Danial B. Hayes, the truck provided the first aerial ladder that was quick, safe, and a convenient means of elevating a ladder. In 40 seconds the ladder could be elevated and extended against a building.

OKLAHOMA
Fort Sill Museum, 437 Quanah Road, Fort Sill, OK 73503-5100 phone 405-442-5123 Contact the curator, Towana Spivey. This 1870's era historic post is located within an active army installation. The museum occupies 26 of the original buildings and features over 60 horse drawn vehicles, (U. S. Army Escort Wagons, Wagonette, Phaeton, Ice Wagon, Ambulances, Chuck Wagons, Mountain Wagons, Conestoga Wagon, Roof Seat Break, Hearse), 30 artillery caissons and limbers for horse drawn artillery, 3 machine gun carts, 2 instrument carts and 2 battery reel carts.

OREGON
Oregon Historical Society, 1200 S. W. Park Avenue, Portland, Oregon 97205 phone 503-222-1741. Has one of the most outstanding collections of horse-drawn models made by Ivan Collins. Plans are available from the Oregon Historical Society Press, 1200 S. W. Park Avenue, Portland, Oregon 97205 or phone orders 503-306-5233. The available plans, copied from the originals in the collection of the Oregon Historical Society's Regional Research Library; are: Adams Express Wagon, Albany Sleigh, Armour Express, Army Escort Wagon, Army Escort covered Wagon, Bakery Wagon, Birdsell wagon, Bobsled, Boiler Wagon, Break, Brooklyn panel-side delivery wagon, Brougham, Bundle Rack, Civil War Cannon and Limber, Concord Coach, Conestoga Wagon, Dump Wagon, Express Wagon, Fire Dept. Wagon, Fuel Wagon, Garbage Wagon, Grain Box Wagon, Hearse, Hose Wagon, Ice Wagon, Lumber Wagon, Milk Wagon, Pleasure Wagon, Pleasure Phaeton, Red River Coach, Road Coach, Rockaway, Roll-off Lumber Wagon, Sheepherder's Wagon, Sprinkler Wagon, Union Oil Tank, Wagonette, Yellowstone Coach.

Museums

PENNSYLVANIA

Gruber Wagon Works, Park & Recreation Dept. of Berks Co., 2201 Tulpehocken Road, Wyomissing, PA 19610 phone 610-374-8839. The Gruber Wagon Works, located at the Berks County Heritage Center, survives as one of the most complete examples of an integrated rural manufactory of its kind in the nation. Erected in 1882 by Franklin H. Gruber, the Wagon Works evolved from a single craftsman shop, having a variety of specialized tools, into a family operated business which employed up to twenty men who utilized mass production methods. The Grubers produced hayflats, box wagons, wooden truck bodies, box sleds, specialty wagons and socket wrenches used on the Model A Ford. The Heritage Center currently has 24 vehicles in the collection, 10 are on display. During the winter of 1976-77, the Gruber Wagon Works was moved from its original location near Mt. Pleasant (Obold) by the Army Corps of Engineers. In 1978, the Wagon Works was designated as a National Historic Landmark and was opened to the public for tours in 1982. The Heritage Center, which also includes the Hiester Canal Center, is open for tours May through October, Tuesday - Saturday, 10 am - 4 pm; Sunday 12-5 pm; and open summer holidays.

VERMONT

Shelburne Museum, Route 7, Shelburne, VT 05482, phone 802-985-3346 has a collection of over 200 horse-drawn vehicles which is one of the largest and most comprehensive public collections of early vehicles in the United States. Ranging in scope from utilitarian to luxurious. Shelburne's collection focuses primarily on vehicles made and/or used in New England between 1800 and 1910 and includes owner-driven vehicles such as the chaise, curricle and various forms of the runabout, rockaway and Phaeton families, as well as such elegant coachman-driven carriages as the landau, Victoria, town coach, private omnibus and the vis-a-vis. The finest vehicles of the collection are the Berlin and caleche made for Dr. Webb about 1890 by the famous firm of Million and Guiet, Paris, France. The Museum also owns over 50 sleighs, many with outstanding paint decoration. The Museum's conservation philosophy is to preserve historic evidence of daily use while stabilizing the original structure and finish. The Shelburne Museum maintains their own conservation lab and staff of conservators.

VIRGINIA

Colonial Williamsburg Foundation, Post Office Box 417, Williamsburg, VA 23187 phone 804-229-1000. This 173 acre Historic area, consists of restored houses, shops, taverns and trade sites, that authentically recreates the capital of Britains largest and most populous colony in North America. For those interested in carriages and horses, this historic site has much to offer. The coach and livestock department has up to 30 horses used with reproduction 18th century carriages, carts, and wagons. This is the most extensive collection of working 18th century vehicles in the world. To support this there are trade shops, such as the wheelwright, where the 18th century trade is carried out, and they keep all the carriages, carts and wagons in working order. Also there is the harness and saddlery shop that makes all the harness and saddlery needed for use in the historic village. Both these shops have a full 6 year apprenticeship programs to ensure the continuation of these trades. There are many other trade shops dealing with 18th century trades, such as the blacksmith, foundry, cabinet makers etc. that lend support to the carriage operation. Colonial Williamsburg also has a very extensive library specializing in all aspects of 18th century life, including books on carriages and livestock.

Museums

WASHINGTON
Yakima Valley Museum, 2105 Tieton Drive, Yakima, WA 98902, phone 509-248-0747, fax 509-453-4890, E-mail museum@wolfenet.com. The 55,000 square foot facility offers historical exhibits on the Yakima valley - its natural history, American Indian culture, pioneer life, early city life, and the roots and development of the Valley's fruit industry. The museum has a superb collection of 47 horse-drawn vehicles, including a hearse, an American road coach, three stagecoaches, phaetons, rockaways, landaus, a brougham, farm and delivery wagons, an army escort wagon, and an 1889 steam fire pumper. An Aggressive program of conservation and stabilization was begun in 1995. There are approximately eleven linear feet of books, advertising pamphlets, broadsides, photographs, and bills of sale related to carriages and wagons in the museum's Sandquist Research Library.

WISCONSIN
Circus World Museum, 426 Water Street, Baraboo, WI 53913, phone 608-356-8341. Circus World Museum is owned by the State Historical Society of Wisconsin, and is operated by the non-profit Historic Sites Foundation, Inc. The Museum's collection includes over 150 circus, wild west and carnival wagons, dozens of circus vehicles, and close to 50 railroad cars, not to mention thousands of other circus artifacts. The circus wagon collection, the largest in the world, represents the work of American wagon builders, although the collection also contains several English examples. The wagons range in construction date from the early 1880s to the 1950s, with styles representative of both the largest and smallest shows. The Museum maintains an active restoration program, restoring several wagons annually, The holdings of the Museum's Robert L. Parkinson Library and Research Center include a large collection of circus wagon photographs and several wagon design elevations. The Museum and Library are open year-round, although the majority of wagons are only on exhibit from May through October.

WISCONSIN
Old Wade House and Wisconsin Carriage Museum, Post Office Box 34, Greenbush, WI 53026, phone 414-526-3271 The Wesley W. Jung Carriage Museum is part of the Wade House Historic Site. The museum features carriages and wagons collected by Wesley W. Jung, grandson of Jacob Jung, who operated a carriage making company in Sheboygan, WI from the mid -19th century to the early 1900's. The collection now includes over 125 horse and hand-drawn vehicles, with about 40% of them made by the Jung Carriage Company, which specialized in business and farm wagons. One of the rarest vehicles in the collection is a self-unloading coal wagon made about 1900 by Streich Co., of Oshkosh, WI. Among the other items on display are a Concord buggy, heavy meat wagon, Portland cutter, racing sulky, light farm wagon, brougham cab, main street livery omnibus, cut-under coupe rockaway, ladies basket phaeton, Velvet tobacco wagon, park drag, wood-tank sprinkler wagon, firefighting vehicles, and a collection of vehicles for children.

Museums
WYOMING
Cheyenne Frontier Days Old West Museum, Post Office Box 2720, 4501 North Carey Avenue in Frontier Park, Cheyenne, WY 82003, phone 307-778-7290, is a comprehensive museum dedicated to conserving and preserving the story and related artifacts of Cheyenne Frontier Days, the City of Cheyenne, Laramie County and Wyoming with emphasis on the "Old West" tradition. The Museum has a total of 132 horse drawn vehicles. They fall into the general categories of buggies; phaetons; luxury carriages; four wheel traps; carts, gigs, and sulkies; road and stage wagons; overland wagons; hunting and excursion wagons; farm and ranch wagons; commercial and service wagons; military wagons and sleighs. Thirty-one of the vehicles have been completely restored, two are reproductions and the balance are being conserved and preserved in their original condition. Accessories include lamps, whips and some covers for protection from the weather. A small harness collection is available. Harness is being researched with the intent of enlarging the collection so that the museum has appropriate harness for each vehicle in the collection.

An attempt is made to keep a provenance and history for each vehicle. A large and growing horse-drawn vehicle and related topics library of books, monographs, periodicals and video tapes is available.

Much of the preservation and restoration of carriages is done in-house by a group of trained volunteers called Wagon Doctors. The museum obtained grants to bring in exerts on restoration to conduct workshops to train the Wagon doctors in the many aspects of preservation and restoration.

LIBRARIES
Library of Congress
Washington, DC 20540-5591
long runs of Carriage Monthly, Hub, Blacksmith and Wheelwright, Spokesman, Rider & Driver

National Museum of American History
Smithsonian Institution
14th and Constitution Ave.
Washington, DC 20560
phone 202-357-2700
long run of Le Guide du Carrosier, Hub, & Carriage Monthly

New York Public Library
Rare Books and Manuscripts
Room 324
Fifth Avenue & 42nd Street
New York, NY 10018
phone 212-930-0801
fax 212-302-4815
Brewster & Co. records from #17450-25903

The Museums at Stony Brook*
1208, Route 25A
Stony Brook, NY 11790
phone 516-751-0066x222
Extensive library

Carriage Museum of America-Library
Post Office Box 417
Bird-In-Hand, PA 17505
phone 717-656-7019
large collection of drawings, mail order reference services, books for sale

National Sporting Library
Post Office Box 1335
301 West Washington Street
Middleburg, VA 22117
phone 540-687-6542

United States Department of Agriculture, Forest Service Forest Products Laboratory
One Gifford Pinchot Drive
Madison, WI 53705-2398
information on woods and wood bending

MUSEUMS-ALABAMA
Museums of the City of Mobile
355 Government Street
Mobile, AL 36602
phone 334-434-7427
9 carriages, 2 steam engines

MUSEUMS-ALASKA
Eagle Historical Society & Museum
Post Office Box 23
First Street
Eagle City, AK 99738
phone 907-547-2325
2 wagons, 2 sleighs, 2 farm machinery

MUSEUMS-ARIZONA
Sharlot Hall Museum
415 West Gurley St.
Prescott, AZ 86301
phone 602-445-3122
2 carriages, 3 wagons, 1 sleigh, 1 farm machinery, less than 100 related items

MUSEUMS-CALIFORNIA
Death Valley National Monument
Post Office Box 579
Death Valley, CA 92328
phone 619-786-3287
1 light spring wagon, 1 light stage wagon, 1 mule wagon, 1 dumb wagon, 1 set of borax wagons(lead wagon, 2nd wagon, water wagon), numerous parts and pieces

200

Furnace Creek Branch
Post Office Box 187
Death Valley, CA 92328
phone 619-786-2345
Several wagons, set of borax wagons, and water wagons

U.S. Borax , Inc.
Valencia, CA
phone 805-287-5773
set of borax wagons

Oakland Museum
1000 Oak Street
Oakland, CA 94607
phone 510-238-3842
2 carriages, 7 wagons, 2 sleighs, 4 farm machinery

San Jose Historical Museum
1600 Senter Road
San Jose, CA 95112-2599
phone 408-287-2290
27 carriages, 27 wagons, 3 sleighs, 10 farm machinery, horse drawn trolley car, large collection of harness & saddles, also collection of archival materials & patent models & models from Knapp Plow works local manufacturer of agricultural equipment from 1870s to 1924.

San Mateo County Historical Association
1700 West Hillsdale Blvd.
San Mateo, CA 94402
phone 415-574-6441
30 horse-drawn vehicles

Parks-Janeway Carriage House *
Post Office Box 181
Santa Ynez, CA 93460
phone 805-688-7889
35 horse-drawn vehicles, stage coach, implement annex, blacksmith shop, library, saddles, reatas, bits,

Mendocino County Museum
400 East Commercial Street
Willits, CA 95490
phone 707-459-2736
8 horse-drawn vehicles on exhibit, 10 in storage

Museums
Banning Residence Museum
Post Office Box 397
401 East Main Street
Wilmington, CA 90748
phone 310-548-7777
6 carriages, 2 wagons

MUSEUMS-COLORADO
Carriage House Museum
Broadmoor
Colorado Springs, CO 80906
phone 719-634-7711
carriage collection

MUSEUMS-CONNECTICUT
Barnum Museum
820 Main Street
Bridgeport, CT 06604
203-331-1104
3 carriages 1 wagon, all items used by Tom Thumb & other midgets in Barnum's show.

Allegra Farm
Living History Museum
Route 82 Town Street
Post Office Box 455
East Haddam, CT
phone 860-873-9658

MUSEUMS-DELAWARE
Historical Society of Delaware
505 Market Street
Wilmington, DE 19801
phone 302-655-7161
farm sleigh & buggy

Hagley Museum and Library
298 Buck Road East
Post Office Box 3630
Wilmington, DE 19807-0630
phone 302-658-2400
5 carriages, 5 wagons, 3 sleighs, highlights: Conestoga wagon, gun powder delivery wagon, folk art sleigh, paten models.

MUSEUMS-DISTRICT OF COLUMBIA
Smithsonian Institution
National Museum of American History*
14th St. & Constitution Avenue North West
Room 5010, MRC 628
Washington, DC 20560
phone 202-357-2700
28 carriages, 14 wagons, 8 sleighs, 6 carriages on display, 1 wagon on display, mail-order drawings for vehicles available

MUSEUMS-FLORIDA
Continental Acres
Post Office Box 68
3024 Marion County Road
Weirsdale, Florida 32195-0068
large collection of horse-drawn vehicles, driving of horses

John & Mabel Ringling Museum of Art
5401 Bay Shore Road
Sarasota, FL 34243
phone 941-359-5700
circus wagons

MUSEUMS-GEORGIA
Pebble Hill Foundation
United States 319 South
Tallahasse Road
Post Office Box 830
Thomasville, GA 31799
phone 912-226-2344
11 carriages, 6 wagons, 1 farm machinery, 9 carts, wagon jacks, single & double trees

Washington-Wilkes Historical Museum
308 East Robert Toombs Avenue
Washington, GA30673-2038
phone 706-678-2105
1 coach of the civil-war period, 1 sleigh

MUSEUMS-ILLINOIS
Aurora Historical Society
Post Office Box 905
Aurora, IL 60507
phone 630-897-9029
hearse, 2 sleighs, 1 extension top phaeton, drop front phaeton, early buggy

Museums

Blackberry Historical Farm Village*
Barnes Road & Galena
Rte 31
Aurora, IL 60506
phone 708-264-7405
43 carriages

Museum of Science & Industry
57th Street & Lake Shore Drive
Chicago, IL 60637
phone 312-684-1414
stagecoach and carriages

Ellwood House Museum
509 North First Street
DeKalb, IL 60115
phone 815-756-4609
25 carriages and sleighs, silican cart

Lena Area Historical Society
427 West Grove Street
Post Office Box 620
Lena, IL 61048
phone 815-3369-2215
hearse, John Adams buggy, fire fighting equipment

MUSEUMS-INDIANA

Studebaker National Museum Inc.*
525 South Main Street
South Bend, IN 46601
phone 219-235-9108
7 wagons, 2 army wagons, 1 U. S. Ambulance, 6 special carriages, 3 carriages, hearse, sleigh, extensive advertising and photograph archives pertaining to Studebaker horse drawn vehicles

MUSEUMS-KANSAS

Frontier Army Museum
100 Reynolds Ave Bldg 801
Fort Leavenworth, KS 66027-2334
phone 913-684-3767
10 carriages, 10 wagons, 3 sleighs, and 5 others

U. S. Cavalry Museum
Post Office Box 2160
Building 205
Fort Riley, KS 66442-0160
phone 913-239-2737
2 wagons, ammunition and lumber wagon

MUSEUMS-KENTUCKY

International Museum of the Horse*
4089 Iron Works Road
Lexington, KY 40511
phone 606-233-4303
37 carriages, carved miniatures collections of horse-drawn vehicles, numerous items related to all kinds of horses

MUSEUMS-MAINE

Colonel Black House
Post Office Box 1478
Ellsworth, Maine 04605
phone 207-667-8671
6 carriages: Brewster victoria, buckboard, early rockaway, omnibus.

Colonel Black House
Post Office Box 1478
Ellsworth, ME 04605
phone 207-667-8671
6 carriages: Brewster victoria, buckboard, early rockaway, omnibus.

Willow Brook at Newfield
Elm Street
Post Office Box 80
Newfield, ME 04056
phone 207-793-2784
Concord coach, 28 carriages, 2 hearses, 7 wagons, 19 sleighs, over 100 pieces of farm machinery

Owls Head Transportation Museum*
Post Office Box 277
Owls Head, ME 04854
phone 207-594-4418
Curator Dave Machaiek
12 carriages, 5 sleighs, large museum of air planes, and cars, 1847 stagecoach

MUSEUMS-MARYLAND

B & O Railroad Museum
901 West Pratt Street
Baltimore, MD 21223
phone 410-752-2490
horse car open, horse car-with sides, Conestoga wagon, fire engine, 3 hose reel carts, 1 carriage, express wagon

Thrasher Carriage Museum*
Allegany County Visitor's Bureau
Mechanic & Harrison Street
Cumberland, MD 21502
phone 301-777-5905
100 horse-drawn vehicles

Rose Hill Manor Children's Museum and Park
902 North Market Street
Frederick, MD 21701
phone 301-694-1648
23 carriages, 4 wagons, 9 sleighs, 8 farm machinery, & harness

Fire Museum of Maryland
1301 York Road
Lutherville, MD 21093
phone 410-321-7500
9-10 horse-drawn pieces

Ladew Topiary Gardens
3535 Jarrettsville Pike
Monkton, MD
21111
phone 410-557-9570
7 carriages, 1 wagon, 4 sleighs, 5 farm machinery

Carroll County Farm Museum
500 South Center Street
Westminster, MD 21157
phone 410-848-7775
4 carriages, 14 wagons, 9 sleighs, 45 farm machinery, 11 other

MUSEUMS-MASSACHUSETTS

Bartlett Museum
Post Office Box 692
270 Main Street
Amesbury, MA 01913
phone 508-388-4528

2 carriages, 1 sleigh, 4 farm machinery, photographs & profiles of carriages made in Amesbury, several manufacturers brochures & advertisements

Museum of Transportation
Lars Anderson Park
15 Newton Street
Brookline, MA 02146
phone 617-522-6547

16 carriages, 4 wagons, 6 sleighs, misc. tack, collars, bridles, saddles

Old Sturbridge Village
1 Old Sturbridge Village Rd.
Sturbridge, MA 01566
phone 508-347-3362

5 wagons, 7 sleighs, 3 chaises, 1 sulky, 3 ox carts, 2 wheeled & sleigh hearses, farm machinery, some harness

Gore Place Society
Gore Street
Waltham, MA 02154
phone 617-894-2798

2 carriages, 1 sleigh

MUSEUMS-MICHIGAN

Henry Ford Museum and Greenfield Village*
20900 Oakwood Blvd.
Post Office Box 1970
Dearborn, MI 48121
phone 313-271-1620

100 horse-drawn vehicles

Sloan Museum
1221 East Learsley St.
Flint, MI 48503
phone 810-760-1169

13 horse-drawn vehicles

MUSEUMS-MINNESOTA

Glensheen-University of Minnesota
3300 London Road
Duluth, MN 55804
phone 218-724-1107

7 carriages, 3 sleighs, tack room of bridles, harnesses, saddles, fly net, blankets, restored old stable

Minnesota Historical Society
345 Kellog Boulevard West
Saint Paul, MN 55102-1906
phone 612-296-0148

4 carriages, 10 wagons, 10 sleighs, 1 farm machinery, ox cart, fire hose cart, hearse, caisson

MUSEUMS-MISSISSIPPI

Old Capitol Museum of Mississippi History
North State and Capitol St.
Box 571
Jackson, MS 39205
phone 601-359-6920

1 carriage

MUSEUMS-MISSOURI

State of Missouri Department of Natural Resources-Division of State Parks
Post Office Box 176
Jefferson City, MO 65102-0176
phone 573-751-2479

surrey, stagecoach built by Garette Jorden in 1840 at Palmyra, MO

Kansas City Museum
3218 Gladstone Blvd.
Kansas City, MO 64123
phone 816-483-8300

some of the harness & carriages of Loula Long Combs.

Museum of Transportation
3015 Barrett Station Road
St. Louis, MO 63122
phone 314-965-7998

mule drawn street car, 30 horse-drawn vehicles, rotating collection

MUSEUMS-MONTANA

Montana Historical Society
225 No. Roberts
Post Office Box 201201
Helena, MT 59620-1201
phone 406-444-2694

Kirby Lambert, Curator of Collections
carriage collection

MUSEUMS-NEBRASKA

Fort Robinson Museum
Box 304
United States Highway 20
Crawford, NE 69339
phone 308-665-2919

4 wagons, ambulance

North Platte Valley Museum
11th and J Streets
Post Office Box 435
Gering, NE 69341
phone 308-436-5411

3 carriages, 3 wagons, 1 farm machinery

Arbor Lodge State Historical Park
2300 West Second Ave.
Nebraska City, NE 68410
phone 402-873-7222

10 carriages 1 cutter, 1 stagecoach, phaeton, surrey, brake, taxi with glass windows, brougham, brougham by Kendall Carriage Co., misc. photographs

MUSEUMS-NEW HAMPSHIRE

New Hampshire Historical Society
30 Park Street
Concord, NH 03301
phone 603-225-3381

concord coach, wagons, ox cart

The Brady Family, Six Gun City
Route 2 Presidential Range Highway
Jefferson NH, 03583
phone 603-586-4592

100 carriages and sleighs

Museums

Museum of New Hampshire History
6 Eagle Square
Concord, NH 03301
phone 603-226-3189
1 carriage, 2 wagons, 2 sleighs, 1 buggy

MUSEUMS-NEW JERSEY
Museum of Early Trades & Crafts
Main Street and Green Village Road
Madison, NJ 07940
phone 201-377-2982
harness, harness maker's tools, wheels, wheelwright's tools, carriage maker's tools, farriers's tools, horse shoes

MUSEUMS-NEW MEXICO
Museum of the Horse*
Highway 70 East
Post Office Box 40
Ruidoso Downs, NM 88346
phone 505-378-4142
65 carriages, 20 on display, 10,000 horse related items

MUSEUMS-NEW YORK
New York State Museum
Cultural Education Center
Room 3090
Empire State Plaza
Albany, NY 12230
phone 518-474-5877
20 carriages, 25 sleighs, 10 wagons, farm machinery, horse-drawn fire apparatus, sprinkler wagon, steam engine, hearse, harness, veterinary materials, horse shoes

Seward House
33 South Street
Auburn, NY 13021
phone 315-252-1283
1 carriage 1850's

Granger Homestead
295 North Main Street
Canandaigua, N Y 14424
phone 716-394-1472
50 carriages

Lorenzo State Historic Site
Rippleton Road
R. D. # 5
Cazenovia, NY 13035
phone 315-655-3200 or 3044
35 horse-drawn vehicles

Nassau County, Division of Museum Services
Eisenhower Park
East Meadows, NY 11554
phone 516-571-7901
20 carriages, 20 wagons, 15 sleighs, 10 farm machinery, harness, saddles, wheelwrights tools, books & periodicals

Essex Historical Society
P. O. Box 428
Elizabethtown, NY 12932
phone 518-873-6466
4 horse-drawn vehicles

Montgomery County Historical Society
Old Fort Johnson
14 Tessiero Drive
Fort Johnson, NY 12070
phone 518-843-0300
1 carriage, 1 sleigh

Rose Hill Mansion
Post Office Box 464
Rte. 96A
Geneva, NY 14456
phone 315-789-3848
1 carriage , LaFayette road from Geneva to Syracuse on his 1825 tour of the U.S.

Chapman Historical Museum
348 Glen Street
Glens Falls, NY 12801
phone 518-793-2826
1 sleigh, whips, harness

Harness Racing Museum and Hall of Fame
Post Office Box 590
240 Main Street
Goshen, NY 10924
phone 914-294-6330
fax 914-294-3463
49 surreys, 5 wagons, 3 sleighs
55 harnesses

American Museum of Fire Fighting*
Firemen Home
125 Harry Howard Avenue
Hudson, NY 12534
phone 518-828-7695
2 horse-drawn engines, 5 steam engines, total of 66 engines most are motorized

Vanderbilt Mansion National Historic Site
519 Albany Post Road
Route 9
Hyde Park, NY 12538
phone 914-229-9115
6 carriages, 3 sleighs

Wayne County Historical Society
P O Box 607 21 ButternutSt.
Lyons, NY 14489
phone 315-946-4943
horse bridge for transporting horses across the canal

Museum Village
130 Museum Village Rd.
Monroe, NY 10950
phone 914-782-8247
50+carriages, 20+wagons, 20+sleighs, 20+farm machinery, 2 steam fire trucks, fully outfitted wagon makers shop, collection of tack, full outfitted harness makers shop

Genesee County Museum
Post Office Box 310
Flint Hill Road
Mumford, NY 14511
phone 716-538-6822
60 horse-drawn vehicles

Old Bethpage Village Restoration
Round Swamp Road
Old Bethpage, NY 11804
phone 516-572-8401
7 wagons, hose carriage, 2 sleighs

Hallockville Museum Farm
6038 Sound Avenue
Riverhead, NY 11901
phone 516-298-5292
1 carriage, 1 wagon, 2 sleighs, 4 farm machinery

Museums

Strong Museum
One Manhattan Square
Rochester, NY 14607
phone 716-263-2700
1 carriage, 2 sleighs, child's dog drawn carts, 2 cutter Studebaker Bros., 10 lap robes, 25 buggy whips

Erie Canal Village
5789 New London Road
Rome, NY 13440
phone 315-337-3999
12 restored horse-drawn vehicles, 20 unrestored horse-drawn vehicles, landaulet, local pieces

Staten Island Historical Society
441 Clarke Avenue
Staten Island, NY 10306
phone 718-351-1617
over 50 horse-drawn vehicles

Long Island Museum of American Art, History and Carriages*
1208 Route 25A
Stony Brook, NY 11790
phone 516-751-0066
250 horse-drawn vehicles, library

Lynhurst
635 South Broadway
Tarrytown, NY 10591
phone 914-631-4481
11 carriages, 2 wagons, 4 sleighs, 1 farm machinery

MUSEUMS-NORTH CAROLINA

Biltmore Estate
One North Pack Square
Asheville, NC 28801
phone 704-255-1776
1 carriage, 1 sleigh, farm machinery in storage and not on display

Gaston County Museum of Art & History
131 West Main Street
Post Office Box 429
Dallas, NC 28034-0429
phone 704-922-7681
6 carriages, 7 wagons, 3 sleighs, 6 farm machinery, restored 20th century ice cream wagon

Greensboro Historical Museum
130 Summit Avenue
Greensboro, NC 27401
phone 910-373-2043
1760 covered wagon

Old Salem Inc.
Box F Salem Station
Winston-Salem, NC 27108-
phone 910-721-7300
3 Eskimo sleighs, 1825 & 1910 carriage, horse-drawn fire engine, covered wagon

MUSEUMS-OHIO

Western Reserve Historical Society
Hale Farm and Village
2686 Oak Hill Road
Post Office Box 296
Bath, OH 44210-0296
phone 216-666-3711
break, 2 runabout, 1835 chaise, governess cart, sulky, fire pumper, landau, octagon front coupe, sleigh

Warren County Historical Society Museum
Post Office Box 223
105 South Broadway
Lebanon, OH 45036-0223
phone 513-932-1817
3 carriages, 2 wagons, 4 sleighs, 2 farm machinery

National Road Zane Grey Museum
8850 East Pike
Norwich, OH 43767
phone 614-872-3143
Conestoga freight wagon, concord coach made in ME on sled runners 1847, 3 horse-drawn

MUSEUMS-OKLAHOMA

Fort Sill Museum*
437 Quanah Road
Fort Sill, OK 73503-5100
phone 405-442-5123
60 horse-drawn vehicles, 30 caissons & limbers, 3 machine gun carts, 2 instrument carts & 2 battery reel carts.

Museum of the Great Plains
Post Office Box 68
601 Ferris Avenue
Lawton, OK 73502
phone 405-581-3460
25 farm machinery, 1 hay wagon, 2 buggies, 1 oil tank wagon, Bain wagon, assorted collars, hames, single trees, iron & wooden wheels and various harness

MUSEUMS-OREGON

Eastern Oregon Museum on the Oregon Trail
Post Office Box 182
3rd and Wilcox on the Oregon Trail
Haines, OR 97833
phone 541-856-3233
3 carriages, 5 wagons, 8 sleighs, numerous farm machinery

Oregon Historical Society*
1200 S. W. Park Avenue
Portland, OR 97205
phone 503-306-5233
collection of horse-drawn models by Ivan Collins

MUSEUMS-PENNSYLVANIA

Boyertown Museum of Historic Vehicles
28 Warwick Street
Boyertown, PA 19512-1415
phone 610-367-2090
about 25 horse-drawn vehicles, collection of antique automobiles

Mercer Museum /Bucks County Historical Society
84 South Pine Street
Doylestown, PA 18901
phone 215-345-0210
4 carriages, 7 wagons, 8 sleighs, chaise, milk sled, cart, stagecoach, sulky, 2 hearses, 3 drags, harnesses, animal husbandry equipment, bells, luggage, turnpike signs, mile markers

Museums

Pennsylvania Historical &
Museum Commission
Post Office Box 1026
3rd and North Streets
Harrisburg, PA 17108-1026
phone 717-787-4980 contact John
Zwierzyna, Senior Curator

30 carriages 6 carriages on display, 15 wagons 3 wagons on display, 20 sleighs 1 sleigh on display

Rough and Tumble
Post Office Box 9
Kinzers, PA 17535
phone 717-442-4249

large collection of gas engines, Conestoga wagon , steam powered saw mill.

James Buchanan Foundation for
Preservation of Wheatland
1120 Marietta Avenue
Lancaster, PA 17603
phone 717-392-8721

1 carriage, built by Bringhurst of Philadelphia, c. 1850, restored

Landis Valley Museum
2451 Kissel Hill Road
Lancaster, PA 17601-4899
phone 717-569-0401 ex 225 Sue Hanna

6 carriages, 14 wagons, 10 sleighs, 60 pieces of farm machinery, 500-1000 related artifacts.

Mifflinburg Buggy Museum
523 Green Street
Mifflinburg, PA 17844
phone 717-966-1355

exhibit of step-by-step technology of buggy making; local-made vehicles & buggy makers's home & furnishings, restore buggy shop

Frick Art &HistoricalCenter
7227 Reynolds Street
Pittsburgh, PA 15208-2923
phone 412-371-0600

2 broughams, basket phaeton, spider phaeton, pony size phaeton, chubb phaeton, 6 carriages, 1 wagon, 2 sleighs, bits, harness pieces, few women's riding costumes

Historical Society of Berks County
940 Centre Avenue
Reading, PA 19601
phone 610-375-4375

town coach, Conestoga wagon, 2 sleighs, horse-drawn street car

Railroad Museum of
Pennsylvania
George Deeming, curator
Post Office Box 15
Strasburg, PA 17579
phone 717-687-8628

1855 town coach made by Rodgers, Philadelphia, 4 vehicles.

Drake Well Museum
R. R. # 3 Box 7
Titusville, PA 16354-8902
phone 814-827-2797

3wagons, steam pumper c. 1868, nitroglycerine wagons c. 1890, traveling photographic wagon darkroom c 1860, portable drilling rigs c. 1880-1910.

Gruber Wagon Works
Park & Recreation Dept. of Berks County*
2201 Tulpehocken Road
Wyomissing, PA 19610
phone 610-374-8839

restored wagon factory, 24 vehicles

Agricultural & Industrial
Museum of York County
480 East Market Street
York, PA 17403
phone 717-852-7007

3 freight wagons, 2 box sleds, milk wagon, mail wagon

MUSEUMS-RHODE ISLAND

Preservation Society of Newport
County
424 Bellevue Avenue
Newport, RI 02840
phone 401-847-1000

11 carriages, 1 wagon, 6 sleighs, 1 farm machinery

MUSEUMS-SOUTH CAROLINA

Horry County Museum
438 Main Street
Conway, SC 29526
phone 803-248-1542

1 wagon, 10 farm machinery

Sumter County Museum
Post Office Box 1456
122 North Washington St.
Sumter, SC 29150
phone 803-775-0908

1 carriage, 1 surrey, 4+horse-drawn plows, collars, bridles, harness

MUSEUMS - SOUTH DAKOTA

Friends of the Middle Border
Pioneer Museum
1311 South Duff Street
Post Office Box 1071
Mitchell, SD 57301
phone 605-996-2122

hearse, 3 sleighs, 3 buggies, 3 wagons, sheepwagon, small stagecoach, ice wagon, 22 farm machinery

Museum of the South Dakota
State Historical Society
900 Governors Dr.
Pierre, SD 57501-2217
phone 605-773-6011

5 carriages, 2 wagons, 2 sleighs, dog travois

MUSEUMS-TENNESSEE

Hermitage Home of Andrew
Jackson
4580 Rachel's Lane
Hermitage, TN 37076-1331
phone 615-889-2941

Brewster phaeton, and 1 other carriage partly destroyed

Belle Meade Plantation
5025 Harding Road
Nashville, TN 37205
phone 615-356-0501

12 carriages, 2 wagons, 2 sleighs, 2 racing carts, harness, saddles, late 1880's riding clothing,

MUSEUMS-TEXAS

Panhandle-Plains Historical Museum
2401 Fourth Avenue
WTAMU Box 967
Canyon, TX 79015
phone 806-656-2244

ambulance, buggies, farm wagons, farm machinery, about 25 horse-drawn

Corpus Christi Museum of Science and History
1900 North Chaparral
Corpus Christi, TX
78401
phone 512-883-2862

2 carriages, stagecoach, 2 buggies, various horse collars, hames, tack & bridles, buggy lanterns, lap robes, horse weights, veternarian tools

John E. Conner Museum
Texas A & M University-Kingsville
Campus Box 134
821 W. Santa Gertrudis
Post Office Box 2172 Station
Kingsville, TX 78363
phone 512-593-2810

2 carriages, 1 wagon, 2 plows, 2 oxen yokes, 1 goat cart

Harrison County Historical Museum
Peter Whetstone Square
Marshall, TX 75670
phone 903-938-9680

1 buggy

Witte Museum
3801 Broadway
San Antonio, TX 78209
phone 210-357-1867

10 carriages, mud wagon, 2 hearses, 1 sulky, 1887 mule drawn streetcar, 1881 LaFrance Steam Pumper

University of Texas Institute of Texan Cultures at San Antonio
801 South Bowie at Durango Blvd.
San Antonio, TX 78294
phone 5210-458-2297

2 carriages, 4 wagons, 3 plows, 1 harrow, 1 log hauler(8wheels), harness for one horse

MUSEUMS-UTAH

This is the Place State Park
2601 Sunnyside Avenue
Salt Lake City, UT 84108-1453
phone 801-584-8392

2 carriages, 3 wagons, 2 sleighs

Desert Museum of Science and Industry
Post Office Box 11052
Salt Lake City, UT 84147

large collection of wagons and early buggy on wooden axles

MUSEUMS-VERMONT

Park-McCullough House
Post Office Box 366
Corner of Park & West St.
N. Bennington, VT 05257
phone 802-442-5441

4 carriages, 6 Joubert & White, 3 sleighs, 2 carts, carriage house

Shelburne Museum*
Route 7 P.O. Box 10
Shelburne, VT 05257
phone 802-985-3346

200 horse-drawn vehicles, conservation lab for carriages

Billings Farm & Museum
Post Office Box 489
River Road & Route 12
Woodstock, VT 05091
phone 802-457-2355 or 802-457-1180

32 Billings family vheicles (to be open in 1999) wagons, farm machinery, lumber wagon express wagon, cutter, dray wagon, 2 hay wagons, 1860's carriage

MUSEUMS-VIRGINIA

Appomattox Court House National Historical Park
Highway 24
Post Office Box 218
Appomattox, VA 24522
phone 804-352-8987

1 carriage, 2 wagons, harness

Westmoreland Davis Foundation
Morven Park
P. O. Box 6228
Leesburg, VA 20178
phone 703-777-2414

100 carriages, sleighs, and wagons, plus harness, hearse, fire engine, army wagon, cannon

Stonewall Jackson House
8 East Washington Street
Lexington, VA 24450
phone 640-463-2552

1 carriage

Mount Vernon-Ladies Association of the Union
End of George Washington Parkway South
Mount Vernon, VA 22121
phone 703-799-8662

5 carriages, 2 wagons, 1 sleigh, 2 dump carts, harness, wagon jacks, collars

Chippokes Farm and Forestry Museum
203 Governor St. Room 338
Richmond, VA 23219
phone 804-786-7950

hearse, 3 dump cart, farm wagon, 2 heavy farm truck wagons

Maymont
1700 Hampton Street
Richmond, VA 23220
phone 804-358-7166

outstanding carriage house, 20 carriages, whitechapel cart, childrens vehicles, 1870 wicker phaeton, landau, 2 wagons, hearse

Museums

Museum of American Frontier Culture
Post Office Box 810
Richmond Road
Staunton, VA 24401
phone 540-332-7850

1 wagon

Stratford Hall Plantation, Robert E. Lee Memorial
Stratford, VA 22558
phone 804-493-8038

11 carriages, 1807 landaulet

Colonial Williamsburg Foundation*
Post Office Box 1776
Williamsburg, VA 23187
phone 757-229-1000

18th century vehicles + library

MUSEUMS-WASHINGTON

Yakima Valley Museum*
2105 Tieton Drive
Yakima, WA 98902
phone 509-248-0747

47 horse-drawn vehicles

MUSEUMS-WEST VIRGINIA

Harpers Ferry National Historical Park
Post Office Box 65
Harpers Ferry, WV 25425
phone 304-535-6163

8 horse-drawn vehicles

MUSEUMS-WISCONSIN

Circus World Museum*
426 Water Street
Baraboo, WI 53913
phone 608-356-8341

150 wagons, library

Bayfield Heritage Ass. Inc.
Post Office Box 137
Bayfield, WI 54814
phone 715-779-5958

hearse, landau, bob sleds

Stonefield Historic Site
Cassville, WI 53806
phone 608-725-5210

25 carriages, 20 farm machinery, large collection of McCormick reapers, harvesters, wire binders

Old World Wisconsin
S103 W37890
Highway 67
Eagle, Wisconsin 53119
phone 414-594-6300

13 farm machinery, butter and egg wagon, 4 farm wagons, spring wagon, sleigh, doctor's buggy

Old Wade House* and Wisconsin Carriage Museum
Post Office Box 34
Greenbush, WI 53026
phone 414-526-3271

80 horse-drawn vehicles.

Madline Island
Post Office Box 9
LaPointe, WI 54850
phone 715-747-2415

logging sleds, sleighs, sleds

Rock County Historical Society
Post Office Box 8096
10 South High Street
Janesville, WI 53545
phone 608-756-4509

4 carriages, 1 wagon, 6 sleighs, 4 farm machinery
carriage robes, whip, buggy jack, sleigh bells, hitching post, fly net, hames, thills, Janesvill Carriage Co. Catalog & papers

State Historical Museum of Wisconsin
30 North Carroll Street
Madison, WI 53703
phone 608-264-6555

1 racing sulky

MUSEUMS-WYOMING

Cheyenne Frontier Days Old West Museum*
Post Office Box 2824
4501 North Carey Avenue in Frontier Park
Cheyenne, WY 82003
phone 307-778-7290

132 horse-drawn vehicles

Buffalo Bill Historical Center
720 Sheridan Avenue
Box 1000
Cody, WY 82414
phone 307-587-4771

2 carriages, 2 chuck wagons, passenger wagons, sheepwagon, roundup or freigh wagon, mail coach, 2 light coaches, yellowstone excursion coach, plow, dredge, driving harness, draft harness, coach harness, hames, bells, whips, jacks, grease buckets, chain brakes

Trail Town Museum of the Old West
1831 DeMaris Drive
Cody, WY 82414

sleighs, caissons, spring wagons, ice wagons,

Bibliography of Available Reference Material
Bibliography of Carriage Journal Articles

AXLES
"[Ball Bearing Axle]." Carriage Journal. Vol.23 No. 4 (Spring 1986), p. 188.
Cantle, Gordon. "Mechanics Of Wheel Setting." Carriage Journal. Vol.27 No. 4 (Spring 1980), pp. 174-176.
Cantle, Gordon. "On Axle Flaps." Carriage Journal. Vol.28 No. 1 (Summer 1990), pp. 3-5.
"[Different Oil Axles]." Carriage Journal. Vol.25 No. 3 (Winter 1987), p. 146-147.
"Historical References To Axle Lubrication." Carriage Journal. Vol.27 No. 4 (Spring 1980), p. 176.
Isles, George. "The Collinge Axle." Carriage Journal. Vol.7 No. 1, pp. 22-25.
"A Man Of Ideas : The Story of Henry Timken, Carriage Builder and Founder of a World Wide Enterprise." Carriage Journal. Vol.17 No. 4 (Spring 1980), pp. 185-191.
"What Is The Best Lubricant For Carriage Axles." Carriage Journal. Vol.20 No. 4 (Spring 1983), p. 193.
Ryder, Tom. "Mail Axle." Carriage Journal. vol.27 No. 3 (Winter 1989), pp. 133-135.
Ryder, Tom. "Carriage Axles." Carriage Journal. Vol.15 No.3 (Winter 1977), 327-330.

BAROUCHE OR CALECHE
"Barouche or Caleche : The Principal Of All Open Carriages." Carriage Journal. Vol.24 No. 4 (Spring 1987), p. 193-196.

BODY CONSTRUCTION
Cantle, Gordon. "Fitting An Edge Plate." Carriage Journal. Vol.27 No. 3 (Winter 1989), pp. 112-114.

BRAKES
Cantle, Gordon. "An Analysis Of The Mechanics Of Carriage Brakes." Carriage Journal. Vol.25 No. 2 (Autumn 1987), p. 72-75.
Cantle, Gordon. "An Analysis Of The Mechanics Of Carriage Brakes." Carriage Journal. Vol.25 No. 3 (Winter 1987), p. 117-120.
Cantle, Gordon. "An Analysis Of The Mechanics Of Carriage Brakes." Carriage Journal. Vol.25 No. 4 (Spring 1988), p. 204.
"[Front Wheel Brakes]." Carriage Journal. Vol.25 No. 1 (Summer 1987), p. 38.
Philipson, William. "Brakes For Carriages." Carriage Journal. Vol.14 No. 4 (Spring 1977), pp. 167-172.

BRIZKA
Ryder, Tom. "Britzka." Carriage Journal. Vol.28 No. 1 (Summer 1990), pp. 9-11.

BROUGHAM
"Concerning The Origin Of The Brougham And The Disposal Of The Original Vehicle." Carriage Journal. Vol.6 No. 3 (Winter 1968), pp. 100-109.

BUCKBOARD
Ryder, Thomas. "Buckboard." Carriage Journal. Vol.23 No. 1 (Summer 1985), p. 3-9.

BUGGY
Ryder, Tom. "The Evolution Of The American Buggy." Carriage Journal. Vol.18 No. 4 (Spring 1981) pp. 185-188.

CANEWORK
Kellog, C. W. "Lancewood and Canework for Carriages." Carriage Journal. Vol.10 No.2 (Autumn 1972) pp. 84-85.
Rolph, Gerald A. "Reproducing Canework." Carriage Journal. vol.5 No.2 (Autumn 1967) pp. 92-93.*

"Imitation Cane-Work For Carriage Panels." Carriage Journal. Vol.20 No. 1 (Summer 1982), pp. 14-16.*

CARE AND PRESERVATION

Carriage Monthly, 1901. "How To Clean A Carriage Properly." Carriage Journal. Vol.29 No. 2 (Fall 1991), p. 71.

Carriage Monthly, April 1904. "Rules For Care and Preservation of Vehicles." Carriage Journal. Vol.12 No.3 (Winter 1974) pp. 134-135.

Green, Susan. "Ware Moths!" Carriage Journal. Vol.22 No. 4 (Spring 1985) p. 217-219.

"Rules For Care And Preservation Of Vehicles." Carriage Journal. Vol.31 No. 4 (Spring 1994), p. 177.

"To Remove Grease Spots From Leather." Carriage Journal. Vol.17 No. 3 (Winter 1979), p. 152.

"Squeaky Wheel: A Spring Tune-up." Carriage Journal. Vol.32 No. 4 (Spring 1995), p. 162-164.

Ware, Francis, 1903. "Carriages And Their Care." Carriage Journal. Vol.29 No. 4 (Spring 1992), pp.165-166.

CART

"Long-Shafted Breaking Cart." Carriage Journal. Vol.24 No. 1 (Summer 1986), p. 13-15.

Ryder, Tom. "American Road Cart." Carriage Journal. Vol.21 No.1 (Summer 1983), p. 12-16.

Ryder, Tom. "The Long Island Carts or Mystery of the Meadowbrook." Carriage Journal. Vol.22 No. 1 (Summer 1984), 12-16.

Ryder, Tom. "Governess Cart." Carriage Journal. Vol.22 No. 3 (Winter 1984), 122-125.

COMMERCIAL VEHICLES

Ryder, Tom. "Patrol Wagons." Carriage Journal. Vol.26 No. 1 (Summer 1988), p. 28-29.

CONSERVATION

Ferrell, Merri. "Conservation Treatment Of A Grand Duc." Carriage Journal. Vol.31 No. 2 (Fall 1993), pp. 65-67.

DRAFTING

Cantle, Gordon. "Coach Maker's Cant Board." Carriage Journal. "Vol.26 No. 4 (Spring 1989), p. 173-174.

Cantle, Gordon. "Designing A Carriage Body With Appreciable Side Sweep and Turn Under." Carriage Journal. Vol.29 No. 3 (Winter 1991), p.105-106.

"How To Sketch A Carriage." Carriage Journal. Vol.31 No. 3 (Winter 1993), p. 132.

FIFTH WHEEL

Cantle, Gordon. "Development Of Center-Pivoted Fore Carriages." Carriage Journal. Vol.26 No. 1 (Summer 1988), p. 7-10.

"Fifth Wheel Of American Carriages." Carriage Journal. Vol.19 No. 4 (Spring 1982), pp. 95-98.

GIGS AND HIGH WHEELED CARTS

Cantle, Gordon. "Tilbury's Modification Of The Cabriolet Suspension." Carriage Journal. Vol.33 No. 3 (Winter 1995), p. 103-105.

Cantle, Gordon. "Body Movements In Two-Wheelers." Carriage Journal. Vol.30 No. 4 (Spring 1993), pp. 168-170.

"[Curve In Gig Shafts]." Carriage Journal. Vol.20 No. 2 (Autumn 1982), p. 101.

"Park Gate Gig." Carriage Journal. Vol.16 No. 1 (Summer 1978), p. 41-43.

Ryder, Tom. "Hackney Cart." Carriage Journal. Vol.20 No. 4 (Spring 1983), p. 194-196.

Ryder, Tom. "Jinkers and Gigs and Other Australian Carriages." Carriage Journal. Vol.17 No. 4 (Spring 1980), pp. 193-197.

Ryder, Tom. "Tilbury Gig." Carriage Journal. Vol.28 No. 1 (Summer 1990), p. 37-38.

"Tandem Carts." Carriage Journal. Vol.26 No. 1 (Summer 1988), p. 35-38.

HANSOM CABS

Downing, Paul H. "The Story of the Hansom." Carriage Journal. vol.9 No.1 (Summer 1971), pp.13-26.

IMPERIAL

"Imperial." Carriage Journal. Vol.21 No. 4 (Spring 1984), p. 196-197.

LADDER, FOLDING

"[Folding Ladder For Roof Seat Break]." Carriage Journal. Vol.24 No. 3 (Winter 1986), p. 149.

LAMPS

C. Cowles & Co. "Fine Carriage Lamps." Carriage Journal. Vol.9 No. 4 (Spring 1972) pp. 176-177.

C. Cowles & Co. "Carriage and Coach Lamps From the 1892 Catalog." Carriage Journal. Vol.6 No. 3 (Winter 1968), pp.128-129.

MANUFACTURE

Tuttle, Charles T. "The Manufacture Of Carriage & Harness Furniture." Carriage Journal. Vol.18 No. 1 (Summer 1980), pp. 37-41.

PAINTING

Carriage Monthly Nov. 1880. "Cracking Of Paint." Carriage Journal. Vol.28 No. 4 (Spring 1991), p. 135.

Green, Susan. "Carmine." Carriage Journal. Vol.33 No. 4 (Spring 1996), 144-146.

Hub Dictionary, May, 1879. "Black Parts Of Carriages." Carriage Journal. Vol.19 No. 4 (Spring 1982), p. 94.

Offord, Gordon J. "Coach Painting With Modern Materials." Carriage Journal. Vol.14 No. 1 (Summer 1976), pp.41-42.

Offord, Gordon J. "Paint Making In London In The Early Part Of This Century." Carriage Journal. Vol.13 No. 4 (Spring 1976), pp. 173-176.

Old Hand, "The Restoration Of Carriages." *brush painting* Carriage Journal. Vol.2 No. 1 (Summer 1964), pp.16-22.

Hub, July 1896. "Carriage Colors." Carriage Journal. Vol.17 No. 1 (Summer 1979), p. 46-47.

"Natural Wood Finish." Carriage Journal. Vol.20 No. 4 (Spring 1983), p. 180.

"Removal Of Old Varnish." Carriage Journal. Vol.16 No.2 (Autumn 1978), p. 103.

Swartz, C. Thomas. "Spray Painting." Carriage Journal. Vol.16 No.3 (Carriage Journal), pp. 149-152.

Varnish, 1889. "Hints On The Selection And Care Of Color Brushes." Carriage Journal. Vol.30 No. 1 (Summer 1992), p. 5.

PERCH

Cantle, Gordon. "Development Of The Perch And Reach." Carriage Journal. Vol.31 No. 4 (Spring 1994), p.155-158.

RESTORATION

"The John Brown Chariot." Carriage Journal. Vol.5 No. 2 (Autumn 1967), pp. 67-80.

Ragle, Tim. "Authentic Carriage Restoration." Carriage Journal. Vol.26 No. 4 (Spring 1989), pp. 161-167.

Ragle, Tim. "Authentic Carriage Restoration Part 2. " Carriage Journal. vol.27 No.1 (Summer 1989), pp. 32-34.

Ragle, Tim. "Problem Of Cracking Or Honeycombing Of Paint Finishes." Carriage Journal. Vol.29 No. 1 (Summer 1991), p. 16.

ROCKAWAY

Downing, Paul H. "A History Of The Rockaway." Carriage Journal. vol.4 No.3 (Winter 1967) pp. 99-110.

SHAFTS
Cantle, Gordon. "Shaft Harness Fittings." Carriage Journal. Vol.30 No. 1 (Summer 1992), pp. 33-35.

"[Light Phaeton Shafts]." Carriage Journal. Vol.23 No. 2 (Autumn 1985), p. 88.

Topham, Humphrey. "Shaft And Pole Dimension Tables For Different Sizes Of Animals." Carriage Journal. Vol.28 No. 4 (Spring 1981), pp.153-154.

SHAFT COUPLINGS
"Shaft Couplings, Anti-Rattlers, And Quick Shifts." Carriage Journal. Vol.20 No. 2 (Autumn 1982), p. 95-97.

SHOW BUGGY
O'Connor, Charles J. "The Evolution Of The Show Buggy." Carriage Journal. Vol.14 No.3 (Winter 1976), pp. 140-145.

SICILIAN CART
Alejos, Elizabeth. "The Sicilian Cart." Carriage Journal. Vol.17 No. 3 (Winter 1979), pp. 125-127.

SJEES, FRISIAN
Bouma, Kai. "The Famous Frisian Sjees." Carriage Journal. Vol.15 No. (Winter 1977), pp. 338-343.

SLEIGHS
McNair, Robert E. "Mystery Of The Dated Sleighs." Carriage Journal. Vol.6 No.3 (Winter 1968), pp. 112-117.

des Grange, Jane. "The Sleigh." Carriage Journal. Vol.1 No. 3 (December 1963), pp. 72-73.

SPRINGS
"A Man Of Ideas : The Story of Henry Timken, Carriage Builder and Founder of a World Wide Enterprise." Carriage Journal. Vol.17 No. 4 (Spring 1980), pp. 185-191.

"[Brewster Side Bar]." Carriage Journal. Vol.21. No.2 (Autumn 1983), p. 70.

Cantle, Gordon. "An Appraisal Of The Royal Society's Wooden Spring Experiments Of 1665." Carriage Journal. Vol.29 No. 4 (Spring 1992), pp. 163-165.

Cantle, Gordon. "Sleigh Springing." Carriage Journal. Vol.32 No. 3 (Winter 1994), pp. 111-113.

Cantle, Gordon. "End Fastenings For Side Springs." Carriage Journal. Vol.28 No. 4 (Spring 1991), pp. 144-146.

Cantle, Gordon. "Observations On "Straight Spring" Carriage..." Carriage Journal. Vol.31 No. 1 (Summer 1993), pp. 6-8.

Cantle, Gordon. "On Spring Curvature." Carriage Journal. Vol.30 No. 2 (Fall 1992), pp. 61-63.

Cantle, Gordon. "On Body Loops And Pump Handles." Carriage Journal. Vol.27 No. 2 (Autumn 1989), pp. 78-81.

Cantle, Gordon. "Effects Of Stress On Carriage Springs With Comments On The Heat Treatment Of Spring Steel." Carriage Journal. Vol.26 No. 1 (Summer 1988), p. 26-27.

Carriage Monthly. "Spring Rusting." Carriage Journal. Vol.9 No. 3 (Winter 1971), p. 119.

"Elliotts Specification." Carriage Journal. vol.1 No. 4 (March 1964), p. 118.

"Improvements In Side-Bar And Side-Spring Carriages At The Centennial." Carriage Journal. Vol.14 No. 1 (Summer 1976), pp. 43-45.

"Names Of Carriage Springs And Their Combinations." Carriage Journal. Vol.24 No. 3 (Winter 1986), p. 141-143.

Ryder, Tom. "Steel Carriage Springs." Carriage Journal. Vol. 15 No.4. (Spring 1978), pp. 367-369.

Ryder, Tom. "Steel Carriage Springs." Carriage Journal. vol.16 No. 1 (Summer 1978), pp. 21-23.

Ryder, Tom. "Steel Carriage Springs." Carriage Journal. Vol.16 No.2, p. 99-101.

Ryder, Tom. "Steel Carriage Springs Part IV-American Designs." Carriage Journal. Vol.16 No. 3 (Winter 1978), pp.141-146.

Ryder, Tom. "Suspension of American Carriages." Carriage Journal. Vol.22 No. 3 (Winter 1984), pp. 145-149.

"[Shuler Spring]." Carriage Journal. Vol.24 No. 1 (Summer 1986), p. 29.

STEPS

Cantle, Gordon. "Step Treads For Carriages." Carriage Journal. Vol.24 No. 4 (Spring 1987), p. 182-184.

Hub, Jan. 1878. "How To Make Oval Gridiron Steps." Carriage Journal. Vol.29 No. 2 (Fall 1991), p. 77.

STRIPING

"How Transfers Are Made". Carriage Monthly May 1873. Carriage Journal. Vol.33, No.1 (Summer 1995), pp. 28-29.

Old Hand. "The Restoration of Carriages." Carriage Journal. Vol.1 No. 3 (December 1963), pp.69-71.

Old Hand. "Restoration Of Carriages Heraldry." Carriage Journal. Vol. 1 No. 4 (March 1964), pp. 121-122.

Old Hand, "Restoration Of Carriages." Carriage Journal. Vol.2 No. 2 (Autumn 1964), pp.64-69.

Old Hand. "Further Suggestions For Striping." Carriage Journal. Vol.6 No.1 (Summer 1968), 31-33.

Stegman, Chester. "Discoveries About Striping." Carriage Journal. Vol.16 No. 2, p. 103.

"Striping Wagons." Carriage Journal. Vol.13 No. 2 (Autumn 1975), pp. 106-107.

"[Use Of Pounce Bag]." Carriage Journal. Vol.25 No. 2 (Autumn 1987), p. 92.

Whitney, Stephen T. "The Rebirth Of Number 431." Carriage Journal. Vol.3 No.2 (Autumn 1965) pp. 76-83.

SULKY

Pines, Philip A. "The Story of The Sulky." Carriage Journal. Vol.12 No.3 (Winter 1974) pp. 123-125.

SURREY

"The Surrey Or Should It Have Been Denominated The Whitechapel ?" Carriage Journal. Vol.7 No.2 (Spring 1970), pp. 141-155.

TRAP

Ryder, Tom. "What Is A Trap?" Carriage Journal. Vol.17 No. 1 (Summer 1979), pp. 33-39.

UPHOLSTERY

"Broadcloth For Carriages." Carriage Journal. Vol.27 No. 4 (Spring 1990), pp. 179-180.

Carriage Monthly Jan. 1883. "Driving Seat Boxes." Carriage Journal. Vol.29 No. 1 (Summer 1991), p. 28.

Carriage Monthly, Aug. 1882. "Sleigh Trimming." Carriage Journal. Vol.29 No. 3 (Winter 1991), p. 110.

"Coated Leathers." Carriage Journal. Vol.24 No.1 (Summer 1986), p. 18.

"Curled Horse Hair." Carriage Journal Vol.26 No. 1 (Summer 1988), p. 29.

"[Imitation Leather]." Carriage Journal. Vol.22 No. 4 (Spring 1985), p. 194.

"[How Brass Beading Was Made]." Carriage Journal. Vol.21 No. 1 (Summer 1983) p. 42.

Hub, 1884. "First-Prize Essay On Trimming Physicians' Phaetons." Carriage Journal. vol.3 No.1 (Summer 1965), pp.31-34.

"Notes On Coach Trimming." Carriage Journal. Vol.18 No. 2 (Autumn 1980), pp.79-83.

"Notes On Coach Trimming Part II." Carriage Journal. Vol.18 No. 3 (Winter 1981), pp. 139-144.

"Notes On Coach Trimming Part III. Seat Falls; Brougham Door." Carriage Journal. Vol.18 No. 4 (Spring 1981), pp. 191-192.

"Notes On Coach Trimming Part IV Leather Work." Carriage Journal. Vol.19 No. 1 (Summer 1981), pp. 43-45. *

Old Hand. "Restoration of Carriages, Trimming (Upholstery)." Carriage Journal. vol.2 No. 4 (Spring 1965), pp. 140-142.

Hub, Feb. 1881. "Simple Directions For Setting Buggy (Road Wagon) Top." Carriage Journal. Vol.12 No. 4 (Spring 1975), pp. 207.

Ryder, Thomas. "Coach Lace : Its History, Methods of Manufacture and Use." Carriage Journal. Vol.22 No. 4 (Spring 1985), 196-198.

"[Seat Valances and Metal Beading On Victoria]." Carriage Journal. Vol.20 No. 2 (Autumn 1982), p. 100.

"Top For Victoria." Carriage Journal. Vol.23 No. 1 (Summer 1985), p. 39.

VICTORIA

Downing, Paul. "The Cabriolet And The Victoria." Carriage Journal. Vol.19 No. 2 (Autumn 1981), pp. 68-76.

WAGONETS

Muller, Adolphus. "A Dozen Popular Patterns Of Wagonets." Carriage Journal. Vol.12 No. 4 (Spring 1975), pp. 170-177.

WHEELS

Cantle, Gordon. " Development Of Solid Rubber Tires For Carriages." Carriage Journal. Vol.29 No. 2 (Fall 1991), p. 75-76.

Cantle, Gordon. "Fundamentals Of Fitting Tires." Carriage Journal. Vol.27 No. 1 (Summer 1989), pp. 10-12.

Cantle, Gordon. "Assembling A Wheel For Tiring." Carriage Journal. Vol.26 No. 3 (Winter 1988), p. 114-115.

Cantle, Gordon. "Tire Bending Segment Extant In North Yorkshire." Carriage Journal. Vol.26 No. 2 (Autumn 1988), p. 77.

Cantle, Gordon. "On Dishing And Staggering." Carriage Journal. Vol.25 No. 1 (Summer 1987), p. 39-40.

Foggett, John S. 1881. "The Manufacture of Carriage Wheels." Carriage Journal. Vol.15 No.1 (Summer 1977), pp. 236-242.

"Proportions Of Wheels In Relation To Their "Tire." Carriage Journal. Vol.13 No. 2 (Autumn 1975), pp. 102-105.

"[Staggered Spokes]." Carriage Journal. Vol.24 No. 3 (Winter 1986), p. 150.

Ryder, Tom. "The Manufacture of Carriage Wheels Part II-Factory Made Wheels." Carriage Journal. Vol.15 No. 2 (Autumn 1977), pp. 268-274.

Wheeling, Ken. "Rubber Tires And The Carriage Industry Part I-Solid Rubber Tires." Carriage Journal. Vol.28 No. 1 (Summer 1990), pp. 6-8.

Wheeling, Ken. "Rubber Tires And The Carriage Industry -Part II-Pneumatic Tire." Carriage Journal. Vol.28 No.3 (Winter 1990), pp. 102-105.

Wheeling, Ken. "Rubber Tires And The Carriage Industry - Part III-Contemporary Scene." Carriage Journal. Vol.28 No. 4 (Spring 1991), pp. 138-140.

Vineyard, Ron. "Straking." Carriage Journal. Vol.28 No. 1 (Summer 1990), pp. 17-20.

"[Wheel Chart For Proportions]." Carriage Journal. Vol.26 No. 1 (Summer 1988), pp. 39-40.

WICKER

Green, Susan. "Willow Basket Bodies For Carriages And Sleighs." Carriage Journal. Vol.24 No. 3. (Winter 1986), pp. 121-124.

WOOD

Carriage Builders' and Harness Makers' Art Journal. "Woods For Carriages." Carriage Journal. Vol.7 No.2 (Autumn 1969), pp. 81-82.

Carriage Monthly, April 1904. "Carriage Wood Bending." Carriage Journal. Vol.14 No.3 (Winter 1976), pp. 133-135.

"Hanley Combined Wood Boiler/Steamer." Carriage Journal. Vol.17 No.3 (Winter 1979), p.153.

Kellog, C. W. "Lancewood and Canework for Carriages." Carriage Journal. Vol.10 No.2 (Autumn 1972) pp. 84-85.

"Principles of Wood Bending." Carriage Journal. Vol.17 No. 2 (Autumn 1979), p. 101-102.

Wheeling, Ken. "The Hickory Supply Crisis." Carriage Journal. Vol.27 No. 1 (Summer 1989), pp.5-6.

"Wood Lamination: A Technique For The Carriage Builder And Restorer." Carriage Journal. Vol.19 No.2 (Autumn 1981), pp. 89-90.

Out of print Carriages Journals Vol. 5 No.4, Vol. 6 No.1 &3,4, Vol. 8 No.4, Vol. 10 No.1,2,3,4 Vol. 14 No.4, Vol. 18 No.4, Vol. 19 No.4, Vol. 21 No.2,3&4, Vol. 23 No.4, Vol. 24 No.1,2 & 4, Vol. 25 No. 3 and Vol. 26 No.1 &2.

Current Books About Carriages and other helpful books

19th Century American Carriages. Stony Brook, NY: Museums At Stony Brook, 1987.

Berkebile, Don. Carriage Terminology A Dictionary of Carriages. Washington, DC: Smithsonian Institution Press, 1978.

Berkebile, Don. American Carriages, Sleighs, Sulkies and Carts. New York, NY: Dover Publications, 1977.

Berkebile, Don. Horse Drawn Commercial Vehicles. New York, NY: Dover Publications, 1989.

Brewster Scrapbook. Bird-In-Hand, PA: Carriage Museum of America, 2001.

C and D Cook and Company, New Haven, Connecticut. New York, NY: Dover Publications, 1970. (reprint of 1860's catalog).

Cantle, Gordon. Essays On Horse-Drawn Carriages and Carriage Parts. Bird-In-Hand, PA: Carriage Museum of America, 1993.

Carriage Collection. Stony Brook, NY: Museums At Stony Brook, 1986.

Coson Carriage Collection at Beechdale. Bird-In-Hand, PA: Carriage Museum of America, 1993.

Dresdner, Michael. The Woodfinishing Book. Newtown, CT : Taunton Press, Inc., 1992.

Felton, William. A Treatise On Carriages. Mendham, NJ: Astragal Press, 1995. (reprinting of the 1794 and 1796 editions.)

Fine Wood Working on Bending Wood. Newtown, CT : Taunton Press, Inc., 1985.

Flexner, Bob. Understanding Wood Finishing : How to Select and Apply the Right Finish. Emmaus, PA : Rodale Press, 1994.

Green, Susan Horse Drawn Sleighs. Mendham, NJ: Astragal Press, 1995.

Hannukaine, John. Pinstripping and Vehicle Graphics. Fort Meyers, FL: Sign Craft Publishing Company, 1992.

Henry Hooker & Co. Salem, NJ: Carriage Association of America (reprint of 1895 catalog).

Hillick, M. C. Practical Carriage and Wagon Painting. Mendham, NJ : Astragal Press, 1997 (reprint of 1898 edition).

Horse-Drawn Vehicles: Colored Plates from the Hub November 1881-January 1892. Bird-In-Hand, PA: Carriage Museum of America, 2000.

Hub May 1888.

Hughes, Ralph C. John Deere Buggies and Wagons. St. Joseph, MI: American Society of Agricultural Engineers, 1995.

Lorch, Walter. Competion Vehicles.

Moseman's Directory

Bibliography of Available Reference Material

Peloubet, Don. Wheelmaking. Mendham, NJ : Astragal Press, 1996.
Reist, Arthur. Conestoga Wagon: Masterpiece of the Blacksmith. Lancaster, PA: Forry & Hacker, 1975.
Richardson, M. T. Practical Carriage Building. Mendham, NJ: Astragal Press, 1995 (reprint of 1892 edition).
Split Hickory Vehicles.
T. W. Lane. Amesbury, Massachusetts
Two-Wheeled Vehicles for Equine. Bird-In-Hand, PA: Carriage Museum of America, 2000.
Walborn and Riker-Pony, Cob and Horse Pleasure Vehicles.
Ware, I. D. Coach-Makers' Illustrated Hand-Book. Mendham, NJ: Astragal Press, 1995. (reprint of the 1875 edition).
Working Drawings of Horse-Drawn Vehicles. Bird-In-Hand, PA: Carriage Museum of America, 1998.

Available Publications

A Collection Of Essays On Horse-Drawn Carriages and Carriage Parts by Dr. Gordon S. Cantle. *This is the foremost technical book in print on the construction and engineering of carriage parts. $23.00*

A Treatise On Carriages by William Felton. *Reprinted from the 1794 and 1796 editions, It was the only book printed in English for this time period. An invaluable reference resource for people who want to study this time period and the history of carriages. $70.00*

Horse Drawn Sleighs by Susan Green for the Carriage Museum of America. *A compilation of sleigh designs in old trade journals, this is the only book ever published just about sleighs. $33.00*

The Royal Mews by Mary Stewart-Wilson, Photographs by David Cripps. *This book is illustrated in full color, showing the English state Carriages and stable. Outstanding photography of the harness and carriages. $28.00*

The Coson Carriage Collection At Beechdale. *This is about one of the premiere private carriage collections in the United States. It is illustrated with full color photographs and descriptions of the vehicles by Thomas Ryder. $33.00*

Wheelmaking : Wooden Wheel Design and Construction by Don Peloubet for the Carriage Museum of America. *It is a compilation of the technical articles on wheelmaking from the old trade journals, showing many designs of wheels.$33.00*

Working Drawings of Horse Drawn Vehicles. *100 engineering drawings for 20 different types of vehicles. The drawings come with a text page and dimensions. $55.00.*

Two-Wheeled Vehicles for Equine. *All different types of two-wheeled vehicles, plus comments on supension, old advertisments. Compiled from the Carriage Monthly and Hub. $43.00*

Horse-Drawn Vehicles: Colored Plates from the Hub Novmeber 1882-January 1892. 150 colored plates with text reprinted from the old trade journal the Hub. Very useful book if you have questions about what colors vehicles were painted. $105.00

Manual of Coaching by Fairman Rogers. Reprinted from the 1900 edition. It is the foremost book on driving and coaching. $70.00.

Brewster Scrapbook. Articles from the Carriage Monthly and Hub about the J. B. Brewster & Co., and Brewster & Co. Technical drawings of their vehicles and descriptions. Articles by John Britton, John Mosier, Franklin Gardner, John Gribbon of Brewster & Co. $80.00

Carriage Museum of America
Post Office Box 417
Bird-In-Hand, Pennsylvania 17505 phone 717-656-7019
web site: www.carriagemuseumlibrary.org

ALBANY SLEIGH REBUILDING
Elvin N. Nolt
321 N. Hershey Avenue
Leola, PA 17540
phone 717-656-2530

AUCTIONS
Topeka Draft Horse & Carriage Auction
Post Office Box 279
Topeka, IN 46571
Art Pagel, Carriage Repres
phone 414-675-6471

Martin Auctioneers, Inc.
Post Office Box 99
New Holland, PA 17557
phone 717-354-6671

AXLES
Farmerstown Axle Co.
2816 SR 557
Baltic, OH 43804

BASSWOOD LUMBER
Constantine
2050 Eastchester Road
Bronx, NY 10461
phone 1-800-223-8087
other special lumber

BEESWAX CANDLES
A. I. Root Candle Company
Post Office Box 706
Medina, OH 44258
1-800-289-7668 an asked for the church representative in your state

BLACKSMITH SUPPLIES
Centaur Forge Ltd.
117 North Spring Street
Post Office Box 340
Burlington, WI 53105-0340
phone 414-763-9175

Services, Supplies and Resources
BENDING PLYWOOD
Fessenden Hall of PA, Inc.
3021 Industry Drive
Lancaster, PA 17603
phone 717-394-1047
1/8 Italian poplar & 3/8 Luan bending plywood

Russell Plywood Inc.
401 Old Wyomissing Rd.
Reading, PA 19611
phone 610-374-3206

Thurway Hardwood & Plywood Corp.
75 Lathrop Street
Buffalo, NY 14212
phone 716-893-9663
1/8 Italian popular, 4x8 & 8x4 : 3/8 Luan bending plywood.

BRUSHES
Sid Moses (Seeling Custom)
10458 Santa Monica Blvd.
Los Angeles, CA 90025
phone 310-475-1111
striping brushes & sign painters brushes

Quill, Hair, & Ferrule
Box 23927
Columbia, SC 29224
phone 803-788-4499
imports German brushes, gilding supplies, sign painters paints, varnish brushes

Andrew Mack & Sons Brush Co.
225 East Chicago Street
Post Office Box 157
Jonesville, MI 49250
phone 517-849-9272
striping brushes

Condon Bros. Company
1912-14 Brighton Road
Pittsburgh, PA 15212
phone 412-321-2028
China Bristle brushes

CHUCKWAGONS
Wolf Wagon Works
John F. Wolf
HCR 65, Box 927
Crossroads, NM 88114
phone 505-675-2480

COACH LACE
Patrick Schroven
7 Slameuterstraat
2861 O.L.V. Waver
Belgium
phone 32-15.75.61.82
fax 32-15.7529.16

Rudolf Stief
Eichenstrasse 24
Neusass, 8901
GERMANY

CONSERVATION SUPPLIES
Talas
213 West 35th Street
New York, NY 10001-1996
phone 212-736-7744
some speciality leathers for book bindings, paint conservation supplies

Conservation Resources International
8000-H Forbes Place
Springfield, VA 22151
phone 800-634-6932
fax 703-321-0629

Conservation Resources United Kingdom Limited
Unit 1, Pony Road,
Horspath Industrial Estate
Cowley, Oxfordshire, OX4 2RD
phone (0) 1865-747755
fax (0) 1865-747035

CONSERVATORS
Colorado Artifact Conservation Center
Colorado History Museum
1300 Broadway
Denver, Colorado 80203-2137

American Institute for Conservation of Historic and Artistic Works
1717 K Street N. W.
Suite 301
Washington, DC 20006
phone 202-452-9545
fax 202-452-9328
referral service, list of conservators by speciality and region

Elizabeth Lahikainen Associates
Peabody Essex Museum
East India Square
Salem, MA 01970
phone 508-741-7560
textile conservation

American Conservation Consortium, Ltd.
Marc Williams
85 North Road
Fremont, NH 03044
phone 603-679-8307

BR Howard & Asso. Inc.
120 Sunset Drive
Carlise, PA 17013
phone 717-243-6596

Ralph Wiegandt
51 Park Lane
Rochester, NY 14625
phone 716-248-5307
speciality metal conservation

Jennifer Baker
Post Office Box 611
Shelburne, VT 05482
phone 802-985-3437

DASH & FENDER STITCHING
Ernie Schwartz
Antique Carriage Restoration
13106N 950W
Nappanee, IN 46550
phone 219-546-1122

Services, Supplies and Resources
Woodlyn Coach Company
44310 TownshipRoad 628
Millersburg, OH 44654
phone 216-674-9124
fax 216-674-3589

Intercourse Coach Shop
3572 West Newport Road
Box 38
Intercourse, PA 17534
phone 717-768-8712

Hunt's Harness
W2451 Dunn Road
Mayville, WI 53050
phone & fax 414-387-5057

DRAWINGS
Cobb & Company Museum
27 Lindsay Street
Toowoomba, Q 4350
Queensland, Australia
Atlas of scale drawings

Smithsonian Institution
Division of Transportation
Room 5010 MRC 628
National Museum of American History
Washington, DC 20560
stage coach drawing, etc.

Gerald & Phyllis Wingrove
Lindum House
27 North Street
Digby, London LN4 3LY
England

W. Hobby Ltd.
Knights Hill Square
London SE27 OHH
phone 01817614244
John Thompson drawings & Barrie Voisey plans

Roger Morgan
51 Court Farm Road
Llantamam, Cwmbran
Gwent NP44 3BZ
England
John Thompson plans and books

Kayo Fraser
Northwest Enterprises
167 Boulder Road
Deer Lodge, MT 58733
phone 406-846-3686
imports drawings from England

Nederlandse Vereniging van Modebouwers
Van der Hestlaan 5
1412 HG Naarden, Netherlands

Circus Model Builders
contact Eric W. Doyle
413 Helfer Lane
Minoa, NY 13116
phone 315-656-7032

Metropolitan Museum of Art
Print and Drawing Room
1000 Fifth Avenue
New York, NY 10028-0198
phone 212-570-3920
Brewster & Co. Technical drawings for carriages

Ted Bruner
B & T Wagon Works
Box 501
Evansburg, Alberta TOE OTO
phone 780-727-2129
meadowbrook cart, surrey, spring wagon, chuck wagon, large wagonette, buckboard, prairie schooner

Oregon Historical Society
1230 Southwest, Park Ave.
Portland, Oregon 97205
phone 503-222-1741
Ivan Collins collection of miniatures

Carriage Museum of America-Library
Post Box 417
Bird-In-Hand, PA 17505
phone 717-656-7019
drawings from Le Guide du Carrossier, Carriage Monthly and Hub in book Working Drawings of Horse-Drawn Vehicles.

Services, Supplies and Resources

FABRIC
LeBaron Bonney Company
6 Chestnut Street
Amesbury, MA 01913
phone 508-388-3811

mohair, Bedford cord, Wilton carpet

William S. Hirsch
396 Littleton Avenue
Newark, NJ 07103
phone 201-642-2404

English woolen broadcloth, Bedford cord, Wilton carpet

FRINGE/PASSEMENTERIE
Wendy Cushings Trimmings
8-9 Orient Industrial Park
Simonds Road, Leyton
London E10 7DE
England

Frances Soubeyran
12 Atlas Mews,
Ramsgate Street
London, E8 2NE England
phone (0171) 241 1064

Sullivans USA, Inc.
5221 Thatcher Road
Downers Grove, IL 60515
phone 630-435-1530
fax 630-435-1532
web: www.sullivans.net

Palladia Passementerie
www.palladiapassementerie.com

contact your local interior design center.

GILDING
Peter Achorn
Post Office Box 276
Tenants Harbor, ME 04860
phone 207-372-8824

decorative guilding for fire pieces

HORSEHAIR & HOGHAIR
E. P. Woll & Co.
P. O. Box 52417
Philadelphia, PA 19115-0017
phone 215-934-5966

LAMPS, REPAIR
Peter Appleyard/Lee Appleyard
Limestone Hall Farm
Limestone Cottage Lane
Wadsley Bridge, Sheffield S6 1NJ ENGLAND
phone (++44)1142852555
fax (++44) 1142853555

West Newbury Wagon Works
Donald W. Sawyer
    from June to December
700 Hilldale Avenue
Haverhill, MA 01832
phone 508-363-2983
fax 508-346-4841
    from January to May
Edgewater, FL
phone 904-423-9903

lamp repair, buys and sells lamps and other appointments.

Luminary Shoppe
Rick & Pat Bischoff
R. R. # 1 Box 336A
Joliet, MT 59041
phone 406-962-3677

John Donnelly Enterprises
Post Office Box 26041
Philadelphia, PA 19128
phone 215-483-4228

LEATHER, PATENT
Corral Leathers
1 Peatfield Street
Ipswich, MA 01938
phone 508-356-5701
fax 508-356-9832

5-12 oz. Veg. Black patent

Libra Leathers
259 West 30th Street
New York, NY 10001
phone 212-695-3114

S. H. Frank & Co.
3075 17th Street
San Francisco, CA 94110
phone 415-863-6244

Russo Leather
Los Angles, CA
phone 213-261-0391

LEATHER-UPHOLSTERY
LeBaron Bonney Company
6 Chestnut Street
Amesbury, MA 01913
phone 508-388-3811

William S. Hirsch
396 Littleton Avenue
Newark, NJ 07103
phone 201-642-2404

LEATHER-WORKING
Harness Shop News
347 Elk Road
Sylva, NC 28779
phone 828-586-6389
fax 828-586-8938

large network of leather suppliers etc.

Tandy Leather Company
Post Office Box 791
Fort Worth, TX 76101

retail stores in most states, thread, leather, tools, glue, mail order catalog

Leather Factory
Post Office Box 50429
Fort Worth, TX 76105
fax 817-496-9806

retail stores across the U.S., thread, leather, tools, glue, mail order catalog

LINOLEUM-BATTLESHIP
Tony Lauris
R D. # 2 Box 253B
Landenberg, PA 19350

OIL CAPS
Homar Molds and Models
64 Diane Terrace
Waterbury, CT 06705
phone 203-753-9017

Services, Supplies and Resources

ORGANIZATIONS
Carriage Association of America
177 Pointers-Auburn Rd.
Salem, New Jersey 08079
phone 609-935-1616
fax 609-935-4955

PAINT ANALYSIS
Williamstown Art Conservation Center
225 South Street
Williamstown, MA 01267
phone 413-458-5741
fax 413-458-2314

PAINT FINISHING
Sherwin Williams Co.
Automotive Training Center
5422 Dansher Road
Countryside, IL 60525
phone 708-579-4120
Offer courses in Atlanta, Philadelphia, Reno, Chicago, Dallas

PAINTS/VARNISHES
Joseph Mason P.L.C.
Nottingham Road
Derby, Derbyshire
DE21 6AR ENGLAND
phone 01332 295959
fax 01332 295252
extra pale coach varnish

McCloskey
1191 Wheeling Road
Wheeling, IL 60090-5794
phone product information 800-345-4530

C.P. F.-A Div. Of Courtaulds Coatings Inc.
5300 West 5th Avenue
Post Office 6369
Gray, IN 46406
phone 219-949-1684
1 Shot lettering enamels

DuPont
1-800-338-7668

California Products Corp.
169 Waverly Street
Cambridge, MA 02139
phone 617-547-5300
Larcoloid paints for brushing and spraying, Larcoloid undercoater

Pettit Paint Co.
Kop Coat, 36 Pine Street
Rockaway, NJ 07866
phone 201-625-3100
marine paints and varnishes

Kremer Pigments
228 Elizabeth Street
New York, NY 10012
phone 212-219-2394
dry pigments

Sherwin Williams
101 Prospect Avenue N. W.
Cleveland, OH
phone 216-566-2000
archives contain the old paint sample books for carriages

Witmer Coach Shop
1070 West Main Street
New Holland, PA 17557
phone 717-656-3411
distributor for: Larcoloid high gloss enamel interior/exterior, enamel undercoater California Brand, special mix of Brewster green, and maroon
1 shot lettering enamels

Northwest Wheel and Buggy
Box 9 R. R. # Crotteau Site
Quesnel, B. C. V2J 5E8
phone 604-992-9238
able to supply some custom mixed colors, that were matched to old paint samples

PASTE WOOD FILLER
Ace Hardware Stores
can supply a paste wood filler made by Jasco Chemical Corp.

PARASOL TOP FRAMES
Al Roggeman
Route 1
Stryker, OH 43557
phone 419-682-6435

PARASOL TOP COVERING
John Zimmerman Coach Trimming
859 Martin Church Road
New Holland, PA 17557
phone 717-445-6455

PARTS/HARDWARE
Latex Carriage Works
18 Hunt Road
Post Office Box 77
Beverly, W.A. 6304
AUSTRALIA
phone 61-96-461413
steel wheels, hickory shafts, brass wear

New Farm Carriage Supply
740 Morningside Drive
Englewood, FL 34223
phone 813-474-8711
products from British & American craftsman

Miller Buggy Shop
R. R. 8, Box 37
Bloomfield, IA 52537
wheels, rubber tires, tufted leather

McKee's Horse & Buggy
O. O. Box 27
Drakesville, IA 52552
phone 515-648-5024

Kuhn's Fifth Wheel Shop
1114 Plymouth-Goshen TR.
Route 1
Bremen, IN
ductile single and double reach fifth wheels & whip sockets

Graber Coach
R R. # 3 Box 295A
Loogootee, IN 47553
custom turned axles, wooden hub wheels with roller bearing inserts

Miller Carriage Company
3035N 850W
Shipshewana, IN 46565
full line of parts & accessories wholesale & retail

Services, Supplies and Resources

Chevalier Carriage Co.
42 Summit Street
Belchertown, MA 01007
phone 413-323-4757

Ziller's Carriage Supply
608 West 6th Street
Wilmar, MN 56201
phone 612-235-7841

Valley Brake Company
Benjamin J. Yoder
3119 Street Route 557
Baltic, OH 43804
manufacturer of hydraulic brakes

Buckeye Cart & Supply
33698 C. R. 12
Baltic, OH 42804
brass carriage hardware

Byler's Blacksmith Shop
5504 S. R. 314
Fredricktown, OH 43019
mfg. of axle clips, spring clips, clip mfg. of roller rub irons with larger bearings

Hickory Lane Welding
7330 Salt Creek Road
Fredericksburg, OH 44627
corner braces, shaft eyes, rub irons, single tree yokes, steps, box hangers, block brakes, reach braces, large inventory of steel bars, rounds, flats, angles channels

Simeon B. Martin Mfg.
RR #1, Wallenstein, Ontario
NOB 2SO
phone 519-698-2442
fax 519-698-2154
wheel parts, doubletree, neck yokes, bent cutter dashes, buggy boxes and seats, etc.

Witmer Coach Shop
1070 Main Street
New Holland, PA 17557
phone 717-656-3411
catalog and large supplies of wheel parts, shafts, upholstery trims.

PLATING
Acme Plating
1915 Bend Hill Avenue
Baltimore, MD 21226
phone 410-355-6821 Silver and nickel

RESTORERS
David J. Glass
Post Office Box 266
Granum, ALBERTA
TOL 1AO
phone 403-687-2120

C. J. Smith, Jr.
2005 North 103rd Avenue
Avondale, AZ 85323
phone 602-264-2539
fax 602-936-7015

Phelp's Wagon Wheel & Coach Shop
427 Colusa Street
Orland, CA 95963
phone 916-865-8244

John Jenkel
3325 Highway 116North
Sebastopol, CA 95472
phone 707-823-7083

G. Philip Wine
Post Office Box 2437
Belleview, FL 34421
phone 904-288-8881

Hubert H. Johnson
1603 Oakhaven Drive
Albany, GA 31707
phone 912-432-7669

Welliver's Carriage Shop
Post Office Box 57
Elko, GA 31025
phone 912-987-3400

Bill Twigg
Moscow Carriage Company
3240 Lenville Road
Moscow, ID 83843
phone 208-882-2445

L. G. Bowman Carriage Co.
Rt. 1 Box 89A
Thompsonville, IL 62890
phone 618-627-2461

Miller Buggy Shop
Andrew Miller
Route 8 Box 37
Bloomfield, IA 52537

Graber Coach Inc.
R. R. #3 Box 295A
Loogootee, IN 47553

Ernie Schwartz
Antique Carriage Restoration
13106N 950West
Nappanee, IN 46550
phone 219-546-1122

Bluegrass Carriage Works
Box 966
Danville, KY 40423
phone 606-236-8395

John D. Mikkola
266 South Road
Post Office Box 172
Hampden, MA
phone 413-566-3956

New England Coach & Carriage Works
101 East Main Street
Merrimac, MA 01860
phone 508-346-4841

Silver Ranch Inc.
Route 124 East of Village
Jaffrey, NH 03452
phone 603-532-7363

Southern Coach & Wood Product
Route 10 Box 257
Asheboro, NC 27203
phone 919-629-8201

Services, Supplies and Resources

Green's Carriage Restoration
William Lee Green
10530 Thrailkill Road
Orient, OH 43146
phone 614-877-4254

Woodlyn Coach Company
4410TR, 628
Millersburg, OH 44654
phone 330-674-9124
fax 330-674-3589
mail order catalog for parts and supplies

Penhale Wagon & Carriage Works Ltd.
R. R. # 2 Old River Road
Bayfield, ONTARIO
NOM 1GO
phone 519-565-2107
fax 519-565-5240

Les Voitures Robert et Fils
715 Haut du Petit rang St-Francois St-Pie JOH 1WO
ONTARIO
phone 514-772-5221

Weavertown Coach Shop
3007 Old Philadelphia Pike
Bird-In-Hand, PA 17505
phone 717-354-4374

Hansen Wheel & Wagon Shop
Doug Hansen
R. R. 1 Box 129A
Letcher, SD 57359
phone 605-996-8754
fax 605-996-2686

R. D. Lewis
Post Office Box 91
Cowley, WY 82420
phone 307-548-7377
fax 307-548-6886

SANDBLASTING EQUIPMENT
Skat Blast Inc./ Truman's Inc.
7075 State Route 14 By-Pass
Post Office Box 649
Canfield, OH 44406
phone 800-321-9260
mail order catalog available

SEATS
Stan Teitge
150 Hilltop Road
Salt Spring Island, BC V8K 1V9
phone 250-653-4811
email: teitge@saltsspring.com
custom wooden seats built & joinery

SPRAY EQUIPMENT
Binks Manufacturing Company
9201 West Belmont Ave.
Franklin Park, IL 60131

Sharpe Spray Equip
8750 Pioneer Blvd.
Santa Fe Springs, CA 90670
phone 562-908-6800

SPRINGS
Derry Cook
Post Office Box 136
Erickson, BC VOB-1KO
phone 250-428-8462
email: pcook@kootenay.com
coil Schuler springs for buckboards.

Wana Coach Company
Norman Yoder
1245 North 850 West
Shipshewana, IN
46565
phone 219-768-7336
answering 219-625-2150

STRIPERS
Fawn Marie Sensenig
105-G Sandy Hill Road
Denver, PA 17517
717-468-2941

Jay & Karen Hankee
Route 2 Box 230
Viroqua, WI 54665
phone 608-634-3825

Ernie Schwartz
Antique Carriage Restoration
13106N 950W
Nappanee, IN 46550
phone 219-546-1122

Kathryn Peace
9730 Cosby Mill Road
Quinton, VA 23141
phone 804-932-4360

STRIPING SUPPLIES
Dick Blick
Post Office Box 1267
Galesburg, IL 61402-1267
800-447-8192
sword stripers, striping tools, striping stencil tape, books, gold leaf, gilders's tip, gold leaf accessories, pounce wheels, pounce powders, china markers, 1-shot lettering enamels

Beugler Manufacturing Co.
4318 West Second Street
Los Angeles, CA 9004
striping tool

Sign Craft Magazine
Post Office Box 60031
Fort Myeres, FL 33906
phone 800-204-0204
books and magazine articles

TOP FINISH
Sem Products, Inc.
651 Michael Wylie Dr.
Charlotte, NC 28217-1546
phone 704-522-1006
products for finishing leather

TOP LEATHER
William S. Hirsch
396 Littleton Avenue
Newark, NJ 07103
phone 201-642-2404

Services, Supplies and Resources

TOP WORK-FOLDING
Welliver's Carriage Shop
Post Office Box 57
Elko, GA 310
phone 912-987-3400

TRANSFER ORNAMENTS
Gerber Scientific Products, Inc.
151 Batson Drive
Manchester, CT 06040
phone 860-643-1515
fax 860-290-5568

UPHOLSTERS
Ralph Lane
Leathersmith Industries
Box 233,
Okotoks, AB
T0L 1T0
phone 403-938-7847

UPHOLSTER SUPPLIES
Pacific Fiber Products
122 Howard Avenue
Hamburg, PA 19526
phone 610-562-4578
fax 610-562-5410
foam, good selection of curve needles, horsehair stuffing, coconut batting,

Witmer Coach Shop
1070 West Main Street
New Holland, PA
17557
phone 717-656-3411
vinyl coated nylon topping material, vinyl coated cloth back called crush, tacks, buttons, rubber matting corrugated & pyramid, cotton batting, foam, thread, fringe.

Van Dyke's
Post Office Box 278
Woonsocket, SD 57385
phone 1-800-843-3320
mail order catalog with large selection of supplies

BestWay Foam, Inc.
904 Plum Street
Elkhart, IN 46514
phone 1-800-688-9159
fax 219-522-1058
quality foam, wholesale/retail, custom cutting

WASHER CUTTER
Witmer Coach Shop
1070 West Main Street
New Holland, PA 17557
phone 717-656-3411

WHEELWRIGHTS
Western Canadian Wheelwrights Association
Terry Francis
Box 1107
Athabasca, ALBERTA
T0G 0B0

George McKenzie
Box 3
Brownvale, ALBERTA
T0H 0L0
phone 780-597-3950
Tire benders and rubber tire machines

Dale Befus
Alberta Carriage Supply
Box 4, Site 15, R. R. #7
Calgary, AB T2P 2G7
phone 403-804-0560
fax 403-934-5712
email: dbefus@cbsl.ab.ca
general wheelwrighting

Ellerslie Blacksmithing & Wheelwright
Irv Nessel
6920 2 Avenue SouthWest
Edmonton, ALBERTA
T6X 1A3
phone 403-988-5080

Ted Bruner
B & T Wagon Works,
Box 501
Evansburg, AB T0E 0T0
phone 780-727-2129
wheel repair

R. Bruce Morrison
Box 13 Site 20, R.R. #1
DeWinton, ALBERTA
T0L 0X0
phone 403-938-5954
editor of the Western Canadian Wheelwrights Ass.

Doran Degenstein
MacLeod Livery Ltd.
Post Office Box 852
Fort MacLeod, ALBERTA
T0L 0Z0
email: dordeg@telusplanet.net
general wheelwrighting & wainwrighting.

Morris Irvine
Moe's Wheelwright & Carriage Shop
Box 62
Lindbergh, ALBERTA
T0A 2J0
phone 403-724-4027
General wheelwright, chuckwagon wheels, carts parts, sleighs & cutters rebuilt, vehicles for miniature horses

Rick McAvena
Wild Rose Spoke & Buggy Ltd.
Box 85
Millarville, ALBERTA
phone 403-931-3603
fax 403-931-3538
General wheelwrighting; carriage & stagecoach construction

Mike & Brenda Hartigan
Lost Arts Workshop
Site 9, Box 17, R. R. #1,
Okotoks, ALBERTA T0L 1T0
phone 403-938-2539
fax 403-938-4596
email:mhart@webminder.com
general wheelwrighting, new & used parts

John Jeffrey
Box 333
Ryley, AB TOB 4AO
phone 403-663-3812
wheels built

K and H Carriage House
Harry Harrison
R. R. # 2
Thorsby, ALBERTA
TOC 2PO
phone 403-389-2385
email:democrat@telusplanet.net

Dwayne Danley
Danley Carriage & Wheel
1853 Pleasant Valley Road
Armstrong, BRITISH COLUMBIA VOE 1B2
phone 250-546-9979
wheels built & repaired

Northwest Wheel & Buggy
David Lockyer
Box 9 R. R. # 8 Croteau Rd.
Quesnel, BRITISH COLUMBIA V2J 5E6
phone 250-992-9236
email: llockyear@quesnelbc.com
General wheelwrighting, authentic buggy paint, stagecoach manufacture, general parts catalogue

Tom Bandy & Son Blacksmith
23649 Old Wagon Road
Escondidio, CA 92027
phone 619-745-4424

Wooly Bear Farm
Charles & Barbara Abel
19410 U. S. Highway 285
Nathrop, CA 81236
phone 719-395-8228

Lester Hollenback
2301 Normandy Blvd.
Deltona, FL 32725-2615

Cornett Buggy Shop
542 Law Road, North West
Cartersville, GA 30120
phone 404-336-5458

Services, Supplies and Resources
Welliver's Carriage and Wheel Shop
Bob & Tammy Welliver
Post Office Box 57
Elko, GA 31025
phone 912-987-3400

Augusta Arsenal and Carriage Works
Don Whitaker
332 Sugar Creek Drive
Grovetown, GA 30813
phone 706-860-9096

Miller Buggy Shop
Andrew Miller
Route 8 Box 37
Bloomfield, IA 52537

Moscow Carriage Company
Bill Twigg
3240 Lenville Road
Moscow, ID 83843
phone 208-882-2445
email:mcctwigg@turbonet.com

Pine Creek Industries
Raymond Dose
1442 W. Pine Creek Road
Pinehurst, ID 83850
phone 208-682-2482
fax 208-682-2482
email: buggyparts@aol.com
wheelmaking tools

Schwartz Wheel & Co.
4199 Cedar Road
Breman, IN 46506
phone 219-546-1302

E Z Axle and Hub Mfg.
14735 Cuba Road
Grabill, IN 46741
wheelwright, manufacture hubs and axles

Miller Carriage Company
3035 North 850 West
Shepshewana, IN 46565
phone 219-768-4926
wheel parts

Daniels Wagon Factory
Bruce E. Tompkins
Daniels Road
Rowley, MA 01969
phone 508-948-3815

Montana Wheel & Wagon
7 Forest Park, #5,
Whitehall, MT 59759
phone 406-494-4227
email rmcavena@msn.com

Donald R. Peloubet
39 Dacotah Avenue
Lake Hiawatha, NJ 07034
phone 201-334-0748
talks on early wheelmaking

Wolf Wagon Works
John F. Wolf
HCR 65, Box 927
Crossroads, NM 88114
phone 505-675-2480
wheelwright, chuckwagons

Wheelwright and Buggy Shop
Pete Robertson
Route 53
Prattsburg, NY 14873
phone 607-522-3782

Stutzman Buggy Shaft & Wheel Works
Melvin A. Stutzman
33650 C. R. 12
Baltic, OH 43804

Holmes Wheel Shop, Inc.
7969 C. R. 189
Post Office Box 56
Holmesville, OH 44633

Shetler Wheel Works
Melvin J. Shetler
4809 Kinsman Road
Middlefield, OH 44062

Country View
556 White Oak Road
Christiana, PA 17509

Kirkwood Coach Shop
Levi L. Fisher
425 Maple Shade Road
Kirkwood, PA 17536
phone 717-529-6178
Buggy wheels, spokes & felloes made to order

Nolt's Wheel Shop
Aaron M. Nolt
214 North Shirk Road
New Holland, PA 17557
phone 717-355-9182

Witmer Coach Shop
Jacob and Emma Witmer
1070 West Main Street
New Holland, PA 17557
phone 717-656-3411

Kulp Wheelwright Shop
Richard & Robert Kulp
2233 Little Road
Perkiomenville, PA 18074
phone 610-754-7295
miniature wheels made

Shepherd's Wheelwright Shop
Jack Shepherd
Maple Creek,
SASKATCHEWAN
SON 1NO
phone 306-667-3251
general wheelwrighting, including wagon wheels

G. L. Musgrove Services
Roy Musgrove
R. R. # 5, Box 19
Saskatoon, SASKATCHEWAN
S7K 3J8
phone 306-373-5808

Western Canadian Development Museum
Post Office Box 1910
2935 Mellville Street
Saskatoon, SASKATCHEWAN
S7K 3SS
phone306-9341400
wheelwright school

Services, Supplies and Resources

Crawford & McKee Carriage Works
Box 57
Vanscoony, SLK
phone 306-683-7580
fax 306-683-7587
email:ae301@sfn.saskatoon.sk.ca
general wheelwrighting

Huron Buggy Works
Box 303
Huron, SD 57350
phone 352-9492 or 352-5935

Hansen Wheel & Wagon Shop
Doug Hansen
Rural Route 1 Box 129A
Letcher, SD 57359
phone 605-996-8754
email:dwhansen@hansenwheel.com
web:www.hansenwheel.com

Gary Gaither Wheelwright Shop
Route 4 Box 45F
Gonzales, TX 78629
phone 210-540-4282

Burkholder Buggy Shop
Everette D. Burkholder
Route 4 Box 45
Dayton, VA 22821
phone 703-879-9260

Karl's Custom Wheels
Karl Gayer
152 Skimino Road
Williamsburg, VA 23188
phone 804-565-1997
wooden axles made

Ron Vineyard
Colonial Williamsburg Foundation
Post Office Box 1776
Williamsburg, VA 23187-1776
phone 804-229-1000
demonstrates 18th century wheel making

Chuck and Helga Firkins
Route 5 Box 2325
Game Farm Road
Ellensburg, WA 98926
phone 509-926-2296

WICKER SUPPLIES
English Basketry Willows
R.D. #1 Box 124A S.
New Berlin, NY 13843
phone 607-847-8264

County Seat, Inc.
R.D. # 2 Box 24A
Kempton, PA 19529
phone 610-756-6124
large supply of reed & canning

WICKER WORK
Welliver's Coach Shop
Post Office Box 57
Elko, GA 31025
phone 912-987-3400

Dicks Wicker Shop
207 State Street
Brinkhaven, OH 43006
phone 614-599-7282

Beth Schaffer
785 Morwood Road
Telford, PA 18969
phone 215-723-6510

WINDOW FLIM-UV
3M Products
phone 1-800-354-7355
3M Scotchtint

WOOD BENDING
77 Coach Supply
Atlee Kaufman
Route 5, Box 235
Millersburg, OH
44654
phone 216-674-9124
shafts and felloes

Peter J. Gummow & Paul Gummow
B & G Sulky Shaft Ltd.
175 King Street
Stratford, ONTARIO N5A 482
phone 519-273-2400

Kringle Sleigh Company
2200 Mastodon Ct.
Imperial, Missouri 63052
phone 314 464-9068
parts for albany swell body sleigh

Mary & Christian Weaver
105 Groffdale Church Road
Leola, PA 17540
phone 717-656-8310

Steve Waddell
Chamberlain Hill Carriage Works
562 Chamberlain Avenue SE
Buffalo, MN 55313
phone 612-888-1551
custom woodbending

John's Woodbending
John E. Glick
4000 East Newport Road
Gordonville, PA 17529
phone 717-768-8183

Yoder Woodbending
Orva Yoder
23351 348th Street
Edgewood, Iowa 52042

Thomas Martin
N.W. Woodbending Ltd.
2936 Arthur Street North
R. R. #1, Elmira, Ontario
N3B 2Z1
phone 519-669-0750

WOOD FILLER
Abatron, Inc.
5501 95th Avenue
Kenosha, WI 53144
phone 414-653-2000
liquidwood, wood epox

WOOD WORKING SUPPLIES
Frog Tool Co. Ltd.
2169 IL. Rt. 26
Dixon, IL 61021
phone 800-648-1270
full line of hand tools, books, sandpapers, finishes

Constantine's
2050 Eastchester Road
Bronx, NY 10461
phone 800-223-8087
full line of hand tools, books, sandpaper, finishes

Services, Supplies and Resources

Available Publications

A Collection Of Essays On Horse-Drawn Carriages and Carriage Parts by Dr. Gordon S. Cantle. *This is the foremost technical book in print on the construction and engineering of carriage parts. $23.00*

A Treatise On Carriages by William Felton. *Reprinted from the 1794 and 1796 editions, It was the only book printed in English for this time period. An invaluable reference resource for people who want to study this time period and the history of carriages. $70.00*

Horse Drawn Sleighs by Susan Green for the Carriage Museum of America. A *compilation of sleigh* designs *in* old trade journals, this is the only *book ever published just about sleighs.* $33.00

The Royal Mews by Mary Stewart-Wilson, Photographs by David Cripps. *This book is illustrated in full color, showing the English state Carriages and stable. Outstanding photography of the harness and carriages. $28.00*

The Coson Carriage Collection At Beechdale. *This is about one of the premiere private carriage collections in the United States. It is illustrated with full color photographs and descriptions of the vehicles by Thomas Ryder. $33.00*

Wheelmaking : Wooden Wheel Design and Construction by Don Peloubet for the Carriage Museum of America. *It is a compilation of the technical articles on wheelmaking from the old trade journals, showing many designs of wheels.*$33.00

Working Drawings of Horse Drawn Vehicles. *100 engineering drawings for 20 different types of vehicles. The drawings come with a text page and dimensions. $55.00.*

Two-Wheeled Vehicles for Equine. *All different types of two-wheeled vehicles, plus comments on supension, old advertisements. Compiled from the Carriage Monthly and Hub. $43.00*

Horse-Drawn Vehicles: Colored Plates from the Hub Novmeber 1882-January 1892. 150 colored plates with text reprinted from the old trade journal the Hub. Very useful book if you have questions about what colors vehicles were painted. $105.00

Manual of Coaching by Fairman Rogers. Reprinted from the 1900 edition. It is the foremost book on driving and coaching. $70.00.

Brewster Scrapbook. Articles from the Carriage Monthly and Hub about the J. B. Brewster & Co., and Brewster & Co. Technical drawings of their vehicles and descriptions. Articles by John Britton, John Mosier, Franklin Gardner, John Gribbon of Brewster & Co. $80.00

Carriage Museum of America
Post Office Box 417
Bird-In-Hand, Pennsylvania 17505 phone 717-656-7019
web site: www.carriagemuseumlibrary.org

INDEX

aircraft plywood, 95
Albany cutter, trimming, 163
alkyd resin, 120
aluminum wagon, 8
artificial leather, 158
AXLE, 55-66
    bibliography, 65-66,
    gauge, 55
    inspecting, 64
    manufacture, 56-58
    types, 58-64
barouche, 14, 209
basket phaeton, color, 137
battleship linoleum, 161
bearing axle, 62
bending plywood, 95
BIBLIOGRAPHY, 209-215
black parts, 138
black japan, 48
black varnish, 48
bleaching, 106
body construction, bibliography, 209
book list, 215-216
brakes, bibliography, 209
brass beading, 88, 91-92
brass molding, 88
brizka, bibliography, 209
broadcloth, 154
brougham, color, 136
brougham, parts of, 99
brougham, trimming, 164
Brunswick black, 48
BRUSH PAINTING, 115-127
    brush care, 116-117
Brussels carpet, 161
buckboard, bibliography, 209
buggy, 10, 181
buggy, bibliography, 209
buggy, trimming, 162
buggy, parts of, 100
built up wood, 95
cabinet makes paneling, 96
cabriolet, color, 136
cabriolet phaeton, 5
caleche see barouche
camels hair cloth, 156
CANE WORK, 185-190
    bibliography, 188, 209
    seats, 190
    glued on, 187
    painted, 185-186
care and preservation, bibliography, 210
carriage technology, 20
carriage lace, 159
Carriage Museum of America, 193
carriage varnish, 47
cart, bibliography, 210
chrome tan leather, 157
coach, color, 137
coach lace, 159
collinge axle, 59
COLORS, 135-143
    bibliography, 138
    coats, 118-119
commercial vehicles, bibliography, 210
composite object, 23
CONSERVATION, 15-35
    analytical, 16
    condition reports, 16
    code of ethics, 16, 18
    treatments, 16
    documentation, 19, 23, 31
    integrity of object, 18
    preservation, 16
    professional, 16
    self treatment, 16
    supplies, 36
    structure, 24
    what is?, 17
    why, 15
conservator, selecting, 10
copal, 41
corning buggy, color, 135
decontaminating, 105
Decorative-painters' wagon, 3
delivery wagon, 139
deterioration, 22
disassembling, 101-102
dish in wheels, 70-71
dog cart, color, 137
dog cart, trimming, 164
door trimming, 173
driers, 46
dust covers, 32-33
dusting, 31-32
elastic carriage varnish, 47
elastic hard carriage varnish, 47
English woolen broadcloth, 154
express wagon, 8
extension top barouche, 14
extension top phaeton, 7
FAIC referral system, 11
felloes, 72-74
fifth wheel, bibliography, 210
finishing body varnish, 46
floor coverings, 161
foam, 160
FRINGE, 165-167
furniture car, 8
gather, 55
gigs, bibliography, 210
gilding, 151
glaze coats, 124
gluing, 103
gum drill, 157
hand sewing leather, 175
hansom cabs, bibliography, 211
hard drying varnish, 47
horsehair, 160
hubs, 71-72
imperial, bibliography, 211
inpainting loses, 28
japanners' gold size, 47
ladder, folding, bibliography, 211
laminating, 95
LAMPS,
    bibliography, 211
    correct size, 181
    covers, 180
    parts of, 182
    restoration of, 182-184
    storage, 184
landau, color, 136
landau, trimming, 162
leather, 156
leather hand sewing, 175
leather washers, 58
linseed oil, 41-43
long oil, 120
luxury fabrics, 156
Macintosh cloth, 157
mail axle, 61
maintenance, 31
maker's name, 6
manufacture, bibliography, 211
metal, cleaning, 106-108
metal components, 29-30

INDEX

microscopic analysis, 37-40
MUSEUMS, 193-208
natural wood carriages, 138-139
nicks and scratches, 35
oil cloth, 161
one-horse truck, 8
overpainting, 29
PAINT ANALYSIS, 37-40
    bibliography, 50-51, 211
    colors, 140-143
    finish, 113-114
painting, spray, 132
paint removal, 103-104
paint remover, 104
paint stabilization, 25
PAINTING, BRUSH, 115-127
painting, preparation, 101, 130-132
pale copal varnish, 47
PANELS, 89-99
    applying, 90
    bending, 92-95
    bibliography, 98
    laminated, 95
    lower quarter, 92
    natural wood, 89-90
    painted, 89
    reed molding, 91
    repairing, 97
    top quarter, 90-91
park drag, 137
park wagon, 14
patents, 6
patent, leather, 157
patent wheels, 68-69
perch, bibliography, 211
phenolic resin, 120
physicians' phaeton, 4
piano box, 10
plain axle, 62
plush, 155
pneumatic tires, 76
poles trimming, 176
polyurethane, 120
Portland cutter, trimming, 163
primer coats, 117-118
protective coatings, 29
reed, 191
reed molding, 91
RESEARCHING, 5-7
restoration, bibliography, 211

restoration, getting started, 101, 130-132
revarnishing, 21
rims, 72-74
road wagon, 10
rockaway, bibliography, 212
rubber mat, 161
rubber tire color, 77
rubber tires, 76-77
rusty screws, 102
sand paper, 109
sandblasting, 107
sanding, 108-111
sanding sealer, 111-112
seat falls, 167
SERVICES & SUPPLIES, 217-226
sewing machine, 154
shaft & pole trimming, 174-177
shafts bibliography, 212
sham-caning, 185-187
short oil, 120
show buggy, bibliography, 212
Sicilian cart, bibliography, 212
Sjees, Frisian, bibliography, 212
skinning, 96
sleighs, bibliography, 212
solid rubber tire, 77
Spanish moss, 160
splinter bars, 177
spokes, 72
SPRAY PAINTING, 128-134
    equipment, 129-130
    problems of, 133
SPRINGS, 79-87
    bibliography, 87, 212-213
    fatigue, 85
    fixing, 80
    heat treatment, 81
    manufacturing, 83-87
    new, 79-80
    painting, 113
    setting, 80 spring,
    sizes, 80, 84
    stress effects, 80-81
    taking apart, 79
square box wagon, 10-13
stanhope phaeton, 4
stationary top phaeton, 4
stenciling, 151

steps, bibliography, 213
stripes, 145
striping, 144-152
striping, bibliography, 152,
striping, brushes, 146
stuffing materials, 160
sulky, bibliography, 213
surrey, 14
surrey, bibliography, 213
surrey, color, 136
tanning methods, 157
tapestry cloth, 155
tires, 74-75
tops, cleaning and repairing, 175
transfers, 149-150
trap, 143
trap, bibliography, 213
trimmers tools, 153
trimming materials, 153-161
tufting fullness, 169
turpentine, 43-46
UPHOLSTERY, 153-179
    bibliography, 213
    conservation, 30
valances for folding tops, 178
valances for seat borders, 178
VARNISH, 41-49, 119-120
    applying, 121-124
    bibliography, 126-127
    cleaning, 26
    getting ready, 124-125
    kinds of, 119-120
    making, 46
    maintenance, 34
    problems of, 126
    removal, 27
    recipes, 46-49
vegetable tan leather, 157
veneering, 96
victoria, bibliography, 214
vis-a-vis, trimming, 163
wagonets, bibliography, 214
wagonette break, color, 137
wagons, 8
washer cutter, 58
WHEELS, 67-78
    bibliography, 77-78,
    parts of, 67
    painting, 119
    puller, 59
    work, 69-70

INDEX

whiffletree trimming, 171
whip cord, 155
WICKER, 190-192
    wicker, bibliography, 215
    reed, 191
    willow, 190
Wilton carpet, 161
wood, bibliography, 215
wood bending, 92-95
wood filler, 111-112
wooden axle, 63
wooden axle making, 63-64